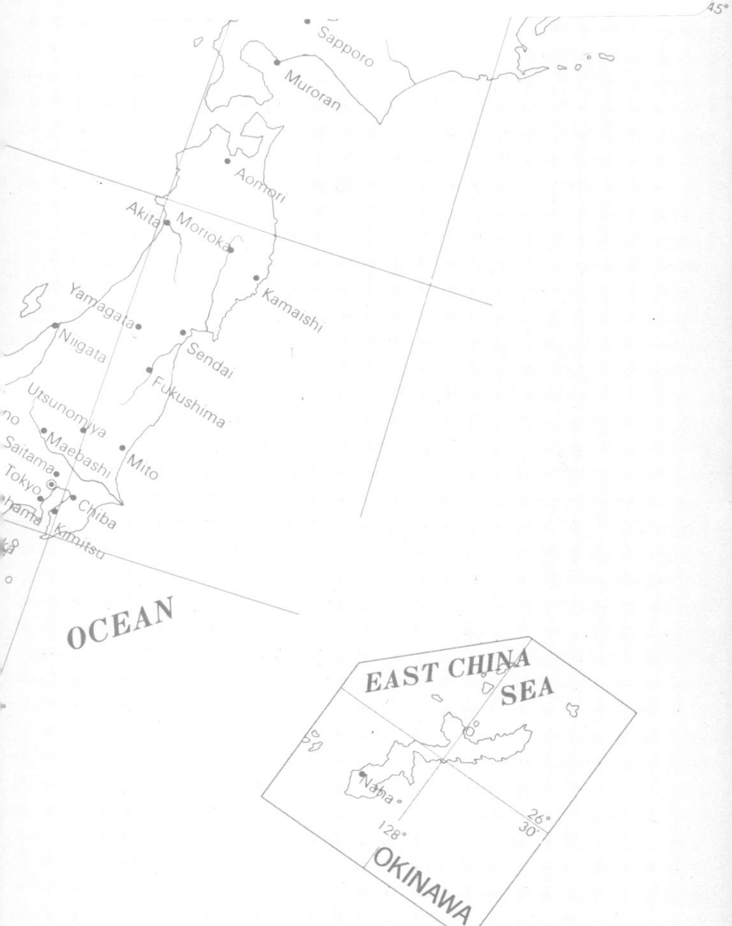

45°

Sapporo

Muroran

Aomori

Akita • Morioka

Kamaishi

Yamagata

Niigata • Sendai

Utsunomiya • Fukushima

Maebashi • Mito

Saitama

Tokyo • Chiba

Kimitsu

OCEAN

EAST CHINA SEA

Naha

128°

26°

30°

OKINAWA

日 本
—その姿と心—

新日本製鐵株式會社
株式会社 日鉄ヒューマンデベロプメント

NIPPON

THE LAND
AND
ITS PEOPLE

学 生 社

第7版の発刊にあたって

「日本―その姿と心―」の初版が新日本製鐵(株)能力開発部の編集によって発刊されたのは、昭和57(1982)年であります。

本書のねらいは、まず日本人自身に日本を知ってもらうこと、さらに国際社会に日本を理解してもらうことであります。幸いにこのねらいが日本内外の多くの読者に評価され、初版以来20年間、好評を得ていることに心から感謝申しあげます。なお、昭和62(1987)年、(株)日鉄ヒューマンデベロプメントが発足した後は、本書の著作に関する一切の業務は新日本製鐵(株)から当社に引き継がれました。

この本は今までに、昭和59(1984)年、昭和63(1988)年、平成5(1993)年、平成9(1997)年、平成11(1999)年の5回にわたり改訂を行ってきました。しかし、前回の改訂から早くも3年を経過し、内容およびデータの更新、追加が必要になっている事項が目立つようになりました。特に、日本経済は未だかつてない経験を重ねており、非常に厳しい環境の中で新しく迎えた21世紀の展望を切り拓くための努力が続けられています。また、環境保全の重要性が日本のみならず世界中で一段と認識されてきております。こうした状況を踏まえ、今回は、時代を経ても変わらない日本の姿と心については初版の記述を残しつつも、大きく変わりつつある日本の現在の姿とその歩みをできるだけ正しく記述するとともに、最新データを補充しました。

具体的には、「外交」「経済」「企業経営」「環境保全」「科学技術」の各項目を全面的に書きかえ、不良債権処理、構造改革、IT産業、雇用関係、新技術の開発など関心を集めている重要事項について、一層の内容充実をはかりました。

今回の改訂については、当社の高岡繁、福澤信二、竹内秀樹が担当し、新日本製鐵(株)の関係各部門、(株)学生社の児玉有

3

平氏にもご協力いただきました。

　また、英文翻訳は、従来と同様に Mr. Richard Foster にお願いしました。

　今後ともこの本が、当初のねらいどおり日本の理解を深めていただくためにいささかなりともお役に立つよう内容充実の努力を重ねていく所存です。引き続き読者の皆様のご支援、ご鞭撻をお願いする次第であります。

　　平成 14 年 9 月
　　　　　　　　　　㈱日鉄ヒューマンデベロプメント
　　　　　　　　　　代表取締役社長　平 山 喜 三

は　し　が　き

　この本はもともと新日本製鐵の従業員のために執筆・編集したものである。

　日本の多くの企業と同じように、当社においても、昨今国際化の進展が著しく、国の内外を問わず、社員が外国人と接触する機会が急速に増加している。

　その際、業務上の話し合いのほかに、日本の実情や文化について話題になったり、質問を受けたりすることがしばしばある。こうしたとき、外国人に適切に対応し、十分な意思疎通をはかることは至難のわざである。

　その理由として、

　第一に、外国人の知りたがっている事柄について、われわれ自身、的確な知識を持っていないこと。第二に、知識を持ち合わせていても、それをうまく表現できないということ、があげられる。

　これらの難点を少しでも解消するための参考に供したいというのが本書の趣旨である。昭和53年5月に原版発行以来、社員のみならず、社外の多くの方々から頒布のご要望をいただいてきた。

　こうした事情を背景に、学生社の鶴岡阯巳社長から再三にわたるおすすめもあり、この本が諸外国との相互理解を深めるうえで、多少なりともお役に立てばという願いをこめて、中身の稚拙をかえりみず、あえて出版していただくことにしたわけである。

　もともと、歴史や文化の基盤が異なる外国人に日本を理解してもらうのは容易なことではない。かつての「フジヤマ・ゲイシャガール」ほどではないにしても、いまだに、日本のほんとうの姿と心が、一般の外国人にはあまり理解されていないの

現実である。

　これは、日本についての紹介や情報が外国人の耳目にふれる機会が乏しかったうえに、ともすると、外国と異なった日本の特殊な面がことさらに強調されてきたことによると思われる。

　日本人は自己表現・自己主張が苦手だといわれている。これは日本人が地理的条件や歴史的経緯から、自国の閉ざされた社会の中で長い間生活してきたために、日本自身を外国に説明する必要性を感じなかったことに起因すると思われる。

　鎖国をといて、世界に門戸を開いたのちも、外国からの情報が大量に流入しているのに反して、日本から外国へ伝達されるものは、比較にならないほど少なく、きわめてアンバランスな状況を呈している。

　本来、国際社会における各国民の相互理解の根底には、国民それぞれの自己主張とその相互容認があるはずである。

　すでに先進国の域に達し、応分の国際的活動が期待されているわが国は、今後あらゆる面で外国との関係をさらに深め、影響力をいっそう強めていくと考えられる。これにともなって、日本と外国との間にいろいろな誤解や摩擦がしばしば発生しかねない。今後われわれは、外国についての認識を深めるとともに、あらゆる機会をとらえて、日本に対する外国の人たちの理解を広めかつ深めてゆく努力が必要である。

　この本の原版を執筆するまえに、外国出張あるいは滞在などで外国人とひんぱんに交際した社員を対象に、話題になる事柄、よく受ける質問についてアンケートを行なった。得られた約500の例を192項目に整理した。それぞれに解説を加え、あわせて英語の対訳を付した。今回市販するにあたっては、さらに項目をしぼって171とし、若干の編成がえを試みた。

　この本の執筆・編集には、主として新日本製鐵能力開発部の青砥安男、百瀬孝、立山恵の諸君があたった。翻訳は永年日本に在住し、その事情にも詳しく、当社の英会話講師になって頂

いている Mr. Richard Foster および Mr. John Bowen にお願い
した。ことに両氏からは、内容についても外国人として見た場
合の疑問の提示と、適切な助言を頂いたことに深く感謝してい
る。

　原稿の校閲などについては、当社の各部門、海外事務所の者
に援助を求め、苦瓜純一氏（原版発刊時の本社能力開発室長）
にもご指導を頂いたことを特記しておきたい。

　また、この本の出版にあたってお世話になった学生社の鶴岡
阨巳社長、三木敦雄常務および土屋晃三氏にも深く感謝の意を
表したい。

　本の構成について、なお多くの大切な事項を見落したり、解
説の内容について的を射ていないものがあるのではないかと危
惧している。ご活用下さる読者諸賢の忌憚ないご批判をお願い
し、後日の改訂に備えたいと思う。

　　昭和 57 年 7 月

　　　　　　　　　　　新日本製鐵　能力開発部長
　　　　　　　　　　　　小　川　一　海

執筆・編集に際して留意した点

1) 各項目の解説は事典的なものではなく、話題の一例を示したものである。具体的な例や客観的なデータをできるだけ引用して、外国との対比・関連性について述べるなど、外国人の理解を得やすいように心掛けた。

2) 和文と英文を対比して収録した。

3) 解説に関する補足を巻末に付記した。

4) 他の文献からの引用については、その文献名・著者名（および訳者名）を引用個所に表示したほか、主な参考文献・資料などは一括して巻末に列記した。

5) 文中の単位などは次の通りとした。

    年　号：西　暦
    時　代：西暦の世紀または日本史で使用されている時代
    　　　　名もしくは元号
    度量衡：メートル法（ヤード・ポンド法を付記）
    金　額：円または米ドル
    温　度：摂氏（華氏を付記）

6) 英文の綴りは米国式とした。

7) 英文中、日本語音をローマ字綴りで表示した語句（標題および固有名詞を除く）はそれが英語化しているか否かにかかわらず、項目ごとにはじめて使用したものについて斜体（イタリック）を用いた。

8) 本の大きさ、装丁は、携帯して手軽に活用し得るように配慮した。

[本文中の写真は毎日新聞社提供]

Foreword to the Seventh Edition

The first edition of Nippon: the Land and its People, compiled by the Personnel Development Department of Nippon Steel Corporation, was published in 1982.

This book was written with two aims: to make Japanese readers more familiar with their own country and to promote a better understanding of Japan throughout the world. The large readership the book has enjoyed both at home and abroad over the past twenty years is most gratifying, as we believe it indicates that both aims have been achieved in some measure.

Since its founding in 1987, Nippon Steel Human Resources Development Co., Ltd. (NHD) has taken over all work related to the preparation and publication of this book from Nippon Steel Corporation (NSC).

Revised editions of the book were published in 1984, 1988, 1993, 1997 and 1999. Still, during the more than two years since the last revision, the need to update content and statistics and to add new material became increasingly apparent. Numerous changes were made necessary, for instance, by the unprecedented developments the Japanese economy experienced in its struggle to open new avenues of progress in the 21st century. Another group of revisions relates to the ever greater emphasis on environmental preservation both in Japan and internationally. In this Seventh Edition, we have attempted to bring all sections of the book up to date so as to describe as accurately as possible the marked changes that have taken place in Japan, and how they came about. Those portions of the earlier editions that remain untouched by time have been left intact.

The sections on diplomacy, economy, business management, preservation of the environment, and science and technology were extensively rewritten. Topics of fresh interest and significance, such as the bad debt issue, structural reform, IT industry, employment relations, and the development of new technologies were expanded.

The writing and editing of new and updated portions of this edition was undertaken by Mr. Shigeru Takaoka, Mr. Shinji Fukuzawa and Mr. Hideki Takeuchi, with invaluable assistance

9

from many persons at NSC and Mr. Yuhei Kodama of Gakusei-sha Publishing Co., Ltd. The English translation was, as before, done by Mr. Richard Foster.

We sincerely hope that this book may continue to make some small contribution toward its goal of furthering understanding about Japan. Reader comments and advice on how this can be better achieved will be greatly appreciated.

September 2002

Kizo Hirayama
President
Nippon Steel Human Resources
Development Co., Ltd.

Foreword

Nippon: the Land and its People was originally compiled for the use of the employees of Nippon Steel Corporation.

Like many Japanese companies, Nippon Steel has been internationalizing its business operations very rapidly the past few years, with the result that the employees are now coming into increasingly frequent contact with foreigners, both in Japan and overseas.

At such times, the conversation often turns to subjects about Japan, and our employees are often asked about Japanese culture and other aspects of their country. Many of these questions are extremely difficult to answer accurately and to the satisfaction of the inquirer.

Two reasons for this are that the employee often does not know enough about the subject, and even when he does know the answer, he is often incapable of expressing it well in a foreign language.

This book was compiled to help eliminate these problems. Since it first appeared in May 1978, it has gained a wide readership both inside the company and with the general public.

This new edition of *Nippon: the Land and its People* has been published in the hope of making some further contribution to mutual understanding between the people of Japan and the people of other countries throughout the world. Especially instrumental in the publication of this new edition was Mr. Masami Tsuruoka, president of Gakuseisha Publishing Co., Ltd., at whose repeated urging the decision to publish an edition for general distribution was finally made.

It is no easy task to explain Japan to people with a fundamentally different historical and cultural background. Although the tendency to look on Japan simply as the land of Fujiyama and the geisha girl may no longer be so strong as it once was, internationally the general level of knowledge about Japan remains low.

One reason for this is that other countries have had little chance to obtain reliable information about Japan. Another is that in the information that has been available there is often too much emphasis on the special aspects of Japan, those which set it apart from other countries.

The Japanese are not good at explaining themselves or expounding their opinions. Geographical and historical factors have long kept Japan an isolated nation and the people have felt no need to explain themselves to the "outside world."

Even after the country was opened up, we still had very little to say about ourselves. Compared with the torrent of knowledge and information that poured into Japan, the amount that flowed out was negligible.

Mutual understanding among the community of nations is based on the principles of self-expression and mutual tolerance.

Japan has now earned a position among the advanced countries of the world and must begin reflecting its new status in its international activities. In doing this, it will become more deeply involved with other countries throughout the world in every aspect of its international relations and will be exerting a stronger influence on world events. The likelihood of misunderstanding and friction arising between Japan and other countries will increase proportionally. From now on, it will be imperative for the Japanese not only to know more about foreign countries but also to take every possible opportunity to assist people everywhere to obtain a broader and deeper understanding of Japan.

Prior to the first edition of this book a questionnaire was circulated among Nippon Steel employees who were in frequent contact with foreigners through overseas trips and assignments. In this way information was obtained on the topics and questions which come up most frequently in meetings with people of other countries. About five hundred topics were mentioned. These were reduced to one hundred ninety-two items through a process of consolidation and elimination and for each of these there was prepared a Japanese commentary along with a corresponding English translation. The present edition being intended for general distribution, the number of topics was further reduced to one hundred seventy-one and a certain amount of reorganization of the material was undertaken.

The writing and editing of this book was done chiefly by the following members of Nippon Steel's Personnel Development Division: Mr. Yasuo Aoto, Mr. Takashi Momose and Mr. Megumi Tateyama. The translation into English was prepared mainly by Mr. Richard Foster and Mr. John Bowen, English instructors at Nippon Steel. Both translators have lived in Japan for many years and are very familiar with the country. In the course of their translation work, they were able to point out problems in the contents of the book as seen from a non-Japanese vantage point and their suggestions and advice were invaluable.

Much of the manuscript was reviewed by persons in other divisions and the overseas offices of the company. Also, special mention must be made of the assistance and advice received from Mr. Junichi Nigauri (General Manager of the Personnel Development Office at the time the original version of this book was published).

Much gratitude is due Mr. Masami Tsuruoka, president of Gakuseisha Publishing Co., Ltd., as well as Mr. Atsuo Miki, a director, and Mr. Kozo Tsuchiya of the same company, for their untiring assistance in the publication of the present edition.

Any shortcomings in the content of the book or the accuracy of the commentary are, of course, the responsibility of the Personnel Development Division of Nippon Steel Corporation. This Division will be grateful to receive any comments, criticism or advice the readers may have and will make every effort to reflect these in future revisions.

July 1982

Kazumi Ogawa
General Manager
Personnel Development Division
Nippon Steel Corporation

Editors' Note

1) No attempt has been made to produce an encyclopedia. Instead, we have tried to limit ourselves to a single aspect of each topic and to make the accompanying commentary easy for those not familiar with Japan to understand by including concrete examples, data and comparisons with other countries.
2) Corresponding Japanese and English commentaries appear on opposing pages.
3) Supplementary information relating to our commentary has been included at the back of the book.
4) Quotations are accompanied by the title of the reference, the name of the author (and translator if any). A list of references appears at the back of the book.
5) Dates are according to the Western calendar. Eras are in some cases referred to by century of the Western calendar and in others by era names commonly used in Japanese history.

   Weights and measures are metric with English system equivalents given in parentheses.

   Monetary values are given in yen and/or U. S. dollars.

   Temperatures are in degrees Celsius with conversions into degrees Fahrenheit given in parentheses.
6) American spelling has been used.
7) All Japanese words used in the book (except those in the headings and proper nouns) are italicized the first time they appear in each topic.
8) A pocket-size format has been used so the book can be easily carried as a handy reference.

目　　次

7 文 化

Contents

7 Culture

日　本

―その姿と心―

1 地理・歴史

(1) 地理

a) 位置・国の広さ

　　日本は、アジア大陸の東側に南北 3,000 km（1,860 マイル）にわたって、弧状に位置している島国である。

　　本州・四国・九州・北海道の四つの主な島のほか、散在する 7,000 弱の島からなっている。これらは日本列島と総称されている。

　　首都東京は東経 140 度（ニューギニア島やオーストラリアの中央とほぼ同経度）、北緯 36 度（中国の青島・イランのテヘラン・地中海のマルタ島・ジブラルタル海峡およびアメリカのグランドキャニオンなどとほぼ同緯度）にある。

　　東京から各地への距離は次のとおりである。

ニューヨーク	10,850 km	(6,740 マイル)
ロサンゼルス	8,740 〃	(5,430 〃)
リオデジャネイロ	18,560 〃	(11,530 〃)
ロンドン	9,560 〃	(5,940 〃)
ベルリン	8,910 〃	(5,540 〃)
カイロ	9,550 〃	(5,930 〃)
シドニー	7,830 〃	(4,870 〃)
シンガポール	5,320 〃	(3,310 〃)
マニラ	3,000 〃	(1,860 〃)
上海	1,770 〃	(1,100 〃)

国土面積は約 37 万 8,000 km²（146,000 平方マイル）で、マレーシアよりわずかに大きく、中国の 25 分の 1・アメリカの 25 分の 1・ブラジルの 23 分の 1・インドネシアの 5 分の 1 にあたる。

　　〔注〕各国の面積は巻末〔統計資料〕欄(1)参照

b) 日本の気候

　　日本列島は、南北 3,000 km（1,860 マイル）におよび、亜熱帯から亜寒帯にわたるうえ、複雑な地形や海流による影響も大きいため、気候の地域差が顕著である。

1 Geography and History

(1) Geography

a) Location and Size of Japan

Japan is an island nation lying off the east coast of Asia. It has the general shape of a crescent and extends 3,000 km (1,860 miles) from tip to tip.

The country is made up of four main islands (Honshu, Shikoku, Kyushu and Hokkaido) which together with a little under 7,000 smaller islands are collectively referred to as the Japanese Archipelago.

The nation's capital, Tokyo, lies at 140° east longitude (on a line with New Guinea and central Australia) and 36° north latitude (about the same as Tsingtao, Teheran, Malta, the Strait of Gibraltar and the Grand Canyon).

Below are the distances between Tokyo and some of the other major cities of the world:

	km	miles		km	miles
New York	10,850	(6,740)	Berlin	8,910	(5,540)
Los Angeles	8,740	(5,430)	Cairo	9,550	(5,930)
			Sydney	7,830	(4,870)
Rio de Janeiro	18,560	(11,530)	Singapore	5,320	(3,310)
			Manila	3,000	(1,860)
London	9,560	(5,940)	Shanghai	1,770	(1,100)

Japan's land area of about 378,000 km² (146,000 square miles) is slightly larger than that of Malaysia, one twenty-fifth that of China, one twenty-fifth that of the United States, one twenty-third that of Brazil and one fifth that of Indonesia.

b) Climate of Japan

The Japanese climate differs greatly from region to region. Although this is largely due to the country's north-south length of 3,000 km (1,860 miles) which puts one of its ends in the subfrigid zone and the other in the subtropic zone, a complex topography and the influence of ocean currents are also important factors.

しかし、大部分の地域は海洋性の温暖な気候で、四季の区別がはっきりしている。

　起伏に富んだ山脈が日本列島を縦断しているため、太平洋側と日本海側の気候の差が大きい。

　太平洋側では、夏は南東の季節風が吹いてむし暑く、冬は乾燥した晴天が多い。日本海側では、冬は大陸方面からの北西の季節風による降雪が多い。この地方は世界有数の多雪地帯で、新潟県下などでは、4〜5m（13〜16フィート）にも達するところがある。

　北海道を除く地域では、6月上旬から7月中旬にかけて高温・多湿の雨期（梅雨）がある。8月から10月にかけては、日本列島の南西部は台風の影響を受けることが多い。

　本州・北海道の内陸部（とくに盆地）では降雨量が少なく、気温の上下差が大きいところがある。また、瀬戸内海の沿岸部は、前述の梅雨期以外は概して雨が少なく、気候温暖である。

　日本の大部分の地域で最もよい季節は春と秋で、とくに新緑のもえる4〜5月ごろと、さわやかで木の葉の色づく9月下旬から11月中旬ごろまでの山野の風景がもっとも美しい。

　梅雨・台風・豪雪はいずれも愉快なものではない。なかでも、風水害の大部分は台風がもたらす。台風のころはちょうど稲の開花〜結実期にあたるので、農家の心配も大きい。しかしながら、これらが与える自然の恵みも大きい。梅雨期の降雨は米作になくてはならないものであり、台風時の大雨や冬の積雪は水資源を豊かにする。

Most of Japan does, however, enjoy a temperate, oceanic type of climate with four distinct seasons.

Ranges of rugged mountains running nearly the full length of the country give the Pacific and Sea of Japan sides of the islands vastly differing climatic patterns.

On the Pacific side, the summers are hot and humid with prevailing seasonal winds from the southeast. The winters are dry and marked by many clear days. On the Sea of Japan side, northwesterly winter winds off the Asian continent bring regular, heavy snows that make this one of the snowiest regions on earth. In Niigata Prefecture, for example, annual snowfalls of 4 to 5 meters (13 to 16 feet) are not unusual.

All areas except the northern-most island of Hokkaido have a hot and very humid rainy season (called the baiu) that lasts from early June to mid-July. And between August and October, the southwestern part of the archipelago is often hit by typhoons.

The inland regions of Honshu and Hokkaido, particularly the basins in these areas, receive little rain and are subject to large temperature variations. On the other hand, the coastal regions of the Inland Sea lying between the islands of Honshu and Shiko-ku, though also quite dry except during the rainy season, have a moderate climate.

In almost all parts of Japan the best seasons are spring and autumn. The countryside is especially beautiful during April and May when all is freshly green, and between late September and mid-November when the air is stimulating and the leaves have changed color.

There is no pretending that the rainy season, the typhoons and the heavy snows are pleasant aspects of the Japanese climate. The typhoons, for example, are responsible for the major share of the wind and flood damage suffered by Japan and they are particularly worrisome for rice-farmers, as it is in the typhoon season that the rice plant blooms and ripens. Still each of the aspects of the climate is in its own way a natural blessing: the rains which fall during the baiu are indispensable to a good rice crop and the precipitation that comes in the form of typhoon rains and heavy snows makes an invaluable contribution to Japan's water resources.

c）東京の気候 （1971〜2000 年の平均値）

東京の年間平均気温は 15.9℃ （60.6°F） である。月間平均気温がもっとも高いのは 8 月で 27.1℃（80.8°F）、もっとも低いのは 1 月で 5.8℃ （42.4°F） である。しかし、真夏には最高気温は 39.1℃ （102.4°F）、真冬には最低気温は− 9℃ （15.8°F） に達する。とくに夏は高温に加えて、湿度が高いためたいへんむし暑い。

年間平均降雨量は 1,467 mm で、温帯地方としてはかなり多いが、もっとも多いのは 6 月で 165 mm、もっとも少ないのは 12 月で 40 mm である。

雨の日は平均して 1 週間に 1 回であるが、梅雨期には期間中の 4 分の 3 は雨天か曇天が続き、冬期は 3 分の 2 が晴天で、時折 1 カ月前後も雨が降らないこともある。

東京の降雪は一冬 1 〜 3 回で量も少ない。

d）日本の地形

日本列島は太平洋や日本海などの海に囲まれ、大陸とは浅い大陸棚で接している。太平洋側には非常に深い日本海溝や伊豆小笠原海溝がある。

日本にはいくつかの火山脈が走っているため、地形は変化に富む。川は短く急流で、山あいでは深い峡谷をなし、海岸線は複雑に入りくんでいる。風光明媚なところが多く、温泉地も点在している。

日本列島は環太平洋地震帯の上にあり、火山活動も活発で世界でも有数の地震多発地帯となっている （1923 年の関東大震災 （マグニチュード 7.9） は、東京をふくむ広い範囲にわたって大規模な損害を与え、1995 年の阪神・淡路大震災 （マグニチュード 7.2） は神戸および淡路島をはじめとする阪神地域に大きな被害をもたらした、二大地震であった）。

c) Climate of Tokyo (Average for 1971~2000)

Tokyo has an annual average temperature of 15.9° C (60.6° F). The month with the highest average is August at 27.1° C (80.8° F) and that with the lowest is January at 5.8° C (42.4° F). The record summer high is 39.1° C (102.4° F) and the lowest winter temperature recorded is −9° C (15.8° F). The hot days of summer are often accompanied by high humidity and are therefore extremely muggy.

Average annual precipitation is 1,467 mm, relatively high for a city in the temperate zone. The wettest month is June with an average rainfall of 165 mm and the driest is December with an average of 40 mm.

On an annual average there is one rainy day per week. In fact, however, it is rainy or cloudy three fourths of the time during the rainy season and is clear two thirds of the time during the winter months. In winter, it is not uncommon to have a dry spell lasting one month or more.

Tokyo generally has between one and three light snows per season.

d) Japanese Geography

The islands of Japan are bounded by the Pacific Ocean on the east and the Japan Sea on the west. They are connected with the Asian mainland by the relatively shallow-lying continental shelf. On the Pacific side of the islands are two regions of extreme depth known as the Japan Deep and the Izu-Ogasawara Deep.

Several volcanic ranges running through the country have given Japan a great deal of variety in its topographical features. Its rivers are short and fast-flowing and form deep gorges in the mountainous areas. All of the major islands have highly irregular coast lines. Wherever the traveler goes in Japan, he will be impressed by the many places of scenic beauty. The countryside is dotted with hot springs, many of which have become popular resorts.

Lying on the Circum-Pacific earthquake zone, the Japanese Archipelago not only is the site of considerable volcanic activity but also is one of the world's most seismologically active areas. (Two particularly disastrous tremors were the Great Kanto Earthquake of 1923 (magnitude of 7.9), which caused extensive damage over a wide area including Tokyo, and the Great Hanshin Earthquake of 1995 (7.2), which devastated much of the

日本の国土は山地が 70 ％近い。その大部分は森林に
おおわれているので、国土の森林の面積は 66 ％と断然
多い。農業用地は 14 ％、宅地は 3 ％で、工業用地にい
たっては、わずか 0.4 ％にすぎない。

e）日本の人口

　　日本の総人口は 1 億 2,692 万人（2000 年）であり、
これは、中国（12 億 6,684 万人、99 年）、インド（9 億
8,661 万人、99 年）、アメリカ（2 億 7,313 万人、99
年）、インドネシア（2 億 926 万人、99 年）、ブラジル
（1 億 6,537 万人、99 年）、ロシア（1 億 4,556 万人、
99 年）、パキスタン（1 億 3,451 万人、99 年）に次いで
世界第 8 位である。
　　人口の分布は、温暖で交通・産業の発達した太平洋側
の海岸沿いの平野に多く、本州の南関東から北九州にか
けて人口の 70 ％が集まっている。また、工業の発展に
ともなって、人口が都市に集中し、農村では著しく減少
した。
　　東京都（区部）の 813 万人（2000 年、郊外をふくむ
と 1,206 万人）を筆頭に、人口 100 万人以上が 13 都市
ある。東京は郊外もふくむと、ニューヨーク 1,994 万人、
ロサンゼルス 1,550 万人、メキシコシティー 1,505 万人、
ムンバイ（ボンベイ）1,260 万人に次いで、世界で 5 番
目に人口の多い都市である。
　　〔注〕日本の主要都市人口は巻末〔統計資料〕欄(4)参照

f）日本の山・川・湖

　　日本の約 70 ％は山地であるが、とくに本州の中央部
には飛騨・木曽・赤石の三つの山脈があって、3,000 m
（9,840 フィート）以上の山々がそびえている。これら
はそれぞれ北・中央・南アルプスとも呼ばれ、また、総
称して日本アルプスといわれる。これは 1896 年に、イ
ギリス人ウェストンによって名付けられたものである。
　　富士山は、標高 3,776 m（12,388 フィート）の日本
最高の山で、典型的な円錐形活火山（1707 年に大噴火
があったが、それ以後過去約 3 世紀噴火活動はない）で、
美しく広い裾野を持つ。冬には中腹まで雪におおわれ、
一層美しさを増す。

Hanshin area, including Kobe, and Awaji Island.)

Nearly 70% of Japan's land area is mountainous. Since most of this is forested, far over half of the country's total area (66%) is covered with forest. Agricultural land accounts for 14% and residential land for 3%. A mere 0.4% is devoted to industrial purposes.

e) Population of Japan

Japan has a population of 126.92 million (2000), putting it in eighth place after China (1,266.84 million, 1999), India (986.61 million, 1999), the United States (273.13 million, 1999), Indonesia (209.26 million, 1999), Brazil (165.37 million, 1999), Russia (145.56 million, 1999) and Pakistan (134.51 million, 1999).

The population is greatest along the Pacific seaboard where the weather is mild and the transportation and industrial facilities are most highly developed. In fact, approximately 70% of the nation's people live on the strip of coastal plain between Tokyo and the northern part of Kyushu. Advancing industrialization has been accompanied by a population shift toward the large cities and a marked population decline in the agricultural areas.

Of the thirteen cities in Japan with populations of over one million, the largest, Tokyo, has 8.13 million inhabitants in its twenty-three wards and a grand total of 12.06 million inhabitants when its suburbs are included (2000). Tokyo thus places fifth in the world after New York (pop. 19.94 million), Los Angeles (15. 50 million), Mexico City (15.05 million) and Mumbai (Bombay; 12.60 million).

f) Mountains, Rivers and Lakes of Japan

About 70% of Japan's land area is mountainous. The most prominent mountains are found in the Hida, Kiso and Akaishi ranges of central Honshu where the highest peaks are over 3,000 meters (9,840 feet). These ranges are, in the order named, often referred to as the North, Central and South Alps. Collectively, they are called the Japanese or Nippon Alps. These designations were introduced into the Japanese vocabulary by Walter Weston, an Englishman, in 1896.

Japan's highest peak at 3,776 meters (12,388 feet) is Mt. Fuji, an almost perfectly conical volcano. Although still classified as "active," Mt. Fuji has displayed no volcanic activity in the nearly

現在、日本には浅間山・阿蘇山・桜島・雲仙岳・三原山など約 60 の活火山がある。

　川は短くて急流が多く、最も長い信濃川でも 367 km（228 マイル）である。落差の大きい急流は水力発電に適し、美しい峡谷をつくっているが、交通にはほとんど利用できず、洪水を起こす危険もある。

　湖は山間にあり、水が澄んでいて眺めのよいものが多い。ただし、規模は小さく、最も大きい琵琶湖が 674 km²（260 平方マイル）である。また、最も深い湖は田沢湖で、水深 423 m（1,388 フィート）である。このほか、砂丘・砂州などによって外海と分離してできた潟として、霞ケ浦 168 km²（65 平方マイル）がある。

g）日本の植物

　日本の気候の地域差は顕著である（b 項）ため、植物の生態は複雑で多極化している。日本にある約 4,500 種の植物のうち、約 1,000 種は日本固有種である。

　北海道をふくむ日本北部には、トドマツなどの針葉樹など、シベリア地域と似かよった植物がみられる。

　日本中央部から九州へかけての平地には、クリなどの温帯落葉樹が多い。

　東北地方から中部山岳地帯ではブナ・カエデなどが広がる。これらの林は 5 月から 6 月には美しい新緑におおわれ、秋には山々は色とりどりの紅葉に彩られる。

　サクラは日本人にはことのほか愛され、日本全土で植林されている。毎春、サクラの季節は沖縄から始まり、北上する。サクラは一週間で散ってしまうが、「サクラ前線」を追って旅行すれば、約 3 カ月間サクラの花を楽しむことができる。

300 years since its last eruption, a major one, in 1707. The beauty of the mountain with its nearly perfect profile and wide-flowing skirts is striking at any time but especially so in winter when its upper half is covered with snow.

Japan has about sixty active volcanoes, the most famous of which are Mt. Asama, Mt. Aso, Mt. Sakurajima, Mt. Unzen and Mt. Mihara.

Most Japanese rivers are short and fast flowing. Even the longest, the Shinano River, is a mere 367 km (228 miles) from source to mouth. Though fast streams which drop from great heights have certain advantages when applied to hydroelectric power generation and are apt to provide picturesque canyons, they are all but impossible to use as waterways and are susceptible to flooding.

Most of Japan's lakes are in the mountains. Many are clear and scenic, but all are of limited size, the largest being Lake Biwa which has an area of 674 km² (260 square miles). Japan's deepest lake is Lake Tazawa which reaches a depth of 423 meters (1,388 feet). The country also has a number of lagoons, bodies of water which have become cut off from the sea by sand banks or reefs. The largest of these is Kasumigaura, which has an area of 168 km² (65 square miles).

g) Plants of Japan

Since the climate differs qreatly between different regions of Japan (see b) of this section), plant life is both complex and diverse. Of Japan's 4,500 or so kinds of plants, around 1,000 are peculiar to the country.

Many of the trees of Hokkaido and other northern regions are similar to those of Siberia, including the fir and other conifers.

The trees at lower altitudes between central Honshu and Kyushu are mainly temperate zone deciduous types such as the Japanese chestnut.

Beech and maple are common through the mountain areas between the Tohoku District and the Chubu Mountain Range. The groves are especially beautiful in May and June, when the foliage is freshly green, and again in the autumn, when they set the hillsides ablaze with red and yellow tints.

The Japanese are particularly fond of the cherry tree and have planted it throughout the country. Each spring, the cherry blossom season begins in Okinawa and moves gradually north-

春は、さまざまな食べられる野草（山菜）が摘める季節である。秋は、山林にキノコ狩りに出かけるシーズンになる。そのなかで、マツタケはその香りから第一とされている。

h) 日本の動物

日本は植物相がきわめて複雑であるので、動物相も寒帯性動物から熱帯性動物まで、きわめて多様に発達している。

北海道には、ヒグマなどシベリアの動物と同種のものがいる。

本州には中国大陸・朝鮮半島と共通した動物がたくさんいる。典型的なものはキツネ・タヌキである。また、本州にはシカ・キジなどの固有種がいる。このほかには、高山地帯の鳥で四季に応じて羽根の色を変えるライチョウがいる。かつて本州に生息していたニホンオオカミは今は絶滅している。

日本には北海道を除くどの地方にも、サル（ニホンザル）が1種だけ生息している。サルは本来熱帯性の動物で、寒帯には野生していない。たとえば、北アメリカ・ヨーロッパにはサルは生息していない。例外はニホンザルで、青森県（北緯40度）にも生息しており、これはサルの北限になっている。雪の中ではねまわるサルが見られるのは日本だけである。

沖縄や南西諸島には、イリオモテヤマネコ・ハブなどの熱帯性動物も多い。

(2) 歴史

a) 日本人の祖先

日本民族の起源には不明な点が多いが、日本人の乳児の多くが、臀部に蒙古斑という青い斑紋があるところから、アジア蒙古人種に属するといわれている。

ward. Although at each place the petals fall after about a week, a person traveling north with the "cherry blossom front" would be able to enjoy the blossoms for nearly three months.

Spring is the time for picking a variety of edible wild plants, and autumn the time for a trip into the woods to gather mushrooms. While many kinds of mushrooms are picked, the matsutake mushroom (Armillaria matsutake) is the favorite for its splendid aroma.

h) Japanese Wildlife

Japan's highly complex flora has led to the development of a multifarious fauna including arctic animals, tropical animals and everything in between.

The island of Hokkaido has many of the same animals found in Siberia: the brown bear and others.

The island of Honshu has many animal species in common with mainland China and the Korean Peninsula. Typical of these are the fox and raccoon dog. Honshu also has a number of animals and birds not found elsewhere, such as the Japanese deer and Japanese pheasant. Another is the snow grouse, a high mountain bird whose feathers change color with the seasons. The Japanese wolf, a former denizen of Honshu, is now extinct.

A single species of monkey inhabits all parts of Japan other than Hokkaido. Monkeys are basically tropical animals not found wild in northern regions. They do not inhabit North America and Europe, for example. The exception is the Japanese monkey, which lives as far north as Aomori Prefecture (about 40° north latitude), a record among simians. Only in Japan can one see monkeys frolicking in deep snow.

Many of the animals in Okinawa and the other Nansei Islands are tropical types, such as the Iriomote wildcat, and habu (a poisonous snake).

(2) History

a) Origin of the Japanese People

It is not altogether clear where the Japanese people came from. However, from the fact that most Japanese babies are born with a blue mark known as the Mongolian spot at the base of the spine, it is generally agreed that the people of Japan are an Asian

日本列島には、1万年以上前の旧石器時代から人間が住んでおり、そのころの石器や人骨も発見されている。

以前は、この人たちは現在の日本人とは異なる先住民族であって、あとから現在の日本人の祖先が入ってきて、先住民族を駆逐したと考えられていた。しかし、最近の研究では、日本人の祖先は旧石器時代からの住人にほかならず、その後、中国・朝鮮・東南アジアなどからたくさんの人が日本に移住して文化を伝え、次第に混血して現在の日本人になったと考えられている。

b）日本国の起源

紀元1世紀ごろ、日本の各地に100余の小国が分立していたが、その後これらの国々はしだいに統一されていった。

4世紀には、関西地方に比較的大きな国ができたが、最後にこれを統一したのが現在の天皇家の先祖である。このころの日本の国の範囲は、本州の西半分と九州の北半分および四国であった。

このように長い期間をかけて徐々に国が統一されていったので、何年何月をもって国が生まれたと決めることはできない。8世紀につくられた史書の『古事記』および『日本書紀』には、紀元前660年に初代の神武天皇が建国し即位したと書かれている。その即位の日が現在の暦では2月11日にあたるため、この日を「建国記念の日」として祝日としている。

c）日本の歴史

1～2万年前までの日本は、アジア大陸と陸続きであったが、地殻変動や海水面の上昇により大陸から離れた。島国であったため外国の侵略を受けにくく、しかも大陸とそれほど離れていなかったので、外国の進んだ文化を取り入れることができた。そこで大陸文化とは共通性を

mongoloid race.

From paleolithic stone implements and human bones which have been discovered, it is known that man has inhabited the Japanese Archipelago for more than ten thousand years.

It was formerly thought that these early inhabitants were aborigines of different stock from today's Japanese and that they were annihilated by the forebears of the islands' present inhabitants. Recent research, however, indicates that these early comers are themselves the true ancestors of the present Japanese people. Later, when large numbers of people began migrating to Japan from China, Korea and Southeast Asia, they and their cultures were gradually absorbed by the earlier settlers. Today's Japanese are the result of this blending.

b) Origin of the Japanese Nation

First-century Japan was a collection of over one hundred small, independent countries located in various parts of the islands. From this time on, the trend was toward coalescence and unification and the number of countries gradually decreased.

By the fourth century one relatively large country in the Kansai area had grown to particular prominence. The family which ruled this country in the final stages of its consolidation was to become the imperial family whose reign continues even to this day. The territory that eventually came under imperial rule extended over the western half of Honshu, the northern half of Kyushu and all of Shikoku.

Thus the foundation of Japan was a gradual process that continued over many years and it is therefore impossible to set any date as that on which the nation came into existence. In the Kojiki and the Nihonshoki, two ancient chronicles written in the eighth century, it is recorded that the Emperor Jinmu began his reign in the year 660 B.C. and the date given for his ascension, February 11, is now set aside as a Japanese holiday called National Foundation Day.

c) History of Japan

Until ten or twenty thousand years ago, Japan was still connected to the Asian continent by land. Its complete separation, when it finally came, was the result of movements of the earth's crust and a rise in sea level. As an island country, Japan has not been susceptible to invasion but, being relatively close to the

持ちながらも、独自性の高い日本文化を育てて今日にいたっている。

○原始時代（3世紀まで）

1万年前から紀元前3～2世紀ごろまでの縄文時代は、おもに狩猟・漁業・採集などによって生活していた。その後、3世紀までの弥生時代には、稲作を行い金属器を使い、日本人の生活の原型をつくった。小さな国々が分立していたが、しだいに統一されていった。

○古代（4世紀～12世紀）

4世紀に天皇が日本を統一し、大陸から文字・制度・仏教・儒教・工芸技術などの文物を導入して国の基礎をかためた。このころ天皇は、有力な豪族の協力によって政治を行っていた。国民は主として稲作中心の農業に従事していた。

7世紀に中国（唐）の制度にならって法治国家体制（律令政治）をつくった。土地や人民は、豪族の支配から離れて国のものとなり、一般農民は1人2,300 m²（0.57エーカー）の土地を国から与えられて一定の税金を納め、国防にも従事することになった。

しかし、この制度も8世紀からくずれ始め、貴族が土地を私有して荘園にしていった。貴族は土地と人民を支配して富を蓄え、独自の貴族文化を形成した。

○中世・近世（12世紀～19世紀前半）

貴族に使われていた武士は、各地方で農民を直接支配することによって力をつけ、12世紀の終わりに政権をとり、以後19世紀まで約700年間政権を持ち続けた。

continent, it has had fairly easy access to advanced foreign cultures. This allowed the country to possess a culture having many points in common with that of the continent while simultaneously developing a highly independent and thoroughly "Japanese" culture.

○ Primitive times (up to the third century):

The period extending from ten thousand years ago up to the third or second century B.C. is referred to as the Jomon period. The main sources of livelihood during this period were hunting, fishing and gathering. Following the Jomon period came the Yayoi period which lasted to around the third century A.D. It was during this period that the Japanese mastered the art of rice cultivation, began to use metal implements and set the fundamental patterns of Japanese life. A large number of small independent countries developed during the Yayoi period and then began to unite.

○ Ancient times (fourth century to twelfth century):

After consolidation of Japan into a single nation in the fourth century, successive emperors strengthened the foundations of the country by introducing various aspects of continental learning and culture. These included the Chinese writing system, various social systems, religion (Buddhism), ideology (Confucianism) and arts and crafts. The emperors of this period ruled in cooperation with a number of powerful families. The common people were for the most part engaged in the production of rice.

In the seventh century, a constitutional form of government modeled after that of China (T'ang) was introduced. The land and the people were no longer under the control of powerful families but were put under the direct rule of the state. Each farmer was granted 2,300 m² (0.57 acres) of land and was required to pay a prescribed tax and contribute a certain amount of his time to defending the nation.

This system crumbled in the eighth century as the nobility began taking private possession of the land and establishing manors. With both the land and the people under their control, the aristocrats of the period were able to amass great fortunes and establish their own independent culture.

○ Middle ages and early modern ages (twelfth century to early nineteenth century):

Warriors employed by the nobility to keep the peasants under control took advantage of their position of direct control over

武士の棟梁は天皇から征夷大将軍に任命されて幕府を設け、各地域の武士の頭（鎌倉時代は「御家人」、室町時代は「守護大名」、江戸時代は「大名」）を支配した。この武士の頭は、土地と人民を支配することについて将軍から承認をうけ、将軍に対して忠誠を誓った。

　17世紀はじめから幕府は外国との交渉を断ち、外国との往来を禁止した。これが鎖国である。この時期の主産業は農業であったが、次第に工業および商業が盛んになり、18〜19世紀には平和な時代が続いたため商人の経済力が武士を圧倒し、幕府の支配体制をゆるがし始めた。また、文化、教育の発展もめざましく、次の近代国家発展期の基礎をつくった。

○近代（19世紀後半〜1945年）

　日本は、1853年のアメリカの提督ペリー来日を契機として鎖国を解き、通商貿易が始まった。しかし、これは幕府を窮地に追いこむこととなった。貿易により経済的危機がもたらされ、これを機会に反幕府勢力が強くなったからである。この勢力が次第に優勢となり、ついに、1867年に幕府は大政奉還を行い、翌68年に明治天皇を上にいただく新政府が成立した。この際、両勢力の賢明な指導者の措置により、大規模な武力衝突は避けられた。

　幕府倒壊後、20年の間に欧州諸国に範をとる諸施策が講じられて、近代国家に発展していった。すなわち、統治制度の面では、内閣制度の設置、憲法の制定（議会の開設、司法権の独立、国民の権利義務を定めた）、ドイツ式陸軍とイギリス式海軍の設立、地方制度の改革などが行われた。経済の面では、土地制度の改革と官営事業による産業振興、貨幣制度の統一が行われた。社会文

the farmers to greatly expand their power, until late in the twelfth century they were able to replace the nobility as the de facto leaders of the country. The rule of the warrior class lasted nearly seven hundred years, finally coming to an end in the nineteenth century.

Formally, the leading warrior would be appointed by the emperor as his "shogun in charge of conquering barbarian territories" and with this designation would set up his feudal government (bakufu) and take leadership over the feudal lords in the various parts of the country. In return for the shogun's recognition of the right of the feudal lords to rule over their territory and people, the lords would pledge their loyalty to the shogun.

Early in the seventeenth century the feudal government broke off all relations with foreign countries, prohibited foreign travel and entered an era of isolation. Although the main industry during this period still continued to be agriculture, manufacturing and commerce became increasingly important. As the result of a long, peaceful period in the eighteenth and nineteenth centuries, the merchants were able to develop economic power far exceeding that of the warriors and, as a consequence, the position of the warriors as the ruling class was badly shaken. This same period was also marked by rapid cultural and educational advances which were to serve as the foundation of Japan' sensuing development into a modern nation.

○ Modern times (from the mid-nineteenth century to 1945):

The arrival of Commodore Perry from the United States in 1853 marked the end of Japan's isolation and the resumption of overseas trade. This turn of events put the bakufu in a very difficult position since international commerce put a severe strain on Japan's internal economy and this in turn strengthened the position of the anti-bakufu forces. Thus it was that in 1867 the bakufu turned over its power to the Emperor, and in 1868 a new government was formed with the Emperor Meiji at its head. That a major military conflict was avoided at the time of this transition is a tribute to the wisdom of the leaders on both sides.

The twenty-year period immediately following this transition saw the new Meiji government implement a wide range of measures modeled on European examples and designed to set Japan on its way to becoming a modern nation. Administrative innovations included the introduction of the cabinet system; the

化の面では、近代的学校制度の樹立、武士の経済的・社会的特権廃止が行われ、欧米文化が摂取された。

　これらの近代化により国力は充実したが、アジア各地におけるアメリカ・イギリス・フランス・オランダ・ロシアなどの既得権益との間で、若干の衝突を経験しなければならなかった。

　国内においては、19世紀の終りごろから産業革命が進展し、資本主義が発達し、第一次世界大戦以後は政党政治も一般化するようになった。しかし、1929年の世界恐慌を契機に軍部が台頭し、逐次日本の政治外交を牛耳ることとなり、37年には日中戦争が勃発した。

　第二次世界大戦勃発のころ、アジアにおける日本と先進諸国との間の権益の角逐は一層激しくなり、日本の海外資産凍結、資源の対日輸出禁止などがあいついだ。

　41年12月にいたり、ついに日本とアメリカ・イギリスとの間に太平洋戦争が勃発した。

　こうして、39年ドイツがヨーロッパで口火を切った戦争は、三国同盟を結んだ日・独・伊と連合国の間の、世界紛争に広がった。

　当初、日・独・伊軍が優勢であったが、やがて形勢は逆転した。日本ははじめの半年間に西南太平洋の広大な地域を占領下においたが、その後、アメリカ軍を主力とする連合国軍は反撃に転じた。1945年アメリカ軍は沖縄に上陸し、さらに、広島・長崎への史上初の原子爆弾投下とソ連の対日参戦が続いた。こうした打撃によって、日本は45年8月無条件降伏をし、太平洋戦争は終わった。すでにイタリアが、続いてドイツも降伏していたので、これによって第二次世界大戦は終結した。

promulgation of a constitution which provided for independent legislative and judiciary branches of government and set forth the rights and obligations of the citizens; the establishment of an army modeled after that of Germany and a navy modeled after that of Britain; and various reforms in the systems of local government. On the economic side, the system of land ownership was revised, modern industries were promoted under direct government management and a uniform monetary system was instituted. A number of social reforms were also adopted: a modern school system was set up, the social and economic privileges of the warrior class were abolished and there was a general effort to assimilate Western culture.

These efforts at modernization greatly enhanced Japan's power internationally, but not to an extent that the nation could avoid occasional conflicts with the United States, Great Britain, France, Holland and Russia, all of which had interests in Asia.

Domestic developments continued to maintain a rapid pace. By the end of the nineteenth century, Japan's industrial revolution was well under way and the groundwork of capitalism had been laid. In the years following the First World War, political parties became an accepted part of the governmental system. Then with the onset of the Great Depression in 1929, the military was able to raise itself to political prominence and gain increasing control over both domestic and international policy. Thus the scene was set for the outbreak of war between Japan and China in 1937.

By the beginning of the Second World War an intense race had arisen between Japan and advanced nations attempting to maintain their foreign interests. Various sanctions were taken against Japan: her overseas assets were frozen and raw material exports to Japan were prohibited.

The Pacific War broke out in December, 1941, with Japan pitted against the United States and Great Britain.

The war touched off by Germany in 1939 had thus grown into a worldwide conflict between the Rome-Berlin-Tokyo Axis and the Allies.

Although the Axis had the upper hand in the beginning, the situation later reversed. The control that Japan had gained over a vast region in the southwestern Pacific during the first six months of action was thereafter pushed back by an Allied counteroffensive led by the United States. The landing of Amer-

○現代（その1）（1945年〜1980年代後半）

　アメリカ軍を主力とする連合国軍の占領と間接統治のもとで、日本は民主主義的平和国家への道を歩むこととなった。

　民主化への基盤は、新憲法の制定（1947年）、婦人参政権を認めた選挙法の施行、労働者の権利を守る労働関係法の制定などによってつくられた。

　1951年、サンフランシスコ平和条約の調印によって、日本は独立を回復した。しかし、米・ソの対立（冷戦）のために、条約に調印したのはアメリカおよび西側自由主義諸国だけであった。同じ日、日本とアメリカは日米安全保障条約を締結し、日本はアメリカに基地を提供することに合意した。こうして日本は西側陣営の一員となった。

　日本はまた、東側社会主義諸国との友好関係を回復する努力を続けた。1956年には日ソ共同宣言がまとまり、その結果、同年日本の国際連合加盟が承認されることとなった。中華人民共和国との国交は72年に回復し、78年には日中平和友好条約が調印された。

　この間の日本の経済的な成功は、全世界の注目を集めた。経済発展の基盤は戦後まもなく敷かれ、アメリカの指導のもとに、いくつかの根本的な改革が行われた。それらは、独占禁止法の制定と財閥の解体、農地改革などであった。また税制改革を中心とする一連の財政政策によって、一時激しかったインフレーションも克服した。

　60年代には、日本の経済は鉄鋼・造船・自動車・化学など重化学工業の主導で、高度成長を実現した。60年代の終わりまでに、国民総生産（GNP）は自由主義諸国の中で第2位に躍進した。この間日本は、国際通貨基金（IMF）8条国となり、経済協力開発機構（OECD）へ加入するなど、世界経済のなかで重要な地位を占めるようになった。

ican troops on Okinawa in 1945 was followed by the dropping of atomic bombs on Hiroshima and Nagasaki, the first use of nuclear weapons ever, and the Soviet Union's entry into the war. These blows led Japan to surrender unconditionally in August 1945, bringing the Pacific War to an end. As Italy had already surrendered and Germany's defeat followed shortly, the Second World War came to a close.

○ Recent times Ⅰ (from 1945 to mid-1980s):

Under the postwar occupation and indirect rule of the Allied Forces, primarily the U.S. military, Japan began to rebuild itself into a peaceful, democratic nation.

The foundation for a democratic society was laid through the enactment of a new constitution (1947), an election law recognizing women's suffrage and a labor relations law for protecting workers' rights.

Japan's autonomy was restored with the conclusion of the San Francisco Peace Treaty in 1951. However, owing to the antagonism (the Cold War) between the United States and the Soviet Union, the treaty was signed only by the U.S. and other free world countries. On the same day, Japan and the United States also concluded the Japan-U.S. Treaty of Mutual Cooperation and Security by which Japan agreed to provide the U.S. with military bases. Japan thus became a member of the Western Bloc.

Japan also made efforts to restore friendly relations with the socialist countries of the Eastern Bloc. A joint declaration agreed on with the Soviet Union in 1956 led to Japan's admission to the United Nations in the same year. Diplomatic relations were restored with the People's Republic of China in 1972 and the Treaty of Peace and Friendship between Japan and the People's Republic of China was signed in 1978.

Japan's economic successes caught the attention of the entire world. The groundwork for the development of the economy was laid in the early postwar years when, under the guidance of the U.S., a number of fundamental reforms were carried out, including the enactment of an antitrust law, the dismantling of the zaibatsu and the implementation of a land reform. Inflation, which once became rampant, was checked by a series of fiscal measures centered on a remodeling of the tax laws.

During the 1960s, the Japanese economy expanded rapidly, driven chiefly by heavy industrial sectors such as steel, shipbuilding, automobiles and chemicals. Before the decade was out,

日本企業は、70年代の石油危機も、ハイテクノロジー機器の導入による省エネルギー、輸出の拡大などによって乗り切った。75年に発足した第1回主要先進国首脳会議（サミット）には、日本は、アメリカ・イギリス・フランス・旧西ドイツ・イタリアとともに参加した（第2回目からカナダも参加）。

　80年代には、日本経済は一層国際競争力を強めた。80年代後半からの日本円の対外為替レートの急激な上昇にもかかわらず、日本の工業製品は世界市場につぎつぎに輸出された。この間における日本の経済指標は、めざましいものがあった。すなわち、巨額の貿易黒字、低い失業率、消費者物価の安定などである。ドル換算による一人あたりの国民所得も、世界のトップクラスに上昇した。

　このような戦後の経済的発展は、日本人のライフスタイルにも大きな変化をもたらした。とりわけ、変化が顕著に認められたのは1964年からである。同年、東海道新幹線が開通し、アジアではじめての東京オリンピックが開催された。また、家庭の電化、乗用車の普及、高速道路網・内外航空路の整備、テレビ・電話・ファクシミリなどの通信網の発達によって、国民の生活は非常に便利で快適になった。また、強い日本円のおかげで、年間1,000万人もの日本人が、外国旅行に出るようになった。このような社会の状況は、終戦直後の日本人には想像もおよばないものであった。

○現代（その2）（1980年代後半以降）

　80年代半ば、日本電信電話公社や日本専売公社など、大きな公共企業体の民営化がなされ、85年にそれぞれ日本電信電話㈱と日本たばこ産業㈱になった。87年には国鉄がJR各社に分割・民営化された。89年には、日本では初めて税率3％の消費税（付加価値税）が導入された。97年に5％に引上げられ、現在にいたっている。

the gross national product (GNP) had risen to second place among the free world countries. During this period, Japan became an International Monetary Fund (IMF) Article 8 nation, joined the Organization for Economic Cooperation and Development and otherwise assumed an increasingly important role in the world economy.

Japanese businesses weathered the oil crises of the 1970s by adopting high-technology equipment to boost energy efficiency, and by expanding exports. Japan joined the United States, Great Britain, France, West Germany and Italy at the first summit conference of leading industrially advanced nations held in 1975. (The second and later summits were also attended by Canada.)

The international competitive strength of the Japanese economy continued to increase in the 1980s. Despite a rapid increase in the value of the yen against other currencies during the latter half of the decade, the country's industrial products continued to pour into world markets. The period was marked by excellent economic indicators: a huge trade surplus, low unemployment and stable commodity prices. Per capita income, as stated in U. S. dollars, rose to the level of the highest anywhere in the world.

This economic development of the postwar years profoundly altered the way Japanese live. The changes became particularly noticeable from 1964, the year when the Tokaido Shinkansen (bullet train line) went into operation and the first Olympiad to take place in Asia was held in Tokyo. The spread of home electrical appliances and private automobiles, the building of an expressway network and domestic and overseas airway networks, and the development and improvement of television, telephone, facsimile and other communications systems combined to make life easier and more enjoyable. Encouraged by the strong yen, people also took to overseas travel, at the rate of 10 million annually. Had the Japanese of the early postwar years been told of these aspects of their country's future, few would have believed it.

○ Recent times II (mid-1980s on):

In the mid-1980s, a number of large government corporations were privatized. Nippon Telegraph and Telephone Public Corporation and Japan Tobacco & Salt Public Corporation became Nippon Telegraph and Telephone Corp. and Japan Tobacco Inc. in 1985. Japanese National Railways was split into seven regional companies and privatized as the JR Group in 1987.

86 年後半から急激な株価と地価の上昇によって生じた資産益をもとに、消費・一般企業の設備投資がすすみ、経済は、いわゆる「バブル経済」にまで雪だるま式にふくらんだ。しかし、金融引き締めなどによって、90 年初頭から株価、土地・建物価格などが暴落し、いわゆるバブルがはじけた。そこに残ったのは、ぼう大な不良債権の処理問題であった。加えて経済・産業のグローバル化が一段と進む中で日本の経済情勢は本格的回復のきざしをみないまま長期低迷を続けている。

d）日本が急速に近代化した原動力

　日本の近代化は 1867 年、200 年余りの鎖国を解いてスタートした。翌年、新しく誕生した明治政府は次のような「五箇条の御誓文」を宣言した。

五箇条の御誓文

一、広ク会議ヲ興シ万機公論ニ決スヘシ
一、上下心ヲ一ニシテ盛ニ経綸ヲ行ウヘシ
一、官武一途庶民ニ至ル迄各其志ヲ遂ケ人心ヲシテ倦マサラシメンコトヲ要ス
一、旧来ノ陋習ヲ破リ天地ノ公道ニ基クヘシ
一、知識ヲ世界ニ求メ大ニ皇基ヲ振起スヘシ

　明治政府の基本的な政策は、国を開いて世界各国と交渉を持ち、国を富まし軍事力を強化して国の独立を維持することであった。進取の精神に富む明治の指導者達は、この政策を断行した。

　上記の政策を含めて、日本近代化の原動力となったと思われる諸要因を次に列挙してみよう。

Another big change was the introduction of a 3% consumption tax (a form of value · added tax) in 1989. The tax was raised to 5% in 1997.

Capital gains produced by a rapid rise in stock and land prices from the latter half of 1986 prompted rampant consumer spending and private sector investment in new plant and equipment, ballooning the economy into what became known as the "Bubble Economy." The bursting of the Bubble in early 1990, mostly because of a credit squeeze, triggered a plunge in stock, land and building values. This left the nation with a massive bad debt problem that, together with the impact of relentless economic and industrial globalization, pushed the economy into a prolonged slump that still persists with no signs of recovery in sight.

d) Force Behind Japan's Rapid Modernization

Japan's modernization began in 1867 following the abandonment of an isolation policy that had shut the country off from the rest of the world for more than two hundred years. A year later, the newly formed Meiji Government issued the following proclamation regarding its basic policies.

Charter Oath of Five Articles

⟨ 1 ⟩ All affairs of State shall be referred to public opinion through general conferences.

⟨ 2 ⟩ The government and the people shall act in harmony in energetically carrying out administrative matters.

⟨ 3 ⟩ No citizen, whether a civil or military officer or one of the common people, shall be discouraged in the pursuit of his aspirations.

⟨ 4 ⟩ Evil practices of the past shall be abandoned and universal justice shall prevail.

⟨ 5 ⟩ The foundation of the Imperial Regime shall be strengthened by the acquisition of knowledge from throughout the world.

The basic policy of the Meiji government was to preserve Japan's independence by opening up the country and building up the nation's military power through intercourse with the rest of the world. This plan was in fact carried through by the progressive political leaders of the time.

Now let us take a look at the specific measures employed in implementing this policy and at some of the other causes behind Japan's modernization.

1）政府は封建時代からの藩制を撤廃し、近代国家における地方行政単位として県をおき、中央集権体制を整備した。

2）士農工商の階級制度を廃止し、全国民に機会均等の教育制度を設置した。日本を近代化するには、それを推進する国民一般の知的水準を高めなくてはならないという考え方から、政府は、国民の教育の普及に力を注いだ。

3）農民に土地を売買する自由を認め、産業の育成をはかり、国営による鉄道・電話・郵便制度を開設した。また、官営のモデル工場を設立して、民間企業が興るのを誘導したり（例：長崎造船所・富岡製糸工場）、貸付金などの援助を積極的に行った。

4）各分野に積極的に外国人顧問を招き、外国の技術や制度の導入・吸収に努めた（たとえばボアソナード［仏］立法および法学教育、ベルツ［独］医学教育、クラーク［米］農業教育、モレル［英］鉄道建設、トッペ［独］八幡製鐵所操業など）。

5）国民が、「文明開化」を旗じるしに、西洋の文明を進んで摂取した。また、よく働き、よく貯蓄して、近代化に必要な資本を造出した。

　以上のような日本の近代化の原動力は、鎖国による平和な封建時代に、すでにその基盤が形成されていたと考えられる。すなわち、武士階級の統治の経験は、官僚制と組織能力を持った人材を育てていたし、貨幣や度量衡の統一、道路や航路の整備がなされており、米をはじめとして、国全体の流通経済がかたちづくられていた。

　　　（吉田茂著『日本を決定した百年』を参考にした）

1) The government centralized its administrative powers by abolishing the fief system and setting up a more modern unit of local administration called the ken (prefecture).

2) The old class distinctions (warriors, farmers, artisans and tradesmen in descending order of rank) were abandoned and all citizens were given equal educational opportunity. Knowing that the nation's modernization could be achieved only if the people had a high level of education, the government put its efforts behind the establishment of a public school system.

3) Farmers were given the right to buy and sell land. Industrial development was promoted. State-operated railway, telephone and postal systems were initiated. The government actively encouraged private enterprise by setting up and managing model production facilities (e.g. a ship building yard in Nagasaki and a silk mill in Tomioka) and by providing financial assistance.

4) Foreign advisors were invited to Japan to promote the introduction and assimilation of Western institutions and technology in various fields. Notable among these men were Gustave Emile Boissonade, a French specialist in law and legal education; Erwin von Baelz, a German educator in the field of medicine; William Smith Clark, an American who gave assistance in agriculture and education; Edmund Morell, an English railroad engineer; and Gustav Toppe, a German engineer who helped to get the Yawata Steel Mill into operation.

5) The people as a whole enthusiastically adopted Western culture and ideas in pursuit of what was called "cultural enlightenment." They were industrious and saved ardently, thus providing the capital required for modernization.

The foundation for Japan's development into a modern nation was to a large extent laid during the peaceful years of isolation of the feudal period. The experience gained by the ruling warrior class during this period accounted for the presence of men capable of running the new bureaucratic government and its institutions. A monetary system and a system of standardized weights and measures already existed. Land and sea routes were extensive enough to support nationwide commodity markets centering on rice but also encompassing other goods.

e）外国と日本との歴史的・文化的関係

　　日本の文化は、中国や欧米の影響を受けたものが多いが、それ以外の地域の文化も、中国や欧米を通じて日本に伝えられたものが少なくない。

　　紀元前3～2世紀に、中国から稲の種が稲作技術とともに伝えられた。これを契機とし、それまでの狩猟時代から稲作中心の農業時代へと社会生活も一変し、発展するようになった。

　　1世紀に九州地方の王が後漢の光武帝から金印を受けたという記事が中国の史書（『後漢書』）にみえ、その金印が18世紀に福岡県で発見された。

　　3世紀にはヤマタイ国の女王が魏に使者を送り、魏からもヤマタイ国に使者が来ている。

　　4世紀に入ると、朝鮮と日本との交流の記録が現れる。5世紀から6世紀にかけて、漢字・美術・農業その他の工芸が朝鮮からもたらされたが、これらは朝鮮独自のもののほか、中国のものが朝鮮を経由して伝えられたものもある。

　　6世紀初頭儒教も伝えられ、日本人の道徳や生活観に大きな影響をおよぼした。

　　7世紀には日本から隋や唐に使者を出し、また多くの留学生を送った。この使者や留学生が彼の地の制度・文物を伝えた。とくに唐のものの影響が大きかった。

　　日本における仏教の歴史は、6世紀に朝鮮から仏像と経文を贈られたことに始まるが、9～10世紀に中国と日本との間で僧侶の往来があり、日本の仏教を発展させた。この間、日本の建築・美術・工芸についても中国の影響が大きかった。

e) Cultural and Historical Relations with Foreign Countries

The strongest cultural influence on Japan has come from China and the West (Europe and America), and through these same channels Japan has also assimilated much from other parts of the world.

Rice and the art of its cultivation reached Japan from China between the third and second century B.C. and this marked the beginning of the rice-centered agricultural age which was to develop and put a close to the hunting and gathering age which preceded it.

A gold seal mentioned in Chinese records as having been presented to a monarch in the Kyushu area by Emperor Kuang Hsu (Later Han Dynasty, first century A.D.) was actually unearthed in the eighteenth century in what is now known as Fukuoka Prefecture.

In the third century, the Queen of Yamatai (exact location disputed but certainly within the boundaries of modern Japan) is known to have dispatched an envoy to Wei (one of three parts China had fallen into) and an envoy from Wei was also received by Yamatai.

The first recorded interchanges between Korea and Japan were in the fourth century. Between the fifth and sixth centuries the flow from Korea into Japan included the Chinese writing system, various arts, agricultural methods and crafts. Thus Korea not only provided Japan with numerous aspects of its own culture but also served as a pathway for the influx of Chinese culture.

Confucianism reached Japan in the early sixth century and had a profound influence on Japanese morals and the Japanese view of life.

During the seventh century, a large number of Japanese envoys and scholars were sent to China during the Sui and T'ang dynasties. These men brought back knowledge of the places they had visited and introduced new social and cultural ideas to Japan. The influence of the T'ang was particularly great.

The first introduction of Buddhism into Japan was in the sixth century in the form of Buddhist statues and scriptures received as gifts from Korea. The religion did not spread widely, however, until Japanese and Chinese monks began actively exchanging visits in the ninth and tenth centuries. This same period also saw growing Chinese influence on Japanese architecture, art and crafts.

10世紀末から12世紀まで、中国と日本の関係は絶えたが、12世紀以後宋・明との間で貿易が行われた。

マルコ・ポーロの『東方見聞録』（1299年）によって、日本はジパングとしてヨーロッパにはじめて紹介された。コロンブスのアメリカ大陸発見も、はじめは西回りでジパングを訪ねようとして出発したものだといわれている。

しかし、ヨーロッパ人と日本人がはじめて実際に接触したのは、1543年ポルトガル人が九州南方の種子島に漂着したときである。このとき、ポルトガル人は鉄砲と火薬を伝えた。

その後スペイン人・ポルトガル人・イギリス人・オランダ人などが相次いで日本に来てカトリックの布教や貿易を行った。

16世紀後半から日本からも華南・シャム・フィリピン・ジャワ・スマトラ・ボルネオなどに向けて200〜800トンの木造交易船が往来し、1592年には豊臣秀吉の朱印状を持った正式な貿易船である朱印船が就航した。これらの船は日本の銀・銅・鉄・硫黄・雑貨などと生糸・絹織物・皮革・鉛・砂糖などとを交換した。

このころすでに交易先の海外各地には日本人が住んでいた。1639年の鎖国後、海外にいる日本人は日本に帰れなくなった。九州出身の「お春」が日本に帰れない淋しさを書いた手紙が、日本の平戸に残っている。

カトリックでなかったオランダだけは、鎖国後も商館を平戸から長崎出島に移して交易を認められた。このため、日本ではオランダの医学は早くから研究され、オランダ語の学習も行われた。

1853年アメリカのマシュー・ペリー提督は、フィルモア大統領の国書を持って、4隻の軍艦を率いて来日し、翌年日米和親条約が結ばれた。1639年の鎖国以来、日本は外国との国交を断っていたが、このようにアメリカ合衆国の積極的な働きかけにより日本は開国することになった。引き続き、イギリス・ロシア・フランス・オランダなどと条約を結ぶことになった。そしてこれらの外交政策の転換を一つの契機として徳川幕府が倒れ、明治維新により日本は近代国家に生まれかわった。

Japan and China had little or no contact with each other between the end of the tenth century and the time that trade relations were restored from the twelfth century during the Sung and Ming dynasties.

Japan was first introduced to Europe as "Zipangu" in the Book of Marco Polo (1299). And it is said that when Columbus discovered America, he was in fact trying to reach Zipangu by traveling west.

The first actual contact between Europeans and Japanese was in 1543 when a Portuguese ship was tossed ashore on the island of Tanegashima just south of Kyushu. It was from these Portuguese sailors that the Japanese first learned about firearms and gunpowder.

From this time on, Japan was regularly frequented by Catholic missionaries from Spain and Portugal and by traders from these two countries as well as from Britain and Holland.

From the latter half of the sixteenth century wooden Japanese trading ships of from two to eight hundred tons began frequenting South China, Siam, the Philippines, Sumatra, Borneo and neighboring regions. From 1592, ships bearing the vermillion seal of Hideyoshi Toyotomi to indicate their official status were commissioned as trading vessels. These merchant vessels traded Japanese silver, copper, iron, sulfur and sundries for raw silk, silk cloth, leather, lead and sugar.

At this time many Japanese were already living at overseas trading posts, and when Japan completed its isolation policy in 1639, they were unable to return home. One of the best known of these was a Kyushu girl named Oharu whose letters expressing her grief at not being able to return to her homeland can still be seen in the city of Hirato.

With the imposition of isolation, only the non-Catholic Dutch were allowed to maintain trade relations, though even they were forced to move their offices from Hirato to Dejima in the city of Nagasaki. The Dutch were thus the source of most of Japan's early knowledge of Western medicine and for many years Dutch was the only foreign language the Japanese could study.

In 1853 Commodore Matthew C. Perry visited Japan with a squadron of four war vessels and presented the Shogun with a letter from U.S. President Millard Fillmore. In the following year the United States and Japan concluded a treaty of amity. This treaty signed by the Japanese in response to strong overtures

日本は近代化を進めるうえで、西欧の文化を吸収し、西欧流の立憲政治体制を取り入れ、西欧の技術による産業を振興して近代資本主義を確立した。日本の近代化とは西欧化にほかならなかった。

　日本から多数の人がヨーロッパやアメリカに赴いて学問や技術を習得し、また、多数のヨーロッパ人やアメリカ人が日本に来て文化を伝達した。1881年から98年まで、イギリスから6,177人、アメリカから2,764人、ドイツから913人、フランスから619人、イタリアから45人の先生や技術者を招いた。

　中東地区と日本との関係は、近代以前には直接的なものはないが、同地域の文化がほかの国を通じて日本にもたらされたものは少なくない。たとえば8世紀にできた正倉院には、ペルシアの宝物や、アッシリア帝国に起源を持つ中国製のハープが納められている。また、アラビア数字や天文学も、ヨーロッパを通じて日本にもたらされた。

made by the United States marked the end of a long period of isolation which began in 1639 when Japan broke off all intercourse with foreign countries. The treaty with the United States was quickly followed by similar treaties with Great Britain, Russia, France and the Netherlands, and this rapid turnabout in the nation's foreign policy was a major factor in the fall of the Tokugawa Bakufu government and Japan's rebirth as a modern nation.

In order to modernize, Japan adopted many aspects of Western culture, as well as the Western system of constitutional government, and established itself as a modern capitalistic nation by promoting the development of its industries with Western technology. For Japan, modernization meant westernization.

Many Japanese traveled to Europe and America to study. At the same time many Europeans and Americans came to Japan to teach Western arts and sciences: between 1881 and 1898, 6,177 Britons, 2,764 Americans, 913 Germans, 619 Frenchmen and 45 Italians visited Japan as teachers and engineers at the invitation of the Japanese government.

Although there was no direct contact between Japan and the Middle East until modern times, various aspects of Middle Eastern culture reached Japan over the years through other countries. Evidence of this is found at the Shosoin, an Imperial Treasury built in the eighth century, which contains a number of Persian treasures and a harp which, though made in China, shows a strong Assyrian influence. Arabic numerals and astronomy, on the other hand, came to Japan through Europe.

2　政治

(1)　天皇

a) 天皇の憲法上の地位

　　　現行憲法では、天皇は日本国の象徴であり、この地位
は主権の存する日本国民の総意に基づくと定められてお
り、憲法の定める国事に関する行為のみを行い、国政に
関する権能を有しないとされる。そして、この国事に関
する行為には、内閣の助言と承認を必要とし、内閣がそ
の責任を負うことになっている。

　　　この国事に関する行為とは、国会の指名に基づいて内
閣総理大臣を任命すること、内閣の指名に基づいて最高
裁判所長官を任命すること、また内閣の助言と承認に基
づき、憲法改正・法律・政令および条約の公布、国会の
召集、衆議院の解散、総選挙施行の公示、栄典の授与、
批准書およびその他の外交文書の認証、外国の大・公使
の接受を行うこと、などに限定されている。

　　　このように、天皇は政治上の権限を有しないが、外交
儀礼上は元首として扱われる。

b) 皇室の歴史

　　　日本の現存する最古の史書によると、紀元前 660 年に
初代の天皇が即位したことになっている。しかし、天皇
の存在を史実に即して説明できるのは、4 ～ 5 世紀以降
である。

　　　7 世紀に中国の法律制度を導入して、天皇は自ら政治
をすることになったが、実際に政治を行った期間は短か
った。

　　　9 世紀以後政治は貴族や武士によって行われた。種々
の変遷はあるが、時の実権者が政治の大権を天皇から預
る形をとったという点では一貫している。

2 Government

(1) The Emperor

a) Constitutional Status of the Emperor

The present constitution of Japan declares that the Emperor is the symbol of the State deriving his position from the will of the people with whom resides sovereign power and that the Emperor shall perform only such acts in matters of state as are provided for in the Constitution without having any powers related to government. It is further stipulated that the advice and approval of the Cabinet is required for all acts of the Emperor in matters of state and that the Cabinet is responsible for these acts.

Acts in matters of state performed by the Emperor are constitutionally limited to appointment of the Prime Minister as designated by the Diet (Japan's national legislative body); appointment of the Chief Judge of the Supreme Court as designated by the Cabinet; promulgation of amendments of the constitution, laws, cabinet orders and treaties; convocation of the Diet; dissolution of the House of Representatives; proclamation of general election of members of the Diet; awarding of honors; attestation of instruments of ratification and other diplomatic documents; and receiving of foreign ambassadors and ministers as approved and advised by the Cabinet.

Thus the Emperor has no governmental powers but is treated as the head of state in diplomatic and ceremonial functions.

b) History of the Imperial House

According to the oldest Japanese history book still in existence, the first Emperor assumed the Imperial Throne in the year 660 B.C. On the basis of more objective historical facts, however, the earliest date for which the existence of an emperor can be confirmed is somewhere in the fourth or fifth century A.D.

After the introduction of a Chinese type legal system in the seventh century, the Emperor did for a time actually govern in his own right but this period of true imperial rule was short-lived.

For a period of about one thousand years beginning in the ninth century, the country was under the control of the nobility and their successors, the warrior class. Although various forms of

19世紀、大政奉還（1867年）によって、天皇は再び国の統治権を行使することになった。しかし、実際は立法・行政・司法の三権分立の形をとった立憲君主制であった。第二次世界大戦後、現行憲法による天皇および皇室の形になった。

　以上のように、日本の天皇は古代以来自ら国政の実権を掌握するということはほとんどなく、そのため政争に直接まきこまれることが少なかった。天皇が日本国民統合の中心であるとする観念を国民の間に強く根づかせたのは、古代以来の伝統と権威に加えて、このように天皇が時の政治の動きに対して超然たる存在であったという史実があるからであろう。

c）天皇・皇后・皇太子

　125代目の今上天皇のお名前は明仁（あきひと）である。1933年12月23日にご生誕、89年1月に践祚（せんそ）した。ご自身戦中派のため、常々平和の大切さを唱えておられる。

　日本では通常、天皇のご存命中はお名前を呼ぶことはしない。崩御後はおくり名をつける。たとえば、124代天皇のお名前は裕仁（ひろひと）であったが、ご在位の元号が昭和であったので、いまは昭和天皇とお呼びしている。

　皇后のお名前は美智子で、民間（正田家）のご出身で、テニスを通じての今上天皇とのロマンスは有名である。

　皇太子のお名前は徳仁（なるひと）で、1960年ご生誕、学習院大学および英国オックスフォード大学に学ばれた。93年、民間ご出身の小和田雅子さんとご成婚になった。2001年12月1日、皇太子ご夫妻に女子のお子さま（内親王愛子さま）がご誕生になった。

government were set up during this period, all had one point in common: the actual rulers of the time based their governments on the sovereign right conferred upon them by the Emperor.

The Meiji Restoration (1867) placed the reins of government back in the hands of the Emperor, not as an absolute ruler but as the head of a constitutional monarchy comprising independent legislative, executive and judiciary branches. The status of the Emperor and the Imperial House in Japan was redefined in its present form by the new constitution adopted following the Second World War.

Only very rarely throughout Japan's long history has the Emperor held actual power over the affairs of state and, as a consequence, he has seldom become directly involved in political struggles. The concept of the Emperor as the center about which the Japanese people are unified is very deeply rooted in the Japanese mind. This view of the Emperor arises not only from the long imperial tradition and respect for imperial authority, but also to a large extent from the fact that the Emperor has remained above day-to-day political matters.

c) The Imperial Family

The name of the present Emperor of Japan, the one hundred and twenty-fifth to occupy the Imperial Throne, is Akihito. He was born on December 23, 1933 and became emperor in January 1989. Having grown up during the Second World War, he frequently speaks of the importance of peace.

The Japanese do not ordinarily refer to living emperors by name and deceased emperors are referred to by names given posthumously. For example, the one hundred twenty-fourth Emperor's name was Hirohito, but he is now called the Emperor Showa because he ascended to the throne in the first year of the Showa Era.

The Empress' name is Michiko. Born a commoner, Michiko Shoda, she and the Emperor first met playing tennis. The story of their tennis court romance is famous among Japanese.

The Crown Prince, Naruhito, was born in 1960. He studied at Gakushuin University and in England at Oxford University. He married Miss Masako Owada, born a commoner, in 1993. The couple's first child, Imperial Princess Aiko, was born on December 1, 2001.

(2) 政治

a）日本国憲法

　　現在の日本国憲法は、太平洋戦争終結の翌年の 1946 年に公布され、1947 年 5 月 3 日から施行された。

　　この憲法は、明治時代に制定された「大日本帝国憲法」の内容を一新したものである。前憲法との違いをいくつか指摘すれば、象徴天皇、主権在民、平和主義、人権尊重、国際紛争を解決する手段としての戦争の放棄などを定めた点である。

　　とくに第 9 条に定められた戦争放棄の条項は、世界の憲法のなかでも稀有の事例である。

b）日本の統治機構

　　日本の統治機構は、立法・行政・司法の各機関の分立した三権分立制をとっている。

　　立法機関たる国会は、国権の最高機関であって、国の唯一の立法機関であり、衆議院および参議院の両議院から成っている。両議院とも全国民を代表する選挙された議員で組織されている。

　　国会の権限として、内閣総理大臣の指名、内閣不信任の決議、法律案の議決、予算の議決、条約の承認、裁判官に対する弾劾裁判、憲法改正の発議などがある。

　　行政権は内閣に属し、内閣は内閣総理大臣とその他の国務大臣で組織し、行政権の行使について国会に対し連帯して責任を負う。内閣は一般行政事務のほか、法律を執行し、外交関係を処理し、条約を締結し、予算を作成し、政令を制定する。これらの業務を分担するため、国務大臣を長とする 1 府 12 省庁がおかれている。これは、1949 年以来、半世紀にわたった行政機構を、行政改革の一環として再編したもので、2001 年 1 月から新体制に移行している。内閣の統一を保つために、内閣総理大臣は国務大臣の任免権を持つ。

(2) Government

a) The Japanese Constitution

Japan's present constitution was promulgated in 1946, the year following the end of the Pacific War, and went into effect on May 3, 1947.

It completely revised the Constitution of the Empire of Japan enacted in the Meiji Era. A few of the points that distinguish it from the earlier constitution are that it defines the Emperor as the symbol of the state, affirms that sovereignty rests with the people, advocates peace, guarantees human rights and forswears war as a means of settling international disputes.

This last-mentioned provision, set out in Article 9, is found in few, if any, of the world's constitutions other than Japan's.

b) Japanese System of Government

The government of Japan is composed of a legislative branch, an administrative branch and a judiciary branch, each of which is independent of the others.

Legislative powers are vested in the Diet, which is the highest organ of state power and its sole law-making body. The Diet is made up of a House of Representatives and a House of Councilors, both of which consist of elected members representing all of the people.

Among the powers of the Diet are the power to designate the Prime Minister; the power to approve nonconfidence resolution in the cabinet; the power to pass laws; the power to approve the budget; the power to approve treaties; the power to conduct trials of impeachment against judges; and the power to amend the constitution.

The administrative power is vested in the Cabinet which consists of the Prime Minister and other ministers of state. In the exercise of its administrative power, the Cabinet is collectively responsible to the Diet. In addition to its general administrative functions, the Cabinet administers the law; manages foreign affairs; concludes treaties; prepares the budget; and enacts cabinet orders. The work of carrying out these functions is divided among one office and twelve ministries and agencies, each of which is headed by one of the ministers of state. This administrative structure was introduced in January 2001 as part of an administrative reform. The organization of Japanese administra-

司法機関として裁判所がある。最高裁判所と下級裁判所（高等裁判所・地方裁判所・家庭裁判所・簡易裁判所）とからなる。すべて裁判官は、その良心にしたがい独立してその職権を行い、憲法および法律にのみ拘束される。最高裁判所の長官は内閣の指名に基づき天皇が任命し、そのほかの裁判官はすべて内閣が任命する。裁判所は一切の法律・命令が憲法に適合するかしないかを決定する権限を有する。

〔注〕日本の統治機構は巻末〔統計資料〕欄(5)参照

c）選　挙

国会議員、都道府県・市町村（東京の区をふくむ）の各首長、および各議会議員は、直接選挙で選ばれる。

選挙権は、20歳以上の男女全員にあるが、被選挙権は参議院議員と都道府県知事は30歳以上、それ以外は25歳以上の者にある。女子は1945年にはじめて選挙権と被選挙権を得た。

現在、国会議員と都道府県の知事および同議会議員の大部分は、政党の党員であるかまたは政党の推薦を受けた者である。しかし、市町村の首長および各議会議員では、特定の政党に属さないという意味の「無所属」を標榜する者が多い。

選挙運動は、ポスター・テレビ・立会演説会・街頭演説などにより行われる。

選挙は無記名自由投票で行い、選びたい人の氏名を、選挙によっては政党名を自分で書く。

国会議員の選挙の投票率では、1958年の77％が一番高かった。

日本の主な政党は、長いあいだ二つの陣営に色分けされてきた。すなわち、一方は政府与党である自由民主党で、他方は日本社会党・公明党・民主社会党・日本共産党などの革新陣営であった。

しかし、93年の衆議院議員選挙では、選挙民の政治不信などにより新勢力が躍進し、自由民主党は過半数を制することができなかった。こうして、38年間続いた自由民主党の一党政権が終り、選挙制度を中心とした「政治改革」の時代の舞台がととのった。その結果、選

tive offices had remained unchanged for more than half a century (since 1949). In order to ensure the solidarity of the Cabinet, the Prime Minister is given the power to dismiss ministers of state as he chooses.

The judiciary branch of government is made up of the Supreme Court and such inferior courts as the high courts, the district courts, the family courts and the summary courts. All judges are independent in the exercise of their conscience and are bound only by the constitution and the laws. The Chief Judge of the Supreme Court is designated by the Cabinet and appointed by the Emperor and all other judges are appointed by the Cabinet. It is in the power of the courts to rule on the constitutionality of any and all laws and orders.

c) Elections

Members of the Diet, prefectural governors and assemblymen, and city, town and village mayors and assemblymen (including those of Tokyo's wards) are chosen by direct election.

All men and women who have reached the age of twenty years have the right to vote. The minimum age for members of the House of Councilors and prefectural governors is thirty and that for all other elected officials twenty-five. Women were first given the right to vote and the right to stand for office in 1945.

Most present members of the Diet, prefectural governors and members of prefectural assemblies belong to a political party or were elected with the support of a political party. On the city, town and village level, however, many mayors and assemblymen proudly proclaim themselves to be "independents," that is, free of any party affiliations.

The election campaigns are conducted through various media including posters, television, speech meetings and street-corner oratory.

Voting is done through free casting of secret ballots, with each voter writing in the name of the candidate of his choice.

The best turnout recorded in a Diet election was in 1958 when 77% of the electorate showed up at the polls.

For many years, Japan's major political parties fell into two distinct camps, with the ruling Liberal Democratic Party on the conservative side and the Social Democratic Party of Japan, the Komeito, the Democratic Socialist Party and the Japan Communist Party on the reformist side.

挙法は 94 年に改正された。衆議院の総選挙を中選挙区制から小選挙区比例代表並立制に改正した。この改正後の選挙ではどの政党も安定過半数が得られず、自由民主党を軸に連合政権的な政治運営がなされている。政党としては、2002 年現在では、自由民主党、民主党、自由党、公明党、日本共産党、社会民主党（旧日本社会党）、保守党などがある。

d) 自衛隊

　日本は、第二次世界大戦終了時、降伏の条件に基づいて全陸海軍が解体された。

　1950 年、日本の治安維持のため警察予備隊が設置された。52 年保安隊に再編され、54 年現在の自衛隊になった。

　47 年施行の現行憲法では、国際紛争を解決する手段としては、国権の発動たる戦争を放棄する旨規定している。しかし、このことは国家の固有の権利である自衛権の放棄を意味するものではない。

　自衛隊は、「わが国の平和と独立を守り、国の安全を保つため、直接侵略および間接侵略に対し、わが国を防衛することを主たる任務とし、必要に応じ公共の秩序の維持に当る」（自衛隊法第 3 条）ものとして設置されている。

　自衛隊の最高指揮権は、内閣を代表して内閣総理大臣が有しているが、通常の業務は国務大臣である防衛庁長官があたっている。自衛隊には、陸上自衛隊・海上自衛隊・航空自衛隊がある。自衛隊員はすべて志願制度によっている。

At the time of the House of Representatives election in 1993, however, political distrust among the electorate led to strong gains by emerging political forces and prevented the Liberal Democratic Party from securing a majority. This brought to a close 38 years of one-party rule by the LDP and set the stage for a period of political reform that focused mainly on the election system. As a result, the Election Law was revised in 1994. The old system of electing members of the House of Representatives proportionally from medium-sized districts was replaced by a system combining small, single-member districts with large proportional representation districts. An election was held under the new system in 1996 but no party emerged with a stable majority. Power has since been in the hands of a coalition government headed by the Liberal Democratic Party. The major political parties as of 2002 were the Liberal Democratic Party, the Democratic Party of Japan, the Liberal Party, the New Komeito, the Japan Communist Party, the Social Democratic Party and the New Conservative Party.

d) Self Defense Force

At the end of the Second World War all of Japan's military forces were demobilized as one of the conditions of surrender.

The present-day Self Defense Force grew out of a National Police Reserve which was set up to maintain the peace in 1950 and then reorganized as the Peace Preservation Corps in 1952. Today's Force came into existence in 1954.

The present Japanese Constitution promulgated in 1947 renounces the sovereign right of the State to use war as a means of settling international disputes. This does not mean, however, that the people of Japan have renounced the right of the State to defend itself.

The purpose of the Self Defense Force is stated in Article 3 of the Self Defense Force Law as follows: "The main mission of the Self Defense Force shall be to protect the peace and independence and preserve the safety of Japan by defending it against direct and indirect attack and, when necessary, to help preserve public order."

Although the highest right of command of the Self Defense Force rests with the Prime Minister in his capacity as chief of the Cabinet, the actual day-to-day affairs of the Force are under the control of the Director of the Defense Agency, an official whose

定員はそれぞれ次のとおりである（2001）。
　　陸上自衛隊　　　163,784 人
　　海上自衛隊　　　 45,812 人
　　航空自衛隊　　　 47,266 人
　1992 年 6 月「国連平和維持活動協力法（PKO 協力法）」が国会で成立し、これによって日本は、はじめて自衛隊海外派遣の明確な法的根拠を持つこととなった。この PKO 法に基づき、92 年から 2000 年までにカンボジア、モザンビーク、ソマリア、ボスニア、東チモールなど世界各地に 40 回にわたり自衛隊の部隊が派遣されている。自衛隊は国内での災害派遣でも活躍している。
　また 2001 年 9 月のアメリカでの同時多発テロ対策への国際協力の一環として制定された「テロ対策特別措置法」に基づき、自衛隊の艦艇、航空機が後方支援活動のためインド洋に派遣された。

(3)　外交

a）日本の外交の基本原則

　日本は、1956 年国際連合に加盟して以来、一貫して次の外交 3 原則を守り、今日にいたっている。
1）国際連合の目的と原則にしたがって、国際社会の平和と安全に寄与するよう努める。
2）自由・民主主義・基本的人権・不平等の是正、市場経済、多角的自由貿易体制などの普遍的価値を共有する自由主義諸国の一員として行動をともにしながら、自らの安全と繁栄を求める。
3）アジア・太平洋地域の一国として、同地域の平和と安全に貢献する。

rank is that of a minister of state. The Self Defense Force is divided into three branches: the Ground Self Defense Force, the Maritime Self Defense Force and the Air Self Defense Force. All members of the Force are volunteers.

The authorized full strength of each branch is as follows:

Ground Self Defense Force 163,784 members
Maritime Self Defense Force 45,812 members
Air Self Defense Force 47,266 members

The Law Concerning Cooperation for United Nations Peace Keeping Operations and other Operations (PKO Law) passed by the Diet in June 1992 first established a clear legal basis for sending Self Defense Force members overseas. Between 1992 and 2000, forces were deployed under the PKO Law on 40 occasions, to Cambodia, Mozambique, Somalia and Bosnia and other regions around the globe.

Further, under the special legislation enacted to increase Japan's contribution to the international fight against terrorism following the terrorist attacks in the United States in September 2001, Japan sent naval vessels and airplanes to the Indian Ocean on a logistic support mission. The Self Defense Force has also actively provided assistance to disaster-struck regions inside Japan.

(3) Diplomacy

a) Basic Principles of Japanese Diplomacy

Since becoming a member of the United Nations in 1956, Japan has consistently adhered to three basic principles in its foreign relations.

1) To contribute to the peace and security of the international community in accordance with the purpose and principles of the United Nations.

2) To promote the nation's security and prosperity while playing a cooperative role as a member of the family of free nations which share such universal values as liberty, democracy, basic human rights, rectification of inequalities, market economy and multilateral free trade.

3) To promote the prosperity and peace and security of the Asian and Pacific region as one member of this area.

b）経済協力

　　現在世界では、総人口 60 億人のうち 12 億人が 1 日当り 1 ドル以下、別の 30 億人が 1 日当り 2 ドル以下の生活をしているなど、発展途上国における援助のニーズはますます高まっている。このような状況の下で先進国からの二国間援助という時代は過ぎ去り、近年は途上国のオーナーシップを尊重した上で、先進諸国、国際機関、民間センター、NGO（非政府組織）など広範な組織が相互に連絡・協力し合って援助に取り組むことが求められている。

　　日本は、政府開発援助（ODA）を基本として、国際経済協力を行っている。世界最大の援助国の一国であり、1991 年から連続世界第 1 位の援助国であった。2000 年の実績は 134 億ドルであった。現在援助を行っている国や地域数は 150 を越えている。援助額だけでなく、質の面も大きく改善されてきており、アンタイド援助の向上、援助分野の重点化、援助要因の拡充などがある。また、最近は、環境問題や開発途上国の人造りなど、従来以上に重点分野を明確にし、管轄官庁の枠を超えた総合調整を行った援助協力を実施している。

　　また、2000 年には非政府組織（NGO）、経団連、外務省の 3 者による緊急人道援助機関、ジャパン・プラットフォームを設立し、NGO、経済界を含む国民参加型の援助を推進している。

c）科学技術協力

　　日本の科学技術政策の重点施策の一つは、「国際的な科学技術活動の強化」である。具体的には次のようなものがある。

1）アメリカ・イギリスをはじめ約 30 カ国と科学技術協定を結び、二国間の協力関係を通じて国際的研究の積極的推進をはかっている。

b) Economic Assistance

The increasing need of developing countries for economic assistance is brought home by the fact that of the 6 billion people on earth today, 1.2 billion must get by on less than 1 US dollar a day and another 3 billion on less than 2 dollars a day, This situation has brought a close to the era of unilateral assistance by economically advanced nations and ushered in a new philosophy, founded on respect for developing nation ownership, that calls on a broad range of organizations-including economically advanced nations, international organizations. private centers and non-government organizations (NGOs)-to cooperate in offering carefully coordinated assistance.

The Japanese Government extends overseas economic assistance primarily in the form of Official Development Assistance (ODA). One of the world's major providers of economic assistance, Japan has been at the top in economic assistance since 1991. Grants in 2000 amounted to $13.4 billion. Currently, more than 150 countries and regions are receiving assistance. Considerable progress has been made not only in increasing the amount of ODA but also in improving the quality of the assistance by, for instance, upgrading untied aid, focusing assistance for maximum effect, and responding to a wider range of factors. Recently, the Government has particularly tried to pinpoint critical needs-such as environmental protection and development of human resources in developing countries-and to plan assistance and cooperation unconstrained by agency borders.

On the other hand, the Japan Platform, an emergency humanitarian aid organization set up jointly by Japanese NGOs, the Federation of Economic Organizations and the Ministry of Foreign Affairs in 2000, is promoting broad-based assistance initiatives by all sectors of Japanese society, including NGOs and the business community.

c) Scientific and Technical Cooperation

One of the key aims of Japan's policy regarding science and technology is to strengthen international scientific and technological activities. Some of the specific moves Japan has made for this purpose are:

1) It joined a science and technology agreement with the U.S., the U.K. and 30 other countries and is now positively engaged in international research projects with each country.

2）日本は、ヒューマン・フロンティア・サイエンス・
プログラム（HFSP）をはじめ、いくつかの国際プ
ログラムを提唱した。このなかには、国際熱核融合
炉開発（ITER）・宇宙ステーション計画などがある。
3）国際研究交流をいっそう推進する。たとえば、外国
人研究者の受入れを拡大したり、重要な国際共同研
究では研究者が直接意見交換できるようにしている。

d）世界の平和と安定
1）軍備管理・軍縮
日本は非核三原則（核兵器を開発しない、保有し
ない、持ち込まない）を依然堅持している。その基
礎に立って日本は 1999 年まで毎年「核兵器の全面
的廃絶への軍縮決議案」およびその「道程決議案」
を国連総会に提出し、2000 年に圧倒的多数で採択
された。また包括的核実験禁止条約（CTBT）の発
効要件である 44 か国の批准獲得のため積極的説得
を行っている。
通常兵器についても小型武器の不正取引の禁止、
対人地雷禁止条約（オタワ条約）加盟国の拡大、地
雷除去活動、犠牲者支援などに向け国際的貢献をし
ている。

2）環境
日本は世界の環境の保全に努力している。高い経
済成長を維持しながら産業公害を克服してきた経験
から、環境と経済との調和は達成できると確信して
いる。こうした考え方に基づき地球温暖化・砂漠化
の防止、オゾン層保護、野生動物保護、森林保全な
どを推進している。また発展途上国の環境問題への
対処能力を向上させるために、資金援助、環境管理
技術の移転、共同作業への参加など数々の協力活動
を展開している。

2) It proposed the Human Frontier Science Program as well as a number of international programs, including one for the development of a thermonuclear fusion reactor (ITER), and one for building a manned space station.

3) It is promoting international research exchanges by, for example, inviting more foreign researchers to Japan and making it easier for researchers engaged in important international joint research projects to communicate directly with each other.

d) World Peace and Stability

1) Arms control and disarmament

Japan remains firmly committed to three non-nuclear principles: no development, no possession, and no entry into the country of nuclear weapons. In the spirit of this commitment, Japan in every year up to 1999 submitted two resolutions to the UN General Assembly, one proposing disarmament toward total abolition of nuclear weapons and the other setting out an itinerary for achieving this goal. In 2000, both resolutions were passed by an overwhelming majority. Japan is also pressing ahead with a campaign to secure ratification of the Comprehensive Test Ban Treaty (CTBT) by at least 44 nations, the number needed for the CTBT to take effect.

Also concerned about the dangers of conventional small arms, Japan is actively participating in international efforts to prohibit small arms trafficking, persuade more countries to join the Ottawa Treaty (an international accord prohibiting production and use of antipersonnel landmines), eliminate already deployed landmines, and offer help to landmine victims.

2) The environment

Japan is endeavoring to protect the world environment. The success it achieved in overcoming industrial pollution while still maintaining a high level of economic growth convinced it of the feasibility of realizing a balance between environmental and economic concerns. It is pursuing a broad range of programs based on this thinking, in such areas as prevention of global warming and desertification, protection of the ozone layer, and preservation of wildlife and the forests. Further, in an effort to assist developing nations in strengthening their ability to deal with environmental problems, Japan engages in numerous cooperative activities involving, for example, financial assistance, transfer of environment protection technology and participation

とくに地球温暖化問題に関しては、1997年京都
で開催された気候変動枠組条約第3回締約国会議の
議定書（京都議定書）の早期発効をめざし、日本は
それぞれに意見の対立するヨーロッパ、アメリカ、
途上国間の調整役として努力を重ね、2001年よう
やくアメリカ抜きではあるが締約国合意に達した。
日本は今後もこの問題についてのアメリカの協力を
得る努力を続ける。

3）麻薬対策

　日本は麻薬対策にも協力している。日本は麻薬の
密造国ではない。しかし、日本は世界の三大麻薬生
産地域のうち2地域が存在するアジア・太平洋地域
に位置している。こうした地域との協力に重点をお
き、資金協力を行い、麻薬対策国際会議を開催して
いる。また、92年に日本が提唱した東南アジア地
域麻薬対策国際機関が設置された。

4）テロリズム対策

　日本もテロリズムを有効に防止するための国際協
力に積極的に参加している。人質の安全救出に最大
限の努力を払うことは当然であるが、「テロリスト
に対して譲歩しない」という断固たる原則を堅持し
ている。
　2001年9月、アメリカのニューヨークを中心に
同時多発テロ事件が発生した。ハイジャック旅客機
の自爆によるビル破壊で3,000人以上の犠牲者が出
るという未曾有の惨事であった。この事件は日本国
民にも非常な衝撃と悲しみを与えた。犯行はイスラ
ム原理主義組織によるものと断定された。これに対
しては中国、ロシア、イスラム諸国をふくむ国連加
盟国の大多数がテロ撲滅のために協力することに同
意した。こうした国際世論を背景に、日本は「テロ
対策特別措置法」を制定し、国連と協調しつつ自衛
隊の艦艇、航空機のインド洋派遣など憲法の範囲内
で可能な後方支援活動を行なった。〔注〕日本国憲
法は、戦争を国際紛争解決の手段とすることを禁じ
ている。

in joint projects.

Japan has worked particularly hard to further the cause of global warming prevention through early implementation of the protocol adopted at the Third Conference of the Parties to the UN Framework Convention on Climate Change held in Kyoto in 1997 (the Kyoto Protocol). Japan's persistent efforts to bring the conflicting positions of Europe, the United States and the developing countries into accord finally came to fruition in 2001, when all parties to the Convention other than the United States reached agreement. Securing the cooperation of the United States on this issue continues to be a high-priority objective.

3) Anti-drug measures

Japan cooperates in the fight against drugs. Japan itself is not a source of illegal drugs. It is, however, part of both Asia and the Pacific, where two of the world's three largest marijuana producing areas are located. Working mainly with the countries of these regions, Japan provides financial assistance and sponsors international conferences on drug control. In response to a Japanese proposal, an international organization for controlling narcotics in the Southeast Asian region was established in 1992.

4) Antiterrorism

Japan actively cooperates with the international community in the effort to prevent terrorism. While it acknowledges the need to place top priority on the rescue of hostages, it adheres strictly to the principle of not negotiating with terrorists.

On September 11, 2001, suicidal terrorists flying hijacked passenger planes crashed into buildings in the United States, killing more than 3,000 people in New York City and elsewhere. The Japanese people were shocked and saddened by this unprecedented tragedy, which was concluded to be the work of an Islamic fundamentalist organization. The response of China, Russia, the Muslim countries and other member states of the United Nations was an almost unanimous commitment to cooperate toward the total eradication of terrorism. Against the backdrop of this international consensus, Japan enacted special antiterrorism legislation to establish a legal basis for an ensuing cooperate effort with the United Nations that involved the dispatch of Self Defense Force ships and airplanes to the Indian ocean to engage in logistic support and other activities within the limits of the Constitution (which forswears war as a means for settling international disputes).

5）難民問題への対応

　　今日世界で国連が保護・支援の対象としている難民・国内難民は 2,600 万人にのぼる。大多数は民族、宗教の対立抗争により発生したものである。日本は難民問題の解消は人道上の要請であるとともに世界全体の平和と安全のために重要であるとの基本認識に立って難民の人道支援を国際貢献の重要な柱の一つと位置づけ積極的に取り組んでいる。

　　また、政府は人道支援における非政府組織（NGO）の役割に注目し、次のような組織・基金の設立に積極的な役割を果した。
　　・「ジャパン・プラットフォーム」…政府、NGO、財界との共同支援組織
　　・「アジア・大洋洲地球国際人道支援センター」…国連緊急人道支援のトレーニングセンター
　　・「人間安全保障基金」…上記の組織活動支援のための財政基盤

　　日本の難民問題への国際貢献を語る上で特筆すべきは緒方貞子氏の働きである。緒方氏は 1991 年から 2000 年までの 10 年間、国連難民高等弁務官として 5000 人のスタッフを指揮してイラク、ルワンダ、旧ユーゴ、東チモールなど世界各地の大規模難民の救済のため精力的な活動を続けた。その献身的努力と貢献は国際社会から高い評価と尊敬を得ている。

e）国際交流の推進ー文化的貢献

　　日本は国際社会に政治、経済、文化など各分野での調和のとれた貢献をする努力をしてきた。しかし日本の国際社会でのイメージと期待はとかく経済面に偏りがちであった。日本は今後とも各国、各文明との対話を進め、各国文化に対する理解と尊敬の念を一層深めるとともに日本文化を更に積極的に発信することが大切である。

5) The refugee problem

Refugees and domestic refugees receiving protection and assistance from the United Nations number some 26 million worldwide. Most refugees are the result of religious conflicts. Japan's basic view is that solving the refugee problem is both a necessity from the humanitarian viewpoint and also essential for ensuring peace and security throughout the world. Programs for offering humanitarian assistance to refugees are therefore being vigorously pursued as a key element in Japan's effort to contribute to the international community.

In recognition of the role of non-government organizations (NGOs) in providing humanitarian aid, the Japanese Government moved positively to help establish the following organizations :

- Japan Platform··· an assistance organization set up jointly among the Government, NGOs and the business sector
- Regional Center for Emergency Training in International Humanitarian Response (e-Center)··· an organization that provides training for people engaged in offering UN emergency humanitarian assistance
- The Human Security Fund··· a source of funds for supporting the activities of the e-Center

Of particular note regarding Japan's contribution to alleviating refugee problems is the work of Mrs. Sadako Ogata. During ten years as the United Nations High Commissioner for Refugees (from 1991 to 2000), Mrs. Ogata energetically led a staff of 5,000 in carrying out large-scale refugee relief operations in Iraq, Rwanda, the former Yugoslavia, East Timor and other regions around the globe, Her total devotion to her work and tremendous contribution to the international community have won her the praise and respect of people worldwide.

e) **International Exchange: Cultural Contribution**

Although Japan has endeavored to maintain a harmonious balance among the political, economic, cultural and other contributions it makes to the rest of the world, the international community's view of and expectations for Japan often tend to be dominated by economic overtones. This makes it essential for the Japanese to continue to expand their dialog with countries and societies all over the world so as to cultivate deeper understanding and appreciation of other cultures, while at the same time

（文明間の対話、文化の多様性の保持）

　国連は 2000 年を「平和の文化国際年」、2001 年を「文明間の対話国連年」に指定し文明間の対話促進を各国政府に呼びかけている。日本もこの考え方を支持し、2001 年に外務大臣の下に「イスラム研究会」を発足させるなど、他の文明、文化の理解に努めている。

　また 2000 年の九州・沖縄サミットにおいては、日本のイニシアテイブにより文化の多様性の保持と無形文化遺産の保護・振興方針を確認した。日本は国連機関を通じてこの方針実現に努力している。

（青少年教育・交流）

　世界の明日をになう若い世代の交流は将来の各国相互理解のためきわめて重要である。2000 年の G 8（先進8 カ国）教育大臣会議で教員、研究者、学生の国際交流を今後 10 年間で 2 倍にする方針が合意された。

　日本は対日理解の大きな柱である JET プログラム（Japan Exchange and Teachihg Program）により、外国人青年が日本を訪問し、各地方で語学指導、国際協力活動をする援助をしている。JET プログラムによる訪日外国青年は 2000 年には 6,000 人を超えた。

　1998 年の海外における、日本語教育機関の数は約11,000、日本語教育者数は 27,600 人、日本語学習者数は 210 万人に達した。

working more aggressively to acquaint people in other countries with Japanese culture.

(Dialog among civilizations, preservation of cultural diversity)

Designating the year 2000 as the International Year for the Culture of Peace and 2001 as the International Year of Dialogue Among Civilizations, the United Nations has called on governments throughout the world to encourage dialogues among different civilizations. In response, the Japanese Government has stepped up efforts to promote understanding of other civilizations and cultures among the Japanese people. The launching of the Study Group for Islam under the Minister of Foreign Affairs is one of a number of steps taken in this direction. On the other hand, at the Kyushu Okinawa Summit Conference of eight leading industrial nations (the G8) held in 2000, a Japanese initiative led to affirmation of G8's commitment to maintaining cultural diversity and preserving and cultivating intangible cultural assets. Japan has since been working to implement this commitment through United Nations organizations.

(Youth education and exchanges)

Exchanges among world youth, those soon to be responsible for mankind's future, are indispensable for ensuring mutual understanding among nations in coming years. One agreement coming out of the G8 Education Ministers'Meeting and Forum of 2000 was to explore ways to double the rate of international exchange of teachers, researchers and students over ten years. A cornerstone of the Japanese initiative for promoting better understanding of itself, while also supporting international cooperative activities among world youth, is the JET (Japan Exchange and Teaching) program, under which young men and women are invited to Japan to assist in foreign language instruction at schools throughout the country. During 2000, around 6,000 young people visited Japan under the JET program.

About 11,000 overseas institutions offer courses in the Japanese language. The number of teachers who teach Japanese as a second language is around 27,600 and the number of non-Japanese studying the language worldwide is roughly 2.1 million (1998 figures).

(4) 国旗・国名

a) 国　旗

　　日本の国旗は日の丸または日章旗といわれている。両方とも昇る太陽の旗という意味である。白地の中心の赤い円は太陽を表す。

　　昔から神社の旗やのぼりに用いられ、16世紀ごろから日本を表す旗として船に揚げられた。

　　「太陽の出る所」という意味の国号（日本）とも合致するので、1870年に商船に揚げる国旗として制定された。1999年には日章旗が国旗として法制化された。

　　国旗としての正式な寸法は、縦横比が2対3、日章の直径は縦の長さの5分の3、日章は旗面の中央となっている。

　　国章は日本では定められていない。

b) 国　歌

　　日本の国歌として歌われてきた「君が代」の歌詞は、古今和歌集（1,000年以上前につくられた）に収録されている和歌であるが、作者は不明である。曲は明治時代になって宮内省の伶人（れいじん）、林広守により作曲され、慣習的に「国歌斉唱」のさいに用いられるようになった。

　　歌詞の意味は、「天皇の御世は、千代も八千代も続くように。小さな小石が岩になって、それに苔が生えるほど先まで永遠に続くように」ということである（昔の人は、岩は小石や砂が長年かかって凝り固まってできるものと信じていたといわれている）。なお、1999年に「君が代」は国歌として法制化された。

c) 国花・国鳥

　　日本では昔から桜が国を代表する花と考えられている。桜は日本の神話にも現れており、桜の花の散り方の潔（いさぎよ）さが、武士の人生観に結びつけられた。

(4) The National Flag and the Name of the Country

a) The National Flag

The national flag of Japan is called the Hi-no-Maru or the Nisshoki. Both words mean "the flag of the rising sun." The sun is represented by a red circle at the center of a white field.

The design had been used on shrine flags and banners for many years before being adapted to a flag for indicating the nationality of Japanese ships in the sixteenth century.

So well did the flag match the name of the country (meaning place from where the sun rises) that it was formally designated as the national flag for use on merchant ships in 1870. It became Japan's national flag by law in 1999.

In its official size, the flag has a hoist of two against a fly of three and the sun is a circle whose center is at the center of the flag and whose diameter is three fifths the hoist.

Japan has no officially designated national emblem.

b) The National Anthem

The words of Kimigayo, which has for many years been sung as Japan's National Anthem, were taken from a waka poem found in Kokinwakashu, a collection of waka poems dating back more than one thousand years. The poet's name is unknown. The Anthem's melody was written by Hiromori Hayashi, an Imperial Court musician in the Meiji Era. By custom, this is the song the Japanese sing together as their National Anthem.

The words of the Anthem mean: "May the reign of the Emperor continue for a thousand, nay, eight thousand generations and for the eternity that it takes for small pebbles to grow into a great rock and become covered with moss." (Ancient Japanese apparently thought that great rocks were formed by the aggregation of pebbles and sand over many years.) Kimigayo became Japan's national anthem by law in 1999.

c) National Flower and National Bird

The Japanese have long thought of the sakura (cherry blossom) as the flower which symbolizes the nation.

It is mentioned in ancient myths, and the way its petals fall while still at the height of their beauty was interpreted by the old warrior class as symbolic of resignation and grace in death,

日本各地に桜の名所があり、満開の桜の木の下で酒宴を開くのが日本人の楽しみになっている。

　また、皇室の紋章が菊であるため、菊も日本を代表する花とされている。

　神話や昔話にしばしば登場するキジが、1947年日本鳥学会で国鳥に指定された。キジは日本固有の鳥で、渡り鳥でないので、一年中みられる。雄と雌とで大きさ・色彩が非常に異なる。雄は顔が赤く、頸・胸・腹部は暗緑色、背は紫がかっており、尾は長く多数の黒帯がある。雌は淡褐色で、黒斑があり尾は短い。草原や耕地の近くの灌木林に棲み、地上に巣をつくる。食物は木の実・昆虫などである。

d）元　号

　東洋の国には時代ごとに呼び名をつけるところがある。古代中国には、皇帝が時をも支配するという思想があった。これに基づいて漢の時代（紀元前2世紀）から元号が用いられるようになった。東アジアでは他国を支配すると、自国の元号を使わせる習慣があった。そのため、強国は元号制度を独立の証として誇示した。日本では、7世紀に「大化」と号したのが最初である。日本の制度では、天皇が元号の終わりと次の元号の初まりを定めてきた。

　しかし、19世紀後半の「明治」以降は、おのおのの天皇の代は一つの元号を用いるという原則（一世一元制）が定められた。すなわち、天皇が前天皇の位をついだ年を元年とし、天皇が亡くなるまで、同一元号を使用する。

　現在は、元号の制定の手続きは、法律によって定められている。現在の元号は「平成」で、1989年から始まる。現在、公文書には日本の元号が使われているが、西暦も広く使われている。

qualities which the warriors rated highly.

There are numerous cherry blossom viewing spots throughout the country and one of the pleasures of life among the Japanese is the chance to hold a sake drinking party beneath a grove of cherry trees in full bloom.

The chrysanthemum is another flower which, because of its use in the Imperial Crest, is considered to be symbolic of Japan.

The pheasant, a bird which makes frequent appearances in Japanese myths and folklore, was designated the National Bird by the Japanese Bird Society in 1947. The pheasant (kiji) is peculiar to Japan, and since it does not migrate, can be seen the year around. The male and female of the species differ greatly in both size and color. The male has a red face and dark-green neck, breast and stomach. Its back is purplish and it has a long tail with numerous black stripes. The female is light brown with black spots and has a short tail. The pheasant lives mainly in wooded areas near grassy fields or cultivated land. It makes its nest on the ground and lives on berries and insects.

d) Use of Eras in Reckoning Years

Some oriental countries name (number) years by eras. In ancient China, even time was thought to come under the emperor's rule. This thinking led to the naming of years by era from the Han dynasty (from about 200 B.C.). In East Asia, it became the custom for a stronger country to force weaker countries under its control to reckon years according to its own era. Stronger countries were therefore proud of their era systems as evidence of their independence. Japan began reckoning years by era in the seventh century, starting with the Taika Era. Under the Japanese system, it was the emperor who decided when one era would end and the next begin.

In the latter half of the nineteenth century, however, it was decided that from the Meiji Era on each emperor's reign would constitute one era. That is to say, the year in which an Emperor ascended to the throne would be the first year of a new era which would continue to his death.

Today, the procedures for deciding a new era are prescribed by law. The present era, named Heisei, began in 1989 (Heisei one). Although official documents are still dated using the Japanese era, the Western calendar is also widely known and used.

e）国名のいわれ

　　日本人は、自国をニッポンまたはニホンと呼んでいる。これは、7世紀のはじめ、政治を行っていた聖徳太子が中国に送った国書に、自国のことを「日の出るところ」と表現したことが起源になっている。その意味をとって漢字で表記したもの、すなわち「日本」が国名として使われるようになった。「日本」は、はじめヤマトと発音されていた。奈良時代にニホンまたはニッポンが用いられるようになった。

　　二つの読み方は現在どちらも使われている。両者を区別する法的根拠または一般ルールはない。ただし、国際スポーツ大会や郵便切手などに使われる場合は、通常ニッポンと発音される。

　Japan、あるいはこれに類するヨーロッパの言語での呼び方の由来には、2説がある。

　その一つは昔、中国北部地方で、日本国のことを Jih pen kuo と呼んでいたのを、ポルトガル人がジパング Zipangu または Jipangu と聞いたという説である。

　今一つは、中国南部地方で日本のことを Yatpun というのを、オランダ人が Japan と聞いたという説である。

　なお英語による日本の正式国名表示は、Japan である。

e) The Name of the Country

The Japanese refer to their country as "Nippon" or "Nihon." These two names have their origin in the words "place from where the sun rises" used by Prince Shotoku, an early seventh-century Japanese ruler, to designate his country in a letter he sent to China. The meaning of "place from where the sun rises" was translated into a pair of Chinese characters that came to be used to indicate the name of the country in writing. At first the characters were read in the Japanese way as "Yamato." "Nippon" and "Nihon" used today were adopted in the Nara Period.

At present, both readings are in common use. There is no general rule, legal or otherwise, for deciding which to use. However, "Nippon" is used, for example, at international sporting events and on postage stamps.

There are two widely held explanations regarding the origin of "Japan" and similar names used in the European languages.

According to one of these, these names come from "Zipangu" or "Jipangu", which are Portuguese attempts at pronouncing "Jihpenkuo," the name used for Japan in northern China.

The other has it that they come from the Dutch "Japan" taken from "Yatpun," the name of Japan used in Southern China.

"Japan" has been chosen as the formal name designating the country in the English language.

3 経済

(1) 全般

a）戦後の日本経済の流れ

　日本経済は、第二次世界大戦後、いくつかの段階を経て今日にいたっている。まず戦前水準への回復期、ついで重化学工業を牽引力とした高度成長期、それから2度の石油危機を経た後の技術集約産業主導による安定成長期、そして1980年代後半からのバブルの生成とその崩壊による1990年代の長期景気低迷期である。景気はその後2000年、2001年に入っても回復せず、企業の倒産、失業者の増大、他方660兆円を超える国家、地方財政の赤字などの深刻な状態が続いている。こうした事態を打開し、日本経済の抜本的建て直しを図るため、2001年4月に成立した小泉内閣は画期的「日本構造改革」政策を打出した。現在この政策を具体的に実施することにより日本経済を再生させるため、官民あげての懸命の努力が続けられている。

1）回復期・高度成長期・安定成長期（終戦～1980年代前半）
　① 戦前水準への回復期（終戦～1950年代前半）
　　終戦直後の日本の鉱工業生産は、戦争勃発当時（1941年）の水準の7分の1に減少し、国民は深刻な食糧危機とインフレーションに苦しめられていた。
　　日本を占領した連合軍は、日本経済の民主化のために、三つの基本政策を導入した。すなわち、(1)財閥解体（別項「財閥」参照）、(2)農地制度の改革、(3)労働権の確立である。戦後の日本経済発展の大きな枠組みとなったのは、まさにこれら3本の柱であった。日本政府は、産業の基礎である石炭・鉄鋼のために、資材・資金・労働力を重点的に投入するいわゆる傾斜生産方式を実施した。こうして、日本経済は1948年ごろから回復に向かったが、その間日本経済は激しいインフレとそれに続く深刻な不振に

3 Economy

(1) The Overall Economy

a) Postwar Development of the Japanese Economy

The Japanese economy has gone through a number of stages since the end of the Second World War: first, a recovery period during which Japan built its economy back up to the prewar level; next, a high growth period driven by the heavy chemical industry; then, after the two oil crises, a stable growth period driven by technology intensive industries; and in the 1990s, a prolonged recession triggered by the expansion and contraction of an economic bubble in the latter half of the 1980s. With the years 2000 and 2001 also failing to see any improvement in the business situation, the economy continued to confront an array of harsh realities, including a spate of business failures, surging unemployment, and combined national and local government budget deficits of more than 660 trillion yen. Upon coming into power in April 2001, the Koizumi Cabinet sought to overcome this impasse by launching a sweeping initiative aimed at restructuring Japan and fundamentally rebuilding the Japanese economy. In line with this program, the government and the private sector are today moving aggressively ahead with concrete measures for economic revitalization.

1) Recovery, rapid growth and stable growth periods (from end of the war to mid eighties)
① Recovery (from the end of the war to the mid fifties)

In the early postwar years, production in the mining and manufacturing industries was down to one seventh the level at the start of the war (1941), and there were severe food shortages and rampant inflation.

In order to put the Japanese economy on a democratic footing, the occupying Allied Forces introduced three fundamental policies: (1) the dissolution of the zaibatsu (see section on The Zaibatsu), (2) the reformation of the agricultural land ownership system, and (3) the establishment of the rights of workers. It was these three policies that formed the overall framework within which the country's postwar economy was to develop. The Japanese Government implemented a "priority production system" for focusing a major part of the available material, financial

落ち込んだ。

　　この状態から立ち直る契機となったのは、1950
年に勃発した朝鮮戦争にともなう在日米軍向けの資
材・サービスの供給（朝鮮特需）であった。こうし
て日本経済は復興の歩みを速め、50年代半ばまで
に、ほぼすべての経済指標が戦前の水準にまで回復
した。

② 　高度成長期（1950年代後半～60年代）
　　1950年代後半から1960年代末まで、日本経済は
「もはや戦後ではない」（1956年経済白書）を合い
言葉に国民総生産（GNP）は年平均10％の高い成
長率を示した。この間、日本の産業は重化学工業の
飛躍的な発展によって、生産規模・生産性などを大
幅に向上させる基盤を固めた。さらに、この時期に
は、国際競争力の強化をはかるための、大型合併が
目立った。
　　日本はまた、輸入・為替の自由化をすすめ、62
年には輸入自由化率が88％に達し、64年にはIMF
8国に移行（為替制限の原則撤廃）した。また資
本の自由化も進んだ。60年代後半には輸出が拡大
し、国際収支も黒字基調に転じた。
　　一方、高度成長の陰の部分としてインフレや公害
問題が発生した。

③ 　安定成長への転換（1970年代～80年代前半）
　　1970年代に入ると、経済成長にもかげりがみえ
はじめた。さらに、国外からも重大な攪乱要素があ
いついで生じてきた。そのひとつは、71年のニク
ソン米国大統領によるドルの金兌換停止であった。
これにより、23年間続いた1ドル360円時代が終
わった。1ドル308円の一時期を経て、円は変動相
場制に移行し、73年には1ドル260円台になった。

and labor resources on the two most fundamental industrial sectors, coal and steel. The economy began to recover from around 1948. The recovery was, however, punctuated by a period of severe inflation and an ensuing slump.

The opportunity to pull out of this recession came with the outbreak of the Korean War in 1950, when the U. S. forces stationed in Japan began making special procurements of supplies and services. The recovery was accelerated to such an extent that nearly all economic indicators had reached prewar levels by the mid fifties.

② Rapid economic growth (from the mid fifties through the sixties)

Buoyed by the sentiment that the Japanese economy could "no longer be termed postwar" (as expressed in the 1956 Economic White Paper), Japan's gross national product (GNP) expanded at a high average annual rate of 10% between the mid fifties and the end of the sixties. The rapid development of the heavy and chemical industries during this period served as the basis for major increases in production capacity and productivity. The period was further marked by a number of large scale mergers between companies attempting to strengthen their international competitive power.

Japan also liberalized imports and lifted foreign exchange restrictions. By 1962, liberalization of imports had reached 88%, and in 1964 Japan acquired IMF Article 8 status (meaning that, in principle, it abandoned foreign exchange controls). It also freed capital investment. It was from the latter half of the sixties that the country began consistently maintaining a favorable international balance of payments.

On the dark side of the rapid growth were the problems of inflation and pollution.

③ Transition to an economy with a stable rate of growth (from the seventies to the mid eighties)

The rate of economic expansion started to slow from the early seventies. In addition, the economy was shaken by a series of major changes outside the country. The first of these was the announcement by President Nixon of the U. S. in 1971 that the U. S. would no longer convert dollars to gold. This brought an end to the fixed exchange rate of 360 yen to the dollar that had been in effect for 23 years. After briefly being revalued to a fixed rate of 308 to the dollar, the yen was allowed to float. By 1973,

73 年の第一次石油危機の衝撃は、日本のような資源輸入国にはとくに痛烈であった。当時日本経済はインフレ基調にあったため、「狂乱物価」と呼ばれる激しいインフレが発生した。

　物価急騰は、政府の総需要抑制により 76 年にはいったん沈静した。しかし、日本経済はその後 5 年余りの低迷の中で、再び第二次石油危機による世界経済の大混乱に巻き込まれた。

　日本の各産業は、省エネルギー技術や自動化技術開発・導入を推進し、産業構造の「重厚長大型」から「軽薄短小型」への転換によりこの危機を乗り切った。米国の高金利によるドル高・円安を背景に、輸出も日本経済の牽引力となった。

　こうして、80 年代前半、日本経済は年率 4 〜 5 ％の安定成長軌道に乗った。

2）"バブル"の生成と崩壊（1980 年代後半〜90 年代初め）

　この間、貿易黒字は増えつづけ、対日批判は強まった。これを解消するため、88 年から公定歩合を引き下げ、各種規制を撤廃するなど、民間活力による内需拡大路線が推進された。この政策は企業の要請にマッチし、経済は非常に活性化した。たとえば、民間設備投資が 3 年連続（88〜90 年度）2 桁の伸び率を示した。株価と地価は、とどまるところを知らず上昇を続けた。このいわゆる「バブル景気」に対処するため、89 年半ばから日本銀行は金融引き締めに転換した。これを契機にいっきょに 90 年初頭から株価の暴落が始まった。91 年 4 月をピークとしてこの景気は下降に向かい、やがて株価は最高値（89 年 12 月 38,915 円）の半分以下に急落し、土地の取引も急速に縮小し、地価も下落してきた。まさに「バブル」がはじけたのであった。

3）90 年代の長期景気低迷（90 年代初め〜2000 年）

　バブル崩壊後の 90 年代の経済は、全般的には低成長を余儀なくされているが、内容は一様ではない。

it had appreciated to 260 yen to the dollar.

The impact of the first oil crisis of 1973 was particularly severe for countries like Japan that depended mainly on imported natural resources. Coming at a time when the Japanese economy was already inflationary, the oil crisis was enough to set off a vicious price spiral.

Government measures to hold down total demand temporarily brought prices under control in 1976. Following this, however, came five years of sluggish growth in the course of which the economy was drawn into the global economic chaos set off by the second oil crisis.

Japanese industries weathered the difficulties of this period by developing and applying energy conservation and automation technologies, and also by a structural shift away from the "heavy and sluggish" toward the "light and nimble." With the value of the yen against foreign currencies being low owing to high interest rates in the United States, exports became a major force behind the economy.

Economic growth during the first half of the eighties was a steady 4 to 5%.

2) The expansion and contraction of the Bubble Economy (from the mid eighties to the early nineties)

During this period, Japan's swelling trade surplus drew increasing criticism from trading partners. In 1988, the Government responded with interest rate cuts, deregulation and other measures designed to increase internal demand by vitalizing the private sector. As these were changes business had been demanding, they gave strong impetus to the economy. For example, private-sector capital spending posted double-digit growth in three consecutive years (fiscal 1988 · 1990). Stock and land prices skyrocketed. To control this Bubble Economy, as it came to be known, the Bank of Japan switched to a tight money policy in the second half of 1989. This precipitated a sharp fall in share prices from the beginning of 1990. The economy went into a tailspin after cresting in April 1991, share prices eventually fell to half their peak level 38,915 yen in December 1989, real estate transactions dwindled and land prices tumbled. The Bubble had burst.

3) Protracted recession of the nineties (from the early nineties to 2000)

The collapse of the Bubble Economy marked the beginning of

この期間は３区分される。まず、第一期は94年度までの３年連続国内総生産（GDP）の成長率が年平均0.5％の不況期である。92〜94年度の３年間にバブル期の設備能力の過剰を解消するため、設備投資は19％減少した。また、地価、株価も暴落した。

　第二期は平均３％の経済成長率を達成した95と96両年度である。設備能力の調整を終えたことを背景に民間設備投資が年率８％の伸びに回復した。また、公共投資追加、円高対応への公定歩合引き下げ（95年９月、史上最低の0.5％へ）、消費税率引き上げ（97年４月、５％へ）を目前にした駆け込み需要などが成長要因として挙げられる。この期は95年の異常な円高（「第２次円高」期でピークは95年４月：79円/＄）にも見舞われたが、公定歩合の引き下げ、新たなる製造業の海外立地・生産、安い輸入品活用などの対応により、景気への悪影響を極力小さくした。

　第三期には従来みられなかった次のような深刻な事態が生じている。第一は、97年11月、大手金融機関の証券会社および銀行が破綻した。これは金融システム全般への動揺、信頼性低下を招いた。民間・政府系ともに金融機関の不良債権増加とその処理もいわゆる金融ビッグバンを迎え大問題になっている。これにともない貸し渋りも生じ、設備や新規事業への投資を阻害している。第二は、企業は長引く不況からの脱出のためいわゆるリストラ、競争力強化を推進しているが、その結果97年７月から連続４年以上も雇用・所得が減少している。

　とくに失業率は年々増えつづけ、1999年３月には300万人を超え、失業率は4.8％となった。

a prolonged slump in the 1990s. Although growth was incessantly slow, different factors were at work at different times.

The period falls into three stages. The first, from 1992 to 1994, was a three-year recession stage in which the gross domestic product (GDP) was held to an annual average growth rate of 0. 5%. During this phase, the private sector cut investment in new plant and equipment by 19% to adjust for the excesses of the Bubble period. Land and share prices plummeted.

During the second stage, from 1995 to 1996, the economy achieved average annual growth of 3%. This growth was powered chiefly by an 8% annual increase in private-sector capital investment following completion of facility capacity adjustment. Other factors included increased public works spending, reduction of the official discount rate (to a record low of 0.5% in September 1995 in a move to counteract the high yen), and a surge in consumer spending in anticipation of a consumption tax hike (from 3% to 5% in April 1997). Another feature of this stage was a wild rise in the value of the yen against foreign currencies. The yen went as high as 79 yen to the U. S. dollar in April 1995, but the adverse effect of this appreciation on the economy was minimized by the lowering of the official discount rate, a fresh wave of private-sector production shifts to overseas locations, and utilization of cheap imported products.

The third stage saw the emergence of two serious situations never before experienced by Japan. The first is exemplified by the failure of two major financial institutions, a securities company and a bank, in November 1997. These collapses were caused by rising anxiety and declining confidence regarding the financial system as a whole. Japan's financial sector underwent rapid and extensive reformation (a process popularly referred to as the financial "Big Bang"). This made the financial institutions still more concerned about swelling bad debt and how to deal with it. Banks, for example, became reluctant to extend loans. Companies therefore found it hard to secure the funds they needed for investment in new facilities and businesses. The second was a decline in employment and personal income starting in July 1997 and continuing for more than four years. This was caused mostly by corporate restructuring efforts aimed at building the competitive strength needed to pull out of the unrelenting economic doldrums. Unemployment continued to increase annually. As of March 1999, the number of jobless exceeded 3 million and the

政府はこうした事態に対処するため、70兆円という過去に例のない公的資金を投入して金融秩序の安定・回復を図るとともに、税収不足をカバーするため多額の国債を発行し財政面からの景気刺激策を実施した。これらの諸施策にもかかわらず景気回復のきざしはみられず、失業者数は2001年12月には360万人余り、失業率は5.6％と政府による現行調査開始以来最高を記録した。

　　このような不況とはいえ、**GDPの規模、国民1人当りのGDP**、対外純資産などで見れば日本の世界経済におけるプレゼンスは依然大きく、日本経済の建て直しと国際的貢献への期待は強いものがある。

4）日本経済の今後の課題—日本の構造改革

　　日本の構造改革の必要性はバブル経済の崩壊後1991年からくり返し論議されてきたが、2002年現在いまだ本格的には実現していない。

　　1997年、当時の橋本内閣は金融、財政、行政など6つの改革を掲げたが、景気の低迷、変革への抵抗、不良債権問題などにより挫折した。その後も日本の経済・社会は金融機関の膨大な不良債権に起因する破綻、600兆円を超す国家・地方の公的赤字、社会保障制度財源の絶対的不足など、危機的様相を深めてきた。2002年6月末現在、780兆円を超えている。

　　2001年4月、国民の広範な支持を得て発足した小泉内閣は、改革のためのいわゆる「失われた10年」を回復するため、①経済・財政、②行政、③社会の相互に関連する3つの構造改革を打ち出し、これらの実施に当たっては「聖域なき改革」と「国民の痛みをともなう改革」への協力を広く国民に訴えた。改革の主要点は次の通りである。今回の日本の構造改革は国際公約でもある。

unemployment rate stood at 4.8%,

To cope with this situation, the government implemented an economic stimulation package that included the unprecedented step of using 70 trillion yen in public funds to stabilize and restore financial order and called for issuing a huge amount of government bonds to cover the tax revenue shortfall. Despite these measures, however, the economy showed no signs of rebounding, while the number of unemployed shot up to more than 360 million and the unemployment rate rose to 5.6% (as of December 2001), the highest recorded since the government started compiling statistics under the current system.

Despite its economic woes, however, Japan remains a strong presence on the world economic scene in terms of GDP, per capita GDP, net foreign claims and other key indicators. Hopes that Japan can rebuild its economy and contribute still more to the international commununitity are running high.

4) Problems Facing the Japanese Economy: Structural Reform

The need for structural reform at the national level was a continual topic of discussion in Japan following the collapse of the economic bubble in 1991. Still, little of substance was accomplished up to the end of 2001.

Although the Hashimoto Cabinet announced a six-point initiative for financial, administrative and other reforms in 1997, the plan soon foundered owing to an economic downturn, resistance to change, and an intensifying bad debt problem. In the years that followed, Japan and its economy were pushed deeper and deeper into crisis by an array of adverse developments, including the collapse of a number of financial institutions under the weight of huge amounts of bad debt, the ballooning of national and local government deficits to more 600 trillion yen, and an absolute insufficiency of social security system resources. These deficits amounted to more than 780 trillion yen end at the June 2002.

After sweeping into power with wide popular support in April 2001, the Koizumi Cabinet hammered out three interwoven initiatives for ① economic and financial reform, ② administrative reform and ③ social reform. Declaring that he intended to make up for ten years of lost time, Prime Minister Koizumi appealed broadly to the Japanese people for their cooperation in implementing reforms he said would be painful but would be pursued without recognizing any sanctuary. The main points of

（経済・財政）
- 各金融機関の膨大な不良債権の処理と金融システムの健全化。

- 金融制度の規制緩和の一層の推進
　　先の商法、銀行法の改正に基づく金融持株会社の設立（1998年認可）、株式交換による銀行合併、金融機関による銀行業・証券業・保険業の兼業、異業種の銀行業への参入などによる金融システムの画期的再編成を図る。
　〔注〕1.日本の預金金利の完全自由化は11年を費やして1995年に実現した。
　　　　2.異業種の銀行業への参入については、イトーヨーカ堂・セブンイレブンの8,500店舗でのATM（現金自動受払機）による金融業務の開始、ソニー銀行（インターネット専業銀行）の開業（いずれも2001年6月）、トヨタ自動車の金融統括会社・証券会社設立などの動きが始まっている。

- 国家財政再建
　　2001年末現在666兆円におよぶ国と地方の財政赤字の解消と財政の健全化のため、国債発行額の規制、道路公団などの特殊法人の統廃合、公共事業投資の見直しなどを実施する。（次項参照）

（行政）
- 政府行政機構の改革
　　2001年1月省庁再編成が実施され1府21省庁が1府12省庁にスリム化された。
- 郵政3事業の民営化
　　郵政3事業（郵便事業・郵便貯金・簡易保

the initiatives are outlined below. The achievement of these reforms is also an international commitment.

(Economic and financial reforms)

- Cleaning up the massive bad debt mess of Japan's financial institutions and putting the financial system back on a sound footing.
- Further deregulation of the financial system

The financial system is to be radically reorganized to reflect recent changes to the Commercial Code and Bank Law, which, for example, allow establishment of financial holding companies (approved in 1998), permit banks to merge by exchanging shares, enable financial institutions to engage in multiple businesses among banking, securities and insurance, and allow companies in unrelated fields to enter the banking business.

>Remarks: 1. Liberalization of interest on bank deposits was completed in 1995, eleven years after the process was begun.
>
>2. A number of companies outside the financial sector have already entered, or have plans to enter, the banking business. Ito-Yokado, the supermarket chain, and 7-Eleven, the convenience store chain, began offering teller machine -based banking services at a total of 8,500 stores in June 2000, and the Sony Bank, which operates on the Internet, went into business in the same month. Toyota Motor Co. has announced plans to establish a financial administration company and a securities company.

- Rebuilding national finance

Measures are to be taken to eliminate national and local government budget deficits of 666 trillion yen (as of the end of 2001) and restore soundness to the financial system. These include limiting the amount of government bond issues, consolidating, abolishing or privatizing special government corporations like Japan Highway Public Corporation, and reappraising public works spending. (See the following section for details.)

(Administrative reforms)

- Reforming the administrative structure

The number of natinal government administrative offices was reduced from one office and 21 ministries and agencies to one office and 12 ministries and agencies in January 2001.

- Privatization of three postal services

険）の現業部門は 2001 年の中央省庁の再編で外庁の郵政事業庁に移行した。今後は 2003 年の郵政公社化を経て民営化への道を推進する。

・特殊法人の改革

　日本道路公団、石油公団など約 80 の特殊法人すべてを現在における存立意義、民営化などの運営形態の妥当性の観点から点検し、廃止、統合、民営化、独立行政法人化などの改革を断行する。

（社会）

　年金、健康保険、雇用保険、介護保険、高齢者医療などの社会保障制度を「将来とも持続可能なレベルにする」ため国家、地方自治体医療機関、国民の負担の適性化をはかる。また改革にともなう雇用問題に対して新産業による雇用の吸収、人材の育成制度の充実を策す。

　いずれにせよ今後 21 世紀初頭には IT 革命の浸透にともない経済・産業・社会が歴史的変容を遂げることは世界の趨勢である。その過程で日本においても政治の運営、企業の経営、個人の経済・社会生活などあらゆる面において従来の固定観念が破られ、自己責任が明確に求められるようになることが予想されている。

b）戦後の日本経済の成長プロセス

　日本は、第二次世界大戦後、奇跡ともいわれる高度成長を実現した。また、2 度の石油危機や急激な円高の影響を迅速に克服した。この理由についての国内外の見解

At the time of the reorganization of the central government offices at the beginning of 2001, the front-line operations of the three postal service sectors previously administered by the Ministry of Posts and Telecommunications (mail, postal savings and postal insurance) were transferred to a newly established Postal Services Agency. After being placed under a public corporation in 2003, they will be progressively privatized.

· Reforming special government corporations

All of the approximately 80 special government corporations, including Japan Highway Public Corporation and Japan National Oil Corporation, will be reexamined to determine whether they are still needed and whether they should be privatized or operated in some other manner. They will then be abolished, consolidated, privatized or reestablished as independent government corporations.

(Social reform)

The sharing of social security system costs (for the pension program, health insurance, unemployment insurance, at-home care insurance, medical care for the elderly etc.) among the national and local governments, the medical institutions and the people is to be appropriately balanced to ensure future sustainability. In order to alleviate employment problems caused by the reform initiatives, steps are to be taken to increase employment opportunities by promoting the development of new industries and offering more and better vocational training programs.

Still, regardless of what Japan may do, the early years of the 21st century will see the relentlessly spreading IT revolution power an economic, industrial and social transformation of global scale and historical significance. As this process moves forward, the Japanese people will be forced to discard many long-held concepts about government, business management, personal economy, social life and virtually ever other facet of their lives. They will also be called on to accept more clearly defined personal responsibilities.

b) Growth of the Japanese Economy after World War II

In the postwar years, Japan achieved what has often been referred to as an economic miracle. It also quickly overcame the effects of the two oil crises and the sharp upswing of the yen. The

をまとめると次のようである。

1) 高度成長
①教育水準が高く勤勉な人的資源があった。
②古い設備が戦争で破壊されたため、世界最新の設備・技術で装備できた。
③自由貿易体制の下で、原燃料を世界中から自由に輸入でき、また、各国、とくに米国が日本の商品をかなり自由に受け入れてくれるなど、輸出市場にも恵まれた。
④企業と労働組合がヨーロッパや米国に追いつくという共通の目的を持ち、まず経済的なパイを大きくするために協力した。
⑤国民の貯蓄性向が高く、また銀行が積極的な融資を行ったため、投資のための資金が十分に供給された。
⑥平和国家の道を選んだため、資金や人材を経済活動に集中できた。
　日本の高度成長には、国民各層の一致した努力に加えて、米国をリーダーとする自由貿易体制の存在など、外的条件が大きく寄与したことも忘れてはならない。

2) 1970年代の石油危機と円高の克服
①新技術の開発による、エネルギー消費の大幅な削減（たとえば、鉄鋼業や化学工業では、製品単位あたりエネルギー消費量は、73年以降の10年間に約20％前後低下した）。
②工場のオートメーション化やコンピュータを活用した管理技法の導入によって、生産効率と品質の向上を実現した。
③「重厚長大」から「軽薄短小」への産業構造転換が進んだ。すなわち、モノ産業からサービス産業へ、またモノ産業のなかでも重工業からエレクトロニクスなど高付加価値産業への移行が進んだ。
④円高は、日本が大量に輸入する原燃料のコストを引き下げ、輸出への抑制効果を相殺した。
⑤インフレの早期克服に成功した。これには、労働

opinions of Japanese and foreign observers as to why this was possible can be summarized as follows:

1) Rapid economic growth

① A well-educated and industrious workforce.

② The opportunity to adopt the world's most advanced equipment and technologies that was provided by the destruction of old production facilities during the war.

③ The free trade system, which enabled Japan to import raw materials freely from around the world and provided it with good export markets in many countries that put few restrictions on the import of Japanese goods, particularly the United States.

④ That enterprises and labor unions agreed on a common goal of catching up with Europe and the United States and therefore gave priority to building a bigger economic pie.

⑤ The propensity of the Japanese to save, which, combined with positive financing by the banks, provided an adequate supply of investment funds.

⑥ The national commitment to peace, which made it possible to concentrate both capital and human resources on economic activity.

What every Japanese must not forget, however, is that the country's rapid economic growth was only in part the result of a concerted effort among Japanese at all levels; it was also largely the product of external conditions, such as the free trade system maintained under the leadership of the United States.

2) Oil crises and rapid appreciation of the yen in the seventies

① Japan dramatically reduced energy consumption through the development of new technologies. For example, energy consumption per product unit in the steel and chemical industries fell about 20% in the decade after 1973.

② It increased production efficiency and product quality by automating its factories and applying computers to management.

③ It moved the center of its industrial structure away from the "heavy and sluggish" toward the "light and nimble" That is from product industries to service industries and, within the product industries, from heavy industries to high value-added industries such as electronics.

④ It offset the adverse effect of the high yen on exports by capitalizing on its effect of lowering the cost to Japan of the

組合が、生産性向上限度内で賃金要求を行ったことが大きく寄与している。これは、第二次石油危機のさいとくに顕著であった。

3）1985 年〜88 年の円高の再克服
　　① 70 年代からのオートメーション化が一層徹底され、コストが削減され効率が向上した（94 年時点、世界の産業用ロボットの 62 ％が日本で稼働していた）。
　　②コンピュータを活用した多品種少量生産システムの開発で、多様化する市場の要請に対応するなど、製品の高級化・高付加価値化をすすめた。
　　③エレクトロニクスの応用による情報・通信システムを広範囲に採用し、管理業務・輸送・在庫管理など種々の分野で、コスト削減とサービスの質的改善を実現した。
　　④米国・欧州などの需要地への工場進出によって、円高の影響を軽減した。
　　　〔注〕円とドルの為替レートの推移は巻末〔統計資料〕欄(6)を参照

c）独占禁止政策

　　第二次世界大戦後、占領軍の主力であった米国の指導によって、1947 年、日本は独占禁止法（正式には、私的独占の禁止および公正取引の確保に関する法律）を制定した。同時に公正取引委員会が設置された。制定当初は、この法律は独占の原則禁止主義に立つきわめて徹底したものであった。しかし、この法律はその後の時代の流れに対応して、何回か改定されている。最初の大きな改定は、米国の対日政策が日本の経済強化に変更されたことにともない、独占の原則禁止から独占の乱用防止を基本とするものになった。不況カルテルの容認や合併条件の緩和で 60〜70 年代にかけて三菱重工業の再統合や八幡製鐵と富士製鐵の再統合による新日本製鐵の誕生など大型合併が実現した。

large quantities of raw materials the country imports.

⑤ It quickly brought inflation under control. The labor unions made a major contribution to inflation control by keeping their wage increase demands within the limits of productivity increases, particularly during the second oil crisis.

3) Response to the high yen from 1985 to 1988

① Costs were reduced and efficiency increased by furthering the automation started in the seventies. (In 1994, 62% of the world's industrial robots were operating in Japan.)

② Computerized manufacturing systems were developed for producing small quantities of a wide variety of products, enabling manufacturers to respond to diversifying customer tastes and requirements with more sophisticated, higher value-added products.

③ Electronic information and communication systems were widely adopted to lower costs and improve quality in various fields, including management, shipping and stock control.

④ The effect of the high yen was mitigated by setting up production facilities in the United States, Europe and other product markets.

c) Antimonopoly Legislation

Under the guidance of the United States, which was dominant among the forces occupying Japan after the Second World War, Japan in 1947 enacted an antimonopoly law (formally called the Law Concerning the Prohibition of Private Monopolies and Maintenance of Fair Trade Practices). The Fair Trade Commission was established at the same time. At the time of its enactment, the Law was a thorough piece of legislation based on the principle of absolute prohibition of monopolies. But it has since undergone several amendments in line with the changing times. The first major revision, made after the United States switched to a policy of encouraging a stronger Japanese economy, changed the law from one basically prohibiting monopolies to one for preventing monopolistic abuses. By permitting formation of depression cartels and relaxing the conditions for mergers, the revised law opened the way for a number of large mergers in the '60s and '70 s, including the reunification of Mitsubishi Heavy Industries and the reuniting of the Yawata and Fuji steel companies to form Nippon Steel Corporation.

90 年代に入って違法行為に対する課徴金引き上げや特定企業間の継続的取引（いわゆる系列取引）や、同業者間の情報交換（いわゆる談合）に対して、運用面で規制を強化した。しかし、97 年には国際競争力を高めるために持ち株会社を許容し、また消費者重視の観点から、再販売価格慣習の見直しなどがなされた。ただ、これからの国際競争に勝ち抜くには依然としてこの独禁法の規制は厳しすぎるとの意見もある。

d) 財　閥

財閥とは、明治時代から第二次世界大戦の終結まで存続した大資本グループである。特定の一族が所有する持株会社が、株式保有を通じて、多業種にわたる傘下企業の人事・経営を支配するという閉鎖的で中央集権的な組織であった。財閥は、当時の日本における産業近代化の推進者として大きな役割を果たした。しかし後には、経済活動を独占したとの批判も受けた。

財閥は一般に 4 つのグループに分類できる。産業界の多くの分野にわたる総合力を持っていた三井・三菱・住友、金融主体の安田・野村、産業主体の浅野・大倉・古河などがあり、さらに 1930 年代に成立した鮎川・森などの「新興財閥」である。

これらの財閥は、第二次世界大戦後占領軍の政策によって解体されたが、その後占領軍の政策の緩和や講和条約の成立によって、企業グループの形で再登場してきた。しかし、新グループはかつての財閥とは性格を異にし、独立企業が緩やかに結びついた形になっている。企業間に支配関係はなく、各企業はグループを超える提携も自由に行っている。

さらに、最近では競争力強化のため、グループの壁を越えた提携も実現している。

Later, in the '90s, the fines imposed on violators were increased and tighter restrictions were placed on continuous transactions between specified companies (keiretsu transactions) and information exchanges between companies in the same line of business (dango). In 1997, the ban on holding companies was repealed and the policy regarding resale price maintenance practices was refocused to protect consumers. Still, some hold that the excessive severity of the Antimonopoly Law provisions limits the ability of Japanese businesses to meet the increasing challenges of international competition.

d) The Zaibatsu

The zaibatsu were large capital holding groups that existed in Japan between the Meiji Era and the end of the Second World War. They were closed, centrally controlled organizations in which a holding company owned by a single family used the shares it held in affiliated companies in various business fields to control their personnel and management decisions. Although the zaibatsu played a leading role in Japan's early industrial modernization, they were later criticized for monopolizing the nation's economy.

The zaibatsu can be generally classified into four groups: those spanning a broad range of industrial sectors such as the Mitsui, Mitsubishi and Sumitomo zaibatsu; those centered on the financial sector such as the Yasuda and Nomura zaibatsu; those centered on the manufacturing sector such as the Asano, Okura and Furukawa zaibatsu; and the "new zaibatsu" of the 1930s, such as the Ayukawa and Mori zaibatsu.

Although the zaibatsu were completely disbanded following World War II in line with the policy of the occupying forces, later, as this policy was relaxed, and then with the signing of the peace treaty, they reappeared in the form of industrial groups. These new groups are different in character from the zaibatsu, however, and are more of the nature of loose associations of independent companies. The members of the groups have no control over each other and each is free to enter cooperative agreements with outside companies.

In fact, some companies have entered alliances across group barriers in order to strengthen competitiveness.

(2) 対外経済

a）貿　易

1）概　観

　　日本は、貿易額では米国・ドイツに次いで第3位
である。2000年には、世界の輸出の7.8％、輸入
の6.5％を占めた。

　　日本の貿易が輸出超過基調に転換して20年以上
たち、今や貿易黒字減らしが、国内的にも国際的に
も重要課題となってきた。83年には、かつて輸出
振興を叫んでいた通産省が、輸入拡大に最も貢献し
た企業を表彰するようになった。

　　しかし、日本経済にとって、輸出は今後とも重要
である。というのは、日本は原料やエネルギー資源
のほとんどを輸入しなければならず、その調達のた
めには輸出による収益が必要だからである。つまり、
日本の貿易においては、輸出・輸入が双方ともに不
可欠なのであり、一方のみに片寄ることは許されな
いのである。

　　とはいえ、日本はシンガポールのような通商国家
とも本質的に違う。2000年には、日本の国民一人
あたり貿易額は、輸出3,777ドル、輸入2,991ドル
であった。貿易依存度（貿易額÷GNP）は、輸出
10.3％、輸入7.6％であった（1999）。これらの数
字は、いずれも米国と大差なく、欧州各国と比べて
半分程度である。

2）輸　出

　　2001年の輸出は前年に比べて5％減の49兆円で
あった。貿易黒字額は6.6兆円であった。

　　商品構成では、機械類（一般機械類・電気機器類
の合計で輸送用機器類を含まず）が圧倒的に多く、
輸出総額に占める比率は44.4％である。次いで多
いのは、自動車の14.7％で、そのほか精密機械の
5.4％、自動車部品の3.8％、鉄鋼の3.4％、有機
薬品の2.5％、船舶の2.1％などがある。

　　地域的にみると、2001年ではアジアが43.1％、
北米が31.7％、欧州が17.4％、中南米が4.4％、
オセアニアが2.3％であり、アフリカは1.1％であ
った。

(2) External Economic Relations

a) Trade

1) Overview

Japan ranks third in international trade volume after the United States and Germany. In 2000, it accounted for 7.8% of world exports and 6.5% of world imports.

Today, more than twenty years after exports first overtook imports, the lowering of Japan's trade surplus has become a major issue both at home and internationally. In 1983, the Ministry of International Trade and Industry, which had long championed exports, began instead to commend companies making the biggest contribution to imports.

Yet exports will continue to be important to the Japanese economy. The country has to import most of the raw materials and energy it uses, and to purchase these it needs the revenues from its exports. This makes both exports and imports equally indispensable aspects of the country's international trade and means that Japan cannot afford to let either take precedence over the other.

Still, Japan is basically different from trading countries like Singapore. In 2000, the per capita value of goods exported and imported by Japan amounted to $3,777 and $2,991, respectively. The degree of dependence on foreign trade (amount of exports/ imports divided by GNP) was 10.3% for exports and 7.6% for imports. (1999). These figures do not differ greatly from those for the United States and are less than half those for, the European countries.

2) Exports

Exports during 2001 were down 5% from the preceding year, to ¥49,000 billion. The trade surplus was ¥6.6 trillion.

Machinery (total of general machinery and electrical machinery, but not including transportation machinery) accounts for 44. 4% of the total value of exports, making it by far the largest export product category. The next largest category is automobiles at 14.7%. Other major categories include precision machinery 5. 4%, automobile components 3.8%, steel 3.4%, organic chemicals 2. 5% and ships 2.1%.

By region, Asia accounted for 43.1%, North America for 31.7%, Europe for 17.4%, Central and South America for 4.4%, Oceania 2.3%, and Africa 1.1%.

国別にみると米国が断然多く30％を占める。これに次ぐ上位相手国はほぼ安定していて、中国、台湾、韓国、ホンコン、シンガポール、マレーシア、タイ、ドイツ、イギリスである。多少の順位入れ替えはあるが、2〜8％の輸出である。

3）輸　入

輸入は、輸出よりは変動の振幅が大きい。その主な理由は、輸入が輸出に比べて景気の影響を直接受けること、日本が大量に輸入する石油や一次産品の価格変動が大きいことなどである。94年から輸入は増加傾向を示していたが、98年は日本国内の需要冷え込みで減少した。

2001年の主なものは、機械類24.8％、原燃料18.3％（うち原油11.1％）、食料品12.2％（魚介類3.8％、肉類2.4％）、衣類5.5％などである。

地域的にみると、アジアが55.2％、北米が20.3％、欧州が15.5％、オセアニアが4.9％、中南米が2.8％であり、アフリカは1.3％である。

国別にみると、米国が18.1％で輸出と同じように首位、2位中国が16.6％であった。以下、韓国、台湾、オーストラリア、インドネシア、ドイツ、マレーシア、サウジアラビア、アラブ首長国が3〜6％台で続く（2001年）。これら諸国はほぼ安定的に上位を占めている。

b）国際収支

1）概　観

日本の国際収支は、貿易の巨額黒字と資本収支の大幅赤字が特徴となっており、貿易で稼いだ金を、資本輸出という形で海外に投資している。

60年代半ば以降は、石油危機の後など例外的な時期を除いて、貿易収支・経常収支のいずれにおいても黒字基調が続いている。

国際収支の内訳を細かくみると、貿易外収支と移転収支はほぼ恒常的に赤字であるが、貿易収支の大幅な黒字がこの赤字を上回っている。また、貿易外収支のなかでは、サービス、輸送・旅行などが赤字であり、投資収益は黒字でその幅が急速に拡大しつつある。また近年、対外投資の活発化などのため、国際収支に占める資本収支の重要性が著しく増大し

By country, the U. S. was by far the biggest customer with 30%. After the U. S. came China, Taiwan, Korea, HongKong, Singapore, Malaysia, Thailand, Germany and the U. K. These countries have consistently stayed at the top of the list, although with some change in ranking. Each accounted for 2-8% of exports.

3) Imports

Imports fluctuate more than exports. The main reasons for this are that imports are more directly affected by business conditions than exports and that the oil and other primary products Japan imports in large quantities are subject to large price fluctuations.

In 1998, sluggish domestic demand led to a decline in imports, ending an upward trend that had continued since 1994.

The major import categories during 2001 were: machinery 24. 8%, raw materials and fuels 18.3% (petroleum 11.1%), foods 12.2% (marine products 3.8%, meat 2.4%) and clothing 5.5%.

Imports by region were Asia 55.2%, North America 20.3%, Europe 15.5%, Oceania 4.9%, Central and South America 2.8%, and Africa 1.3%.

By country, the U. S. was at the top, as in exports, with 18.1%, and China second with 16.6%. Coming next were Korea, Taiwan, Australia, Indonesia, Germany, Malaysia, Saudi Arabia and the United Arab Emirates with 3-6% each (2001). The top-ranking countries are always pretty much the same.

b) International Balance of Payments

1) Overview

Japan's international balance of payments is characterized by a huge trade surplus and a capital account deficit. In simple terms, this means that money earned from trade is invested overseas as exported capital.

Since the mid-sixties, both the trade account and the current account have stayed in the black, except during a few exceptional periods, most notably the periods following the oil crises.

On close examination, a breakdown of the international balance of accounts shows that although the invisible trade account and the transfer account almost constantly run deficits, these are more than offset by the huge trade surplus. Within the invisible trade account, deficits are being posted by such categories as services, shipment and travel, while investment earnings

ている。

　　日本の貿易収支は、相手国によって著しく状況が
異なっている。たとえば、主として製品輸出の市場
である米国・EU・東南アジアに対してはほぼ恒常
的に黒字であるが、主として原燃料の購入先である
中東の産油国やオーストラリアに対しては赤字が続
いている。

2）推　移

　　日本の貿易収支の黒字は、80年の68億ドルから
81年には200億ドルに急増した。その後も増加を
続け、86年には964億ドルに達した。この時期に
は貿易外収支の赤字が減少していたため、同年は、
経常収支でも870億ドルの大幅黒字となった。この
ピークを過ぎると、経常収支の黒字は90年まで縮
小を続けた。これは、内需拡大や円高の効果で輸入
が大幅に伸びた結果貿易黒字が減少し、また貿易外
収支の赤字が拡大したためである。

　　しかし91年には、輸出の増加と輸入の頭打ちで、
黒字が再び拡大し、729億ドルになった。92年から
94年にかけては、1,200〜1,300億ドルと高水準で
あったが、95年は減少し、96年には600億ドル台
にまで減少した。97年からまた増加し、2000年に
は996億ドルと大幅黒字になった。

　　資本収支は大きく変動した。対外直接投資・間接
（証券）投資が急増したために、88年には1,309億
ドルの巨額の赤字を計上した。その後赤字幅が縮小
し、91年には371億ドルの黒字に転じた。

　　しかし、92年から再び赤字になり、93年から94
年は800億ドル強まで増大した。その赤字は95年
から96年にかけては減少を示したが、97年〜98年
は増加し、98年の実績は1300億ドル、2000年は減
少し、850億ドルとなっている。

are posting a rapidly increasing surplus. In addition, more active Japanese overseas investment in recent years has markedly increased the importance of the capital account as a factor in the international balance of payments.

The trade balance situation differs greatly from one trading partner to another. Trading surpluses are the norm with the U. S., the EU, and Southeast Asia, which are the largest markets for Japan's manufactured products, while the balances with raw material supplier countries such as the Middle East oil producers and Australia are invariably in the red.

2) Trends

Japan's trade surplus soared from 6.8 billion dollars in 1980 to $20.0 billion in 1981. It then stayed on its upward trajectory and reached $96.4 billion in 1986. Since the invisible trade deficit decreased during this period, the current surplus for the same year swelled to $87.0 billion. Following this peak, the current surplus shrank until 1990. This was in part due to a decline in the trade surplus, the result of a big increase in imports triggered by a surge in internal demand and the appreciation of the yen, and in part to an increase in the invisible trade deficit.

In 1991, however, an increase in exports and a leveling off of imports pushed the current surplus back up to $72.9 billion. Between 1992 and 1994, the trade surplus maintained a high level in the $120-130 billion range. This was followed by successive declines in 1995 and 1996 that brought it down as far as the $60-70 billion range. Then, after turning up in 1997, the surplus surged to a massive $99.6 billion in 2000.

The capital account has fluctuated wildly. After a sharp rise in overseas direct and indirect (securities) investment pushed it into an enormous deficit of $130.9 billion in 1988, it rebounded to a $37.1 billion surplus in 1991.

After going into the red again in 1992, it posted deficits exceeding $80 billion between 1993 and 1994. The deficit shrank between 1995 and 1996 but then swelled during the next two years, reaching $130 billion in 1998. It declined again in 2000, to $85 billion.

(3) 産業

a) 産業構造

　　日本の戦後の高度成長期は、第二次産業が大きく成長したのが特色であった。やがて、経済の発展とともに第三次産業が急速に拡大し、1970年代以降国内総生産（GDP）の50％を超えるまでに至った。2001年現在、一次・二次・三次産業の比率は、就業者数でそれぞれ4.9％、30.0％、64.5％、GDP（2000年）では1.5％、28.9％、69.6％（分類不能、調整項を含む）であった。

b) 産業基盤

　　日本は石灰石など限られたものを除いて、見るべき鉱物資源を持たない。また、木材・羊毛など、動・植物原料についても輸入依存度が高い。したがって、資源の安定的な入手と効率的な利用が、常に重要な課題である。

　　国土が狭いため、工業用地も少ない。そこで、重化学工業化を推進した時には、海面を埋め立て、専用港をもった新立地を造成した。

　　産業用インフラストラクチャーは、比較的良く整備されている。

　　人的資源には恵まれており、そのため産業構造の変化にも円滑に適応できた。しかし最近では就業人口の高齢化が問題になっている。さらに、近い将来は、若年労働力の減少が問題になろう。

c) エネルギー事情

　　日本の一次エネルギー供給量は、22,967千兆ジュールである。その内訳は石油52.0％、石炭17.4％、原子力13.0％、天然ガス12.7％、水力3.6％、新エネルギーその他1.1％である（1999年）。

　　しかし、エネルギー資源は、水力と石炭の10分の1を除けば、ほぼ全量を輸入に依存している。そのため、日本は大きな努力と資金を投入して、エネルギー資源を確保しエネルギーを節約してきた。また、政府は緊急事態にそなえて、石油の備蓄体制の整備を進めている。

　　原子力発電は、80年代以降急速に拡大した。2000年

(3) Industry

a) Industrial Structure

Japan's postwar high-growth period was marked by the rise of the secondary industries. Then, as the nation's economy grew stronger, the tertiary industries began to expand rapidly, to the point of accounting for more than 50% of the gross domestic product (GDP) since 1970. As of 2001, the primary, secondary and tertiary industries employed 4.9%, 30.0% and 64.5% of the nation's workers and accounted for 1.5%, 28.9% and 69.6% (including non-classifiable and adjustment categories) of the GDP (2000).

b) Industrial Foundation

Aside from a very limited number of items such as limestone, Japan has no mineral resources to speak of. It is also highly dependent on imports for lumber, wool and other animal and plant resources. Little wonder that the Japanese are constantly concerned about securing a stable supply of resources and making optimum use of them.

The country's small land area leaves little room for industrial facilities. When the heavy and chemical industries were the focus of development, the construction sites were obtained by reclaiming land from the sea—so that each had its own port facilities.

Japan has a relatively sound industrial infrastructure.

The country has an excellent workforce, thanks to which it has been able to adapt smoothly to changes in the industrial structure. However, the aging of the workforce has become a problem. A shortage of young workers is likely to arise in the near future.

c) Energy

Japan's primary energy supply amounts to 22,967 quadrillion joules. The breakdown is: oil 52.0%, coal 17.4%, nuclear power 13.0%, natural gas 12.7%, hydroelectric power 3.6%, and new energies and other 1.1% (1999 figures).

Except for the hydroelectric power and a tenth of the coal, all of these energy resources are imported. Japan therefore invests a great amount of effort and funds to secure energy resources and conserve energy. In addition, the government is building oil storage facilities to cope with emergencies.

Nuclear power generation has risen sharply from the eighties.

には、全発電量の 34.2 ％が原子力発電になっている。しかし日本人は、核の取り扱いについては極めて敏感なので、原子力発電の安全性や核廃棄物の処理をめぐって、議論が続いている。したがって、発電所新設は非常に難しくなっている。

また、太陽熱、ごみ発電などの新エネルギーの利用も進められているが、まだその絶対量は少ない。

今後は 97 年に義務づけられた炭酸ガス等の排出量削減（別項「環境保全」参照）の実現を重視したエネルギー諸施策が取られるであろう。

d）第一次産業

1）農林業

日本の農業（畜産を含む）は、297 万人が就業し（2000 年）、国内総生産（GDP）の 1.4 ％を占めている（2000 年）。農用地面積は国土の 14 ％で、農家一戸あたり 1.60 ヘクタール（4.0 エーカー）にすぎない。農業界の重要な課題としては、就業者の高齢化が進んでおり、若年後継者をどう確保するかということがある。また、食糧自給率が低いことも大きな問題であり（2000 年は 40 ％）、いかにして輸入食料に対抗して国内生産を維持していくかという課題もある。

主な作物は、農業生産額の 30 ％を占めるコメで、95 ％自給できている。そのほか生鮮野菜・牛乳・乳製品などは比較的自給率が高い。しかし、大量に消費される小麦・大豆は大部分を輸入に依存している。最近では、輸入品のリストは緑茶・そば粉など日本の伝統食品にまで拡大されている。

畜産の経営規模は、養鶏を除いて極めて小さく、輸入自由化の進展によって畜産の経営はますます厳しくなっている。99 年には、飼料全体の約 60 ％が輸入された。

林業は、 7 万人が就業している（2000 年）。日本の国土面積の約 3 分の 2 は森林であり、99 年は伐採量が 2,470 万 m³ であった。しかし、国内木材需要の約 52 ％は輸入に依存している（2000 年）。

In 2000, it made up 34.2% of the total electric power supply. Since the Japanese are extremely sensitive about anything nuclear, however, a sometimes emotional public discourse has arisen concerning the safety of nuclear power facilities and the disposal of nuclear wastes. This makes the building of new nuclear power plants extremely difficult.

Progress is also being made in the use of new energies, including solar energy and electricity generated from garbage, but the amounts utilized are still small.

Under a global accord signed in 1997, Japan is required to reduce emissions of carbon dioxide and other greenhouse gases. To meet this commitment, various measures will have to be taken to control energy use. (See section on Preservation of the Environment.)

d) Primary Industries
1) Agriculture

Agriculture (including livestock farming) has a workforce of 2.97 million (2000) and accounts for 1.4% of the gross domestic product (GDP) (as of 2000). About 14% of the total land area is used for agriculture; the area per farming household is only 1.60 hectares (4.0 acres). One important issue for the farming community is how to attract and retain more young successors for rejuvenating the aging workforce. Japan's low self-sufficiency in food (40% in 2000) is also a problem. Ways must be found to keep domestic production competitive with imports.

The main product is rice, which accounts for about 30% of the value of agricultural production and meets 95% of demand. Japan is also relatively self-sufficient in fresh fruits and milk and other dairy products. However, it depends on imports for most of the large quantities of wheat and soy beans it consumes. Recent years have seen the list of imports being extended even to such traditional Japanese foods as green tea and buckwheat flour.

With the exception of poultry farming, all livestock farming is conducted on a very small scale and the progressive freeing of imports is making it increasingly difficult for livestock farming to survive. In 1999, about 60% of all feed had to be imported.

Forestry has a workforce of 70 thousand (2000). Forests cover about two-thirds of Japan's total area and the timber cut in 1999 was 24.7 million cubic meters. Still, around 52% of domestic demand is met by imports (2000).

2）水産業

　　魚介類は日本人の主要蛋白源になっている。1人1日あたり魚消費量は 188（99年）グラムで、これは米国，英国の3倍である。

　　2000年には、日本の水産業は、29万人が就業し、中国、ペルーに次ぐ638万トンの漁獲量をあげている。このうち21％が国内養殖および内水面漁業、25％が沿岸漁業、54％が遠洋または沖合漁業である（2000年）。このように遠洋漁業への依存度が高いため、水産業界は、200海里漁業水域の設定や公海上でのサケ・マス漁の規制には、大きな打撃を受けている。

　　日本では、鯨は大事な蛋白食糧源であったが、国際捕鯨委員会の決定に従い捕鯨からは撤退した。

　　これらの事情により、日本が魚介類を自給するのは不可能となっており、輸出を上回る輸入をはかっている（26万トン対588万トン：2000年）。

e）第二次産業

1）建設業

　　建設業は、2000年には、就業者総数の 10.1％を雇用し、国内総生産（GDP）の7.3％を占めた。

　　企業数は 59万に達する。このなかには、売上高が1兆円を超える大手のゼネコン（総合建設業者）数社も含まれるが、数のうえでは、小規模な工務店や下請けの専門企業が圧倒的に多い。全企業数の99.0％が資本金1億円未満である。

　　建設業はバブル崩壊後も、景気対策による公共事業により事業が支えられてきた。が、これにも限界があり、多額の不良債権に加え、不況による受注競争激化で受注価格が下落し、2001年には 5,852件の建設会社が倒産した。最近では、過剰雇用も指摘されるなど建設業界の環境は非常に厳しい。

2) Marine Products Industry

Fish and shellfish are a primary source of protein for the Japanese people. Daily per capita fish consumption was 188 grams in 1999, about three times the amount in the United States and the United Kingdom.

In 2000, Japan's marine products industry had a workforce of 280 thousand and a fish haul of 6.38 million tons, the world's third largest after China and Peru. Of this, 21% came from fish farms and freshwater fishing in Japan, 25% from coastal fishing and 54% from deep-sea and off-shore fishing (2000). Owing to this high dependence on deep-sea fishing, the fishing industry has been strongly impacted by the enforcement of two hundred nautical mile economic zones and the prohibition of salmon and trout fishing on the open seas.

While whale meat was previously an important source of protein for Japan, commercial whaling has been abandoned in line with the resolution of the International Whaling Commission.

Since these circumstances make it impossible for Japan to supply all of the fish and shellfish it needs, the country imports more of these than it exports (5.88 million tons vs. 0.26 million tons in 2000).

e) Secondary Industries

1) Construction Industry

In 2000, the construction industry employed 10.1% of the workforce and accounted for 7.3% of the gross domestic product (GDP).

The industry comprises 590,000 companies. While a few of these are general construction firms with annual sales of over ¥1 trillion, the overwhelming majority are small private housing contractors and subcontractors that specialize in particular aspects of construction. Companies capitalized at less than ¥100 million account for 99.0% of the total.

Public works projects undertaken to simulate the economy have helped to offset the decline in private-sector orders received by the construction industry since the bursting of the economic bubble in 1991. But they have been no panacea. In 2001, huge amounts of bad debt, plus price declines triggered by intensifying competition, pushed 5,852 construction companies into bankruptcy. Recently, the business environment of the construction

2) 製造業

　　製造業は日本の高度成長の立役者であった。近年、経済全体における比重は低下しているとはいえ、なお1,321万人（2000年）が就業し、国内総生産（GDP）の21.6％（2000年）を占めている。現在構造変革が進行している。かつて中心であった鉄鋼や造船から、まず自動車や産業機械へ、さらにエレクトロニクスへと、主体は次第に付加価値の高い技術集約型の製品に移っている。

　　以下、主要業種について概観する。

①鉄鋼業

　　日本の鉄鋼業は、積極的に技術導入をはかり、つぎつぎに効率的な臨海製鉄所を建設し、旺盛な需要にこたえて急速に拡大した。1973年のピーク時には、粗鋼生産量は、戦前の17倍の1億1,930万トンに達した。

　　その後、2度の石油危機や円高の影響によって、生産量は一時9,700万トン台まで落ち込んだ。しかし各企業は、大胆な新技術導入、非効率設備の閉鎖などをはかり、需要低迷をはじめとする困難な事態に対処してきた。こうした努力に、需要の回復も加わって、80年代初めには粗鋼生産量で米国を上回り、ソ連に次いで世界第2位の鉄鋼生産国となった。

　　その後、生産は1億トン前後に留まっている。このように量的拡大を望めない中で、国際競争に打ち勝つべく更なる生産効率化、設備集約、要員合理化などが強力に進められている。一時日本は世界一の生産量（93〜95年）を誇っていたが、今は量の面では中国にその地位を譲った。

　　また鉄鋼業は、顧客の要求が高度化するのに応じて、新製品・新技術を開発してきた。これらの技術の多くは、ヨーロッパ・米国をはじめ世界各国にも提供されている。また、日本と外国企業との合弁事業も数多く設立されている。

industry has grown extremely severe because of overstaffing and other problems.

2) Manufacturing

The manufacturing sector was the prime mover behind Japan's rapid economic growth. Though it does not dominate the overall economic picture the way it once did, it still has a workforce of 13.21 million (2000) and accounts for 21.1% of the workforce and 21.6% of the gross domestic product (2000). The industry is moving forward with structural reforms. Originally centered on steelmaking, shipbuilding and the like, it has been making a steady transition to more technology-intensive product sectors with higher value-added, first to automobiles and industrial machinery and more recently to electronics.

The main manufacturing industries are outlined below.

① Iron and Steel Industry

The Japanese steel industry achieved rapid growth in response to strong demand for its products by vigorously introducing advanced technologies and investing in the construction of many new and highly efficient seaside steel mills. At its peak in 1973, crude steel production reached 119.3 million tons, 17 times the highest prewar level.

Production later fell as low as 97 million tons under the pressure of the two oil crises and the appreciation of the yen. Faced with flagging demand and other difficulties, the industry's companies responded by implementing bold measures centered on the development and application of new technologies and the closing of inefficient facilities. As a result of these efforts, plus a recovery in demand, the industry's crude steel output overtook that of the United States in the early eighties, making Japan the world's second largest producer after the Soviet Union.

Annual production has since leveled off at around 100 million tons and cannot be expected to increase appreciably. The industry's focus is therefore on enhancing international competitiveness by streamlining production, consolidating facilities and optimizing the workforce. Japan was the world's largest steel producer from 1993-1995. This status now belongs to China.

The industry has consistently developed new products and technologies to meet the increasingly sophisticated needs of customers. Many of the technologies developed have been licensed to companies in Europe, the U. S. and other countries throughout the world. A large number of joint venture com-

鉄鋼はかつて日本の主な輸出品であったが、生産量に対する輸出の比率（粗鋼換算）は、80年の30％から90年には17％に低下した。最近増加傾向にあり、2000年は29.5％であった。一方、輸入は大幅に増加し、90年には日本の消費量の7.6％を占めた。が、最近は少し減少し、2000年は6.9％であった。

　日本の鉄鋼業は、鉄鉱石、石炭とも、ほぼ100％を輸入している。鉄鉱石はおもに、オーストラリア・ブラジル・インドからの輸入である。石炭の主な供給国は、オーストラリア・カナダなどになっている。

②非鉄金属産業

　国内資源が乏しいため非鉄金属製品は大半を輸入原料で生産されている。その際、鉱石を輸入して精錬から行うのと、地金を輸入して圧延・加工以降を行う方法がある。

　日本のアルミニウム需要は急増している。2000年には、新地金の消費量は216万トンであった。以前は、日本においてもかなりの量のアルミニウムを精錬していたが、石油危機後の電力コストの上昇によって、大部分の企業が精錬から撤退した（アルミニウム生産には多量の電力が必要である）。そのため、94年以降は、必要量の99％を輸入しなければならなくなった。

　一方、銅については、2000年には144万トンを生産した。ほぼ需要にみあう量である。国内鉱からの精錬は生産の1％で大部分は輸入鉱に頼っている。鉛については、2000年には24万トンを生産した。需要の95％である。国内鉱からの精錬は生産の4％で大部分は輸入鉱に頼っている。亜鉛については、2000年には65万トンを生産した。需要を上回る量である。国内鉱からの精錬は生産の10％で大部分は輸入鉱に頼っている。

③一般機械・精密機械

　日本は、機械工業の基礎をなし「機械の機械」といわれる工作機械については、2000年に9.1万台、8,150億円を生産した。そのうち、5.4万台（59％、金額では88％）がコンピュータ制御

panies have also been established between Japanese and foreign companies.

Although steel was previously one of Japan's main export products, the percentage of all steel produced that is exported fell from 30% in 1980 to 17% in 1990 (in terms of crude steel), although it has since rebounded, reaching 29.5% in 2000. On the other hand, imports, which rose sharply, accounted for 7.6% of the steel used in Japan during 1990. The figure for 2000 was slightly lower, at 6.9%.

The industry imports nearly 100% of the iron ore and coal it needs. Ore is imported mainly from Australia, Brazil and India, and coal from Australia and Canada.

② Nonferrous Metals Industry

Because of the shortage of domestic resources, nonferrous metal products are generally produced from imported materials, starting either with the refining of imported ore or with the rolling and processing of imported metal.

Japanese demand for aluminum has been increasing rapidly. In 2000, 2.16 million tons of new metal were used. Although Japan also previously refined a substantial share of the aluminum it used, the high cost of electric power since the oil crises has forced most companies to abandon their refining operations. (Aluminum production requires large amounts of electricity.) Since 1990, Japan has had to import 99% of the aluminim it requires.

Japan produced 1.44 million tons of copper in 2000, an amount that substantially matched demand. Dependence on imported ore was almost total, with only 1% being produced by refining domestic ore. Lead production amounted to 240,000 tons in 2000, 95% of demand. Dependence on imported ore was high, with only 4% being produced by refining domestic ore. Lead production came to 650,000 tons, an amount that exceeded demand. Dependence on imported ore was high, with only 10% being produced by refining domestic ore.

③ Machinery Industry

In 2000, Japanese production of machine tools, known as "the machine of machines" because of their fundamental role in the machine industry, amounted to 91 thousand units. Of this total, 54 thousand (59%, 88% in terms of value) were computer-

の NC 機であった。日本の工作機械工業は、質・量ともに世界の最高水準にあり、生産額の76％が輸出されている。

　産業用ロボットの生産量は、80 年代の間に 4 倍に増加し、90 年には約 8 万台が生産された。その後景気後退で減少をつづけ、99 年には 7.1 万台弱にとどまっている。しかし、2000 年には 9 万台の生産に戻った。2000 年末には、国内で 39 万台が稼働しているが、これは世界全体の 52 ％、米国の 4.3 倍にあたる。

　このような工作機械と産業用ロボットは、機械技術とエレクトロニクスの結合したいわゆるメカトロニクスの成果である。これらの技術は、建設機械・農業機械・事務機械などにも活用され、各種機械工業製品の機能を著しく高度化している。

　精密機械工業では、カメラ・時計・医療機器など幅広い製品を生産している。2000 年には、日本は約 3,100 万台のカメラを生産した（カメラ970 万台、ビデオ一体カメラ 1,170 万台、デジタルカメラ 960 万台）。

　最近パソコンへの取込が可能なデジタルカメラの伸びが特に著しい（2001 年速報 1,280 万台）。技術面でも日本は世界をリードしている。時計工業も 2000 年には 5 億 7,000 万個を生産し、世界市場で圧倒的な地位を占めている。

④家庭用電気機器産業

　日本の家庭用電気機器産業は、2000 年に電子レンジ、カラーテレビ、電気洗濯機、電気冷蔵庫、電気掃除機、電気がま、換気扇、エアコン、VTR、テープレコーダー、DVD をそれぞれ 300 ～800 万台生産した。

　家電機器は、日本の電気機器メーカー発展の原動力であった。しかし最近では、テレビやテープレコーダーなどの生産は、コスト節減や貿易摩擦に対処するため、国外に移転される傾向にあり、国内生産は高級機種主体になっている。また、多くの製品の市場が成熟化しているので、マイクロコンピュータやファジー制御などの先端技術を活

controlled numerical control (NC) type machines. Japan's machine tool industry ranks with the world's best in terms of both quality and quantity. It exports 76% (in terms of value) of the machines it produces.

Industrial robot production increased fourfold during the 1980s. About 80 thousand units were manufactured in 1990, but production then began to slip because of the economic downturn, falling to slightly under 71 thousand units in 1999. By 2000, however, annual production had rebounded to over 90 thousand units. As of the end of 2000, there were 390 thousand industrial robots operating in Japan, which is 52% of the world total and 4.3 times the number being used in the United States.

Both machine tools and industrial robots are the result of an advanced blend of mechanical and electronic technologies ("mechatronics"). These technologies are now being applied to various other types of machinery—in fields such as construction, agriculture and business—to provide a broad range of machines and manufactured products with highly sophisticated functions.

The precision machinery industry produces cameras, watches, medical equipment and a wide range of other products. Japan produced 31.0 million cameras in 2000 (9.7 million film cameras, 11.7 million camcorders and 9.6 million digital cameras.

Recently, digital cameras, popular because they can export image data to a personal computer, have made particularly rapid advances. (Unconfirmed data for 2001 pegs production at 12.8 million units.) Japan also leads the world in camera technology.

The watch industry, with an annual output of 570 million units (2000), commands an overwhelming share of the world market.

④ Home Appliance Industry

In 2000, Japanese home appliance manufacturers produced 3-8 million each of microwave ovens, color TVs, washing machines, refrigerators, vacuum cleaners, rice cookers, ventilating fans, air conditioner, VCRs, tape recorders and DVDs.

The growth of Japan's electrical and electronic equipment manufacturers was powered by home appliances. In recent years, however, these companies have been moving to transfer production in sectors such as televisions and tape recorders overseas in order to reduce costs and ease trade tensions. Today, most of their domestic production is in top-of-the-line products. Also, since the markets for many of their products have reached

用して、高度な機能を持つ製品を開発し、新しい需要を生みだそうとしている。

輸出は伸び悩んでいるが、家電製品は依然として重要な輸出品目となっている。

たとえば、2001 年には、約 1.6 兆円の輸出をしている。

⑤コンピュータ・エレクトロニクス産業

コンピュータ産業は、今日の情報社会において不可欠な役割をもち、急速に発展し続けている。2001 年には、総数 1,463 万台のコンピュータが生産された。

このほとんどがパーソナルコンピュータ（パソコン）である。コンピュータ産業の生産額は、2000 年で総額 3.3 兆円で、ソフトウェアの国内出荷額は、2000 年には 7.3 兆円、ほかに端末などの関連機器の生産額は 1.9 兆円であった。

パソコンが普及しはじめたのは 80 年代半ばからであり、それにともないコンピュータ全体の生産額は、85 年から 90 年までの間に、年平均 14.3 ％の急増を示した。その後も、日本におけるパソコンは企業内ネットワーク化、小売店での商品管理、個人のビジネスやゲーム用など幅広い利用層に支えられて広範囲に普及が進んでいる。

日本は、半導体素子および集積回路の世界有数の生産国である。2001 年には、877 億個、4.3 兆円（そのうち集積回路 246 億個、3.4 兆円）を生産した。

なお、コンピュータの普及にともなって、サービス産業に属するソフトウェア産業も急成長している。

⑥自動車産業

日本の自動車生産は 1910 年代にさかのぼるが、産業として本格的に基礎が固まったのは 50 年ごろであった。その後の発展はめざましく、80 年には、四輪車の生産量が 1,104 万台に達し、米国を抜き世界第 1 位の生産国となった。しかも、その過半数の 597 万台が輸出された。90 年には、生産量 1,349 万台までに達した。しかし、その後円高による輸出減らし、海外現地生産推進、国内販売の不振などで、94 年には生産台数は 1,055

maturity, they are trying to develop new demand by using microcomputers, fuzzy control and other advanced technologies to develop products with sophisticated functions.

Although the volume of exports has leveled off, home appliances remain an important export category.

The value of exported home appliances in 2001, for example, was about ¥1.6 trillion.

⑤ Computer and Electronics Industries

Because of the indispensable role it plays in today's information-oriented society, the computer industry continues to expand rapidly. A total of 146.3 million computers were produced in Japan in 2001.

Most of these were personal computers. In 2000, the production volume of the computer industry amounted to ¥3.3 trillion plus an additional ¥1.9 trillion in terminals and other computer-related equipment. Domestic software shipments in 2000 came to ¥7.3 trillion.

Personal computer market penetration advanced so rapidly after taking off in the mid-eighties that the increase in personal computer production pushed the average annual growth in the value of all computers produced up 14.3% between 1985 and 1990. Personal computers have since continued to spread into a broad range of applications, including intracompany networks, retail store merchandise control, family-owned businesses and games.

Japan is one of the world's largest producers of semiconductor devices and integrated circuits. Production in 2001 stood at 87.7 billion units valued at ¥4.3 trillion (including 24.6 billion integrated circuits valued at ¥3.4 trillion).

The spread of computers has also triggered vigorous expansion of the service sector software industry.

⑥ Automobile Industry

Though Japanese production of automobiles can be traced back to around 1910, it was not established as a full-blown industry until about 1950. Once established, however, the industry grew with astonishing speed, overtaking the United States and becoming the world's leading automobile producer in 1980, when production of four-wheeled vehicles hit 11.04 million. Of these, over half (5.97 million) were exported. In 1990, 13.49 million vehicles were manufactured. By 1994, however, production was down to 10.55 million owing to a fall in exports caused

万台に止まり、15 年振りに米国に抜かれ世界一の座を奪われた。国内外の自動車産業を取り巻く環境は厳しさを増しており、部品の共有化、部品点数の削減などのコストダウン対策に必死に取組んでいる。また、生き残りをかけて、国内だけでなく海外同業メーカーとの提携なども模索されている。2001 年の生産台数は 978 万台で、そのうち輸出は 417 万台であった。

二輪車についても状況は同様である。2001 年には、日本の二輪車生産は 233 万台、輸出が 158 万台に達し、ともに世界最大であった。また海外生産は拡大、国内生産は減少している。

⑦造船業

日本は、1956 年以降世界一の造船国であったが、2000 年のロイズ統計では、韓国が竣工量、受注量、手持ち工事量の同時首位を達成した。しかし、2001 年には竣工量と受注量で日本は再び首位に返り咲いた。日本の造船業は、高い生産技術と工程管理能力で世界的な信頼を得ており、世界の造船量の約半分を生産してきた。世界の造船需要は、70 年代のピークの後大きく落ち込んだが、最近やや持ち直している。2001 年における鋼船竣工量は 1,170 万総トンで、世界の 41 ％で、韓国は 1,060 万総トン（37 ％）であった。

⑧化学工業

化学工業は、日本最大の基礎素材型産業である。1999 年の出荷額は 31 兆円で、製造業全体の 10.6 ％にあたり、就業者数では 4.1 ％を占めた。

日本の化学工業の主体をなすのは石油化学工業で、化学工業の総生産額の約半分を占める。石油化学工業は 60 年代以降急速に発展した。その背景には、安い輸入原料を確保できたこと、および生産拠点としてコンビナートが臨海埋立地に建設できたことがある。

日本の石油化学工業が利用している主な原料は、石油からとれるナフサである。一方、米国におけ

mainly by the strengthening of the yen, the shifting of production overseas and sluggish domestic sales. Overtaken by the U. S., Japan's reign at the top ended after 15 years. Against the backdrop of an increasingly severe global business environment, the automotive industry is desperately trying to reduce costs, such as by adopting shared component types and low parts counts. As part of the effort to survive, the industry companies are also seeking alliances with other automakers both within and outside the country. Japan's auto makers produced 9.78 million vehicles in 2001, of which 4.17 million were exported.

The situation is substantially the same for two-wheeled vehicles. In 2001, production of motorcycles and the like came to 2. 33 million and exports to 1.58 million, making Japan the world leader in both categories. Overseas production is increasing, domestic production decreasing.

⑦ Shipbuilding Industry

Japan was the world's leading shipbuilding country between 1956 and 1999. In 2000, however, the Republic of Korea captured top position in all three categories of completions, orders, and work in progress (based on Llyod's statistics). But then in 2001, Japan again moved into first place in two categories: completions and orders. Respected internationally for its excellent production technology and process control capability, the Japanese shipbuilding industry constructs about half of the world tonnage. Demand for ships fell off sharply after peaking in the seventies but has revived somewhat in recent years. In 2001, the total of new steel ship completions in Japan was 11.7 million tons, 41% of the world total. The corresponding Korean figures were 10.6 million tons and 37%.

⑧ Chemical Industry

The chemical industry is the largest of Japan's basic material industries. In 1999, it posted shipments of ¥31 trillion, 10.6% of the manufacturing industry total, and employed 4.1% of all manufacturing industry workers.

The petrochemical sector, which dominates Japan's chemical industry and accounts for about half of its production, began to grow rapidly in the 1960 s. It owes its prosperity to the access it has had to cheap imported materials and the fact it was able to construct its production facilities in large industrial complexes built on land reclaimed from the sea.

The main raw material used by Japan's petrochemical industry

る石油化学工業は、天然ガスからとれる安いエタンを原料としている。2度の石油危機によるナフサの高騰に対処して、業界は大規模な設備合理化を実施し、需要の増加にも助けられて立ち直った。

90年代に入り、景気低迷で、再度設備過剰になって、さらなる体質改善が迫られている。

化学工業の製品は、基礎素材型とファインケミカル型とに大別される。前者はプラスチック、合成繊維、洗剤原料など、後者は医薬品、写真材料、化粧品など多様である。

代表的な製品の一つであるプラスチックの出荷額は、99年に2.9兆円にもなっている。その特性から天然素材に代わって、日用品、包装材料、家電や自動車の部品など身近に大量に使用されている。そのプラスチックのうち、加熱すると硬化する特性のものが全体の10％を占める。近年、プラスチックの欠点を克服して、工業材料分野で金属に代わる新素材として、エンジニアリングプラスチックが注目をあび、電機や自動車産業などに使われ、2000年に92万トンも出荷された。

⑨繊維工業

日本の工業化初期の段階を支えたのは繊維工業であった。現在日本は、次第に在来型製品の国内市場を発展途上国に譲りつつあるので、業界では、高機能の新繊維の開発、高級織物、ファッション製品など、付加価値の高い分野への展開に力を入れている。一方、繊維以外の新素材事業などにも進出しており、また、縫製を中心に海外への工場進出も活発である。

1999年の工業製品出荷額に占める比率は、繊維工業と縫製工業を合わせて2.5％であった。2000年の繊維の生産量は109万トンで、うち82％が化学繊維である。天然繊維の原料は、大部分を輸入に依存している。

また、現在では最終製品の輸入が急増しており、特に中国製が2000年現在、輸入点数の約90％近くを占める。

is naphtha, a product of petroleum. Its U. S. counterpart uses ethane, a cheap product of natural gas. In response to the sharp rise in the price of naphtha caused by the two oil crises, the industry carried out large-scale equipment rationalization, which, together with an increase in demand, led to its recovery.

In the 1990 s, the industry was again forced to scale back facilities, because of the economic recession.

The chemical industry's products, although diverse, fall in two major categories: basic materials and fine chemicals. The former group consists of products like plastics, synthetic fibers and detergent raw materials. The latter group includes such items as pharmaceuticals, photographic materials and cosmetics.

Among these various products, plastics are typical. In 1999, the industry shipped 2.9 trillion yen worth of plastics. Large quantities of plastics are used as a substitute for natural materials in numerous everyday items, packaging, home products, car parts and other familiar products. Ten percent of the plastics are of the thermosetting (hot-set) type. Technologies for overcoming the shortcomings of conventional plastics have led to the development of a new class of engineering plastics that are attracting attention as new materials capable of taking the place of industrial-use metals. In 2000, several industries, most notably the electrical machinery and automotive sectors, used 920 thousand tons of engineering plastics.

⑨ Textile Industry

The early stage of Japan's industrialization was supported by the textile industry. Today, however, since much of the domestic market for conventional textile products is being taken over by the developing countries, Japanese textile companies are concentrating on the development of new, high-performance textiles and shifting the focus of their business to quality fabrics, fashion goods and other high value-added sectors. They are also diversifying into new materials unrelated to textiles and actively moving some operations overseas, particularly garment manufacturing.

In 1999, the textile and garment manufacturing industries together accounted for 2.5% of all manufactured goods shipped. In 2000, synthetic fabrics made up 82% of the 1.09 million tons of textile products produced. The industry imports most of the natural fibers it needs.

Final product imports have also risen sharply in recent years.

⑩窯業・製紙業・ゴム産業

　窯業にはセメント・ガラス・陶磁器などが含まれ、1999年の出荷額は約8.9兆円であった。

　窯業の製品で新素材として注目されているのは、ファインセラミックスである。これは酸化物などの合成微粉末を焼き固めた磁器である。耐熱性、耐食性など保ちながら、電気的、光学的機能がすぐれていて、電子部品や触媒に使用されている。2001年には約2,080億個生産された。ガラス工業でも、加工ガラスやガラス繊維に続いて、ニューガラスなどの高機能ガラスの需要創出が期待される。

　日本における紙・板紙の生産は、1970年から90年にかけて2.2倍に伸び、その後は伸び悩んでいるが、2000年には3,180万トンになった。これは米国に次いで世界第2位である。

　パルプ用原木とチップの消費は3,760万トンで、その70％が輸入材であった。なお、最近は森林資源保護のため古紙利用が推進されており、古紙利用率は90年にはじめて50％を超え、2000年は58％であった。

　ゴムの需要も拡大を続けている。2000年には、日本は、米国、中国に次ぐ、世界第3位の189万トンを消費した。消費量が最大のゴム製品は自動車用タイヤで、約62％を占める。

⑪食料品工業

　食料品工業の製品出荷額（飲料・飼料・たばこなどを含む）は1999年には35兆円に達し、全工業の約12.0％を占めた。

　この産業は成熟段階に入っているとされるが、レトルト食品や冷凍食品などの加工度の高い製品は需要が拡大している。また、消費者の健康志向から、無農薬食品の輸入増加や清涼飲料、特に茶系飲料の伸びが目立つ。酒類のなかでは、ビールは伸びているが、日本酒の生産は減少気味である（別項「酒」参照）。

The number of Chinese products is particularly high, accounting for 90% of the total in 2000.

⑩ Ceramics, Paper and Rubber Industries

Shipments by the ceramics industries, which encompass cement, glass, china, porcelain and the like, amounted to ¥8.9 trillion in 1999.

Fine ceramics, produced by fusing fine synthetic powders composed of oxides and other materials at high temperatures, are receiving particular attention as a new class of raw materials. Excellent in electrical and optical performance, while also resisting heat and corrosion, they are used, for instance, in electronic components and catalysts. About 208 billion units were produced in 2001. The glass industry is moving to reinforce its success in processed glass and glass fiber products by developing markets for high-performance glasses including so-called new glasses.

Japanese production of paper and cardboard expanded 2.2 times between 1970 and 1990 but has since experienced slow growth. Production in 2000 amounted to 31.8 million tons, second in the world after the United States.

The industry imported 70% of the 37.6 million tons of pulp logs and chips it used in the same year. Thanks to the promotion of paper recycling as a forest preservation measure, the used paper reutilization rate rose over 50% for the first time in 1990 and reached 58% in 2000.

Demand for rubber has continued to expand. In 2000 Japan used 1.89 million tons of rubber, placing it third after the United States and China in rubber consumption. The consume using the most rubber is automobile tires, which account for about 62% of total rubber consumption.

⑪ Food Industry

Shipments by the food industry (defined broadly to include beverages, animal feed, tobacco products etc.) came to ¥35 trillion in 1999 and accounted for about 12.0% of the total for all industries.

Although this industry is believed to be reaching maturation, demand for retort, frozen and other highly processed foods is expanding briskly. Two notable trends, reflecting stronger consumer health concerns, are a rise in organic food imports and surging demand for soft drinks, especially tea-based beverages. Among alcoholic beverages, beer is doing well but sake produc-

タバコの販売数量は、1985年のたばこ事業民営化以降ほぼ横ばいである（約3,300億本）。87年の関税無税化に伴い外国産が増え、2000年度には25％を占めている。わが国の喫煙者率は暫減傾向にあるが、2001年で52％（男性）14.7％（女性）となっている。

f) 第三次産業

1) 商　業

　　　商業（飲食店を除く）は、99年には商店数で183万店、就業者数で1,250万人、年間販売額で640兆円を占める。

　　　この業界には、従業員を千人以上抱える総合商社や百貨店もあるが、事業所のほとんどは小さい。たとえば、99年の調査によると、小売店の87％が従業員10人未満で、49％が2人以下であった。卸売業の73％も10人未満である。

　　　ただし全般的なトレンドとしては、伝統的な個人商店は減少しつつあり、チェーン店（コンビニエンスストアやディスカウントストアなど）が増加している。コンビニ店とディスカウント店は集客に成功しているが、コンビニ店は消費者ニーズに合わせた品揃えや営業時間の拡大、ディスカウント店は価格破壊がその要因となっている。通信販売業も普及過程にある。

　　　日本の「総合商社」は、その広範な活動で世界に知られている。90年以降、その取引は大きく落ち込んでいる。主因は輸出入取扱い高の減少である。このような苦境を克服するため、各社はリストラを行いそれぞれの得意分野に経営資源を集中するとともに、単なる商品の取扱い機能から事業の推進主体への転換を計りつつある。

　　　飲食店については、ライフスタイルの変化にあわせて売上が伸びている。

2) 金融・保険業

　　　金融・保険業は、2000年には、就業者総数の3.8％にあたる248万人を雇用し、国内総生産（GDP）の6.4％を産出した。

tion is declining. (See section on Sake and Other Drinks.)

Cigarette sales volume has remained substantially unchanged at around 330 billion pieces since the privatization of the tobacco business in 1985. The share of imported brands has increased since the elimination of all tariffs in 1987, reaching 25% in 2000. Although the number of smokers is gradually decreasing, 52% of men and 14.7% of women were still smoking in 2001.

f) Tertiary Industries
1) Commerce

In 1999, the commercial sector (not including restaurants) encompassed 18.3 million shops and 12.5 million workers. Annual sales amounted to 640 trillion yen.

Although the sector includes a number of trading companies and department stores with more than a thousand employees, most of the businesses are small. According to a 1999 survey, for example, 87% of the retail stores have fewer than ten employees and 49% have only one or two. Seventy three percent of wholesalers were found to have fewer than ten employees.

As a general trend, however, traditional privately owned shops are on the decrease and chain stores (e. g. convenience stores and discount stores) on the rise. The convenience stores and discount stores have succeeded in attracting large numbers of customers, the former by offering a selection of merchandise optimized to customer needs and staying open long hours, and the latter by selling merchandise at "smashed" prices. The media-sales business is growing steadily.

The Japanese sogo shosha (general trading companies) are known throughout the world for the broad range of their activities. Trading company business has fallen sharply since 1990, mostly because of decreases in both export and import transactions. To break out of this bind, the companies are restructuring to focus corporate resources on their strongest areas and attempting to convert themselves from mere commodity traders to business developers.

Restaurant sales are on the rise, largely because of changing lifestyles.

2) Finance and Insurance

In 2000, the finance and insurance sector employed 2.48 million workers, 3.8% of the total for all industries, and generated 6.4% of the gross domestic product (GDP).

日本の金融機関は、積極的な資金供給によって、日本の経済の発展を支えてきた。しかし、90年代の長期景気低迷により、97年に中堅の生命保険会社、そして、大手金融機関の証券会社および銀行が破綻した。それまでの「金融機関の倒産はない」という神話は崩れ、金融システムへの不安が突如湧き起こった。98年には「健全行」とされた名門銀行の二つも破綻し、これら二行は一時国有化による特別公的管理の下におかれた。これら両行の債務超過の実態が明らかにされるにつれ、市場の不信・危機感は他の大手銀行へも向けられるようになった。事実、多くの銀行が多額の不良債権をかかえ、その処理に苦慮していることも判明した。国としては、金融安定化二法を成立させ、公的資金投入などにより銀行の早期健全化のバックアップ体制を作った。今後はこの不良債権の処理を急ぐとともに市場原理を徹底し、金融機関への信頼を早急に回復する必要がある。

　一方では、97年6月に日本版ビッグバン（金融制度の抜本改革）の具体的内容とそれらのスケジュールが決まった。その第一弾として、98年4月に改正外国為替法が施行され、金融ビッグバンが始動した。対外資本取引も原則自由になり、日本の金融・資本市場が「世界市場」への第一歩を踏み出した。これにより、外国の金融機関が続々と上陸してきた。これに対抗するためと国内での生き残りをかけて、国内の銀行や証券会社は金融機関間での異業態連携、グループ間の結束強化、地域連合、外資系金融機関との提携などを盛んに実行するとともに、新商品の開発や財務体質の改善にも一層力を入れている。

　2000年に入って規模の利益を狙った大手銀行の再編が進み、日本に四つの巨大銀行グループが誕生した。2000年9月のみずほホールディングス（第一勧業、富士、日本興業）、2001年4月の、三菱東京フィナンシャルグループ（東京三菱、三菱信託、日本信託）、UFJホールディングス（三和、東海、東洋信託）と三井住友銀行（さくら、住友）がその四つのグループである。UFJ銀行が2002年1月に、みずほ銀行・みずほコーポレート銀行が2002年4月にそれぞれ発足した。

Japan's economic progress would have been impossible without the positive financing activities of the Japanese financial institutions. In 1997, however, the prolonged recession forced a medium-sized life insurance company, a major securities company and a large bank into bankruptcy. This sound disproval of the myth that "Japanese financial institutions don't fail" immediately triggered a wave of apprehension about the financial system. Then, in 1998, two prestigious banks thought to be "rock-solid" folded. Both were provisionally nationalized and placed under special official management. As the extent of their insolvency became clear, the mistrust and anxiety of the market turned toward other large banks, which were also found to be carrying tremendous amounts of bad debt they had little capability to deal with. Against this backdrop, the government moved to set up a backup system for restoring the nation's banks to a sound footing. Two laws (the "financial system stabilization laws") were enacted to enable use of public funds and other measures this required. To rebuild confidence in the financial institutions promptly, the bad debt situation must be quickly brought under control and market mechanisms given full play.

On the other hand, in June 1997, a detailed blueprint was announced for the Japanese edition of "Big Bang" (the drastic overhaul of the U. K. financial system carried out in 1986). Japan's Big Bang entered the first round with the implementation of new Foreign Exchange Law provisions in April 1998. These in principle deregulated foreign currency transactions, marking a first step in the transformation of Japanese financial and capital markets into "world markets." Foreign financial institutions responded by moving into Japan in a virtual procession. Japanese banks and securities companies, sensing a threat to their very existence, clambered to form complementary alliances across traditional business sector boundaries, reinforce group solidarity, establish regional confederations, and strengthen ties with foreign-owned institutions. They also stepped up the development of new products and intensified efforts to improve their financial position.

Starting from 2000, Japan's major banks, seeking scale merit, realigned into four huge banking groups: Mizuho Holdings (Dai-Ichi Kangyo Bank, Fuji Bank and Industrial Bank of Japan) formed in September 2000, Mitsubishi Tokyo Financial Group (Bank of Tokyo-Mitsubishi, Mitsubishi Trust & Banking and

不良債権処理を主体とした体質強化とフリー、フェア、グローバルを原則とする金融ビッグバンへの対処如何が今後の金融機関の存続を決めよう。

3）運輸業

　　運輸は、2000年、国内総生産（**GDP**）の4.7％を産出した。

　　国内輸送についてみると、1965年から96年にかけて、旅客量（距離×人数）は3.7倍、貨物量（距離×重量）は3.1倍に増加した。とくに自動車と航空機輸送の伸びが大きい。自動車の保有台数は、2001年末で7,480万台に達した。自動車輸送は、2000年度の旅客輸送の67％、貨物輸送の54％を占めた。航空機は旅客輸送の5.6％を担った。

　　鉄道は、旅客で27％、貨物で4％を占めるが、いずれも以前よりシェアは低下している。ただし、鉄道貨物は70年代より絶対量では減少したが、鉄道旅客は依然増加している。なお、日本国有鉄道（それまで国内全路線の約80％を保有）は、87年に地域別の7社に分割・民営化され、**JR**グループとなった。

　　国際輸送についてみると、旅客者のほぼすべては航空が、貨物の大部分は海運が担っている。しかし、貿易品目の高付加価値化にともない、航空貨物が伸び、金額ベースで国際貨物輸送の約30％に達している。

4）マスコミ

　　日本は、人口一人あたりの日刊新聞の発行部数が、世界でもっとも多い（毎日の発行部数7,190万部、2000年）。

　　日本の新聞の特徴は、全国紙がいくつかあることである。これらには、朝日・毎日・読売・産経・日

Nippon Trust & Banking) formed in April 2001, UFJ Holdings (Sanwa Bank,Tokai Bank and Toyo Trust & Banking), and Sumitomo Mitsui Banking Corporation (Sakura Bank and Sumitomo Bank). UFJ Bank (operated by UFJ Holdings) emerged in January 2002 and Mizuho Bank and Mizuho Corporate Bank (Mizuho Holdings) in April 2002.

The future of Japanese financial institutions will depend on how successfully they restructure, particularly how well they deal with bad debt, and how positively they respond to the Free, Fair and Global principles of the financial Big Bang.

3) Transportation

In 2000, the transportation sector generated 4.7% of the gross domestic product (GDP).

Looking first at domestic transport, between 1965 and 1996 the volume of passenger transport (distance times number of passengers) increased 3.7 times and freight transport (distance times weight) 3.1 times. The growth was particularly large for automobile and air transport. The number of automobiles in use was 74.8 million at the end of 2001. During the same year, automobiles accounted for 67% of passenger transport and 54% of freight transport. Airplanes handled 5.6% of passenger transport.

Railways accounted for 27% of passenger transport and 4% of freight transport, both smaller shares than in earlier years. In absolute terms, railway freight transport has been decreasing since the seventies, whereas railway passenger transport continues to increase. In 1987, the Japanese National Railways, which had up to then owned about 80% of all railway mileage in Japan, was broken into seven regional companies and privatized as the JR Group.

Turning next to international transport, nearly all international passengers travel by air and by far the largest percentage of overseas freight goes by ship. Air freight is on the rise, however, owing to the increasing value-added of exported goods. It accounted for about 30% of international freight transport in terms of value.

4) Mass Communications

Japan has the highest ratio of newspaper circulation to population of any country in the world (71.9 million copies per day, in 2000).

A distinctive feature of newspapers in Japan is that there are several national papers. These include the Asahi, Mainichi,

経がある。発行部数が最も多い新聞は読売新聞で、全国で朝刊 1,022 万部、夕刊 418 万部を発行している（2000 年 1 月から 6 月の月間平均）。

日本国内の英字新聞は、朝刊 3 紙、夕刊 1 紙が発行されている。また近年、海外に駐在する日本人が増えたために、衛星による日本の新聞の海外版も多くなっている。

日本放送協会（NHK）は公共放送で、さらに全国各地に多くの民間放送がある。NHK は、テレビ受像機の持ち主すべてと受信契約を結び、受信料を徴収している。その契約数は 3,727 万になる（2000年）。日本のテレビ放送は、すべてカラー化されている。

番組は、「NHK 教育テレビ」を除き、クイズ・スポーツ・ドラマ・グルメ料理・マンガなど、娯楽的なものが多い。最近の調査では、日本人は一人平均 3 時間テレビを見ている。

1987 年 7 月から衛星放送（BS）が本格的に開始され、2000 年 12 月のデジタル化もあり、それ以降受信機の数も着実に増えている。この放送は、赤道上空の静止軌道にある放送衛星から直接放送されているので、どこでも鮮明な画像を受信できる。通信衛星（CS）を利用したデジタル多チャンネル衛星放送は 96 年に導入され、現在は 100〜200 チャンネルの放送がなされている。2002 年 3 月には、新しい CS 放送も始まった。

CATV は、たとえばアメリカのように、テレビ放送の主流のメディアにはなっていない。新しい住宅地で CATV が導入されているところもあるが、本格的な利用はこれからである。

東京首都圏で配達されている朝刊には、テレビ関係では、VHF 放送 7 局（うち公共放送 2 局）、UHF 放送 5 局、衛星放送 10 局、衛星音声放送 1 局の番組が紹介されている。

一方、ラジオ放送は、東京首都圏では、少なくとも AM 放送 6 局、FM 放送 9 局、短波放送 1 局を選べる。

Yomiuri, Sankei and Nikkei. One of the largest in terms of circulation is the Yomiuri, which in November 1996 had a national circulation of 10.22 million for the morning edition, and 4.18 million for the evening edition (average for January–June 2000). Four English-language newspapers are published in Japan, three morning and one evening. On the other hand, the use of satellite communications to publish Japanese-language papers at overseas locations has increased in recent years owing to the larger number of Japanese residing outside the country.

Nippon Hoso Kyokai (NHK) is the public television organization, and there are numerous regional private broadcasting stations throughout the country. NHK solicits funds by making contracts with all television set owners and charging them a viewing fee. The number of such agreements came to 37.27 million in 2000. All television broadcasting in Japan is in color.

Except for the NHK educational station, most TV stations feature entertainment programs, such as quiz shows, sports events, drama, gourmet cooking shows and cartoons. Recent surveys show that each Japanese watches television an average of 3 hours a day.

Satellite TV broadcasting (BS) moved into full swing in July 1987 and the number of sets equipped to pick up satellite broadcasts has increased steadily ever since, especially since the advent of digital broadcasting in December 2000. Since the signals are beamed directly from geostationary satellites located above the equator, they can be picked up clearly anywhere in the country. Digital multichannel satellite broadcasting services utilizing communications satellites (CS) were commenced in 1996. Station provides services on 100-200 channels. New CS broadcasting was started from March 2002.

Cable TV is not the major medium for television distribution that it is, for example, in the United States. Although available in some newly developed residential areas, cable has yet to come into its own in Japan.

The TV columns in the morning newspapers distributed in and around the Tokyo metropolitan area show the programming of seven VHF channels (including two public channels), five UHF channels, ten satellite channels and one satellite audio channel.

Radio is also popular. People around Tokyo have a choice of at least six AM stations, nine FM stations and one shortwave station.

　　　　日本での書籍の年間出版点数は、中国、イギリス、
　　　ドイツ、アメリカに次いで5番目に多く、スペイン、
　　　ロシア、イタリアと続く（1996年）。
　5）その他のサービス業
　　　　その他のサービス業（洗濯・理容・浴場・旅館・
　　　娯楽・修理・物品賃貸・調査・広告・医療・宗教・
　　　教育・社会保険・社会福祉など）は、2000年に国
　　　内総生産（GDP）の26％を生み出し、就業者総数
　　　の27％を雇用している。
　　　　多様化する社会の要求に応じて、常に新しい事業
　　　が誕生している。たとえば、女性の社会進出にとも
　　　なって、従来主婦の仕事とされた家事労働を肩代わ
　　　りする会社がつぎつぎに生まれている。また、従来
　　　製造業などに含まれていたいくつかの業務——設
　　　計・研究・情報処理など——が拡大・複雑化し、効
　　　率性・経済性などの観点から、それらの業務部門を
　　　分離してサービス会社を設立する例が増加している。

g）情報通信産業
　1）情報通信産業の現状
　　　　日本政府発行の「情報通信白書」は情報通信産業
　　　を、①郵便、②電気通信、③放送、④情報ソフト、
　　　⑤情報関連サービス、⑥情報通信機器製造、⑦情報
　　　通信機器賃貸、⑧情報通信設備建設、⑨研究の9分
　　　野に分類している。日本の情報通信産業の2000年
　　　の実質国内総生産額は113.8兆円で、全産業に占め
　　　るシェアーは11.6％であった。1995年から2000
　　　年にかけては情報通信産業は建設業を上回り国内最
　　　大規模の産業となった。また成長率も情報通信産業
　　　は最も高く、7.5％で第2位の電気機械の6.1％を
　　　大きく引き離している。この他に一般企業内で情報
　　　通信関連業務に従事している人達の生産活動が約7
　　　兆円あると通信白書は試算している。
　　　　わが国の経済活動が低迷を続ける中で情報通信産
　　　業は、このように堅調な成長を示している。

In number of books published, Japan is fifts after China, the UK, Germany and the US and is followed by Spain, Russia and Italy (1996).

5) Other Services

In 2000, other services (laundry, hairdressing, public bath, lodging, amusement, repair, rental, survey/investigation, advertising, medicine, religion, education, social insurance, social welfare etc.) generated 26% of the gross domestic product (GDP) and employed 27% of all workers.

New services responding to new social needs appear almost daily. For example, now that women are playing a more active role outside the home, companies have sprung up that offer to take over the household chores traditionally considered to be the work of housewives. In addition, a number of jobs that have always been handled within the manufacturing industry—such as product design, R&D, and data processing—have grown too large and complex for many manufacturers to deal with easily. In the interest of efficiency and economy, therefore, the related departments are frequently being divided out and set up as independent service companies.

g) Information and Telecommunications Industry

1) Industry Overview

The Japanese Government's *Information and Communications in Japan White Paper* divides Japan's info-communications industry into nine sectors: ① Postal services, ② Telecommunications, ③ Broadcasting, ④ Telecommunications software, ⑤ Information and telecommunications services, ⑥ Information and telecommunications equipment manufacturing, ⑦ Information and telecommunications equipment leasing, ⑧ Information and telecommunications facility construction, and ⑨ Research and development. In 2000, the industry's real gross domestic output of ¥113.8 trillion accounted for 11.6% of that of all industries. Between 1995 and 2000, the industry overtook the construction industry to become Japan's largest industrial sector, It is also top in annual growth rate, which averaged 7.5% between 1999 and 2000 and far exceeded the 6.1% of the second place electrial machinery industry. The white paper estimates that, in addition to the output of the industry itself, the value of the productive activities of people engaged in info-communications-related work at private corporations in other industrial sectors

情報通信産業の雇用者数は 2000 年において 382 万人で、小売業の 630 万人、建設業の 530 万人に次いで第 3 位で全産業に占めるシェアは 7.1 ％である。

　2000 年における情報通信産業内部の部門間比較では、実質国内生産額が最も大きいのは情報通信機器製造の 28.6 兆円で、次いで関連サービス業の 24.9 兆円である。また、雇用者数が最も多いのは情報通信関連サービス業で 115 万人と全体の 3 割を占めている。しかし雇用者数の成長率をみると情報ソフト、機器リース業が大きく伸びており、機器製造業ではやや減少気味である。

2 ）進む IT 社会の構築

　日本政府は IT （情報通信技術）革命が 18 世紀に始まった産業革命に匹敵する歴史的大変換を社会にもたらすものとの基本認識をもっている。すなわち「IT は新世紀の日本の発展基盤として、経済的側面では経済構造改革を実現し、産業活動をより効率的にし、国民生活の側面では多様なライフスタイルを実現し、生活をより便利にするための鍵であり、情報と知識が付加価値の源泉となる高度情報通信ネットワーク社会への移行がわが国でも現実のものとなりつつある」と考えている。そして、このような認識と期待が、社会全体にほぼ定着したものと考えている。

　この考えに立って政府は 2001 年に「高度情報通信社会ネットワーク基本法」の制定および同法推進本部（IT 戦略本部）の設置、5 年以内に世界最先端の IT 国家となることを目指す「e-Japan 戦略」および「e-Japan 戦略計画」の策定、さらに同戦略を 2002 年に各府省庁の施策に反映させるための「e-Japan 2002 プログラム」の策定などの政策を次々と打ち出してきた。

amounts to some ¥7 trillion per year.

The strong growth of the info-communications industry stands in contrast to the sluggish pace of the overall Japanese economy.

In 2000, the industry employed 3.82 million workers, 7.1% of the total workforce, putting it in third place after the retail industry with 6.30 million workers and the construction industry with 5.30 million workers.

The sector with the largest real gross domestic output in 2000 was equipment manufacturing, with output of ¥28.6 trillion. Services came in second with ¥24.9 trillion. The services sector was the biggest employer, with a workforce 1.15 million accounting for 30% of the industry total. The workforces of the services and equipment leasing sectors grew the fastest, while that of the equipment manufacturing sector declined slightly.

2) Building an IT Society

The Government of Japan expects the IT (Information Technology) revolution to produce a sweeping social transformation comparable to that caused by the industrial revolution that started in Europe in the 18th century. By providing the basic building blocks for Japan's development in the new century, IT will, it says, "impact the economy by powering a ground-up reform of the nation's economic structure and enhancing industrial efficiency, change the way people live by opening the way to still more diverse lifestyles and offering new amenities, and enable the nation to continue its ongoing transition to an advanced info-communication network society in which information and knowledge are the primary sources of added value." The Government believes that this view of IT and its potential benefits are today accepted substantially throughout Japanese society.

Such thinking led to the enactment of the Basic Law on Formation of an Advanced Information and Telecommunications Network Society in 2001 and the ensuing establishment of the IT Strategy Headquarters for promoting the Law's implementation. These moves were rapidly followed by a series of fresh initiatives, including the e-Japan Strategy and the e-Japan Strategy Program, which were launched to build Japan into a world leader in IT within five years, and the e-Japan 2002 Program, which was aimed at ensuring that these strategies would be reflected in the policies of all Government ministries during 2002.

政府は、2000年から2001年のわが国のITの特徴をIT発展の基盤整備となる光ファイバー網支援・DSL（Digital Subscriber Line：デジタル加入者線）やケーブルインターネットの急速な普及、常時接続サービスの普及、価格の低廉化が本格的に進みだした年、すなわち「ブロードバンド元年」と位置づけている。

〔注〕ブロードバンドとは音楽データなどを簡単にダウンロードできる「高速インターネットアクセス網」および映画などの大容量映像でも簡単にダウンロードできる「超高速インターネットアクセス網」のことをいう（e-Japan戦略より）。たとえば音楽用CD1枚をダウンロードする場合、ISDN（64 kbps）では2時間半、DSL（600 kbps）では15分、ケーブル（1.5 Mbps）では6分、FTTH（100 Mbps）では6秒で可能となる。

3）ITが先導する経済・行政

ITは、IT関連企業の成長が日本の経済成長を牽引し、さらに電子商取引が普及したり企業内のIT活用の進展により生産性が向上することなどを通じて、わが国の経済構造を変革する原動力として機能しつつある。

（電子商取引）

最終消費財の電子商取引の2001年の市場規模は1.2兆円であるが対前年比で96％増加しており、2005年には約8兆円に拡大するものと予測されている。電子商取引の上位品目はコンピュータおよび周辺機器、航空・鉄道乗車券、ホテル予約、有料デジタルコンテンツ、食品・酒などである。

原材料・部品などの中間材電子商取引の2001年の市場規模は53.9兆円で対前年比で41.5％の増加を示しており、2005年には約100兆円に達すると予測されている。目下のところは電機・自動車などの2業種で全体の約8割を占めている。

別の電子商取引市場形態として複数の売手と複数の買手企業との間のインターネット電子商取引市場である「e-マーケットプレイス」が立ち上がり始めた。2000年の市場規模は800億円に過ぎないが、2005年には17兆円にまで成長すると予測されてい

The Government further proclaimed a period straddling 2001 and 2002 as "The First Year of Broadband," a year in which the tone of Japanese IT would be set by major advances in the establishment of the basic infrastructure for IT development, most notably the building of an optical fiber network, solid progress in making DSL (Digital Subscriber Lines), cable networks and continuous connection services widely available, and quantum price reductions.

Remark: e-Japan Strategy defines "broadband" as including "high-speed Internet access networks" that enable easy downloading of music and similar data and "ultra-high-speed Internet access networks" that enable easy downloading of movies and other high-volume video data. The time required to download the contents of a single music CD, for example, is 2.5 hours by ISDN (64 kbps), 15 minutes by DSL (600 kbps), 6 minutes by cable (1.5 Mbps) and 6 seconds by FTTH (100 Mbps).

3) IT at the Forefront of Economic and Administrative Reform

Companies operating in IT-related sectors are today the main engines of economic growth in Japan. Electronic commerce has become commonplace and businesses are utilizing IT internally to upgrade productivity. In these and other ways, IT has become a primary force behind the reformation of Japan's economic structure.

(Electronic commerce)

The value of goods for final consumption transacted on the e-commerce market in 2001 was ¥1.2 trillion, up 96% from the preceding year. The market is expected to expand to around ¥8 trillion by 2005. The most heavily traded items are computers and peripherals, air and train tickets, hotel reservations, chargeable digital contents, food and alcoholic beverages.

The e-commerce market for raw materials, parts and other intermediate goods amounted to ¥53.9 trillion in 2001, a 41.5% increase from the preceding year, and is expected to balloon to about ¥100 trillion by 2005. Up to now, the electrical equipment and automotive sectors have accounted for approximately 80% of the market's business.

Another emerging e-commerce format is the Internet-based e-marketplace. Trading on these markets, which offer a venue for trading among multiple buyers and sellers, amounted to only ¥80 billion in 2000 but is thought likely to grow to ¥17 trillion

る。この事例としては 300 社が 8000 種類の花きを
インターネットで 24 時間取引できる「フラワーワイ
ズ」が登場し、年間取引額 10 億円にまで成長し
ている。この他 2000 年に設立された e-マーケット
プレイスの主要商品は、鋼材一般、加工食品、建設
資機材・工事、トラック荷台の空きスペース、電機
通信工事用部材などがある。

(電子政府)
　○政府・地方公共団体内部の情報化
　　政府は「e-Japan 重点計画」に基づき国・地方公
共団体の行政の情報化を積極的に推進している。そ
の前提としての「職員 1 人 1 台パソコン整備」につ
いては、政府本省庁においては 1998 年に 100 ％完
了した。設置されたパソコンは資料作成などの単体
利用は 1/4 程度で、3/4 近くは LAN を主体とする
ネットワークシステムの端末として利用されている。
国の行政機関には各省庁間のネットワーク「霞が関
WAN」が 1997 年から運用開始され、各省庁間の
情報交換、国会関係事務支援、総合統計データベー
スなど共通情報検索などに利用されている。政府は
現在行政事務のペーパーレス化（電子化）を推進し、
2002 年までに 57 の内部事務をペーパーレス化する
計画である。
　　地方公共団体においても「1 人 1 台パソコン」は
完成に近づきつつあり、各庁内 LAN の整備は都道
府県・政令指定都市については 100 ％に達している。
また、国の行政機関ネットワーク「霞が関 WAN」
に対応して、全国 3,300 の地方公共団体を相互に結
ぶ「総合行政ネットワーク」の整備が進められてい
て、このシステムは将来的には国の「霞が関
WAN」との接続も視野に入れている。

　○電子政府の国民・企業へのサービス
　　政府の各府省庁は「行政情報の電子提供政策」に
基づき、ホームページを活用した行政情報の提供を
図ることとしている。また、およそ 1 万種類の政府
関係申請・届け出手続きについては、現在は 123 件
に止まっているが、2003 年には全面オンライン化

by 2005. One typical e-marketplace, Flower Wise, allows 300 member companies to engage in 24-hour trading of 8,000 kinds of flowers and ornamental plants. Annual trading volume has already risen to ¥1 billion. Major items traded on other e-marketplaces established in 2000 include general-purpose steel materials, processed foods, construction equipment, materials and jobs, available truck space, and telecommunication facility materials.

(Electronic government)

○ Computerization at national and local governments

In implementing the e-Japan Priority Policy Program, the Japanese Government has put high priority on computerizing administrative work at both the national and local level. One prerequisite for this, putting a personal computer on every government worker's desk, was fully realized at the central ministries and agencies in 1998. About a quarter of the PCs are used as stand-alone systems for compiling data and materials and the remaining three-quarters as network (mainly LAN) terminals. The central government offices are interconnected by a network called the Kasumigaseki WAN that has been in operation since 1997. The offices use this network to exchange information, provide the National Diet with clerical support, and retrieve shared information from an integrated statistical database. The Government is also trying to process a greater percentage of internal work electronically rather than on paper. As of 2002, 57 categories of administrative work had been rendered paperless.

The goal of equipping every local government worker with a computer is also near achievement, and the installation of LANs at prefectural and ordinance-designated city governments has reached 100%. In addition, an Integrated Administrative Network modeled after the central government's Kasumigaseki WAN is being built to interconnect 3,300 local governments throughout the country, with an eye to interconnecting the two networks at some future date.

○ Electronic government services

The central ministries and agencies are utilizing homepages as a way to improve public access to government information. They are also putting in place a system that will allow businesses and the general public to electronically submit many different types of applications and notifications. Although the system can cur-

を目標としている。

　公共事業などの政府調達・入札についても 2003 年の全面電子化をめざしている。

　地方公共団体の行事・観光・物産・施設利用などに関する情報提供の 60 ％から 100 ％程度はすでにホームページによっても行われている。また、住民が最も多く希望している住民票・印鑑登録などの届出・申請手続きについても一部で先行的な取組を行う事例も出始めている。

4) 国民生活に浸透する IT

　日本の 2000 年における世帯当りの情報機器普及率をみると、携帯電話約 6,912 万契約、パソコン 50 ％、ワープロ 36 ％、ファクシミリ 50 ％で、ワープロを除き保有率は増加している。また、携帯電話、パソコンのインターネット接続率も急速に伸びつつある（2000 年 34 ％、2001 年 60.5 ％）。

　生活面におけるインターネットの利用方法として現状では、レジャー、娯楽、商品などの情報入手と個人間の情報交換が突出していて、時事情報（ニュース）はテレビ・ラジオが多く、航空券・ホテル・コンサート・レストランの予約などは固定電話が多い。そのほか一般商品の電子取引、ネットオークションによる特殊な商品の取引、複数の対戦者がインターネットのウェブサイトで行うオンラインゲーム、サーバーを介さずに不特定多数のコンピュータ同士で直接音楽ファイルを交換できるシステム「ピア・トゥ・ピア」（P to P）なども登場してきた。

　また、医療・福祉面では遠隔地診療所と大学病院をオンラインでつなぐ遠隔診療システム、介護を要する高齢者の自宅に通信機能をもつペット型ロボットを置き、安否確認・会話の状況確認・緊急時の迅速対応を行う遠隔介護システムも一部で開始されている。

rently handle only 123 of the approximately 10,000 types of legal forms in existence, online processing of all types will become possible in 2003.

All public works related purchases and tenders will also be conducted electronically starting from 2003.

Local governments throughout the country maintain homepages that provide information regarding local events, tourism, products and facility utilization. Coverage of these topics ranges between 60 and substantially 100%. The local government services most frequently used by residents are those related to address and seal registration and certification, and some of the more progressive local governments are moving to offer electronic services in these areas as well.

4) IT in Daily Life

In 2000, the number of mobile phone subscriptions in Japan was 69.12 million, while 50% of Japanese households owned a personal computer, 36% a dedicated Japanese word processor, and 50% a facsimile machine. With the exception of word processors, the ownership rate of all of these IT devices is increasing. The number of mobile phones and personal computers with access to the Internet is also growing rapidly (2000: 34%, 2001: 60.5%).

In their private lives, Japanese are using the Internet mostly to communicate with friends and to obtain information regarding recreation, entertainment and products. They tend to rely on television for news and use fixed-line telephones for flight, hotel, concert and restaurant reservations. Still, more and more people are using the Internet for a variety of purposes, such as to shop for general consumer goods, bid for special items on net auctions, play games on sites that allow simultaneous participation of multiple players, and use peer-to-peer systems (P2P) that allow computer users to swap music files directly (i. e., without going through a server).

Medical and welfare systems are also emerging. A few university hospitals have set up systems for online diagnosis of patients at remote clinics. Remote home-care systems for the elderly are also appearing. In one such system, a pet-like robot with communication capabilities is installed in the person's home to watch for signs of trouble and exchange simple greetings and the like with the care recipient. When the robot senses an emergency, it promptly takes appropriate action and calls for help.

仕事の面では、情報通信機器を利用して自宅で仕事を行うテレワーク、あるいは自宅を独立小オフィスにしてビジネスを行う SOHO（Small Office/Home Office）などの勤務形態が広がりつつある。

5）IT 革命の今後の課題
（情報格差の解消）
　　　IT 革命の進展は市民生活に多大な利便性と多様性をもたらすことが期待される。それ故に今後はまず国民が等しく、最大限に IT の恩恵を享受できる環境（デジタル・オポチュニティー）の確保が第 1 の課題である。言い換えれば、インターネット利用における地域格差、個人間能力格差、身体の障害事情による格差など（デジタル・ディバイド）をいかに埋めていくかということである。

（情報リテラシーの向上）
　　　次には、インターネット利用の拡大に向けて国民一般の情報通信システムを自由自在に使いこなす能力（情報リテラシー）を向上させることと企業における IT 技術者の不足の解消が重要な課題となっている。
　　　一般市民に対する情報基礎技能講習を支援するために、「IT 講習特別交付金」制度が 2001 年 1 月に創設され 2002 年 3 月までに 550 万人の受講が見込まれている。
（情報セキュリティの確保）
　　　一方、IT 社会の影の部分としての「不正アクセス」、「コンピュータウィルス」、「サイバーテロ」、「違法、有害情報」、「個人情報の流失」などが社会的大問題となっている。IT 革命が進展し、IT の国民生活・社会経済活動への浸透が進めば進むほど情報セキュリティの確保がより一層重要な課題となってきている。

IT is also affecting the way people work. Some company employees now work at home as "teleworkers" using computers and telecommunications equipment. And an increasing number of people are operating businesses out of an independent home office known as a SOHO (Small Office/Home Office).

5) IT Issues

(Eliminating digital divides)

The advancing IT revolution can be expected to add considerably to the convenience and diversity of people's lives. The foremost IT issue is, therefore, how to establish an environment in which everyone in the country has a chance to share the benefits of IT equally and to the utmost (how to equalize digital opportunity). In other words, attention must be focused on how to bridge the various digital divides by, for example, eliminating disparity in Internet utilization between different regions, leveling differences in individual capability, and compensating for differences caused by disabilities.

(Boosting information literacy)

The expanding use of the Internet has created two other urgent needs: (1) to improve public information literacy to the point that that the average citizen is able to make free use of telecommunication and information systems and (2) to eliminate the shortage of IT engineers and technicians in the business sector.

A government-subsidized IT Workshop program was launched in January 2001 to help train ordinary citizens in computer and telecommunication fundamentals. The number of people taking courses is expected to reach 5.5 million by March 2003.

(Ensuring information security)

The IT society also has its dark side. Unauthorized access, computer viruses, cyberterror, illegal/harmful contents, and leakage of personal information have become major social issues in Japan. The importance of ensuring information security is increasing in proportion as the IT revolution advances and IT finds its way more and more deeply into the fabric of Japanese life and the country's social and economic activities.

4　企業経営

a）企業経営の特徴

　　日本の企業経営については、従来いわゆる「日本的経営の特徴」といわれる独特のシステムがあり、これが日本経済を成功に導いたという認識が国の内外において一般的であった。これらのシステムが戦後日本企業の発展に歴史的役割を果たしたことは事実であり、また、この特徴が現在も日本の多くの企業の経営体質に多分に残っていることも否定できない。

　　しかし、グローバル化が急速に進展し企業に強力な競争力が求められる現在の状況下で、これらのシステムを維持したままでは企業の体質改善は困難であるという認識が深まり、これらのシステムは総合的見直しを迫られている。

（日本的経営の特徴とその歴史的役割）

　　従来指摘された「日本的経営の特徴」とは次の諸点である。

1）意思決定方法……稟議（りんぎ）制度や会議方式により集団的に意思決定が行われる。

2）雇用関係……原則として所定の年齢（定年）までは雇用関係は継続する。雇用期間中は年功と能力の向上に従い給与と地位が上昇する。

3）労働組合は、船員などを除いて企業別が主であり、職種別ではない。

4）資金関係……多くは自己資本（株式など）よりも銀行借入などの他人資本により設備資金を調達する。

5）生産体制……組み立産業（自動車、電機など）や装置産業（鉄鋼、化学など）では、部品調達、設備操作を多く外部企業（いわゆる系列会社）に委託する。

6）貿易依存度……原料輸入、製品輸出など産業の海外依存度が高い。

4 Business Management

a) Business Management Characteristics

Both internal and external observers have generally viewed Japanese business management as characterized by unique systems or "Japanese management features" and considered these to have led Japan to economic success. These features did in fact play a historical role in the postwar development of Japanese businesses. And they undeniably remain strongly present in the management culture of many companies even today.

Now that rapidly advancing globalization is making powerful competitiveness indispensable, however, more and more companies are realizing that it will be difficult to carry out the corporate streamlining they require while keeping these traditional systems intact. These features of Japanese-style management therefore need to be thoroughly reassessed.

(Characteristics and historical role of Japanese-style business management)

Some features that have been pointed to as characterizing the management of Japan's private enterprises are:

1) Decision making—Decisions are reached by a collective decision making process through the ringi system and the kaigi system.

2) Employment—Under most circumstances, employment continues up to a prescribed age (retirement age). Salary and position rise according to seniority and performance.

3) Labor unions—Aside from the seamen's union and a few others, most unions are enterprise unions rather than trade unions.

4) Funds—Most funds invested in plant and equipment are not owned capital funds (are not funds raised on the open market by selling shares etc.) but are procured as borrowed capital from banks and similar sources.

5) Production—Outside companies (affiliated companies) are relied on heavily to supply parts in assembly industries (like automobiles and electrical equipment) and handle equipment operation in the process industries (like steel and chemicals).

6) Dependence on foreign trade—Industry dependence on raw material imports and finished product exports is high.

戦後55年余りの日本の経済・社会情勢の歴史を通してみると、1945年終戦直後の荒廃と混乱のなかから立ち上がった日本経済は、1955年ころを境として急速な発展をとげた。上記のシステムはおおむねこの1955年から1975年までの日本経済の高度成長・急速拡大期に最も適合したものであった。

　すなわち、東西冷戦体制における日・米の緊密な友好関係、保革両勢力のバランスの上に立った国内政治の安定、西欧に追いつき追い越そうとする国民の勤労意欲などを背景に、主としてアメリカの先進技術の導入、規格工業製品の大量生産方式により経済は大発展をとげ、旧西ドイツと並んで「奇跡の復興」と称賛された。

　その急速な発展の一例を鉄鋼業でみると、日本の鉄鋼生産量は1955年の1000万トンを起点として、5年ごとに2000万トン、4000万トン、9000万トン、と文字通り倍々ゲームで伸びて、1970年代には1億2000万トンのピークに達した。鉄鋼は主要な基幹産業であるから、日本経済もおおよそこの線に沿って伸展したわけである。このようにして、日本は1975年代には「経済大国」として国際的ステージに立ち、唯一の非欧米国メンバーとして主要先進国首脳会議（サミット）にも連なった。

　この事実は戦後の日本人の一致協力した努力の成果であったこと、また同時にそのプロセスにおいて「日本的経営」システムが一定の歴史的役割を果したことを示すものとして記憶されてよい。

(「日本的経営」の転換)

　しかしながら、その後東西冷戦体制の解消と機を一にして、日本は押し寄せる市場開放の強い圧力、急速なグローバル化による熾烈な国際競争の波に直面することとなった。

　この状況のなかで、これまでにも厳しい国際競争環境

The over 55-year postwar history of Japanese economic and social trends begins with the rise of the economy from the devastation and turmoil at the end of the war in 1945. This process continued until around 1955, when the pace of economic development shifted into high gear. It was during this high-growth, rapid-expansion period of the Japanese economy, between about 1955 and 1975, that the Japanese-style management systems worked best.

This period was marked by cordial U.S.-Japan relations during the East-West standoff known as the Cold War, by internal political stability underpinned by a good balance between conservative and progressive forces, and by the availability of a highly motivated workforce intent on overtaking Western Europe. Against this backdrop, Japan had ready access to sources of advanced technology, most notably the United States, and moved forward to grow its economy around a system focused on mass production of standardized industrial products. This success, paralleling that in the former West Germany, won both countries international acclaim for their "economic miracles."

A typical example of this rapid development can be seen in the steel industry. Taking Japan's total steel production of 10 million tons in 1955 as the starting point, production substantially doubled during each succeeding 5-year period, climbing to 20 million tons, 40 million tons and 90 million tons, and finally peaking at 120 million tons in the 1970s. As steel is a basic industry, it follows that the whole Japanese economy developed more or less along the same trajectory. Thus, by 1975, Japan stood on the international stage as an economic superpower and was the only member of the G-7 from outside Europe and North America.

Although this achievement was the product of the combined efforts of postwar Japanese, the considerable part that Japan's unique management systems played in this process is also worth noting from the historical perspective.

(Transforming Japanese management)

The end of the Cold War was, however, a turning point that put Japan under intense pressure to open its markets and brought it face to face with fierce international competition triggered by rapid globalization.

While some sectors with well established track records in the

のなかを歩んできた鉄鋼、自動車、電機、機械、電子機器などの比較的競争力が強いとされてきた産業に加えて、政府のいわゆる護送船団方式によって保護されてきた金融、農業、航空、各種特殊法人などの比較的競争力が弱いとされてきた産業もすべてが独力で国際市場における競争に立ち向かわざるをえなくなった。

こうした事態を受けて、日本企業は従来の成功体験の思い出と長年の環境への過剰適応体質からの脱却、いわば「ユデガエル」からの脱却を迫られている。企業は「日本的経営」の長所は残しつつも、その欠点を改善すべくさまざまな改革を実行しつつある。

〔注〕ユデガエルの例話：カエルを熱湯の中に投げ入れると、カエルは驚いて必死で飛び出して助かる。しかし、水の中に入れて徐々に熱するとカエルはぬるま湯の中にじっとつかっていて、やがてゆでられて死んでしまう。快適環境への安住を戒めた例話である。（テイシー米ミシガン大学教授の来日講演より）

b) 企業における意思決定の仕組み

日本の大企業の意思決定方法はその集団的方式に特徴があるとされている。その典型的な方法が稟議制度と呼ばれる一連の事務手順で、現在も企業、官庁で一般に行われている。まず、プロジェクトの提案部署の担当者は企画案を文書形式（伺い書）で作成し、直属の上司から組織の序列に沿って順々に上位者の承認を得る。さらにその案件に関係ある部門の各級責任者にも同意を求め、最後に決裁者の決裁を得る。決裁者はその案件の重要度に従い、社長、取締役、部長などと決められている。承認、決裁の意思表示は捺印によって行われる。捺印者は時に20人を超える場合もあった。現在はこの制度もかなり簡素化され、またITインターネットによる電子決裁も採用されているが基本的性格は同じである。企画の起案者は計画段階であらかじめ関係者の意見を聞いて内々の了解を取っている（いわゆる根回しができている）ので、成案が修正・廃案となることは稀である。

international arena, like the steel, auto, electrical equipment, machinery and electronic equipment industries, were fairly strong competitors, the competitive strength of others, including the financial, agriculture, airline and a number of government-run business sectors, was relatively weak because they had long been sheltered under the government's "convoy system." So, suddenly, all industries, strong or weak, had to contend with the challenges of international markets on their own.

Faced with this reality, Japanese businesses must now stop clinging to their outdated formula for success and shed their tendency to go on adapting perpetually without taking decisive action (in a word, their boiled-frog syndrome). Most are in fact moving steadily forward with reforms for eliminating the draw-backs of Japanese-style management but preserving the merits.

> The boiled-frog parable: Put a frog into hot water and it will frantically jump out and save itself. But when the same frog is put in room-temperature water and the water is slowly heated, the frog will complacently endure the rising temperature until it dies. The lesson in this parable is that we should not be too complacent about a comfortable environment. (From a talk given by Prof. Tichy of the University of Michigan while in Japan.)

b) Business Decision Making Process

The decision making process of large Japanese companies is characterized by its collective nature. The process typically takes the form of a series of procedures called the ringi system, which is widely used at corporations and government offices even today. First, the person in charge at the department proposing the project draws up the plan in written form (the ukagaisho) and gets the approval of his or her immediate supervisors at successively higher levels of the organization. Then, after obtaining the approval of officers in the other departments involved in the plan, the person obtains the final executive decision. The final decision is made by the company president, a director, a department head or other officer as appropriate for the importance of the matter. Each person indicates approval by affixing his or her seal. In the past, the document might bear the seals of 20 or more persons by the end of the process. Although most organizations have considerably simplified their systems in recent years, some now even handling the whole process electronically via the

この意思決定方式は関係者のいわば全会一致の同意を前提としているので実施に当たっては各部門の協力が得られやすいという一定の利点が認められる。

　反面、この方式は意思決定に時間がかかり、管理部門の生産性の低下、実施のタイミングを逃すなどのデメリットをともなう。さらに経営上の基本問題としては責任が余りに分散してその所在が明確でないことである。これが従来の日本の経営がお神輿（みこし）経営と呼ばれた理由である。

　　〔注〕神輿（みこし）：日本の神社の神体または霊が
　　　　乗ると信じられる壮麗な櫓（やぐら）状の輿
　　　　（こし）で、神社の祭りの時に大勢の信徒がか
　　　　ついで街を練り歩く。神輿経営とは企業を神輿
　　　　に例えて、皆でかつぐので誰が責任を取ってい
　　　　るのかわからない経営方式をなかば揶揄（や
　　　　ゆ）した表現である。

　このほかに、同時に多数の人の賛同を得て意思決定を行う方法として会議方式がある。企業経営の意思決定機関として法律に定められているものに株主総会、取締役会がある。このほかに、意思決定の場として各レベル、各分野の委員会・会議があり、ここで情報提供、意見交換を通じてコンセンサスが得られる。

　近年のメガ・コンペティション時代を迎え、企業は国際競争力の観点から、意思決定についても形式の整合性よりもスピードと責任の明確化を迫られている。このため企業は、会社分割、事業部制、カンパニー制などにより責任と権限を大幅に各組織に委譲し、意思決定の迅速化・効率化ともに結果に対する責任を追求できるシステムを導入している。

Internet, the basic nature of the system remains unchanged. Since the person making the proposal informally secures the acceptance of those concerned beforehand at the planning stage (through nemawashi or consensus-building), revision or withdrawal of an approved plan is rare.

One advantage of this decision-making system is that the cooperation of the people concerned is easy to obtain when the plan is implemented because they have all approved it in advance.

On the negative side, the long time it takes to arrive at a decision lowers administrative productivity and may result in opportunities being lost owing to delays in plan implementation. The system is also flawed from the viewpoint of management fundamentals. It spreads responsibility so widely that accountability is blurred. This is why Japanese-style management has been called mikoshi (leaderless) management.

A mikoshi is an ornate palanquin-like portable shrine in which the ghost or spirit of a Shinto shrine deity is believed to ride. During shrine festivals, scores of believers wind through the town carrying the mikoshi on their shoulders. "Mikoshi management" is a term mildly poking fun at a management system that makes pinpointing responsibility impossible because the company's course is set by everyone.

Decision-making is also conducted through the kaigi system of meetings for obtaining the agreement of many persons simultaneously. Some meetings, such as the general meeting of shareholders and the board of directors meeting, are legally prescribed corporate management decision-making bodies. Other decision-making venues include meetings and conferences held at every level in every division for the purpose of reaching a consensus through exchange of information and opinions.

Owing to the emergence of the megacompetition era in recent years, businesses are coming to require increasingly powerful international competitive strength. This means Japanese companies now need to develop decision-making schemes that stress speed and clear accountability over formal consistency. They are therefore speeding up and streamlining decision-making by using spin-offs, divisionalized organization, company-based organization and other measures to transfer responsibility and authority to the individual operating divisions on a wholesale basis. In parallel, they are introducing systems for holding

またサービス産業では、例えばファーストフード店やコンビニのようにた正社員は店長１人だけで残りの従業員はすべてパートタイマーかアルバイターで、店長がすべての決定権と責任をもっている事業所も多い。

　さらに、近年来企業の意思決定についての注目すべき動きは、企業の最高責任者たる社長が自らの責任と権限に基づき、確かな経済的合理性と見通しをもって明確な意思決定を行ない組織をリードしていく、いわゆるトップダウン方式のケースである。

c) 雇用関係の特徴

　戦後かなり長期にわたり終身雇用、年功序列賃金、企業別労働組合は日本的雇用制度の「３種の神器」といわれてきた。これはアメリカの経営学者で日本の企業経営を研究したジェームズ・アベグレンがその著書『日本の経営から何を学ぶか』の中で日本の雇用関係の特徴としてあげた次のような指摘に呼応するものである。

1 ）企業は、学校を卒業した直後の若者を従業員として採用する。（定期採用）
2 ）採否は個人の属人的要素により決められ、特定の職務のために人を雇うのではない。必要な職務訓練は採用後企業内で行う。（企業内訓練）
3 ）雇用は、その個人の全生涯にわたる。（終身雇用）
4 ）給与は勤続年数により決まる。（年功序列）
5 ）労働組合は１企業１組合である。（企業別組合）

　これらの日本の雇用慣行が、欧米の実態との対比においてはじめての欧米人に驚きと興味を抱かせたことは容易に想像できる。また、この時期は旧西ドイツと並んで日本の急速な経済発展が世界的注目を浴びていた背景から、日本の研究が内外で盛んであった。アベグレンの著書もその１例である。

　しかし、これらの指摘は戦後のある期間のある範囲の大企業の観察に基づくものであることに注目しなければならない。経済史研究者たちによれば、これらの特徴は

employees responsible for their performance.

In the service industry, many places of businesses, such as fast food shops and convenience stores, have only one full-time employee, a manager who makes all decisions and takes total responsibility, and all other employees are part-timers.

Another noteworthy trend in corporate decision-making is that some company presidents are adopting a top-down approach. Utilizing their positions of responsibility and authority as chief executive officers, they are moving to lead their companies by issuing unambiguous decisions based on sound economic reasoning and projections.

c) Employment Characteristics

For a considerable time after the Second World War, people spoke of the Three Sacred Treasures of the Japanese employment system, meaning lifetime employment, seniority-based pay, and the enterprise labor union. The term was coined in response to the following features of employment in Japan pointed out by James Abegglen, an American expert on Japanese business management, in his book *Management and Worker: The Japanese Solution* (1974).

1) Japanese enterprises employ young people fresh out of school. (Periodic hiring)

2) The decision to employ or not is based on personal qualities rather than suitability for a specific job. The enterprise provides any special job training necessary after the person is hired.

3) Employment in Japanese enterprises extends over the whole working life of the employee. (Lifetime employment)

4) Pay is determined by the number of years of employment in the company. (Seniority-based wages)

5) For each enterprise there is one labor union. (Enterprise union)

As might be expected, these employment practices at first surprised and intrigued people in the West because of the strong contrast with their own practices. At the time, Japan (along with the former West Germany) was a focus of international attention for its rapid economic development. Studies on Japan were therefore very active and Abegglen's book was one among several on Japan published.

It should be noted, however, that Abegglen's analysis was based on his observation of large Japanese corporations during

ずっと昔から日本に存在したわけではなく、日本文化の伝統に根ざすものでもないというのが多数説である。時期的にはこれらの制度のきざしは第1次大戦後の1920年代からでさらに普及したのは第2次大戦後の1955年以降の高度成長期のころである。これらの制度はアメリカに追いつこうとするキャッチアップ型経済体制のもとで新卒労働者の定期的大量採用、規格品の大量生産により製造業を基幹として日本経済が急速に拡大発展した時期にうまくフィットし、有効に機能して十分に歴史的役割を果たした。

ここで、日本全体の雇用関係を考えるには、現在における約250万の会社・法人とそこに就業するおよそ6,400万人の労働者を対象とする必要がある。その観点からみると現在の日本の雇用関係はきわめて多様であり、またその伝統的特徴とされた諸点は、次のような諸現象が示すようにきわめて大きな変容を遂げつつある。

○パートタイマー、派遣会社社員、フリーターと呼ばれるアルバイト暮らしの若者、在宅勤務者などの就業者が増加し、雇用形態・雇用期間が多様化している（パートタイマー、派遣社員などの正社員外の労働者の比率は、2001年には27.7％に達している）。
○産業の情報化・ソフト化（サービス業のウェイトの増大）にともない労働市場が流動化している。
○昇給・昇進制度が年功序列型から実力主義・成果主義へ転換しつつある。
○経済情勢の長期的停滞、企業のグローバル化、熾烈な国際競争、組合組織率21％という環境のなかにおける労働組合の社会的役割の変化。

a limited postwar period. In the opinion of most scholars of Japan's economic history, these features cannot be traced far back into Japan's past or be considered deeply rooted in Japanese tradition. They first emerged in the 1920s, after the First World War, and set in after the Second World War, during the period of high economic growth starting from 1955. The Japanese economy of this period can be characterized as a "catch -up" economy aimed at closing the economic gap with the United States. The strategy followed was to focus chiefly on mass production of standardized products and to take advantage of the spring graduation season to hire the large numbers of new employees needed for further expansion. The systems were well fitted to the needs of this period of rapid economic growth. They worked well and played a significant role historically.

Still, any serious study of the overall Japanese employment situation must encompass all of the country's roughly 2.5 million companies and the approximately 64 million people they employ. When viewed from this perspective, employment in Japan is very diverse. Moreover, many of what have been considered traditional characteristics are undergoing dramatic changes, as can be seen from the following trends.

○ Employment is diversifying in format and length of the employment period. This can be seen, for example, in the larger number of young people who make a living as non-regulars (part-timers, temporaries dispatched by employee-leasing agencies, and free-timers) and the increasing number of regular employees becoming telecommunicators. (As of 2001, part-timers, temporaries and other non-regulars accounted for 27.7% of the labor force.)

○ The stronger focus of businesses on information, systems and services (the expansion of the service sector) is fluidizing the labor market.

○ The basis for deciding pay increases and promotions is shifting away from seniority toward ability and performance.

○ The social role of labor unions is changing under the pressures of a protracted economic slump, business globalization, intense international competition and a decline in union membership to 21%.

d) 終身雇用、定期採用、年功序列、定期昇給、定年退職

（終身雇用）

これは企業が一度雇った従業員は定年まで雇い続けるという長期雇用慣行の呼び名であって、実際に生涯にわたって雇用を保証するという意味ではない。さきに述べたように戦後日本の大企業は学校新卒者を大量に定期採用した。日本にはアメリカのようなレイオフ制度がないので、この若者たちは不況時にも解雇されることなく本人の任意退職以外は原則的に定年まで雇用された。

しかし、中小企業においては、従来から必要時期に、必要要員を通年採用する所も多かった。また近年、企業が予測外の困難な経営状況に陥った場合に一定の条件を示して希望退職を募ったり、企業の倒産により雇用が突然に消滅するケースも無視できない数に達している。また、管理職など労働組合員以外の社員については、労働協約に定められた定年よりかなり前倒しに退職するのも大企業では一般的慣行である。

このような実状から、日本の雇用関係の特徴とされた終身雇用は必ずしも普遍的でなくなりつつある。

（年功序列・定期昇給）

年功序列は年齢や勤続年数に応じて賃金が上昇し、社内の職務資格も昇進する制度である。もとより、年齢と勤続年数だけで給与や資格が画一的に決まるわけではなく、さきの終身雇用慣行のもとで長期にわたり能力・業績に応じて賃金を決定していくという制度である。

この慣行は、定期採用・終身雇用という雇用関係を前提として、次のような基本的考えと期待に基づく制度であった。

①日本の労働者は採用時に学歴ごとにその能力が一定水準以上に均質化されている。

②企業は従業員を採用後に長期的観点から計画的に教育訓練を行う。

d) Lifetime Employment, Periodic Hiring, Ranking by Seniority, Periodic Wage Increases, and Fixed-age Retirement

(Lifetime employment)

The term "lifetime employment" refers to the practice of companies continuing to employ the people they hire up to a mandatory retirement age. It does not mean that employees are guaranteed employment throughout their lives. As mentioned earlier, in the years following the Second World War, Japanese businesses hired large numbers of new graduates at a fixed time each year. As Japan had no layoff system like that in the United States, these employees were kept on the payroll no matter how bad the times. Unless they retired of their own will, their employment basically continued up to retirement age.

Still, many small businesses have long adopted a year-round system of hiring the number of employees they need when they need them. And, in recent years, it is not uncommon for a company that has run into severe difficulties to encourage voluntary retirement by offering certain incentives. Cases in which bankruptcy suddenly deprives all employees of their jobs have also reached a significant level. At large corporations, managers and other nonunion members frequently retire well before the retirement age prescribed by the labor agreement.

Thus the lifetime employment system, long considered a characteristic of Japanese employment relations, is becoming less and less the norm.

(Ranking by seniority and periodic salary increases)

Seniority ranking is a system in which salary and job position rise in accordance with age and length of service. But Japanese companies have never implemented the system to the point of deciding salary and position solely on the basis of these two factors. Rather, they have operated it within the context of lifetime employment, with salaries being increased at different rates over the long term based on capability and performance.

The system is founded on the employment practices of periodic hiring and career-long employment with the same company. The underlying assumptions and expectations can be outlined as follows:

① At the time of hiring, Japanese workers with like educational backgrounds have the same capabilities.

② Companies systematically educate and train hired employees with an eye to the long term.

③従ってその業務遂行能力は経験年数に従い向上する。

④企業は個々の業績に対してではなく、全雇用期間を通じてみた業績に報いる。

⑤この制度では年齢の上昇にしたがって増加する結婚、子供の教育、住宅取得などの生活経費に対応する賃金カーブを設定できる。したがって従業員はさきの終身雇用制度と相まって安心感と企業に対する忠誠心もって業務に専念する。

こうした観点から、各人の職務レベル、学歴、勤続年数、年齢をベースとし設定されているテーブルの昇給基準額に各人の能力・業績を加味した昇給額が初任給に毎年加算されていく。この昇給は、毎年定期的に全従業員に対して行われる。これが定期昇給である（一般的には毎年4月）。

(年功序列の功罪)

この制度は、日本の高度成長期には期待通りの効果を発揮した。しかし、同時に次のようなマイナス面を内蔵するものであった。

①能力があり、実績を上げた者も所定の勤続年数に達しないと期待通り昇給・昇進が与えられないという不公正感が生ずる。

②一方普通に過ごせば一定の処遇が保障される安心感から自己啓発・業務効率改善の意欲が薄れる。

③従業員の高齢化とともに企業の能力の総和に関係なく総労務費は増えつづける。

こうした年功序列制の問題点は、1980年代のいわゆる右肩上がり経済成長の停滞、さらにはグローバル・スタンダードの波に乗って押し寄せる激烈な国際競争、バブルの崩壊後の長期不況という環境下で、一挙に顕在化した。

各企業では非効率かつ際限ない労務費増をともなう年功序列賃金体系を見直す必要に迫られ、一定年齢以降は賃金、職務資格が水平または下降線をたどるいわゆるS字型賃金カーブが一般化した。

③ Job performance therefore improves with years of experience.

④ Companies reward employees for their contributions throughout their years of service rather than separately for each achievement.

⑤ The system makes it possible to set a wage curve that keeps pace with outlays that increase with age, such as those involved in marrying, raising a family, education, and building a house. The effect of this, together with the lifetime employment system, is that the employee will concentrate on his or her job with a sense of security and loyalty to the company.

Each employee's salary is increased annually by the amount of a base increase set out in a table categorized by position, educational background, years of service and age, plus an increase taking into account the employee's ability and performance. All employees receive their raises at the same time every year (usually in April). This is called the "periodic salary increase."

(Merits and demerits of seniority ranking)

This system produced the desired results during Japan's high-growth period. But it also included some negative aspects:

① It is unfair that able employees with strong achievement records are not given the pay increases and promotions they deserve until accruing the prescribed number of years of service.

② Employee motivation to develop and become more efficient workers is dampened by a sense of security that comes from knowing even the average worker will be rewarded to some degree.

③ An aging workforce steadily increases overall labor costs without necessarily contributing to aggregate corporate capability.

The effect of these drawbacks of the seniority ranking system first emerged with the flattening of the economic growth curve in the eighties, grew stronger as Japan was increasingly forced to abide by tough global business standards that brought it face to face with intense international competition, and reached full force during the prolonged slump following the bursting of the Bubble Economy.

Businesses had no choice but to reassess their seniority-dominated wage systems, which they now saw as inefficient and a source of endlessly rising labor costs. Most switched to a wage

さらに、情報通信技術（IT）の浸透、産業構造のソフト化にともない、職務の知識・技能と年齢・年功とが平行せず、ときに逆転するという状況のもとで、現在ますます多くの企業が、年功序列体系を色濃く残しながらも成果主義に基づく年俸制など経営体質強化につながる賃金システムを導入するか、または検討している。

なお、賃金の年功制という性格は欧米諸国にもみられるが、日本ほど顕著ではない。

（定年退職）

一定の年齢を設定し、これに達すると本人の意思とは関係なく自動的に退職となる制度である。日本では 30 人以上の規模の企業では 90 ％以上が定年退職制度を採用している。現在、定年は法律の定めに従い 60 歳以上となっているが、60 歳と定めている企業が 90 ％以上である。

なお、アメリカでは「雇用における年齢差別禁止法」により定年退職制度は認められていない。

e）企業別労働組合組織、労使関係、賃金要求「春闘」

（企業別労働組合）

日本の労働組合は、個々の企業を単位として組織されている労働組合が主で企業別または企業内労働組合と呼ばれている。これは産業別あるいは職種別に組織されている欧米の産業別労働組合、職種別労働組合と対比されるもので、現在においても変わらずに日本の労働組合の特徴である。

（組織）

2001 年現在、日本には 67,700 余りの個別の労働組合があり、組合員総数は約 1,150 万人である。組合員数の雇用者数に占める割合を示す組合組織率は 20.7 ％である。近年、労働組合数、組合員数および組合組織率はいずれも減少傾向にある。

curve, called the S curve, that peaked at a certain age and then leveled off or declined. This curve was applied to both salary and position.

Then, with the penetration of information technologies (IT) and the emergence of a more service-intensive industrial structure, it became apparent that job proficiency (knowledge and expertise) does not always increase, may in fact decrease, with age and seniority. This is leading more companies to introduce new wage systems, e. g., annual salary systems based on performance, that help to strengthen the company's financial and business position. Usually, however, many features of the seniority raking system still remain clearly evident.

While facets of the seniority system can also be seen in European and American wage practices, they are not so pronounced as in Japan.

(Fixed-age retirement)

Under this system, employees are automatically retired at a prescribed age without consideration to their personal wishes. Over 90% of Japanese companies with 30 or more employees adopt fixed-age retirement systems. The law requires the mandatory retirement age to be set at sixty or higher. Actually, sixty is the age specified by more than 90% of the companies that adopt the system.

The situation in Japan contrasts sharply with that in the United States, where mandatory retirement at a fixed age is prohibited by the Age Discrimination in Employment Act.

e) Organization of Unions by Enterprise, Labor-Management Relations, and the Spring Wage Offensive

(Organization of unions by enterprise)

Most Japanese labor unions are organized separately by enterprise and are therefore called enterprise unions. This still persists as a feature of Japanese labor unions that sets them apart from European and American unions organized by industry or trade.

(Organization)

In 2001, Japan had more than 67,700 separate labor unions with a total membership of around 11.5 million. The unionization rate (percentage of union members among all employees) was 20.7%. Recent years have seen a decline in the number of unions as well as in the number of union members and the unionization rate.

企業別労働組合は同一産業内でまとまり産業別労働組合を組織している。さらにこの民間の産業別労働組合および諸官庁・自治体労働組合の大部分が合流して全国労働組合総連合会（連合）という中央組織を構成している。連合は労働組合最大のナショナルセンターで700万人の組合員を擁している。

　また、このナショナルセンター・連合と産業別労働組合との中間レベルに複数の主要産業別労働組合で構成する組織がある。これには鉄鋼・電機・自動車・造船などの産業で構成する金属労協（IMF-JC）や化学・エネルギー・繊維・紙パルプ産業で構成する化学・エネルギー労協などがある。

（労使関係）

　日本の労使は、先進国へのキャッチアップという共通の目標のもと、戦後の一時期を除いては、民間労働組合の経済条件重視の運動路線に沿い、相互の理解と信頼の基盤に立って良好な協力関係を維持してきた。大きな労働争議も1960年代以降は起っていない。

　労使関係は2000年以降の厳しい経済状況下にあってもきわめて良好で、賃金、雇用問題などにつき労使間で真剣な協議を重ねている。

　このような労使の協力関係が1960年代以降の日本の高度経済成長を支えた大きな要因の一つであったことは広く認められているところである。

（労働組合の賃金の引き上げ要求「春闘」）

　賃金の引き上げ要求については、1955年以降「春闘」と呼ばれる日本独特の賃金要求方式が定着し、方式としては2002年現在も行われている。春闘は1955年以降の日本経済の高度成長を背景に「ヨーロッパ並みの賃金」をスローガンとして、鉄鋼、造船、自動車、電機、化学、紙・パルプ、私鉄などの主要産業別労働組合および公共企業体労働組合が合同して賃金要求額、闘争のスケジュールなどを各産業ごとにあらかじめ統一し、春に合わせて一斉に全国闘争を展開する方式である。これは賃金の全国的・全産業的規模での引き上げ・平準化を目的とし

The enterprise unions are federated by industrial sector. Moreover, most of these private-sector federations and the national and local government worker unions (public-sector unions) are merged into a central organization called the Japan Trade Union Confederation (Rengo). With 7 million members, Rengo is Japan's largest national center of labor unions.

In addition, there are a number of key industrial sector labor union federations organizationally positioned between Rengo and the private-sector federations. These include Kinzoku Rokyo (IMF-JC) made up mostly of unions in the steel, electrical machinery, auto and shipbuilding sectors, and Kagaku Energy Rokyo composed of unions in the chemical, energy, textile and paper pulp industries.

(Labor-management relations)

Except during a short period in the postwar years, Japanese labor and management have maintained an excellent cooperative relationship founded on mutual understanding and trust growing out of their commitment to the common purpose of catching up with the industrially advanced nations and the adherence of the private-sector unions to policies with strong emphasis on economic progress. No major labor disputes have occurred since the 1960s.

Despite the severe economic conditions since the advent of the 21st century, labor-management relations have remained extremely good, with both sides cooperating to resolve wage and employment issues through earnest discussions.

This collaborative relationship between labor and management is widely recognized as one of the main reasons Japan was able to achieve such a high rate of economic growth from the 1960s onward.

(Spring wage offensive)

Every spring since 1955, Japanese labor unions have engaged in a wage increase campaign, called Shunto (literally, "spring battle"), without counterpart elsewhere in the world. The campaign continues to be held annually (as of 2002), at least in form.

Shunto took shape during the years of rapid economic expansion starting from 1955. Converging under the banner of "Wages On A Par With Europe," the labor unions of the major industrial sectors, such as the chemical, private railway, electrical machinery, paper pulp, steel and shipbuilding industries, and those of the public sector would coordinate their wage demands and

たものであった。この運動方式はほぼ20年間かなり有効に機能した。

しかし、企業は1975年以降の経済成長の停滞、1990年代のいわゆる経済バブルの崩壊に引き続く長期不況、2000年以降は5％を超える高い失業率、加えて国際競争の一層の激化という深刻な諸問題に直面し、従来の産業別横一列の統一回答、賃金体系全体を底上げする「ベースアップ」という考え方そのものの是非が問われることとなってきている。

その結果、賃金引き上げは雇用問題をも含めて個別の労使関係の場で、それぞれの企業の実情に応じた総合的労働条件の決定という枠組みの中に組み入れられる方向にある。

f）労働時間

日本人労働者の年間総実労働時間は、1960年に2,426時間でピークになった後、2000年には1,854時間に減少してきている。これは、経済的豊かさに見合った生活実現を求めている社会的要請に加え日本政府が1980年以来、労働時間短縮に積極的に取り組んできたことが背景にある。その具体的な動きとしては、次のようなものがある。

1）1987年、労働基準法が40年ぶりに改正された。従来の週48時間労働制から、40時間労働制に向けて、政令による段階的移行をはかることとしている。

2）政府は1988年、「世界とともに生きる日本 - 経済運営五ヵ年計画」や、その他の関連計画を策定した。それらの計画では、「週40時間労働制の実現を期し、年間総実労働時間を1,800時間程度に向けてできる限り短縮する」ことをうたっている。この目標を達成するためには、完全週休2日制、年次有給休暇の20日付与・20日取得、所定外労働時間の削減が必要であるとされている。

これに対して、民間企業や労働組合も、労働時間の短

campaign schedules industry by industry. Then, with the coming of spring, they would march forward in a unified nationwide offensive. This was a strategy aimed equalizing pay raises on a nationwide and industry-wide scale. It worked quite well for about 20 years.

But in the years that followed, the business world was seriously impacted by a number of adversities, most notably the stagnation of economic growth after 1975, the prolonged recession that followed the collapse of the economic bubble of the 1990s, the high unemployment rate of over 5% starting from the year 2000, and intensifying international competition. Companies were therefore forced to reconsider not only their traditional practice of giving a single industry-wide response to union demands but even the underlying "base-up" concept of implementing pay increases by hiking the whole pay structure.

Increasingly, therefore, wage and other employment-related issues are being included within the framework of the overall process of deciding working conditions, at every labor-management negotiating table and in accordance with the circumstances of each company.

f) Working Hours

After peaking at 2,426 hours in 1960, the total hours actually worked per year by the average Japanese worker fell to 1,854 by 2000. While the improvement was powered by the demand of the Japanese people for a quality of life commensurate with the country's economic wealth, it was also accelerated by the vigorous efforts of the government starting from 1980. Specific measures taken include:

1) In 1987, the Labor Standards Law was revised for the first time in 40 years. The new law stipulates that Cabinet orders are to be used to gradually reduce the work week from 48 to 40 hours.

2) In 1988, a five-year plan called "Economic Management within a Global Context" was launched along with other related programs. The plan calls for "realizing a 40-hour work week and reducing total hours actually worked per year to as close to 1,800 as possible." Achieving these goals is expected to require nationwide adoption of the five-day work week, 20-day paid vacations actually taken by all workers, and a reduction in overtime work.

Thanks to the efforts of private enterprises and labor unions in

縮に取り組んだ結果、国際比較では、英米にほぼ並ぶまでになった。厳密に言うと、1999年の製造業労働者の年間総実労働時間は、日本の1,942時間に対してアメリカ1,991時間、イギリス1,902時間、フランス1,672時間、ドイツ1,517時間であった。

こうした日本、アメリカに対するドイツ、フランスなどヨーロッパ大陸諸国の年間労働時間の格差の要因としては、所定外労働時間が長いこと、年次有給休暇の所得日数が少ないことなどがあげられる。ヨーロッパには長期バカンスの習慣があり、労働者は年間20〜30日の休暇を取っている。それに対して、日本の労働者に与えられている年次有給休暇は平均18日であり、そのうち実際に使われているのは5割程度で推移している（2000年）。また、日本の労働者は年間約140時間の所定外労働時間があり、残業を行っている労働者は、約9割に達する。

残業時間を少なくする対策として、1日の所定労働時間は変えずに出勤・退勤時刻を個人別に前後に数時間スライドさせるフレックスタイム制を採用する企業もある。これは通勤時の混雑緩和の効果もある。

今後の労働時間に関わる課題としては、休暇の消化、残業の削減とともに余暇時間を安い出費で楽しめるようにする方策も重要である。

g) 賃金水準

従業員30人以上の企業の平均月額賃金は28万5,000円であるが、このほか、年2回の賞与があるので、これを含めた月額は39万7,400円である（2001年）。

日本の賃金の特徴として、大企業と中小企業の差が大きいことがあげられる。また、年齢や勤続に応じて賃金が上がる、いわゆる年功序列の傾向が強い（雇用の項参照）。

賃金の国際比較においては、各国為替レートで換算すると、日本の賃金水準は非常に高く、製造業生産労働者の賃金水準は欧米諸国に肩を並べている。この事情から日本製品の価格競争力は徐々に弱まり、国内市場で輸入品製品に押されるため農産物などの輸入をめぐってアジア諸国との貿易摩擦が顕在化している。また、国内企業が低い労働コストを求めて生産拠点を海外に移すいわゆる産業の空洞化も憂慮されている。

line with this plan, working hours in Japan have decreased substantially to the level of those in the United States and the United Kingdom. Specifically, total hours worked per year by manufacturing industry workers in 1999 was 1,942 in Japan as against 1,991 in the U. S., 1,902 in the U. K., 1,672 in France and 1,517 in Germany.

The gaps between Japan and the European countries arise mainly because Japanese work many overtime hours and do not use all of their vacation days. In Europe workers take 20 to 30 days of paid vacation a year. In contrast, the average Japanese worker takes only about half of the 18 days of paid vacation he is allowed by company regulations (2000). In addition, the average Japanese worker puts in around 140 hours of overtime per year, and 90% of Japanese workers work overtime.

In order to cut overtime hours, some companies are introducing flextime, i. e., allowing employees to shift their own times for starting and finishing work up to several hours in either direction. Flextime also helps to decrease congestion during commuting hours.

Two important issues regarding working hours in Japan are therefore getting workers to use their vacation time and reducing overtime. Another is finding ways to allow workers to enjoy their vacations inexpensively.

g) Salary Levels

The average monthly wage of employees in enterprises of 30 or more is ¥285,000. There are, however, semi-annual bonuses. When these are included, the monthly average becomes ¥397,400 (2001).

One characteristic of the pay scale in Japan is the great difference between the large and small enterprises. Another is the strong tendency for pay to increase with age and years of service under the seniority ranking system. (See Employment Characteristics.)

When wage levels are compared internationally using the going currency exchange rates of the individual countries, Japanese wages turn out to be extremely high. For example, the wage levels of production workers in Japanese manufacturing enterprises exceed those in Europe and the United States. As this situation has gradually weakened the price-competitiveness of Japanese products, causing them to lose ground to imports in the

一方、国民の生活実態の観点から購買力平価で賃金比較すると、1999年においては旧西ドイツは日本の1.8倍、アメリカは1.5倍である。このように日本においては、為替レートでの賃金と購買力平価での賃金とに大きなギャップがあり、所得の高さほどには豊かさの実感を味わえないのが実情である。

h）通勤方法

　大都会における通勤手段は、公営または民営の電車・バスが主であり、自家用車は少ない。自家用車の使用が少ないのは、道路が混雑するのと駐車場の確保難（少なく、高値）のためである。都会への人口集中により、通勤電車・バスは混雑が激しい。さらに、住宅地が都市の中心部から遠い郊外に広がったため、通勤時間がのびている。片道1時間半以上かかる人が半数以上である。さらに遠隔地に住む人では、「新幹線」利用の通勤者が増えている。一部企業では「新幹線通勤」を認め、費用を負担している。

　大都会以外の工場などでは、通勤のため自家用車の利用が多く、また専用の通勤バスなどもあり通勤はかなり便利である。

i）日本における外国人労働者

　日本の「出入国管理法および難民認定法」によると、船舶・航空機の乗務員を除き、日本に在留できる資格は限定されている。単に日本で働きたいという目的では入国できない。許可される在留期間は、たとえば貿易に従事する者、教育に従事する者、宗教活動を行うために外国の宗教団体から派遣される者、新聞などの派遣員、高

domestic market, trade tensions are emerging between Japan and its Asian trading partners, particularly with regard to agricultural product imports. At the same time, Japanese enterprises are shifting production overseas to take advantage of lower labor costs, raising fears that the nation's industries may be hollowed out.

However, a comparison of wages based on buying power as an index of standard of living shows that former West German and American workers had 1.8 and 1.5 times the buying power of their Japanese counterparts in 1999. Owing to the large gap between the relative levels of Japanese wages as judged based on currency exchange rates and based on buying power, Japanese do not enjoy as much affluence as their incomes might seem to imply.

h) Commuting

In major metropolises of Japan the main modes of commuter transportation are publicly or privately operated trains and buses; the use of private cars is relatively small. The reasons for the low use of private cars are traffic congestion and the difficulty of obtaining parking spaces (which are few and expensive). Because the population concentration in cities is great, commuter trains and buses are terribly crowded. Furthermore, since residential housing has been spreading out from the center of cities to the distant suburbs, commuting time is becoming longer. The one -way journey for over half of the commuters is 1.5 hours or more. An increasing number of workers living particularly far from their workplaces are now commuting by Shinkansen bullet trains. Some companies now accept this as a necessity and bear the travel costs of their "bullet line commuters."

For factories and businesses located outside large urban centers, commuting is relatively convenient, with many private cars and company buses being used.

i) Foreign Workers in Japan

Although making an exception for airplane and ship crews, the Immigration-Control and Refugee-Recognition Act of Japan restricts the reasons considered acceptable for an alien's stay in Japan. For example, one may not enter Japan to find employment. The periods of stay permitted for various jobs are three years for those who are engaged in trade, education, or who have

度の技術者として招かれる者は3年まで、教育を受けよ
うとする者、文化活動を行おうとする者、もっぱら熟練
労働に従事しようとする者、演芸・スポーツそのほかの
興業を行おうとする者は1年まで、観光客は90日まで
である（1998年現在）。

　日本経済の国際化の進展にともなって、円高の影響も
加わり、日本で働きたい外国人がますます増加している。
こうした現状から、政府は現在政策の見直しを検討しは
じめており、受け入れ範囲をどの程度までに拡大するか、
今後日本政府が決断を要する課題となっている。

been sent by foreign religious organizations for religious work in Japan, and correspondents of newspapers, etc. and for technical specialists invited to Japan; one year for those who intend to study, engage in cultural activities, specialize in skilled work, or engage in sporting activities or the performing arts; and 90 days for tourists (as of 1998).

Owing to the internationalization of the Japanese economy and the strength of the yen, more and more foreigners have become interested in working in Japan. In view of these circumstances, the Japanese government is reviewing its policies regarding foreign workers and will have to decide on how far the door should be opened to foreigners seeking employment in the country.

5 社会

(1) 社会一般

a）日本人の平均寿命

日本人の平均寿命は男が 77.7 歳、女が 84.6 歳である（2000 年）。男女共世界一と見られる。

20 世紀初めに比べ、それぞれ 33 年、39 年伸びている。これだけ伸びた最大の理由は、医学の発達による乳児死亡率の大幅な減少と、青年層の肺結核のいちじるしい減少である。

日本人の主な死因は、2000 年の調査によると、ガンによる死亡が全死亡の約 30 ％で最も多く、次いで心臓病が約 15 ％、脳卒中など脳血管疾患による死亡が約 14 ％で、これら成人病による死亡が全死亡の半分以上を占めている。

結核による死亡は 1950 年と比較して約 60 分の 1 に減少しており、最近では自動車事故によるものの方が多い。

b）人口増加率

1 世紀前、日本が近代国家として出発した明治の初めには、日本の人口は約 3,500 万人であった。1990 年には 1 億 2,361 万人になっている。この 100 年の間、年人口増加率は、おおむね 1 ％であった。

第二次大戦後、出生率はかなり減少した。しかし、死亡率は老幼を問わず低下したため、人口増加率はあまり変化しなかった。2000 年 10 月現在、日本の人口構成は、15 歳未満 14.6 ％、15 歳以上 64 歳まで 68.2 ％、65 歳以上 17.3 ％となっており、1950 年にはそれぞれ 35.4 ％、59.7 ％、4.9 ％であったので、急速に高齢化社会に移行していることが分かる。1992 年に発表された推計によると、2025 年には、この割合は 14.5 ％、59.7％、25.8 ％になると予測されている。また、女性が一生の間に生む子供の数が年々低下しているので（2000 年にはわずか 1.36）、今後、日本の若年人口は急速に減って

5 Society

(1) General Outline

a) Average Life Expectancy of the Japanese
The average life expectancy of the Japanese male is 77.7 years and of the Japanese female 84.6 years (2000). The expectancies for both sexes are thought to be the highest in the world.

Compared with the beginning of the twentieth century this represents an increase of 33 years and 39 years respectively. The principal reason for this increase in life expectancy is the marked decrease in infant mortality and the remarkable decrease in pulmonary tuberculosis among the young because of advances in modern medicine.

According to a 2000 survey, the greatest cause of mortality among Japanese is cancer, accounting for 30% of all deaths, followed by heart disease, 15%, then cerebral hemorrhage and other forms of stroke, 15%. Deaths resulting from these adult diseases account for the majority of deaths in Japan.

Deaths from pulmonary tuberculosis have decreased to about one-sixtieth the 1950 level; in recent years, the number of fatalities resulting from automobile accidents has been higher than that from tuberculosis.

b) Rate of Population Growth
A century ago, when Japan began to emerge as a modern nation early in the Meiji era, the country had a population of 35 million. In 1990, the population reached 123 million 610 thousand. Within this span of one hundred years, the annual rate of population increase has been about 1%.

The birth rate has declined markedly since the end of World War II. Nevertheless, because of the decline in the rate of mortality among the old and the young alike, there has been relatively little change in the overall rate of population increase. As of October, 2000, 14.6% of the population was under 15 years of age, 68.2% was between 15 and 64, and 17.3% was 65 or older, whereas the corresponding figures for 1950 were 35.4%, 59.7% and 4.9%, pointing up the rapid rate at which the population is aging. Statistics announced in 1992 predict that the age breakdown will be 14.5%, 59.7% and 25.8% in the year 2025. In addition, the

くることが予想される。

c ）社会保障

　　1999 年、日本の社会保障給付費総額は 75 兆 400 億円、国民所得の 19 ％、国民一人当り 59 万 2,300 円になった。

　　この給付額は、1955 年からの 40 年間で、国民所得の伸びの約 2.5 倍のスピードである。これは、個人に対する給付の向上と高齢化の進展によるものである。とくに日本は世界一の長寿国なので、社会の高齢化の影響は極めて大きい。2000 年現在、65 歳以上の人の全人口に対する比率は 17.3 ％であったが、2015 年までには 25 ％に達すると予想される。こうした状況から、制度と給付レベルの改善とともに、費用負担のあり方が議論の焦点となっている。

　　日本の社会保障は、社会保険・公的扶助プログラム・その他の公的サービスに大別される。

1 ）社会保険

　①　健康保険：1998 年、日本の国民医療費は 29 兆 8,250 億円に達した。これは「国民皆保険」が実施されはじめた 1961 年当時の約 60 倍になる。その 85 ％が保険制度による負担で、残りが患者負担である。

　　　標準的企業労働者を例にとると、本人の傷病については費用の 80 ％、家族の場合は 70 ％が給付される。保険料は、本人と会社が 1/2 ずつ負担している。

　②　年金保険：「国民皆年金」は 1961 年から実施されている。その後の数次の制度改正を経て、全国民共通の「基礎年金」の設定と給付の平準化、給付の物価スライド制などが実現した。年金受給開始年齢は 2001 年より段階的に 60 歳から 65 歳にくり下げられる。

number of young people in the population is expected to drop sharply in coming years owing to the steady decline in the average number of children borne by each female throughout her lifetime (only 1.36 in 2000).

c) Social Security Services

In 1999, total social security benefits paid in Japan came to ¥75.04 trillion, an amount equivalent to 19% of national income and ¥592.3 thousand per capita.

The rate of increase in benefit payments over the 40-year period since 1955 was about 2.5 times that of national income, the result of higher payments to each individual and the aging of the population. The impact of population aging has become particularly great in Japan because the Japanese now have the longest life expectancy of any people in the world. The percentage of the population accounted for by persons aged 65 or more was 17.3% in 2000 and is expected to reach 25% by 2015. This has focused concern not only on how the system and its benefits can be improved but even more on how the costs should be borne.

Social security services in Japan can be broadly classified into social insurance, public assistance programs, and other public services.

1) Social Insurance
① Health insurance

The total spent on medical care in Japan during 1998 was ¥29.825 trillion, about 60 times more than when the system providing health insurance for the whole nation was launched in 1961. Eighty-five percent of the amount was covered by health insurance. Those receiving the care paid the rest.

In the model case for the average company employee, health insurance covers 80% of the expenses for illness or injury of the insured worker and 70% of the expenses incurred through illness or injury of dependent family members. The worker and the company each pay half of the insurance premium.
② Annuity insurance

An annuity system covering the whole nation was implemented in 1961. Having undergone several revisions over the years, it today provides a standard "basic annuity" for everyone and adopts a sliding scale for adjusting payments for the cost of living. The age at which those covered by the program become eligible for an annuity is being progressively

③ 雇用保険：この保険は、労働者が失業した場合、失業前の給与の 60～80 % を 3 カ月ないし 10 カ月間給付するものである。本人が報酬の 0.45 %、会社が 0.80 % の保険料を負担する。

④ 労働者災害補償保険（労災保険）：業務上の災害に対する労働者への補償プログラムである。たとえば、死亡すると、遺族に対して、死亡労働者の給与の 42～67 % の年金が支給される。保険料は、事業の種類ごとに定められた率によって、会社が負担する。

⑤ 介護保険（2000 年 4 月から実施）：痴呆や寝たきりなどで介護が必要になった場合、本人や家族の経済的負担を軽減することを主な目的とする保険である。40 歳以上の人は全員保険料を納めるが、この保険のサービスを受ける人は主に 65 歳以上になる。

2) 公的扶助・公的サービス
① 公的扶助：公的扶助のほとんどは生活困窮者に対する生活保護である。憲法に保障された「健康で文化的な生活水準」の保障に必要な最低生活費を国家が負担する。ただし、受給対象者は 1984 年以降年々減少している。

② 公的サービス：急速な高齢化に対応して、高齢者の医療・介護・施設・生きがい対策などの必要性がますます大きくなっている。これらに関して、90 年には福祉関係八法の改正と、高齢者保健福祉推進 10 ヶ年戦略（ゴールドプラン）の設定をした。ゴールドプランは、94 年見直された。
　一方、子供が健やかに生まれ育つ対策として、働く両親に対する育児休業、受給資格をもつ両親への児童手当などの制度が設けられている。また、心やからだの障害者は年金・教育サービス・就業支援・介護などを受けている。

raised from 60 to 65.

③ Unemployment insurance

This insurance program pays an unemployed worker monthly benefits amounting to between 60% and 80% of his or her former salary for a period ranging from 3 to 10 months. The worker pays 0.45% of his or her salary as premium, and the company 0.80%.

④ Workman's accident compensation insurance

This is a program for insuring workers against the hazards of the workplace. In the case of death, for instance, this accident insurance pays annual benefits equivalent to between 42 and 67% of the deceased worker's salary to his surviving family members. For this insurance, the worker's company pays premiums at the rate specified for the type of business concerned.

⑤ At-home care insurance (starting from April 2000):

This helps to pay for the care of dementia sufferers and the bedridden. It is intended mainly to ease the financial burden of such persons and their families. Everyone 40 or older is required to pay into the program. Services are in general available only to persons 65 or older.

2) Public Assistance Programs and Other Public Services

① Public assistance

Most of the programs in this category provide social welfare for the poor. The national government assumes responsibility for maintaining a minimum income level sufficient for a standard of living consistent with "wholesome and cultured living" as guaranteed by the Constitution. The number of people receiving this type of assistance has been declining since 1984.

② Other public services

With the rapid graying of the society has come a greater need to provide elderly people with medical care, nursing, senior citizen homes, and help in finding ways to enjoy their remaining years. The eight welfare-related laws were revised to this end in 1990, and a Gold Plan (a ten-year strategy for promoting the health and welfare of the elderly) was adopted in the same year and reviewed in 1994.

In contrast, for ensuring that children will have a chance to grow up strong and healthy, working women are allowed special holidays for child-care and qualifying parents can obtain child support. Mentally and physically handicapped

なお、この分野では民間サービスも活発化し、さまざまなサービスが受けられるようになっている。

(2)　教育

a)　学校教育制度

　日本の学校教育制度は、小学校6年、中学校3年、高等学校3年、大学4年が基本になっている。この制度は、第二次大戦後、新しい学校教育法（1947年）によって生まれたものである。

○小学校：子供は6歳で小学校に入学する。小学校では、社会における日常生活に必要な基礎科目を学ぶ。この初等教育期間では、1人の先生が全教科を教えることが多い。
○中学校：国家および社会の一員として必要な資質を養うために、中学校の生徒には、社会に役立つ職業についての基礎的知識・技能が教えられる。また、個性に応じて将来の進路を選択する能力を養う。科目ごとに違った先生が教える。
　この最初の9年間（小学校と中学校）が義務教育になっている。この間の就学率は100％である。憲法26条によって、親は子供に義務教育を受けさせる義務がある。また、市町村は義務教育のために学校を設置しなければならない。

○高等学校：中学校卒業生は入学試験に合格して、高校に入学する。高校では、学生は普通教育科目あるいは専門技能科目を学習する。これらの科目は、国家と社会に有為な人物として必要な資質を伸ばし、さらにそれぞれの使命感を養い、人生の将来の進路を定めさせることを目標にしたものである。専門技能科目は、工業・農業・商業・水産などに分類される。工業はさらに機械・電気・化学・土木・建築・情報処理・冶金などに分かれる。ほとんどの高校は都道府県立または私立である。

persons are given annuities, educational services, assistance in finding work, and nursing.

As the private sector is also becoming more active in this field, more kinds of services are becoming available.

(2) Education

a) The Japanese Educational System

The educational system of Japan is comprised fundamentally of 6 years of elementary school, 3 years of junior high school, 3 years of senior high school and 4 years of college. This system was set up by the new School Education Act enacted shortly after the Second World War (1947).

○ Elementary school: Children enter elementary school at age 6. In elementary school, students learn basic subjects necessary for daily life in society. During the elementary education period, one teacher generally teaches all the subjects in each class.

○ Junior high school: For cultivating the qualities that young people will need to play useful roles in the nation and society, junior high school students are taught fundamental knowledge and skills necessary for socially useful occupations. Their ability to choose the future path which best suits their individual capabilities is also nurtured. Each subject is taught by a different teacher.

The first nine years of education (elementary school and junior high school) are compulsory. The rate of school attendance by children during this period is therefore 100%. Under Article 26 of the Constitution, parents are obligated to send their children to school for this compulsory education, and cities, towns and villages are required to establish the schools needed.

○ Senior high school: Junior high school graduates enter senior high schools upon passing entrance examinations. High school students study general academic subjects or specialized technical subjects. The courses are aimed at developing the qualities required of capable members of society and at helping the students set their goals and decide their future course in life. Specialized vocational subjects include such categories as engineering, agriculture, commerce and fishery. Engineering subjects are subdivided into mechanics, electrical engineering, chemistry, civil engineering, architecture, information processing, metal-

○大学：高校を卒業してから大学に入りたい学生は、入学試験に合格しなければならない。大学での教育科目は、広く知識を授ける一般教養科目と、特定分野の学芸を深く学習・研究させるための専門科目からなっている。大学教育の目的は、知識・人格面とともに応用能力を十二分に開発することである。すなわち、大学は教育機関であると同時に学術研究機関としての役割ももっている。

　大学教育は一般には4年だが、医学・歯学部は6年である。大学院では、修士課程が2年、その上の博士課程が3年である（医学・歯学には修士課程がなく、4年の博士課程だけである）。大学は国立と私立が大部分である。しかし数は、私立大学の方が国立大学よりもはるかに多い。

　上記のほかに、短期大学（2年制）や高等専門学校（中学卒業後5年の課程）がある。また、小学校就学前に、幼稚園（1～3年）に入る子供も多い。

　［補］上記以外に特殊教育の学校・教員養成所・専修学校があり、さらに文部科学省所管外に職業訓練校や各種学校がある。また、高校以上の学校の専攻科・別科・特殊年限のコースなどもあるが、一切省略した。

　〔注〕日本の学校体系図は巻末〔統計資料〕欄(18)参照

b）教育制度の発展

　19世紀前半まで日本は封建時代だったが、国民の間には教育熱が高かった。当時は、武士階級が軍事担当者

lurgy etc. Almost all senior high schools are prefectural and municipal or private.

○ University: Students who want to enter a university after graduation from high school have to pass entrance examinations. Academic pursuits at the university center on a combination of general learning intended to give the student a wide knowledge base and specialized learning intended to allow the student to make deep study and research into a specific field of art or science. The goal of this education is to fully develop the student both in terms of knowledge and character and in terms of practical ability. In other words, the university is an educational organization and at the same time is an institution for academic research.

University education generally lasts 4 years, but medicine and dentistry require 6 years. In graduate school, the masters (M.A. or M.S.) program requires 2 years, while the subsequent doctoral (ph. D.) program requires an additional 3 years. (For medicine and dentistry, there is no master's program, but there is a doctoral program which requires 4 years.) Most of the universities are either national or private, but private universities far outnumber national universities.

In addition to the above, there are also junior colleges (2-year curriculum), as well as specialized vocational high schools (with a 5-year curriculum for junior high school graduates). Moreover, prior to entering elementary schools, many children enter kindergarten (1 to 3 years).

> Remark: Aside from the educational institutions mentioned in the foregoing there are also special education schools, teachers' training schools and special training schools, as well as vocational training schools and various other schools not under the jurisdiction of the Ministry of Education, Culture, Sports, Science, and Technology. Though not mentioned in the foregoing, high schools and universities also offer various courses in special studies, special courses and limited term courses. (Also see Note 18 "Japanese School System" in the reference section at the end of this book.)

b) The Development of the Educational System

Even during the feudal age, which lasted up to the first half of the nineteenth century, the people were enthusiastic about educa-

であると同時に、行政担当者であった。そのため、その務めに必要な教養・道徳・武芸を、武士の子弟たちに教える学校（藩校）が各地に設置されていた。また、農民や町民のためには、生活に必要な読み・書き・算数（そろばんを使った）を教える寺子屋が、全国に2万個所もつくられていた（文字通りには「寺の学校」だが、ふつうは、寺が運営していたわけではない）。この寺子屋への入学はまったく自由で、誰の強制もなく年限も決められていなかった。約40％の農民や町民が、寺子屋で学んだと推定される。

　明治時代に入り、日本の近代化にともなって、政府は西洋の学問を導入して産業・文化を発展させるために、小学校から大学まで一貫した教育制度を整えた。

　1872年学制が発布されたが、ここに、「むらに不学の戸なく、家に不学の人なからしめんことを期す」という言葉とともに、日本で初めて義務教育制度が制定された。

　1900年に、6歳からの4年制義務教育が発足した。この年の就学率は90％であった。1907年には6年制の義務教育となり、就学率は99％になった。

　それ以降、小学校・中学校・高等女学校・実業学校・高等学校・専門学校・大学などがたくさんつくられた。しかし、小学校以外は希望者が選ばれて入学するものであり、進学率は高くなかった。1935年には、中等教育機関（中学校・高等女学校・実業学校など）への進学率は18.5％で、高等教育機関（高等学校・専門学校・大学など）への進学率は3％であった。

　終戦後、1947年に教育制度は全面的に改正され、義務教育の期間は3年延長されて9年になった。

tion. At that time, the military (*samurai*) class was in charge of both military and political affairs. For this reason, schools (*han* schools—schools of the feudal domains) were established all over the country to teach the children of samurai families the cultural, moral and martial subjects necessary for their duties. There were also 20 thousand *terakoya* (literally "temple schools" though they were not generally operated by temples) set up throughout the country to teach reading, writing, and arithmetic (by use of the abacus) to farmers and townspeople who needed such skills in their daily life. Attendance at these temple schools was on a purely voluntary basis; no one was compelled to attend and there was no age limit on those who did. About 40% of the farmers and townspeople are estimated to have studied at such schools.

Early in the Meiji era, as Japan began undergoing modernization, the government established an integrated educational system from elementary school to university in order to foster the development of industry and culture through the introduction of Western learning.

This educational system was promulgated in 1872, and with the words, "We look forward to a time when there will be no illiteracy in any village house, no illiterate in any home," a compulsory educational system was established in Japan for the first time.

In 1900, children were required to begin the 4 years of compulsory education from age 6. In that year, the attendance rate of those required to go to school was 90%. In 1907, when compulsory education was increased to 6 years, the attendance rate was 99%.

After that, many elementary schools, middle schools, girls' high schools, vocational schools, higher schools, colleges and universities were founded. Since only selected students were admitted to schools above the elementary level, however, the proportion of students continuing on to higher education was not high. In 1935, the percentage of elementary school students going on to the secondary schools of the time (middle school, girls' high school, and vocational school) was 18.5%, and the percentage going on to receive higher education (higher school, college, university) was 3%.

After the Second World War, in 1947, the educational system was completely revised, and compulsory education was extended

c ）大　学

　日本で最も古い大学は、東京大学である。江戸時代、幕府が設立した「開成所」と「医学所」がその前身で、1877 年両校が合併して東京大学が設立された。以後 1940 年までに、次の国立総合大学が設置された。すなわち、京都大学・東北大学・九州大学・北海道大学・大阪大学・名古屋大学である。

　このほかに、一橋大学・東京工業大学・東京外国語大学・大阪外国語大学・筑波大学・お茶の水女子大学・奈良女子大学・東京芸術大学など合計 99 校の国立大学がある（2001 年）。

　公立大学は、東京都立大学や大阪市立大学など 74 校が設置されている（2001 年）。

　また私立大学は 496 校あり、慶応大学と早稲田大学が「私学の双璧」といわれている。キリスト教系の大学としては、同志社大学・立教大学・上智大学・関西学院大学・神戸女学院大学・青山学院大学・国際基督教大学などがある。

　上記 669 校の大学のうち 479 校（国立大学 99 校、公立大学 50 校、私立大学 300 校）には、大学院がおかれている。このほかに、559 校の短期大学がある（2001 年）。大学・短期大学・大学院生の総数は約 311 万人である。

　1972 年、国際連合の決議によって国連大学が東京に設置された。これは学生のいない高度の研究機関である。地球環境、都市・人口、世界平和等の様々な課題に取り組んでいる。95 年には研修・研究センターも完成した。

d ）進　学

　近代日本では、職業につくための条件は能力本位であって、出身階級・家柄・親の財産などはほとんど関係が

by 3 years, to a total of 9 years.

c) Universities

The oldest national university in Japan is the University of Tokyo. The Kaiseijo and Igakusho (Medical Institute) founded by the Shogunate during the Edo period were the predecessors of Tokyo University, which was established in 1877 by the merging of these two schools. The following national universities were founded between 1877 and 1940: Kyoto University, Tohoku University, Kyushu University, Hokkaido University, Osaka University and Nagoya University.

Others among the total of 99 national universities (2001) include Hitotsubashi University, Tokyo Institute of Technology, Tokyo University of Foreign Studies, Osaka University of Foreign Studies, Tsukuba University, Ochanomizu Women's University, Nara Women's University, and the Tokyo National University of Fine Arts and Music.

Prefectural and municipal universities number 74 (2001). These include such schools as Tokyo Metropolitan University and Osaka City University.

There are 496 private universities, among which Keio University and Waseda University are referred to as the "twin jewels of the private universities." Notable Christian universities include Doshisha University, Rikkyo (St. Paul's) University, Sophia University, Kwansei Gakuin University, Kobe College, Aoyama Gakuin University and International Christian University.

Of the total of 669 universities of all types, 479 (99 national, 50 prefectural and municipal, and 300 private) have postgraduate courses. In addition, there are 559 junior colleges (2001). The total enrollment of universities and colleges is 3.11 million.

Under a United Nations resolution, a United Nations University was established in Tokyo in 1972. A university without students, it is basically an institute for high level research. It conducts research on a variety of topics, including the world environment, urban and population issues and world peace. A new United Nations University Institute of Advanced Studies was completed at the University in 1995.

d) Ascending the Educational Ladder

In modern Japan, securing a job depends principally on one's personal capabilities. Social background, family lineage and

ない。

その能力の端的な尺度は、どんな学校で何を学んだかであるとされている。したがって、家が貧しくとも、学校を卒業して良い職業につき、高い社会的地位を得ることが人々の念願になっている。

さらに近代化以前から、日本人には読み書きを好む国民性があり、日本社会には教育を尊重する気風があった。

このようなことから、皆が競って進学し、できれば大学まで行こうとする。そのため、進学率が高くなった。

2001年における小学校および中学校での義務教育就学率は100％、高等学校への進学率は96.9％、短期大学および大学への進学率は48.6％、大学院などへの進学率は10.3％である。小学校入学前の幼稚園にも61.1％が就園している。

近年大学進学率が高くなっているが、これは子供を大学に進学させる経済的なゆとりができたことにもよる。

多くの者が大学に進学するので、大学間・学生間のレベル差が大きい。そのため、今では単に大学を卒業したことだけでは、能力があることの証明とはされなくなっている。しかし、伝統ある大学の研究水準は、諸外国の一流大学に劣らず、入学の競争も激しい。

日本では有名校への志願倍率が高く、小学校から「受験戦争」に巻き込まれる。その戦争に勝つ手助けを学校だけでなく、家庭教師、塾や予備校がする。2000年のデータでは小学生でさえ36.7％も塾に通っている。大学入試に失敗すると一年後再挑戦する"浪人"が多数出ている。

wealth have almost no bearing.

Nowadays, the direct measure of this ability is what schools one attended and what subjects one studied. Consequently, all Japanese, even the poor, dream of graduating from a prestigious school, finding a good job, and thereby attaining high social status.

Even before the modernization process, love of reading and writing were part of the Japanese national character and respect for learning was a characteristic attitude among the Japanese.

Because of these factors, everyone competes for opportunities in higher education, and tries to enter a university if at all possible. So, the proportion of students going on to higher education has become quite high.

In 2001, the attendance rate at elementary and junior high schools (compulsory education) was 100%. Of those graduating from junior high school, 96.9% continued on to senior high school, while 48.6% of senior high school graduates continued on to junior college or university and 10.3% of university graduates continued on to graduate studies. The percentage of preschoolers attending kindergarten was 61.1%.

The percentage of students entering university has risen in recent years, partly because more families can now afford to send their children to college.

Because of the huge numbers of people going on to universities, the differences in quality between universities and between their students have become more pronounced. As a result, the mere fact of graduation from a university is no longer considered proof of ability. Nonetheless, the standards of scholarship of those universities which have long and proud scholarly tradition compare favorably with those of the best schools anywhere in the world, and the competition for entering them is extremely intense.

As famous Japanese schools receive many more applications than they can accept, students are frequently drawn into the competition to get in, known as the "entrance examination war," while still in elementary school. The main help in winning this war comes not from the public schools but from private tutors, cram schools and preparatory schools that specialize in exam-taking. According to 2000 figures, even 36.7% of elementary school students attended a *juku* (cram school). Many students fail to get into the school of their choice on the first try and have

e）学生生活

　　日本の大学では、講義が一般的な教授法になっている。施設や教授陣の割に学生数が多いこともあって、何百人もの学生が一つの講義を聴くことも珍しくない。自分の希望する教授に直接個人的な指導を受けたい学生は、ゼミナールを受講する。ゼミナールでは課題が出されたり、グループで調査したり実験したりする。

　　日本の学期は、国の会計年度と同じである。4月から翌年3月までを1年とし、その間を2学期（4〜9月、10月〜3月）に分けていることろがほとんどである。

　　自宅から遠く離れた大学に入学すると、寮に入るか下宿をする。

　　余暇の時間には、クラブ活動・旅行・アルバイト（学費やレジャー費に充てるため）をしている。アルバイトは、大学生にとっては日常的なものになっている。

f）日本人の外国語会話能力

　　19世紀の末まで、中学校以上の理・工系の学科ではイギリスやアメリカの教科書が広く使われていた。また、外国語で講義をする外国人の先生がかなりいた。そのため、このころの教育を受けた人には、外国語の上手な人も多かった。しかし、その後次第に日本語の教科書ができ、学校で外国語を使うことは、外国語の時間に限られるようになってしまった。

　　また、外国語の勉強はもっぱら外国文献から新知識を得るための手段と見られていた。したがって、日本の外国語教育は次第に読み書き、とくに読みに重点がおかれた。このためほとんどの日本人の外国語能力は、時間を長くかけている割には、会話能力が低い。

　　しかし近年、国際化の進展にともなって、外国との往来が非常に増加した。そのため、日本人が外国人と接する機会が多くなり、外国語とくに英語で会話する必要性が高くなった。

to wait another year to take the exam again.

e) Student Life

In Japanese universities, the lecture is the usual method of instruction. Partly because of limited facilities and the high ratio of students to professors, it is not uncommon for lectures to be attended by hundreds of students. Those students who want to receive direct and personal guidance from their professors attend seminars. In a seminar, specific topics are proposed, and investigation and experiments are carried out by the group.

The Japanese academic year coincides with the Japanese fiscal year. From April to March of the following year constitutes one year, which at most schools is divided into two semesters (April to September; October to March).

Students who attend universities far away from their homes usually live in dormitories or in rooming houses.

During their free time, students engage in various club activities, travel, or do part-time work (to help pay tuition or to earn extra income for recreational purposes). Side jobs have become a part of the daily routine for most university students.

f) Ability of Japanese to Speak Foreign Languages

Until the end of the nineteenth century, English and American textbooks were widely used in science and engineering courses from middle school onwards. There were also quite a few foreign teachers who taught in their own language. So among those who were educated in that period, many were fluent in foreign languages. With the gradual production of textbooks written in Japanese, however, use of foreign languages at school came to be limited to foreign language study courses.

The study of foreign languages has therefore long been considered mainly as a means of deriving new knowledge from foreign books. As a result, the emphasis in foreign language study was on reading and writing, especially reading. This is why the speaking ability of most Japanese is poor considering the great amount of time they devote to foreign language study.

In recent years, however, Japan's internationalization has led to a sharp increase in the number of people traveling in and out of the country. This has given the Japanese more opportunities to come into direct contact with foreigners and increased their need to be conversant in foreign languages, especially English.

こうした背景のなかで、地方自治体主導による、国際理解を向上させる教育プログラムも盛んである。地域によって内容にいくらかの違いがあるが、これらには、小学校レベルでの英語教育、高校生の海外派遣、語学指導を支援する外国青年の招致、高等学校の英語科の設置、海外に長期滞在した帰国子女に対する特別教育の配慮などがある。

いっぽう、企業における英会話・国際化教育も盛んである。

(3)　家庭生活

a）結　婚

1995 年以降、日本では、約 90 ％が「恋愛結婚」である。このほかに見合結婚がある。

見合結婚の場合は、間をとりもつ紹介者（仲人・なこうど）が、結婚を希望する男と女を引き合わせる。二人はお互いに相手を観察して、結婚の相手として好ましいかどうかを判断する（見合）。このとき双方の親が立ち合うことが多い。その後しばらく交際して、結婚するかどうかをきめる。お互いに交際のなかった男女を引き合わせる場合の有効な手段であり、また交際範囲の狭い人にとっても、良い相手を見つける有効な方式である。

仲人は、これを職業としているのではなく、好意によりあるいは奉仕として行っており、世話ずきな年配者に多い。

見合結婚の長所としては、人生経験豊かな仲人が双方の条件を見極めて、お互いに結婚相手として適当と判断される人を組み合わせ、結婚後も相談相手になることなどがあげられる。

恋愛結婚の場合は、相手は同じ学校・同じ職場、地域活動・趣味のサークルなどの友人・先輩・後輩さらにその兄弟・姉妹などさまざまである。

Local governments have taken the lead in responding to this situation and are progressively introducing new educational programs for promoting international understanding. While these differ from one locality to another, they include the teaching of English at the elementary school level, overseas tours for high school students, the inviting of young foreigners to Japan to help with language instruction, the establishment of English departments in high schools, and special educational assistance for boys and girls of families returning to Japan after long stays overseas.

Many private companies also actively conduct spoken English and international awareness courses.

(3) Home Life

a) Marriage

Since 1995, about 90% of all marriages in Japan have been "love marriages," the remainder being arranged marriages (*omiai*).

In an arranged marriage, a man and a woman, both of whom are seeking a marriage partner, are brought together by a go-between (*nakodo*) so that they can see and get to know each other. The parents of both sides are often present at the initial meeting. After this, the prospective couple meet each other socially over a period of time and then eventually decide whether or not to get married or not. Such an arrangement provides an effective way of bringing together men and women who have little opportunity to meet persons of the opposite sex and is also an effective way of finding marriage partners for those whose social circles are rather limited.

The go-betweens for arranged marriages are usually not professional matchmakers, but persons who like to help purely out of goodwill.

One of the merits of an arranged marriage is that the nakodo, with his or her experience and familiarity with the situation of both sides, can bring together people who in the nakodo's judgment would make suitable marriage partners. Another is that even after the marriage the nakodo continues to offer advice and discuss problems with the married couple.

Mates in "love marriages" are selected, for example, from

平均初婚年齢は、男は28.8歳、女は27.0歳である（2000年）。

b）結婚式・披露宴

結婚式は神前で行うことが多い。神前で新郎と新婦が結婚の誓約を行った後、三つ重ねの盃で献酬を行う。献酬の媒妁（ばいしゃく）は、仲人に代わって巫女（みこ）が行う（元来、媒妁は仲人の役目であった。このため結婚式では、仲人は媒妁人と呼ばれる）。新郎新婦のほか神主・媒妁人・両親・親族が出席する（恋愛結婚の場合も、結婚式には媒妁人を立てる場合が多い）。

仏式やキリスト教式で、結婚式をあげる者もいる。

結婚式のあと、親族のほか友人や関係のある人々を招待して披露宴を開く。ここで媒妁人は出席者に新郎新婦を紹介する。披露宴は洋式で行うことが多い。

結婚式・披露宴では新郎はモーニングやタキシード、または和服の正装を着用し、新婦は和式の結婚衣装を着ることが多い。披露宴の途中、新婦は中座して衣装を換える（お色なおし）。いろいろの衣装を見せて、美しさを披露するためであろう。披露宴のあと、新郎新婦は新婚旅行に出発する。

c）家族構成

現在の日本では、家族計画の考え方が普及し、子供の数は少なくなっている。また、戦後「家」の観念の変化のほか、深刻な住宅事情ともあいまって小家族化が進み、両親と子供だけという、いわゆる核家族が増えており、一世帯あたり平均家族数は2.63人となっている（2001年）。

among friends and colleagues who attend the same school, work at the same place or are members of the same club or circle, or the brothers and sisters of such people.

The mean age at first marriage for Japanese men is 28.8, and for Japanese women is 27.0 (2000).

b) Wedding Ceremonies and Banquets

Most weddings are conducted according to Shinto rites. At the shrine, after the bride and groom have exchanged nuptial vows, they drink in turn from each of a set of three *sake* cups. In this exchange of drinks, a maiden of the shrine performs the *baishaku* (literally "intermediation in pouring sake"). (Originally, this was the function of the *nakodo*, or "go-between." So, even to this day the nakodo at a wedding ceremony is called the *baishakunin*.) Besides the couple, a Shinto priest, the nakodo, the parents and other relatives also take part in the wedding ceremony. (Even in the case of a "love marriage," someone usually plays the formal role of a "go-between.")

Some couples are married in Buddhist or Christian ceremonies.

Other relatives, friends and acquaintances are invited to join the immediate families of the couple in a wedding banquet following the wedding ceremony. At the banquet, the go-between introduces the newlyweds to the guests. In the cities, most wedding banquets are Western style.

At most weddings and wedding banquets, the bridegroom wears morning dress, a tuxedo or a formal *kimono*, while the bride usually wears a wedding kimono. Partway through the banquet, the bride leaves the room to change her costume. These changes of attire are to display various costumes and to emphasize the beauty of the bride. After the banquet, the newlyweds depart on their honeymoon.

c) Family Structure

With the spread of family planning in contemporary Japan, the number of children per family has decreased. After World War II, changes in the concept of *ie* (family) together with an acute housing shortage gave a strong impetus to the trend toward smaller families, so that now an increasing number of households consist only of parents and their children (nuclear family). As a result, the number of people per household now averages 2.63

欧米諸国ほどではないにしても、以前のように祖父・祖母と同居することが減少しているため、高齢者から生活の知恵を受け継ぐことが少なくなっている。住宅事情が許せば、老夫婦と若い世代の家族とが「スープのさめない距離」に住むことを理想とする考えの人も多い。近年の経済成長の結果所得水準も向上してきたため、三世代同居を可能とする規模の住宅を持ちたいという考えもでてきている。

　また、日本でも古くからの地域共同体が崩れ、高齢者同士の交際の場が減ってきている。このため、とくに都市において孤独な高齢者が増えており、高齢者問題が一つの大きな社会問題となりつつある。

d) 女性の職業と家事

　2001年、日本女性の就労可能な人口は、約半数の2,760万人である（除く、就学・家事・老齢などの事情で働けない女性）。これは15歳以上の女性人口のおよそ半数である。その約95％が仕事に就いている。働く女性の中心になっているのは、35〜54歳の年齢層である。農林業以外の一般産業では、その過半数（67％）が既婚者である。このように近年、女性の職場への進出はますます活発になっている。その背景としては、まず女性の高学歴化の進展があげられる。2001年、短期大学以上の進学率は、男性48.7％に対し、女性は48.5％であった。つぎに、女性が仕事につきやすい条件が整備されてきた。すなわち、サービス産業の拡大、フレックスタイムの導入などによる仕事環境の変化である。さらに、1980年代後半からは、日本の労働力の絶対量の不足も要因となっている。

　女性の進出分野も広がり、企業経営者・管理職・専門職など、職場の第一線で働く女性も急増している。また今では、女性の国会議員・地方議会議員・上級公務員・

persons (2001).

Although the situation may not have reached the extent it has in Europe and the United States, still, differently from what was often the case before World War II, fewer and fewer children in Japan are growing up in the company of their grandparents. As a result, nowadays there are very few children who can benefit from direct contact with the worldly wisdom of the elderly. However, many Japanese think that it would be ideal, housing conditions permitting, if the older and younger generations could live close together ("close enough to bring over some soup before it cools" as the Japanese expression goes). In recent years, as a result of economic growth and the consequent rise in the level of income, it has become possible for some families to consider acquiring a house that can accommodate three generations under one roof.

Moreover, even in Japan the sense of community has become weaker in many regions, so the number of places where the elderly meet socially has been steadily decreasing. In urban areas, especially, the number of elderly people who suffer from loneliness is growing. The plight of senior citizens is becoming an increasingly serious social problem.

d) Women at Work and in the Household

In 2001, 27.60 million Japanese women were potential members of the workforce (not including those who were prevented from working because they were attending school, engaged in housekeeping, too old, etc.). This is about half of all women aged 15 and older. Of these, about 95% had jobs. Most were between 35 and 54 years old. Outside the agricultural and forestry industries, the majority (67%) were married. These figures indicate that women are entering the workforce in ever greater numbers. One reason behind this is the increase in the number of women going on to higher levels of education. In 2001, the percentage of women continuing onto junior college or university was 48.5%, as against 48.7% for men. Changing conditions have also made it easier for women to go to work. These include the growth of the service industry, the introduction of flextime and other changes in the working environment. Another factor has been the absolute shortage of workers in Japan from the latter half of the 1980s.

The jobs in which women are rapidly becoming more involved

大学教授なども珍しくない。

　一方、まだ女性労働者にはパートで働く人が多く、ま
た男性との賃金格差がある場合も多い。しかし、1986
年4月に施行された男女雇用機会均等法をはじめとして、
その後の97～99年のこの法律と関連の法律改正により、
女性をとりまく社会制度面の就労環境は急速に変化して
いる。こうした変化によって、女性の社会進出やステイ
タスの向上が一層進んできている。
　このように女性の社会進出が活発になった反面、女性
の結婚年齢が年々高くなり、出生児の数が減少している。
2000年における女性の平均初婚年齢は27.0歳で、1965
年に比べると2.5歳高くなった。結婚しない女性の数も
増えている。
　日本では、女性が一生の間に生む子供の平均数が
2000年には1.36人になり、長期的には日本の人口は減
少に向かうと憂慮されている。政府は、こうした現状を
ふまえ、女性の仕事と家事・育児とが両立する条件づく
りのため、児童手当制度の改正、育児休業法の施行など
の施策を進めている。
　家事労働は、現在も大勢としては女性が行っている。
家庭電気機器の普及により、従来よりかなり軽減された
とはいえ、女性の家事労働負担は依然として大きい。
　また、日本社会の高齢化にともない、家庭における高
齢者の介護が増加しているが、その負担もより多く女性
にかかる傾向がある。この問題も日本が解決しなければ
ならない大きな課題である。

e）単身赴任

　日本では夫婦が仕事のために一時別居することは珍し
くない。ことに海外へ短期間行く場合は、家族をともな
わないのが普通である。
　長期間の場合でも単身赴任するのは、主として子供の
教育のため、妻が日本に残らざるをえないからである。
子供を外国の学校へ入れた場合、言葉の関係から学力が
低くなってしまい、日本に帰ってから非常に苦しむとい

extend right up to such top echelon positions as business executive, manager and specialist, and it is no longer uncommon for women to become members of national and regional legislative bodies, high-ranking public officials and university professors.

On the other hand, a large proportion of working women are still employed part time and women's wages are often lower than men's. Still, the working environment of women is improving rapidly, thanks in large part to the Law concerning Equal Opportunity and Treatment between Men and Women in Employment implemented in April 1986 and amendments made to this and related laws between 1997 and 1999. Because of this, women are playing increasingly important roles outside the home and enjoying rising social status.

As women have become more active throughout society, they have begun to marry later and have fewer children. In 2000, the mean age for first marriage for women was 27.0 years, 2.5 years higher than in 1965. The number of unmarried women has also increased.

The average number of children born per woman per lifetime in Japan was 1.36 in 2000, posing a danger of a decrease in the Japanese population in the long term. The Government is therefore working on a revision of the child's allowance system, the establishment of a law requiring employers to give working mothers time off for child-care, and other measures that will make it easier for working women to raise a family without giving up their jobs.

Most housework is still done by women. Although home appliances have considerably lightened a housewife's tasks, a woman's work in the home remains heavy.

Much of the work of caring for the aged also tends to fall on women and is increasing as the population grows older. This is another major problem which Japan has to solve.

e) Taking a Post Abroad without One's Family

In Japan, it is not unusual for a husband to live temporarily apart from his wife for business reasons. Especially if a man is going abroad for a short while on business, it is quite common for him to go without his family.

Even when a man is sent abroad for a long period, it is quite usual for the wife to remain in Japan for the sake of the children's education. If the children were to go to school abroad, their

われ、このことが現在大きな問題になっている。

　　外国への赴任の場合だけでなく、国内の転勤の場合で
も子供の教育のため、夫だけ単身赴任するケースがかな
り多い。

(4)　環境保全

a)　戦後の日本の環境問題

　　日本は戦後の復興期とこれに続く 1950 年代後半から
の高度成長期における経済発展優先の政策を推進する過
程で水俣病、イタイイタイ病などいわゆる 4 大公害とよ
ばれる深刻な社会問題を経験した。しかしこれらの問題
は、このほかの大気・水質・土壌の汚染、騒音、地盤沈
下など環境基本法にうたわれている典型 7 公害を含めて、
その後の政府の環境関係の法制整備、企業の公害防止の
技術開発、膨大な公害防止投資などの努力により、おお
むね収束した。

　　こうした経済成長と公害防止の両立を実現した日本
の努力と実績は、国際的にも広く認められ、1992 年の
リオデジャネイロでの「地球サミット」でも高く評価さ
れた。このような他国に例を見ない経験からの教訓を、
今後国際社会に有効に還元するのは日本の責務であると
いえる。

b)　循環型経済社会の構築

　　人類が 20 世紀に展開してきた生活様式、すなわ「大
量生産」、「大量消費」、「大量廃棄」型の経済・社会活動
は、一面では人類に多大な豊かさと利便性をもたらした。
しかしその反面、このような 20 世紀型の活動様式は自

education would be handicapped by their deficiency in the foreign language, and upon their return to Japan it would be extremely difficult for them to catch up with their classmates. This is becoming an increasingly difficult problem.

Not only when a man is sent abroad, but even when he is assigned to a post elsewhere in Japan, it is common for the husband to go alone to avoid disrupting the children's education.

(4) Preservation of the Environment

a) Environmental Problems in Post-War Japan

During the reconstruction period following the Second World War and the period of rapid economic growth that started in the late 1950s, Japan gave top priority to economic development. In the course of pursuing this objective, however, the country experienced a number of serious social issues, most notably the so-called Four Major Pollution Issues (including the mercury pollution that led to the Minamata disease outbreak and the cadmium pollution determined as the cause of the itai-itai (pain -pain) malady). These problems, as well as the other seven typical kinds of pollution identified by Japan's Basic Law for Environmental Pollution Control (air, water, soil and noise pollution, ground subsidence, etc.), were substantially overcome through tougher environmental protection legislation and the efforts of the industrial sector, including development of effective antipollution technologies and huge outlays for installing pollution control facilities

Japan's success in simultaneously achieving economic growth and environmental production, and the effort behind it, attracted even international attention. It was, for instance, spoken of favorably at the Earth Summit held in Rio de Janeiro in 1992. This unique experience provides Japan with many valuable lessons that it must now endeavor to share effectively with other members of the international community.

b) Building a Zero-Waste Economy and Society

The 20th century saw the development of a way of life that put "mass production," "mass consumption" and "mass disposal" at the center of economic and social activity. While this life-style brought people considerable affluence and convenience, the harm

然本来の循環を阻害し、これまでの延長線上では現在の
ライフスタイルそのものの維持が限界に達しているとい
う認識が世界で共有のものとなりつつある。このような
認識から、21世紀の経済社会のあり方として考えられ
たのが「循環型経済社会」である。

　「循環型経済社会」とは、廃棄物の発生を抑制（リデ
ュース）し、廃棄物を再使用（リユース）し、再生可能
なものを再生利用（リサイクル）し、最後に残ったもの
を適切に処理するという、天然資源消費抑制型・環境負
荷低減型の経済社会をいう（循環型社会基本法）。

（法制整備）

　政府は、先の循環型の必要性についての世界共通の基
本認識と上のような事実の認識に立って、2000年「循
環型社会形成推進基本法」を制定し、これとともに従来
の環境基本計画を見直し、「持続可能な社会」に向けた、
「循環」・「共生」・「参加」・「国際的取組み」を基調とす
る基本理念を明らかにした。

　また、政府はこの理念実現のため、容器や家電などの
廃棄物のリサイクル関連法を次々と制定した。

（産業界の取り組み）

　経団連は1997年、環境自主行動計画とあわせて廃棄
物自主行動計画を策定した。廃棄物自主行動計画には
35業種が参加し、各業界ごとにリサイクル率、最終処
分量などの数値目標を設定し、毎年業界ごとの推進状況
をフォローアップしている。

　その1例を鉄鋼業で見ると次のようである。新日本製
鉄の2001年の「環境報告」によると、水の循環率90％、
副生ガス活用率100％、高炉スラグなどのセメント、路
盤材などへの再資源化率99％、排熱回収による鉄鋼製
造エネルギー効率60％などとなっている。また、他産
業で発生する廃棄タイヤ、自治体が回収した家庭からの
プラスチック容器などもコークス炉に装入し製鉄原料な
どとして利用し、CO_2の削減にも貢献している。

it continues to do to the natural environment has prompted an emerging global consensus that it is untenable in its present form. Against this backdrop, the Japanese Government is promoting a new economic and social concept for the 21st century that it calls the Zero-Waste Economy and Society.

The Basic Law on the Zero-Waste Economy and Society envisions a new economic and social order in which consumption of natural resources is minimized and the load on the environment reduced by decreasing the amount of waste generated, reusing discarded products, recycling waste materials whenever possible, and disposing of anything that cannot be reused or recycled in the optimum way.

(Improving the legal system)

In 2000, convinced that the international community had reached a basic understanding on the need to establish zero-waste recycling, the Japanese Government enacted the Basic Law for Building the Zero-Waste Society. In parallel, it reassessed existing environmental initiatives and also announced its intention to work toward establishing a sustainable society based on a philosophy that stresses Recycling, Symbiosis, Participation, and Global Perspective.

As a first step toward realizing this goal, a series of laws were passed to promote recycling of containers, home appliances and a variety of other waste materials.

(Industry Efforts)

In 1997, the Federation of Economic Organizations (Keidanren) added momentum to its Voluntary Action Plan by launching an initiative aimed at improving the handling of industrial wastes. The 35 industrial sectors participating in the initiative are assigned sector-specific numerical targets for recycling rate, final disposal volume and the like. Each sector's performance is audited annually.

One participating company is Nippon Steel Corporation (NSC), a member of the steel industry sector. In its 2001 Environment Report, NSC says it has achieved a water recycle rate of 90%, regenerated gas utilization rate of 100%, reclamation rate of blast furnace slag for cement and paving of 99%, and waste heat recovery enabling a steelmaking energy efficiency of 60%. The company also says it helps to cut CO_2 generation by converting waste materials from outside the company, like plastic containers from household trash and discarded tires, into coke that it uses

また、産業界の努力の一端は、環境マネジメントシステムの国際規格 ISO 14001 の取得件数の国際比較にみることができる。わが国の 1999 年における同規格の認証件数は 3,015 件で第 2 位のイギリスの 1,492 件の 2 倍以上で世界第 1 位である。以下第 3 位ドイツの 962 件、第 4 位スウェーデンの 851 件、第 5 位アメリカの 636 件と続いている。その後、2001 年においては中小事業所、サービス業への普及もあり、5,585 件に達している。

（自治体、市民の取り組み）

　循環型経済社会をめざす資源のリサイクル推進には市民の積極的参加が不可欠である。しかしながら、日本は市民レベルの環境保全への危機感、循環型社会構築の必要性についての認識が浸透しているとはいいがたい状況にある。ゴミの分別排出も自治体により大きなばらつきがみられ、廃棄物の不法投棄も深刻な問題である。今後国、自治体、市民、企業の一体となった一層の努力が求められている。

　このように持続可能な循環型経済社会の構築には、大気環境の保全、水環境の保全、土壌・地盤環境の保全、廃棄物・リサイクル対策、化学物質の環境リスク対策など取り組むべき課題が多いが、つぎにきわめて重要かつグローバルな問題としての地球温暖化防止対策についてやや詳しく述べることとする。

c) 地球温暖化防止

（地球温暖化問題の特質）

　地球温暖化は、科学の発達によって「発見された」環境問題である。大気中の二酸化炭素（CO_2）濃度の上昇が地球温暖化の原因になりうるという理論は、19 世紀末にアレニウスによって発表された。それから約 1 世紀をへたのち、コンピュータによる観測・予測技術により、これが地球の将来を脅かす重大な問題として認識された。いまだ不確定要素は多いが、今後の政策決定に不可欠な情報が提供されるようになった。

to make steel.

One measure of a country's environmental protection performance is how it compares internationally in number of ISO14001 accreditations received. (ISO14001 is the international standard for industry environmental management systems.) As of 1999, Japan ranked first with 3,015 accreditations, more than twice the 1,492 received by the United Kingdom in second place. Germany placed third with 962, Sweden fourth with 851, and the United States fifth with 636. By 2001, the number of accreditations acquired by Japanese companies had risen to 5,585. Small businesses and service sector companies accounted for much of the increase.

(Efforts of Local Governments and Ordinary Citizens)

The resource recycling needed to realize a zero-waste society cannot be achieved without the help of ordinary citizens. Unfortunately, the average Japanese is still complacent about environmental preservation and not very responsive to the need to build a zero-waste society. Most households separate their trash to some extent, but the degree of compliance varies greatly from one community to another. And illegal waste disposal is also a serious problem. Local governments, citizens and companies will need to make a considerably greater and better coordinated effort from now on.

Preservation of air, water and soil/ground quality, implementation of effective waste and recycling measures, and better management of the environmental risks of chemical substances are just a few of the many issues that need to be tackled on the road to building a sustainable zero-waste economy/society. Another, and one of profound worldwide significance, is global warming. That is taken up is some detail in the following section.

c) Prevention of Global Warming

(Special nature of the global warming problem)

Global warming is an environmental problem discovered as a result of advances in science. The theory that a rise in the amount of carbon dioxide (CO_2) in the earth's atmosphere might cause global warming was first put forward by Svante Arrhenius in the late 19th century. It was not until a century later that the application of computer-based observation and prediction technologies brought home the fact that global warming poses a very real and serious threat to the future of the planet. In recent years, while

地球温暖化による将来の影響については、国際公式機関である「気候変動に関する政府間パネル（IPCC）」（1988 設置）は、次のように予測している。すなわち温暖化がこのまま進み、両極大陸の氷の流出、海水の膨張などにより、現在の海水面が 40 cm 上昇したと仮定すると、高潮による浸水を受ける人口が全世界で 7,500 万人から 2 億人増加すると予測される。また、海水面の上昇と熱帯低気圧の強大化によって、アジアの温帯、熱帯の沿岸地方に住む人々が移住を強いられ、マラリアなどの感染症も増大すると予測される。これにより途上国と先進国との格差が一層拡大することも憂慮されている。大気中の二酸化炭素濃度が 2050 年に産業革命以前の 2 倍に達すると仮定した場合の被害総額は年間 3,000 億ドルに達すると試算されているが、一方で最近欧米でも異なる見解が発表されてきており、引き続き冷静な議論が望まれるところである。

　地球温暖化は、人間のほとんどすべての社会活動がその原因となりうるという事情から、その解決に向けては必然的に全地球的協調が要求される。これが地球温暖化が典型的なグローバルな問題であるとされる理由である。

　また、この解決に向けては科学技術的手法のみならず、各種の政策手法をもあわせて実施することが要求される。

（地球温暖化防止の国際的取組み―京都議定書―）

　地球温暖化防止に向けた国際的な取り組みの努力は 1985 年以来のたび重なる国際会議における真剣かつ激烈な討議に現れている。このような中で 1997 年 12 月、「気候変動枠組条約第 3 回条約国会議（COP 3）」が京都において開かれ、『京都議定書』が採択された。

　この議定書は、先進国の温室効果ガスの排出削減につき拘束力のある数値目標を定め、各国の国情に応じた対策の実施を求めているほか、国際的に協調して目標を達成するための仕組みとして、排出量取引、共同実施、グリーン開発メカニズムいわゆる「京都メカニズム」を導

many uncertain elements still exist, global warming-related information indispensable for making policy decisions has become increasingly available.

The Intergovernmental Panel on Climate Change (IPCC), the international organization established in 1988 to deal with the global warming issue, did a study on the assumption that the earth's climate continues to heat up at the current rate. Its conclusion was that by the 2080s the sea water surface will have risen some 40 centimeters owing to melting of the polar ice masses and that the number of people affected by high tides worldwide will increase from 75 million to 200 million. It predicts that people living in costal regions in the Asian temperate and tropical zones will be forced to migrate and that the incidence of malaria and other infectious diseases will rise. This, it is feared, will further expand the gap between the developing and industrially advanced nations. According to one estimate, an increase in atmospheric carbon dioxide to double the pre-industrial revolution level by 2050 would cause damages totaling 300 billion dollars annually. Recently, however, contrary opinions are being heard from Europe and the United States. Such differing views are best resolved through continued calm discussions.

As almost every human social activity can be a cause of global warming, the search for solutions naturally requires broad international cooperation. This is what makes global warming a classic example of an international problem.

It is, moreover, a problem that cannot be solved only by scientific and technical methods. Government's around the world will also have to tackle it by implementing a broad range of strategies.

(The Kyoto Protocol)

The international community's effort to find ways of preventing global warming is reflected in the serious and often fervid debates that have taken place at numerous world conferences. One of these was the Third Conference of the Parties to the UN Framework Convention on Climate Change (COP3) that was held in Kyoto in December 1997 and led to the adoption of the Kyoto Protocol.

This Protocol sets legally binding numerical targets for the reduction of carbon dioxide and other greenhouse gas emissions by the industrially advanced nations and calls on every country

入するとともに、目標達成にあたって森林などのいわゆるシンク（吸収源）による吸収量を算入できるようにした。しかし、諸課題の最終合意は今後の交渉に持ち越されいる。

　　加えて、この間アメリカのブッシュ政権は京都議定書を支持しない立場を表明した。日本は京都議定書の発効のためにも、アメリカの再参加をめざし、ねばりづよい働きかけを続けている。
（日本に課せられた目標と課題）
　　日本は温室効果ガス（CO_2、メタンなど）の排出量において第4位である（1997年の全世界の排出量232億トン中、アメリカ23.6%、中国14.5%、ロシア14.5%、日本5.0%）。また、途上国にくらべると1人当たりの排出量はかなり高水準である。したがって日本は、地球温暖化防止について、大きな責任を負っているといえる。
　　日本は京都議定書で、2008年から2012年の第1約束期間において温室効果ガスの排出量を対1990年比で6%の削減目標を課せられている。しかし、民生、輸送部門の排出量が急増したため、日本は第1約束期間における目標達成のためには現時点における温室効果ガスの排出量を15%（9%＋6%）削減しなければならない。
　　地球温暖化の防止には特効薬が存在しないという現実を踏まえ、今後の日本の課題としては、国の基本方針に基づき、国、地方自治体、企業、国民などすべての主体が協調して対策を実施することが求められている。

(5)　交通

a ）国内輸送

　　旅客輸送手段で輸送量（人・km）が最も多いのは自動車で、次が鉄道である。航空機・船舶の比率は少ない。2000年度には、自動車67.0%、鉄道27.1%、航空機

of the world to implement measures matched to its particular circumstances: The Protocol introduces three "Kyoto Mechanisms" for achieving emission goals through international collaboration: international emissions trading, joint implementation, and the clean development mechanism. It also allows participating parties to include the amounts of carbon dioxide absorbed by forests and other "sinks" in calculating goal achievement. However, final agreement on a number of issues was left to future negotiations.

In addition, the US Bush administration later announced that it would not support the Kyoto Protocol. As part of its effort to ensure that the Protocol goes into effect, Japan will persistently press the United States to rejoin.

(Japan's obligation)

Japan ranks number four in emission of greenhouse gases (mainly CO_2 and methane). (Of the 12.2 billion tons of greenhouse gases emitted worldwide in 1997, the United States accounted for 23.6%, China 14.5%, Russia 14.5% and Japan 5.0%.) On a per capita basis, Japanese emissions are quite high compared with those in developing countries. Japan therefore has a heavy responsibility to contribute to the prevention of global warming.

The Kyoto Protocol obligated Japan to cut greenhouse gas emissions to 6% below 1990 levels during the first commitment period from 2008 to 2012. Meanwhile, however, gas emissions by the Japanese trucking sector shot up sharply, so that as of 2002 Japan needed to reduce greenhouse gas emissions by 15% in order to achieve its target for the first commitment period.

Facing up to the reality that there is no quick remedy for the global warming problem, Japan must now coordinate the forces of the national and local governments, businesses, people and every other element of society in moving forward with measures based on fundamental national policy.

(5) Transportation

a) Domestic Transport

In terms of passenger-kilometers, the most common means of passenger transportation is the automobile and next comes trains. In comparison, airplanes and ships are used much less extensive-

5.6％、旅客船 0.3％となっている。1970年ごろまでは鉄道が一番多かった。

　貨物輸送量（トン・km）では、自動車が最も多く、次は船舶である。鉄道輸送の比率はかなり少ない。2000年度には、自動車 54.2％、船舶 41.8％、鉄道 3.8％、航空機 0.2％となっている。

b）鉄　道

　鉄道の全長は 2 万 300 km（1 万 2,600 マイル）であるが、そのうち 80％近くが、国鉄の民営化により 1987年に設立された JR 7 社の路線で占められている。

　日本の鉄道は英国人技師の指導により、1872年に東京の新橋と横浜の間に開通したのが、最初である。

　日本の鉄道の花形は新幹線で、東海道・山陽新幹線は東京・福岡間 1,176 km（731 マイル）を約 5 時間で走る。現在、このほか東北・山形・秋田新幹線、上越・長野新幹線が開通している。新幹線の最高時速は 300 km（186 マイル）である。

　1988年、本州と北海道の間に青函トンネル（全長 53.85 km で世界一長い）、本州と四国の間に瀬戸大橋（1.1 km）が相次いで開通し、本州と九州の間の関門トンネルを加えて、日本の主要 4 島が、鉄道で直接結ばれた。

　東京・大阪などの大都市では、都市と郊外を結ぶ通勤用鉄道や地下鉄網も整備されている。

c）道路と自動車輸送

　日本の主要道路である国道および都道府県道の全長は、約 18.8 万 km（11 万 8,000 マイル）で、うち 96％が舗装されている。高速自動車道も逐次整備されてきた。しかし、市町村道の舗装率は 73％で、整備が立ち遅れている（2000年）。

ly. The ratios for these four categories in 2000 was automobile, 67.0%; rail, 27.1%; air, 5.6%; and ship 0.4%. Until about 1970, the train was the most popular means of transportation.

In terms of ton-kilometers, road vehicles are the most widely used form of transportation for goods, followed by ships. Trains are not used much for transporting freight. In 2000 the breakdown was truck, 54.2%; ship, 41.8%; rail, 3.8%; and air, 0.2%.

b) Railroads

There is a total of 20,300 kilometers (12,600 miles) of railways in Japan, of which nearly 80% is accounted for by the seven JR companies established upon the privatization of the Japanese National Railways in 1987.

The first Japanese railway, extending from Shimbashi in Tokyo to Yokohama, was built in 1872 under the supervision of British engineers.

The crowning glory of Japan's railway system is the Shinkansen (Bullet Train) lines. The Shinkansen trains can do the run between Tokyo and Fukuoka in Kyushu, a distance of 1,176 kilometers (731 miles) covered by the Tokaido-Sanyo Shinkansen line, in about five hours. Two other Shinkansen lines, the Tohoku-Yamagata-Akita Shinkansen line and the Joetsu-Nagano Shinkansen line, are also in operation. The maximum speed of the Shinkansen trains is currently 300 kilometers per hour (186 mph).

In 1988, work was completed on the Seikan Tunnel (the world's longest, extending 53.85 kilometers or 33.5 miles between Honshu and Hokkaido) and on the Seto Ohashi Bridge (1.1 kilometers or 0.68 mile) between Honshu and Shikoku. These, together with the Kanmon Tunnel between Honshu and Kyushu, now connect all of Japan's four major islands by rail.

In addition, large cities like Tokyo and Osaka also have extensive commuter train and subway networks connecting urban centers with the suburbs.

c) Roads and Motor Transportation

The major part of Japan's roads are accounted for by the national and prefectural highways which have a combined total length of 188 thousand kilometers (118,000 miles), 96% of which is paved. An additional network of expressways is being expanded steadily. In contrast, less progress has been made in the

自動車輸送は年々増加し、全国の自動車の登録台数は7,164万台（2001年、乗用車74.8％、トラック24.9％、バス0.3％）である。これは人口あたりにすればアメリカ・オーストラリア・イタリア・カナダなどの方が多いが、面積あたりでは世界で最も多く、そのため交通事故や排気ガス・騒音などが悩みのたねになっている。

d）海　運

　日本は工業やエネルギー用資源・原料に乏しい。それ
ばかりか近年の工業化にともない、農業人口が減少し、
食料まで外国に依存する割合が大きくなってきた。そこ
で必要な外貨を稼ぐため、輸入した原料を加工し、製品
を再び輸出しなければならない。この輸入・輸出を支え
るのが海運業である。

　輸入する石油・鉱石・石炭・木材などはタンカー・鉱
石専用船・バルクキャリアーなどにより運ばれ、また輸
出する鋼材や消費材などは一般貨物船やコンテナ船によ
って運ばれる。

　日本の船舶保有量は1,530万トンで、世界の2.7％を
占めているが、ここ10年以上、下落傾向が続いている
（2000年）。

　主な港は神戸・横浜・千葉・名古屋・大阪・北九州である。

　なお、多くの日本船名に「丸」がつくのは、日本では
昔の人が男の子の名前や刀の銘など、大切なものの名称
に「丸」をつけたのと同じ理由からであろう。

building of city, town and village roads of which only 73% are paved (2000 figures).

Motor transportation has increased year by year. In 2001 there were 71.64 million registered motor vehicles in the country. (Passenger cars accounted for 74.8% of the total, trucks for 24.9%, buses for 0.3%.) Although Japan does not come up to the United States, Australia or Canada in number of cars per capita, it ranks top in the world in number per unit area and, as a consequence, is plagued with a high accident rate as well as exhaust gas and noise pollution.

d) Marine Transportation

Japan's energy and material resources are much too meager to meet its industrial requirements. What is more, the industrialization of the nation in modern times has led to a decrease in the farming population, so that Japan has become increasingly reliant on overseas sources even for its food. In order to obtain the foreign currency required for these procurements from abroad, Japan is forced to process a large share of the raw materials it imports into finished products for reshipment out of the country as exports. It is the marine transportation industry that supports this import-export cycle.

Petroleum, ore, coal, lumber, etc. are brought into Japan in tankers, ore carriers and bulk carriers while exported steel products, consumer goods and a variety of other finished products leave the country on general cargo and container ships.

The total tonnage of all Japanese ships amounts to 15.3 million tons and accounts for 2.7% of the world total. Japan's share of world total tonnage has been on the decline for more than ten years (2000 figures).

Japan's main ports are Kobe, Yokohama, Chiba, Nagoya, Osaka and Kitakyushu.

As a footnote to the above, it might be noted that the suffix maru appended to the names of most Japanese ships is thought to come from a similar ending which in the past was often added as a term of endearment to the names of boys, as well as to those of swords and other cherished possessions.

6 科学技術

(1) 日本における科学技術の役割

　天然資源に恵まれていない日本にとっては、人間の知的創造力こそが最大の資源である。したがって、国民が安全で潤いがあり、かつ豊かな文化のあふれる生活を営むために、とりわけ科学技術の果たす役割は諸外国以上に大きいといえる。

　また、政府と国民は日本が科学技術によって国際社会・人類全体に貢献していくためは、地球環境、食料、エネルギー、資源など地球規模で取り組むべき人類共通の課題に対して、日本の科学技術を積極的に応用すべきであると考えている。

　さらに、円高による産業の海外シフトや情報通信・輸送システムの飛躍的発展による産業のグローバル化・ボーダーレス化の過程で、発展途上国などへの広範かつ急速な技術移転が進展した。その結果、従来の日本の国際競争力を支えてきた科学技術上の優位差も、縮小しつつある。

　このような諸事情を背景に、日本が 21 世紀の国際社会においても主要な役割を果たすめには、科学技術活動において常に他国に先んずるための不断の努力が必要である。

(2) 科学技術基本政策

　1995 年に制定された「科学技術基本法」にもとづき策定された科学技術基本計画は、2001 年に第 1 期計画期間を終えた。政府は、引き続き 2001 年から向こう 5 年間の第 2 期科学技術基本計画を実行中である。

　この計画は、自然科学と人文・社会科学との総合性の観点および科学技術を未来への先行投資ととらえる戦略的観点から、21 世紀における科学技術と社会との新しい関係の構築をめざしている。

6　Science and Technology

（1）The Role of Science and Technology in Japan

For Japan, the ingenuity of its people is a far greater asset than its meager natural resources. The role of science and technology in helping people to lead a life that is secure, rewarding and culturally rich is therefore probably greater than in most countries.

The government and people of Japan believe that Japanese science and technology should be used to contribute to the international community and all mankind and, for this, should be vigorously applied to solve problems common to people everywhere, particularly in connection with the world-scale issues of environmental preservation, food, and energy and material resources.

Japanese industry has grown increasingly global and borderless owing to the shift of production to overseas locations in response to the strong yen, quantum advances in the field of info-communications and other factors. This process has been accompanied by a sweeping and rapid transfer of Japanese technologies to the developing countries in particular. As a result, Japan's superiority in science and technology, long the source of its international competitive strength, is diminishing.

This means that if Japan is to play a leading role in the international community in the 21 st century, it must strive constantly to keep its scientific and technological activities ahead of those of other countries.

（2）Basic Policy

The Basic Law on Science and Technology was enacted in 1995 and was immediately followed by the launching of a Basic Plan for Science and Technology. When the first stage of the plan was completed in 2001, the government began moving forward with the Second-Stage Basic Plan for Science and Technology, which is to run for five years starting from 2001.

Aimed at building a new relationship between science and society in the 21st century, the Second-Stage Basic Plan is being

日本は、今後の欧米主要諸国の動向をも考慮して、2001年からの5年間に政府研究開発費として国のGDPの1％、総額24兆円を見込んでいる。

(3)　科学技術重点化戦略

　　政府は、日本の経済産業が持続的に発展するため、また、国民が安心して生活できるために、次の4つの重点分野に積極的、戦略的投資を行っている。

a）ライフサイエンス（生命科学）

　　生命科学は、保健医療・環境保全・農林水産・化学・薬品などの分野で大きく貢献することが期待されている。

　　政府は、今後10年程度を見通した「ライフサイエンスに関する研究開発基本計画」において、日本独自の戦略的重点開発分野として脳、発生・再生、ガン、有用植物機能、生態系・植物圏などの総合システム、ゲノムなどの基礎的生体分子に関する研究開発を目指している。また、クローン固体の作製などにかかわる生命倫理の問題について基本的考え方を示した。

　　このなかで、ヒトゲノムの塩基配列解読については、日・米・欧などの科学者で構成する「国際ヒトゲノム計画」が2000年6月に約30億の配列の概要を解読したと発表したが、このプロジェクトにおける日本の研究者の貢献が高く評価されている。

b）情報通信分野

　　情報通信技術は、現代社会を形成する重要な知的・創造的基盤で、個人生活・社会システム・科学技術など社

carried out from the perspective of the natural sciences, arts and social sciences viewed comprehensively and also from the perspective of science and technology as a strategic investment in the future.

The scale of the plan was decided with consideration to trends in Europe and the United States. Total outlays on government R&D during the five years are expected to total 24 trillion yen, or 1% of the national GDP.

(3) Strategic Focus on Science and Technology

The government is promoting scientific technological progress in order to ensure sustainable economic and industrial development and enable the country's people to live secure lives. For this, it is investing aggressively and strategically in the following four key areas:

a) Life Sciences

The life sciences are expected to make large contributions in such fields as hygiene, medicine, environmental protection, agriculture, forestry, fishery, chemical engineering, and drugs.

Under its farsighted (ten-year) Basic Research and Development Plan for the Life Sciences, the government aims to promote R&D in a number of Japan's own strategic, high-priority development areas. These include the brain, genesis, regeneration, cancer, useful plant functions, integrated systems encompassing the ecosystem and the plant world, and the genome and other basic biomolecules. The plan also clarifies Japan's fundamental thinking regarding the cloning of individuals and other ethical aspects of the life sciences.

Japanese scientists worked side by side with their counterparts from the United States, Europe and elsewhere as members of the International Human Genome Project, which, in June 2000, announced the decoding of the entire sequence of the approximately 3 billion DNA bases making up the human genome. The contribution of the Japanese researchers was widely applauded.

b) Info-communications

Info-communications technologies offer a critical intellectual and innovative platform for the evolution of modern society and

会全体の大きな変革の原動力となると考えられる。

政府は、この認識に立って2001年に「高度情報通信ネットワーク社会形成基本法（IT 基本法）」を制定した。これにもとづき政府は、国家、地方自治体、大学、事業者などが連携してIT国家戦略「e-Japan 戦略」を推進することを求めている。

〔注〕 3 経済(3) g 情報通信産業の項参照

c) 環境分野

政府は、1993年に制定された「環境基本法」にもとづき環境基本計画を策定した。さらに2000年には大量生産・消費・廃棄という20世紀型の社会から持続可能な社会への転換をめざして循環型社会推進基本計画を策定した。政府は、科学技術をこの政策実現のための重要な手段の一つとして位置づけている。

〔注〕 5 社会(4) 環境保全の項参照

d) ナノテクノロジー・材料分野

ナノテクノロジー・材料開発は、あらゆる科学技術の基盤として、いわば21世紀の産業革命ともいうべき、科学技術の飛躍的発展を支える分野として期待されている。また、この分野は日本が他の国にくらべて優勢な分野でもある。

諸外国においても、2000年にアメリカ政府が「ナノテクノロジーに関する国家戦略」を発表したほか、各国政府が近年、ナノテクノロジー・材料開発への取り組みを強化している。

日本においても、「2001年度科学技術振興に関する重点指針」において、重点的かつ緊急を要する項目として、ナノ融合物質・材料、安全材料、環境・循環型材料などの開発推進が示された。

この中には、エネルギー半減・環境負荷ミニマムのプロセス技術、新材料（超鉄鋼材料・スーパーメタル・超伝導材料など）、およびナノスケール加工技術などの研究開発がふくまれている。

are expected to provide the driving force behind a major revolution extending through all sectors of society, from the private lives of individuals to infrastructure systems, science, and technology. Recognizing the importance of info-communications, the government passed the Basic Law for Building an Advanced Info-Communications Network (Basic IT Law) in 2001. This law is the basis for an ongoing effort to promote a coordinated national IT strategy (the e-Japan Strategy) among national and local government organs, universities, and the business community.

(See 3, (3) g) Information and Telecommunications Industry)

c) The Environment

The Basic Law for the Environment passed in 1993 served as the basis for implementing the Basic Environmental Plan launched in 1994. Then, in 2000, the government introduced the Basic Plan for Promoting a Zero-Waste Economy and Society, which is intended to remake the mass production, mass consumption and mass disposal society of the 20th century into a sustainable society. The government views science and technology as an effective tool in achieving this transition.

(See 5, (4) Preservation of the Environment)

d) Nanotechnologies and Nanomaterials

Nanotechnologies and nanomaterials provide ground-level support to all branches of science and technology. Their development is therefore believed to be capable of catalyzing dramatic breakthroughs on a scale that may well come to be seen as the industrial revolution of the 21st century. Japan is the world's most advanced country in the field.

But other governments around the world are also stepping up efforts to promote the development of technologies and materials in this sector, as evidenced by the US announcement of a National Nanotechnology Initiative in 2000.

In Japan, the Priority Guidelines for Advancing Science and Technology in 2001 specify nanofusion materials, safety materials and environmental zero-waste materials as categories that must be made the focus of intense and immediate development initiatives.

This R&D encompasses processing technologies that halve energy needs and minimize environmental load, new materials

　　　　以上が日本が指向する最重点の戦略的開発分野である。
　　　　その他の重点分野としては次の各項があげられている。

e) エネルギー分野

①原子力発電

　　　日本は、稼働中の原子力発電プラントを52基もって
いて、発電能力4,508万KWでアメリカ、フランスに
次いで第3位である（2001）。1999年における推定では
日本の総発電量の34.2％（3,213億kwh）を原子力発
電によってまかなっている。

　　　このように、日本が電力供給の1/3以上を原子力発電
に依存している現状から、原子力発電技術の研究開発は
国の科学技術政策上の重要課題である。

　　　日本原子力委員会は、21世紀において日本が採るべ
き原子力開発利用の基本方針について、公開審議をへて
2000年に「原子力研究・開発・利用に関する長期計画」
を策定した。

　　　この計画に沿って、各種の原子力利用に関する科学技
術の研究開発が進められているが、そのすべてについて
最優先・最重要課題は、安全性と信頼性の確保である。

②自然エネルギーの利用開発

　　　エネルギーの安定供給、地球環境保全の観点から、太
陽エネルギー、地熱エネルギー、風力エネルギー、海洋
エネルギー、バイオマスエネルギーなどの自然エネルギ
ー利用の研究開発が経済産業省、農林水産省、文部科学
省などで進められている。

f) 製造技術分野―ものづくり技術―

　　　近年、製造業の国外シフト・国内空洞化と、ものづく
り技術の継承の困難性が憂慮されている。自国および諸
外国に有用な優れた「もの」を持続的に供給するための
ものづくり技術を確保し、開発することは、ものづくり
を国の主要な立脚点としてきた日本にとってきわめて重

(super steels, supermetals) and nanoscale machining technologies.

The three sectors listed above are the ones Japan has singled out for top-priority strategic R&D.

Other high-priority sectors include the following:

e) Energy

① Nuclear energy

Japan has 52 nuclear power plants in operation with a capacity of 45.08 megawatts, placing it third in nuclear power capacity after the United States and France (2001). In 1999, 34.5% (31.65 megawatts) of the country's power needs were met by nuclear power.

As Japan thus depends on nuclear power generation to supply more than a third of the electric power it consumes, research and development of nuclear power technologies is a key priority of the national science and technology program.

Following a series of public hearings on the fundamental nuclear energy development and use policy Japan should adopt in the 21 st century, the Atomic Energy Commission in 2000 drew up the Long-term Plan for Nuclear Power Research, Development and Use.

A variety of research and development projects regarding nuclear power utilization are moving forward in line with the plan. In all, primary emphasis is placed on ensuring safety and reliability.

② Natural energy

As natural energies can help to stabilize energy supply and protect the environment, a number of government organizations, particularly the Ministry of Economy, Trade and Industry, the Ministry of Agriculture, Forestry and Fisheries, and the Ministry of Education, Culture, Sports, Science and Technology, operate programs for R&D into technologies for utilizing solar, geothermal, wind, ocean, biomass and other natural energies.

f) Shop-floor (monozukuri) Technologies

In recent years, the hollowing-out of the manufacturing industry by the transfer of production to overseas bases and the difficulty of handing down traditional shop-floor production (monozukuri) technologies have become sources of rising concern. One of Japan's supporting pillars has long been its strength

要な課題である。

　　このような事態に対処するために、政府は「ものづく
り基盤技術整備基本法」を制定し、ものづくり技術の維
持、発展に努めている。

g）社会基盤分野
　　国民生活を支える基盤分野として安心・安全・快適な
社会の実現をめざして、防災科学技術、地震調査・予知
技術などの研究が進められている。

h）フロンティア分野
　　日本はこれらのほかフロンティア分野として、①宇宙
開発、②航空技術、③海洋開発に関する研究、技術開発
を積極的に推進している。

(4)　日本の科学技術の特質

a）研究開発：体制と資金
　　2000年における日本の研究費は、総額16.3兆円であ
った。これは、28.5兆円の米国に次いで世界第2位で、
ドイツ（5.0兆円）、フランス（3.0兆円）よりも多い。
その対国内総生産（GDP）比3.18％は、他の工業先進
主要国並みの高水準を維持している。
　　研究費の政府負担割合は22.0％で、米国およびヨー
ロッパ主要国の水準以下である。その残りを産業界が負
担している。その民間企業研究費は、1992年以降、景
気の後退等により3年連続して減少したが、95年から
4年間増加に転じた。その研究費の売上高に対する比率
は2000年3.01％で、1990年以降ほぼ横ばいである。
また、その民間企業負担研究費の90％は、製造業が支
出している。
　　研究費総額の14.0％を占める大学では、その52％が
基礎研究に、39％が応用研究に、残り9％が開発研究
に使われている。いっぽう民間企業での使用比率は、そ
れぞれ6％、21％、73％である（2000年）。

in monozukuri. The importance of preserving and developing monozukuri technologies for ensuring the uninterrupted supply of useful products to domestic and international markets is therefore immeasurable.

This situation led to the enactment of the Basic Law for Buildup of Fundamental Monozukuri Technologies and a renewed effort to maintain and improve monozukuri technologies.

g) Infrastructure

Infrastructure level research aimed at realizing a secure and pleasant social environment is progressing on a number of fronts, including disaster-prevention technologies and earthquake forecasting technologies.

h) Frontier areas

Japan is vigorously involved in R&D and technology development in the frontier areas of ① space development, ② aeronautics and ③ ocean development.

(4) Features of Japanese Technology

a) Research: Organization and Funding

Japan spent a total of ¥16.3 trillion on research in 2000. This was second after the United States, which spent ¥28.5 trillion, and larger than the amounts spent by Germany (¥5.0 trillion) and France (¥3.6 trillion). It was equivalent to 3.18% of gross domestic product, a high level on a par with those of other industrially advanced nations.

The government footed 22.0% of total expenditures on research, a smaller proportion than in the United States and Europe. The remainder was borne by industry. Industrial sector outlays on research declined for three consecutive years between 1992 and 1994, mainly because of the economic downturn, but rose from 1995 to 1998. In 2000, the private sector devoted the equivalent of 3.01% of total sales to research, a percentage that has not changed substantially since 1990. Ninety percent of private-sector research funds comes from the manufacturing industry.

Universities, which account for 14.0% of total expenditures, used 52% for basic research, 39% for research in applications

日本における科学技術研究者数は 73 万人である。米国の 111 万人（2001 年）に次いでおり、ドイツ、フランスより多い。また人口 1 万人当りの人員では、日本は米国、ドイツなどを上回り、世界第 1 位である。

b）研究開発水準の国際比較

　文部科学省科学技術政策研究所は、科学技術総合指標を開発した。これは、毎年の理学士・工学士取得者数、研究者数、研究開発費、技術輸出・輸入額、論文数、論文被引用回数、国内・国外特許出願件数、工業製品付加価値額、ハイテク製品付加価値額の 12 の指標の分析により作成されるものである。

　これによると、主要 5 カ国の科学技術総合指標値は 1981 年から 1996 年の間でアメリカが最高かつ常に上昇しつつあり、次いで日本がアメリカの 1/2 程度で第 2 位、続いてドイツ、イギリス、フランスとなっている。例えば特許登録件数をみると、国籍別で日本は 21.8 万件、国別で 12.6 万件とアメリカを上回るか同レベルである。（ただし、特許の出願件数では日本は、1990 年代初頭からアメリカ、EU に追い抜かれ、1999 年においては日本 91 万件に対しアメリカ、EU 250 万件以上と差が開いていることに注目しなければならない。）

　また、スイスの国際経営開発研究所が 8 分野 290 項目の調査・評価結果にもとづき発表している、競争力総合評価では日本は 2001 年の 26 位から 2002 年には 49 か国中 30 位に後退した。しかし科学技術分野に関してはアメリカに次いで第 2 位と高く評価されている。

　しかし、内容的に分析すれば日本の科学技術水準は、研究人材・国内特許数・研究開発費などインプット（入力）の量的側面および工業製品付加価値額、ハイテク製品付加価値額では国際的に高いが、論文被引用回数・国内特許数・技術輸出などのアウトプット（出力）の面では高いとはいいがたい。今後、日本は科学技術活動の一層の質的な充実とともに研究開発の生産性の向上にも努力しなければならない。

technology and 9% for development-related research. The corresponding figures for private industry are 6%, 21% and 73%.

The number of persons engaged in scientific and technological research work in Japan is 730 thousand. This is second after the United States, which has 1.11 million research personnel (2001), and larger than the number of research workers in Germany and France. In terms of the number of research workers per 10 thousand population, Japan ranks first in the world, above the U. S. and Germany.

b) International Standing in R&D

The National Institute of Science and Technology has developed a composite index of capability in science and technology. The index is prepared by analyzing twelve factors: number of persons acquiring bachelor of science and bachelor of engineering degrees each year, number of researchers, R&D expenditures, technology exports, technology imports, number of research papers published, number of times research papers cited, number of domestic and foreign patent applications, added value of industrial products, and added value of high-tech products.

A look at the composite indexes of the top five countries between 1981 and 1996 shows that the United States not only ranked highest but its index rose constantly throughout the period. Then came Japan in second place, with about half the US score, followed by Germany, England and France. Taking the number of patent registrations each year as an example, Japan had 218 thousand on a nationality basis and 126 thousand on a country basis, placing it above the United States. (But it must be noted that the United States and the EU overtook Japan in number of patent applications in the early nineties. In 1999, the number of filings in the EU was over 2.5 million, compared with 790 thousand in Japan.)

Moreover, according to overall competitiveness rankings based on an analysis of 290 items in 8 categories announced by the International Institute for Management Development (IMD) in Switzerland, Japan fell from 26 th (among 49 ranked countries) in 2001 to 30 th in 2002, However, it got high marks in the science and technology category, ranking second after the United States.

When Japan's science and technology level is analyzed in more detail, however, it is found to be high by international standards

c) 技術貿易

　日本の技術貿易収支比（輸出/輸入）の数字は，調査方法や対象により統計値が異なるが、総務庁統計によれば、2000年の技術貿易収支比は、2.39で、この輸出超過は長期的に増加傾向を続けている。

　地域的に見ると、日本技術の最大の輸出先は北米であり、単独の相手国としては米国が最も多い（45％）。輸入は、米国（74％）と欧州からが圧倒的である。業種別にみると、技術輸出額が多いのは、輸送用機械（主に自動車）、通信・電気機械、医薬などで、他方、輸入額が多いのは、通信・電気機械、医薬の順である（2000年）。

(5)　日本の科学技術の課題

　科学技術立国として発展してきた日本が、引き続き国際競争力を維持し、現代の日本社会ならびに国際社会における諸問題を解決し、さらに豊かな未来社会の実現に向けて積極的、先導的貢献を果たしていくためには、一段と新しい科学技術の創出が期待される。

（科学技術創出のシステムの構築）

　そのためには、まず新しい科学技術創出のシステムの構築が重要である。これには国際的研究開発拠点（COE：Center Of Excellence）の育成、「産業技術力強化法」の有効運用、産・学・官の情報・人的交流システムの推進、ハイテク・ベンチャー企業創出の環境整備など

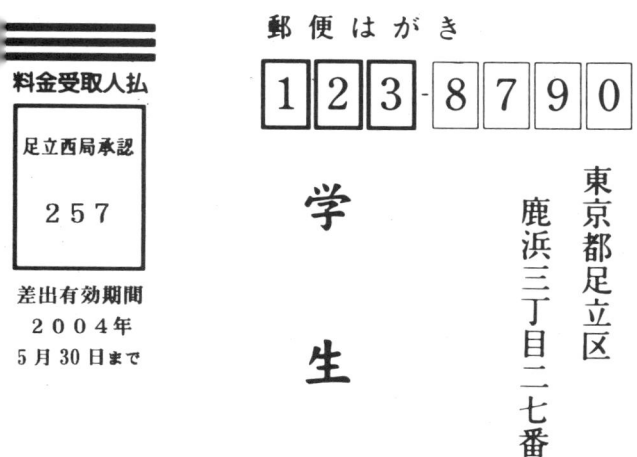

郵便はがき

123-8790

東京都足立区
鹿浜三丁目二七番十四号

学生社 行

料金受取人払

足立西局承認

257

差出有効期間
2004年
5月30日まで

| お買いになった 本の書名 | 日 本 -その姿と心- | [第7版] |

この本についてのご感想・ご要望をご記入下さい

学生社愛読者カード

ふりがな お名前		(自宅 Tel － － (自宅 fax － － (勤務先Tel － －
(年齢　才)		

ご住所	都道 府県	区市 町村
〒　－		

Eメール

ご職業 学校名		購読の　朝日　読売　毎日　日経　産経 新聞名　その他(　　　　　　)
お求めになっ た書店の名	都道 府県	区市 町村　　　　　　　書店

お求め 1 新聞広告(　　新聞) 2 書店で見て 3 書評を見て(掲載名　)
の動機 4 人にすすめられて　5 DMを見て　6 その他(　)

学生社の図書目録の送付を希望　　(　する　・　しない　)

学生社の図書のお求めの方法

①お近くの「書店」にてお求めください。

②「通信販売」···下記の注文書欄にご希望の書名・定価・冊数をご記入のう
この葉書をご投函してください。また、小社ホームページ http://gakusei.co
Eメール info@gakusei.co.jp でもご注文ができます。

本が届いてから、郵便振替または現金書留で本の代金、消費税と送料(冊数
かかわりなく 200 円)を小社までお送りください。

ホームページでは、書名・著者名・本体価格などがご覧いただけます。

【ご 注 文 書】

書　　名	本体価格	冊 数

in terms of quantity of input, including researcher resources, domestic patents, and R&D expenditure, and also in added value of industrial products and added value of high-tech products, but not so high in terms of output, such as number of times research papers are cited, domestic patents and technology exports. From now on Japan needs to upgrade the quality of its scientific and technological activities and increase R & D productivity.

c) Technology Trade

While figures reported for Japan's technology trade ratio (exports/imports) differ depending on how the import-export survey was conducted and what was included, the Management and Coordination Agency pegged it at 2.39 for 2000 and predicted that the export surplus would continue to grow over the long term.

Although the region receiving the most Japanese technology is Asia, with Korea at the top, Japan's biggest single technology customer is the United States (taking 45%). An overwhelming share of imports come from the U. S. (74%) and Europe. The industrial sectors that export the largest amounts of technology are transportation equipment (mostly automotive equipment), electrical equipment, chemicals and general machinery, while those that import the most are electrical machinery, chemicals, transportation equipment and general machinery (2000).

(5) Issues in Science and Technology

Japan's development was underpinned by science and technology. Today, it needs to create new technologies at an even faster pace if it expects to maintain its international competitiveness, overcome the problems confronted by Japanese society and the international community, and make a positive forward-looking contribution toward the realization of a more prosperous world in the future.

(Building systems for scientific and technological innovation)

For this, Japan must by all means establish systems for achieving new scientific and technological advances. This will require the development of international centers of excellence (COEs),

の課題がある。

(国際協力)

　地球環境、エネルギー、資源の開発利用などの地球規模の諸問題の対応には科学技術の国際的協力活動が不可欠である。日本はこの分野においても積極的、先導的役割を果たすことが期待されている。

　また、増大する人口と豊かな資源を保有する発展途上国の、国際社会における重要度がいよいよ高まっている。この状況下で、これらの国が国際的協力活動に十分に参画できる環境整備に努力することは、日本の責務であるとともに、日本の持続的安定と繁栄のためにもきわめて重要な課題である。

(人材の育成)

　これらの国内的・国際的な諸課題に取り組みにあたって、その大前提・基盤要件となるものは創造性豊かな科学技術の人材の育成である。

　このためには、大学院、大学をはじめとする教育機関において、高度な専門技術とともに、柔軟かつ広い視野をもって課題探究、総合判断能力の養成を目指して、学際的・総合的教科や教養教育の充実が求められている。また、産業フロンティア創出と産業の国際競争力の観点からは、技術士制度の改善・推進、技術者資格の国際的整合性の確保と、国際相互承認制度の推進などによる高度な科学技術分野の人材の質的、量的確保が課題である。

(科学技術者の職業倫理の確立)

　さらに、ヒトゲノムの解読、ヒトに対するクローン技術応用の可能性など急速に高度化・複雑化する科学技術

effective implementation of the Law for Strengthening Industrial Technologies, promotion of systems for information and personnel exchanges among industry, academia and government, and fostering of an atmosphere the encourages the emergence of high-tech venture businesses.

(International cooperation)

Scientific and technological cooperation on the international level is indispensable for tackling worldwide issues like global warming and the development and use of energy and material resources. The international community expects Japan to play an active role as a leader in this regard.

Japan must also respond to the reality that the developing countries, with their expanding populations and abundant natural resources, are emerging as ever more important players on the international stage. Specifically, Japan has a responsibility to help to create an environment that allows these countries to participate fully in international cooperative activities. This is also essential for ensuring Japan's own continuing stability and prosperity.

(Development of human resources)

The foremost prerequisite for effectively tackling these domestic and international issues is the development of creative people with sound capabilities in science and technology.

Postgraduate schools, colleges and other educational institutions are therefore being called on to enrich their inter-disciplinary, polytechnic and liberal arts programs with an eye to going beyond merely offering instruction in advanced specialized technologies to help students develop the ability to approach research projects flexibly from the broad view and to make decisions based on the overall picture. Further, the need to create new industry frontiers and boost industry's competitive strength in the international marketplace can be met only by ensuring Japan has a sufficient number of high-caliber people in the advanced scientific and technological sectors. This requires improvement and revitalization of the consultant engineer system, harmonization of engineer qualifications with international standards, and promotion of a system of mutual international recognition.

(Professional ethics for scientists and engineers)

As can be seen from the decoding of the human genome and the development of cloning techniques that are potentially usable

には、ますます期待が寄せられるとともに信頼性、安全性、安心感が求められている。

ダイナマイトや核エネルギーの例をみても、これらの利用が人類に偉大なる福祉、すなわち利便性と豊かさを与えたと同時に、また多大な惨禍をももたらしたことは、歴史的事実である。

こうした事実に鑑みれば、急速な発展の道をたどる科学技術の将来をになう研究者には、より深い専門性とともにこれを正しい方向に先導するための一層高い倫理性が要求される。科学技術者に、いかにしてこの倫理性を与えるかが、今後の世界に課せられた共通の重要課題である。日本はこの課題についても積極的役割を果していかなければならない。

on human beings, science and technology have rapidly increased in sophistication and complexity. While this has raised hopes for the benefits that may be reaped, it has also made people more concerned about reliability, safety and peace of mind.

There is a lesson to be learned from technologies developed in the past. Take dynamite and nuclear energy, for example. Both benefited mankind tremendously, by making life easier and more rewarding. But the great misfortune they wrought is also a historical fact.

From this viewpoint, the researchers on whose shoulders the future of rapid scientific and technical progress rests require not only deep specialized knowledge but also high ethical standards to keep them on the proper course. How to instill such ethics is a weighty issue common to people throughout the world. Japan also needs to work positively toward finding an answer to this question.

7 文化

(1) 文字・言語・文学

a) 文 字

　　日本では漢字・平仮名・片仮名の3種類の文字を使うが、このほか、ローマ字も使われることがある。

　　漢字は中国から伝わった表意文字である。漢字の音訓で国語を表現した万葉仮名が考案され、これを簡略化して書いたものから、平仮名・片仮名が発生した（9世紀ごろ）。平仮名・片仮名はいずれも音節文字で、現在はそれぞれ46文字を使う。

　　日本語を書くとき名詞・動詞・形容詞などは多くは漢字で書き、動詞および形容詞の活用変化の部分や助動詞・助詞は仮名で書く。副詞は漢字でも仮名でも書く。現在は平仮名が広く使われ、片仮名は外来語を表す場合に用いられる。

　　学校で最初に教えられる文字は平仮名である。しかし現在は、学校へ入学する前に仮名の読み書きのできる子供が多い。

　　日本の文字は縦書き用にできているが、横書きもできる。縦書きの場合は右から左へ行を移す。昔は縦書きが多かったが、数字の表記や外国語の引用に便利な横書きが逐次普及してきた。しかし、読みやすさは縦書きの方なので、一般の新聞・雑誌・書籍は縦書きのものが多い。

b) 漢 字

　　漢字は紀元前十数世紀からすでに中国で用いられてい

7 Culture

(1) Writing System, Language and Literature

a) Writing System

There are three main types of written characters in Japan: *kanji, hiragana* and *katakana.* Roman letters are also used, but to a much lesser extent.

Kanji characters are ideograms which were brought in from China. On the basis of the Chinese and Japanese readings of these characters a system of phonetic *manyogana* characters was devised. This in turn was simplified into the hiragana and katakana systems in about the ninth century. The characters of the hiragana and katakana systems represent single syllables. Each system presently has 46 characters.

In writing Japanese, most nouns, verb roots and adjectives are represented by kanji while the verb and adjective endings indicating the various tenses etc., the auxiliary verbs and the particles are written in one of the *kana* systems (hiragana or katakana). Adverbs can be written in either kanji or kana characters. Of the two kana systems, hiragana has by far the wider usage in modern times. Katakana characters are used mostly for the spelling of loan words brought into Japanese from other languages.

The first characters taught at school are those of the hiragana system. In fact, however, a fairly large percentage of Japanese children are able to read and write kana characters even before they enter school.

All three types of Japanese characters are designed to be written in vertical lines, though they can also be written horizontally. When written vertically, the first line comes on the right of the page and succeeding lines follow it to the left. Years ago, almost all writing was vertical but the horizontal style has gradually become more popular since it is more adaptable to inclusion of Arabic numerals and passages in foreign languages. From the reader's point of view, however, vertically written sentences are easier to assimilate and for this reason most newspapers, magazines and popular books are printed in this style.

b) Kanji

Kanji characters were already in use in China more than three

た象形・指事（しじ）から発達した表意文字である。太陽を表わす文字（日）は太陽の形から、樹木を表わす文字（木）は樹木の形に似せてつくられた。また、林を表わす文字は木を二つ並べてつくられ、森を表わす文字は木を重ねてつくられている。漢字は中国から朝鮮・日本・ベトナムに伝えられた。漢字は全部で5万くらいあるといわれる。

　　これは「字」数であり、「語」数はこれの数倍に達する。日本では一般の社会生活で使用する漢字の目安として常用漢字1,945字を選定している（1981年）。しかし、人の姓や地名にはこれ以外にもたくさん使われているため、これよりはるかに多くの漢字を知らないと新聞や書籍を読めない。
　　なお、日本でつくられた漢字（国字）も多い。
　　中国から伝わった漢字には、中国式に読む音（おん）読みと日本式に読む訓（くん）読みとがある。

c）日本語

　　日本語は、独特の文章構造をとり、固有の文字を持ち、ほかの言語とあまり類似していない。系統的には、朝鮮語・アルタイ諸語との同系説が有力であるが、その証明はまだされていない。
　　現代日本語の特徴のいくつかをあげると次のとおりである。

1）漢字・平仮名・片仮名・ローマ字など異なった種類の文字をまじえて用いる。

2）使用する文字の数が多い（一般通用漢字約3,000字〔そのうち常用漢字1,945字〕、平仮名・片仮名各46字）。

3）文章は、縦書きも横書きも行われる。

4）音韻組織が単純で、音節の種類が少ない（標準母音は、ア・イ・ウ・エ・オの五つ、音節は母音または子音と母音とからなり、常に母音で終わる。単独使

thousand years ago. They are ideograms developed from pictograms and signs. For example, the character meaning the sun was drawn in the form of the sun and that meaning a tree was made to resemble the shape of a tree. Going a step further, two trees were combined in a single character to indicate a wood and three trees were combined to represent a forest. The kanji characters developed in China gradually began to be used in Korea, Japan and Vietnam. There are said to be about fifty thousand characters in total.

This is only the number of characters; the number of words that can be formed by combining characters is many times this. In Japan, 1,945 kanji characters have been selected as those most suitable for ordinary purposes. Still one must know considerably more characters than this in order to read even the newspapers and ordinary books since the characters for many personal and place names are not included in this limited number.

The Japanese have also invented a fair number of kanji characters (called Japanese characters) for their own use.

Most of the kanji introduced from China can be read in two ways: in the "*on*" or Chinese reading and in the "*kun*" or Japanese reading.

c) The Japanese Language

The Japanese language has its own peculiar sentence structure and writing system and has little in common with other languages of the world. Although the theory that Japanese belongs to the Altaic and Korean family of languages is widely accepted, this has never been fully substantiated.

Below are listed a few of the characteristic features of modern Japanese:

1) It uses a mixture of different types of characters, namely, *kanji* characters, *hiragana* characters, *katakana* characters and Roman letters.

2) The number of characters used is large. (There are about 3,000 commonly used kanji characters including the 1,945 "daily use characters," 46 hiragana characters and 46 katakana characters.)

3) Sentences can be written either vertically or horizontally.

4) Having few sounds, it is phonetically simple. (It has only five standard vowels: "a" as in father, "i" as in piano, "u" as in flute, "e" as in red and "o" as in cord. Syllables are

用の子音はンのみ)。

5) 同じ事物を指すのに、いくつもの単語が用いられる。とくに一・二人称代名詞は種類が多い(わたし・ぼく・おれ、あなた・きみ・おまえなど)。
6) 同じ音で異なった意味を表わす単語が多い(対象・対照・対称、公正・厚生・構成など)。
7) 職業・年齢・性別などによる用語の違いが著しい。
8) 助詞(が・をなど)、助動詞(ない・だろうなど)が文の成立に大切な機能を果たしている。
9) 主語は述語の前におき、述語は文の終わりにおくが、文節の順序はかなり自由である。主語は述語の使い方で省略されることも多い。

10) 敬語が発達していて、複雑である。

d) 外国人の日本語学習

　　日本語はそれ自体は、学びはじめるのに容易な言語の一つであるとされている。発音が簡単で、文法規制も例外が少なく、構文上の制約もゆるい。難しさは主として漢字の読み書きにある。

　　日本語は話す主人公が男であるか女であるか、大人であるか子供であるか、によって用法が少しずつ異なる。たとえば「私」を意味する言葉も、その主人公によって幾通りかに使い分けられる。さらに面倒なことは、相手との関係によっても使い分けられる。そのほか、同じ音で違う意味の言葉が多かったりして、外国人にはすぐ理解しにくい面がある。また敬語といわれる用法がかなり広く使われている。これには二つのタイプがある。ひとつは相手のものや行為に尊敬語をつける用法で、もうひとつは自分のことを謙遜して表現する用法である。敬語を正しく使うには、日本人でもかなりの訓練がいる。

　　しかし、日本人は自分達が外国語を話すことが下手なため、外国人が日本語を間違えて話しても、できるだけよく理解しようと努める。

formed by a single vowel or a consonant-vowel combination, "n" being the only consonant that can stand alone.)

5) The same thing or idea can often be expressed with a number of different words. For example, there are a number of words that would translate into English as "you."

6) There are many words having the same sound but expressing different ideas.

7) There are pronounced differences in the words and expressions used by persons of different occupation, age, sex etc.

8) Particles are used to indicate part of speech (subject, object etc.) and auxiliary verbs play an important role in sentence structure.

9) Aside from the restriction that the subject must come before the predicate (which comes last), the speaker has considerable freedom in choosing the order of the phrases. The subject is often omitted when the meaning is clear from the predicate alone.

10) It has a complicated system of honorific expression.

d) Learning Japanese

Purely from the linguistic point of view, Japanese is generally considered as one of the easier languages for a beginner to approach. It has a simple pronunciation scheme and few exceptions to grammatical rules. Restrictions on sentence structure are not severe. Probably the most difficult aspect of the language is the reading and writing of *kanji* characters.

The way Japanese is spoken differs somewhat depending on whether the speaker is a man or a woman, an adult or a child. For example, there are numerous words meaning "I" and each speaker refers to himself using the one that is most appropriate for his situation. What is even more troublesome is that the speaker must choose his words considering the relationship between himself and the person he is speaking to. Another aspect of the language that makes it difficult for foreigners to grasp quickly is the presence of many words which are pronounced the same but have different meanings. Still another is the relatively common use of especially polite (honorific) speech forms. These are of two types: one which uses special words of respect in connection with the acts and possessions of the person or persons one is speaking to and one which uses special words of modesty with respect to oneself. Even native speakers require considerable

日本語は他の言語と異なったところが多いため、難しいと思われがちであるが、基礎的な会話は決して難しくない。

　　その証拠に、日本に来ている外国人は、１年もすると日常会話は十分できるようになる人が多い。

　　現在世界各国における日本語学習者は 200 万ないし 300 万人といわれており、その数は次第に増加しつつある。とくに ASEAN 諸国・中国・韓国などで、日本語の学習者が急増している。

e) 日本語のなかの外来語

　　日本語には多くの外来語が取り入れられている。このうち最も古く、多いのが漢語である。しかも、その大部分は漢語本来の意味とは別に、日本語としての意味が与えられた。したがって、この場合漢語は外来語とはいいがたい。

1) 英語から

　　19 世紀以来非常に多い。

　　ポスト、ボール、バス、プール、オートメーション、ラッシュ、メリット、テレビ、ミシン、コンピュータ、ナイフ

2) オランダ語から

　　17 世紀から 19 世紀まで、日本はヨーロッパの国としてはオランダとのみ貿易していたため、オランダ語からきたものも多い。

　　コック、ピント、ホース、ポンプ、ポン酢、ボール盤、ホップ、ビール、ドイツ、おてんば、コンパス、アルカリ、コーヒー、ガラス、ゴム、ペンキ、マンガン、モートル

3) ジャワ語から

　　サラサ

4) ポルトガル語から

　　日本に初めて来たヨーロッパ人がポルトガル人だったため、ポルトガル語からも多い。

　　金平糖、天ぷら、カッパ、ボタン、パン、タバコ、

training and practice before they can use honorifics properly.

The Japanese themselves are not good at speaking foreign languages, and therefore they understand the problems of the foreigner and will make every effort to understand him even if he makes mistakes.

Because of the many differences between it and other languages, Japanese tends to be considered difficult. In fact, however, basic spoken Japanese is not difficult at all. This is evidenced by the fact that many foreign visitors master the language well enough for their daily needs after only a year's stay.

It is estimated that worldwide anywhere between 2 and 3 million people are studying Japanese, and the number is increasing rapidly, especially in the ASEAN countries and in China and Korea.

e) Loan Words

Japanese has borrowed a large number of words from other languages. The oldest and largest group of borrowed words is from China. However, as the meanings assigned to most of the Chinese words used in Japanese are different from the original Chinese meanings, it does not seem quite proper to call them loan words.

1) From English

A great many English words have been adopted in Japanese from the nineteenth century on.

post, ball, bus, pool, automation, rush, merit, television, (sewing) machine, computer, knife

2) From Dutch

Holland was the only European country with which Japan had trade relations between the seventeenth and nineteenth centuries. As a consequence, a large number of Dutch words came into Japanese.

kok, brandpunt, hoos, pomp,pons, boor-bank, hop, bier, Duitsch,ontembaar, kompas, alkali, koffie, glas, gom, pek, mangaan, motor

3) From Javanese

saraça

4) From Portuguese

As the first European visitors to Japan were from Portugal, Japanese has adopted many Portuguese words.

confeito, tempero, capa, botao, pão, tabaco, carta,

カルタ、ブランコ、ピン、キリ、オランダ、ギリシ
ャ、ジュバン
5）韓国語から
韓国語からきた言葉は極めて多いが、現在外来語
として、日本語と区別できるものは少ない。
チョンガー、パッチ
6）イタリア語から
音楽用語・料理用語を中心に比較的多い。
チェンバロ、メゾピアノ、オペラ、ソナタ、ソルフ
ェージ、スタッカート、スパゲティ、マカロニ、チ
ャオ、フィナーレ
7）フランス語から
デッサン、リットル、メートル、ポロネーズ、シャ
ッポ、オートクチュール、オブジェ、グラム、サボ
タージュ、シルエット、フィアンセ、モルモット、
ブルジョア、ビフテキ、バカンス、スイス、コロッケ
8）ドイツ語から
ゼミナール、テーマ、アルバイト、カルテ、ガーゼ、
リンパ、クレゾール、デマ（ゴギー）、ノイローゼ、
ボンベ、ルンペン、ルーペ、ヒステリー、ナトリウ
ム、セレナーデ、チフス、ヘモグロビン
9）マレーシア語から
ペケ、トンカチ、トカゲ
10）ロシア語
インテリ、カンパ、ノルマ

f）日本語の文書事務処理

　　日本語のタイプライターは1900年代から利用される
ようになったが、特別な訓練を受けたタイピストだけし
か使えなかった。したがって、最近まで一般の人は手で
すべて書かざるを得なかった。
　　1978年に日本語ワードプロセッサ（俗称ワープロ）
が開発された。これにより漢字仮名まじり文の文書の作
成・編集が、英文の文書と同様に、容易にできるように
なった。
　　80年代の後半から、このワープロは会社・官庁に急
速に普及し、オフィスの文書業務に欠かせないものにな
った。
　　これに並行して、90年頃からパソコン用のワープ
ロ・プログラムが利用されるようになり、日本語の文書
事務の効率化は、ますます進んでいる。

balanço, pinta, cruz, Holanda, Grécia, gibão

5) From Korean
Although an exceedingly large number of words have entered Japanese from Korean, only very few of them can presently be labeled loan words as distinguished from true Japanese words.

chonga, pat-chi

6) From Italian
The number of loan words from Italian is relatively large, particularly in connection with music and food.

cembalo, mezzo piano, opera, sonata, solfège, staccato, spaghetti, maccaroni, ciao, finale

7) From French
dessin, litre, mètre, polonaise, chapeau, haute couture, objet, gramme, sabotage, silhouette, fiancé, marmotte, bourgeoisie, bifteck, vacances, Suisse, croquette

8) From German
Seminar, Thema, Arbeit, Karte, Gaze, Lymphe, Kresol, Dema(gogie), Neurose, Bombe, Lumpen, Lupe, Hysterie, Natrium, Serenade, Typhus, Hämoglobin

9) From Malaysian
pergi, tongkat, takék

10) From Russian
intelli gentsiya, kamp anija, norma

f) Japanese Word Processing

Although Japanese-language typewriters became available from the early 1900s, only specially trained typists could use them. Until recently, therefore, the ordinary person had to write everything by hand.

With the development of the first Japanese–language word processor in 1978, however, the production and editing of Japanese–language documents became as easy as ones in English.

From the mid 1980s, word processors rapidly became indispensable for the production of all types of documents at companies and government offices.

Word processor programs for personal computers appeared from around 1990 and are further increasing the efficiency of Japanese document preparation.

g）日本の文学

　8世紀の初め、皇室を中心とした国家体制が完成すると、日本古代の神話と歴史が『古事記』と『日本書紀』にまとめられた。

　『古事記』は、故事を記憶することを職としていた宮廷の役人が暗唱していたものをまとめた記録である。『古事記』は、和漢折衷的な漢文体で書かれ、天皇を中心としたより強力な国家を形成しようという意図で編纂されたものだが、日本最古の文学と考えられている。

　『日本書紀』は、本格的な史書である。先進隣国であった中国に敬意を払い、純粋な漢文体で書かれている。

　また8世紀の後半には、現存する最古の歌集『万葉集』が登場した。これは、20巻からなり、450年にわたって天皇から庶民まで各階層の作者がつくった約4,500首もの歌が含まれている。その歌の約9割が万葉仮名で書かれた短歌（別項258頁参照）である。万葉仮名は、日本語の音を表すために、漢字（中国の表意文字）の中国語と日本語の読み方を利用した表現法である。

　9世紀末の仮名文字の発明によって、多くの物語が生み出されるようになった（「仮名」は音節文字で、書くのがやさしく、数も限られているので、日本語を標記するのがたいへん楽になった）。政治の権力が貴族に移ったこととあいまって、この仮名の出現によって多彩な平安文学の時代の基盤ができあがった。そして、11世紀の初めに、この時代の文学は紫式部の作品『源氏物語』によって最盛期を迎えた。この物語のなかで、紫式部は皇子として生まれながら天皇となれなかった主人公光源氏の華やかな宮廷生活を描いている。『源氏物語』は、和歌をまじえた和文体で書かれている。登場人物たちの心理描写は見事である。『源氏物語』は54帖におよび、世界最古の長編小説である。

　12世紀、武士階級が台頭し、動乱のなかで人々は宗教に救いを求めるようになった。こうして仏教が武士や庶民の間に広まった。これを反映して、この時代の文学は仏教的無常観から描かれた作品が多い。その代表作が『平家物語』だが、作者は不明である。この物語は13世紀に登場し、琵琶の音楽を伴奏として語り継がれ民衆の中に広まった。作品の内容は、12世紀後半の平家一門の繁栄と滅亡を描いた物語であり、作品の根底には、奢れる者は必ず滅びるという仏教観が貫かれている。

g) Japanese Literature

Once Japan had been consolidated as a single nation around the imperial family, the country's ancient myths and history were gathered together in the *Kojiki* and *Nihonshoki* in the early eighth century.

The *Kojiki* is a record of ancient events as recited by a court official responsible for memorizing such matters. Written in a blend of Japanese and classical Chinese (*kanbun*), it is considered Japan's earliest literary work, despite being compiled with the political motive of building a stronger nation around the emperor.

The *Nihonshoki* is a straightforward historical record. It is written in pure kanbun with deference to China as an advanced neighbor.

Also in the late eighth century, there appeared what is now the oldest existing anthology of poetry, the *Manyoshu*, which consists of 20 scrolls and includes approximately 4,500 poems written by poets in all walks of life, from emperors to common people, over a period of about 450 years. Around 90% of the poems are *tanka* (see p. 259) written in *manyogana*, a style that uses the Chinese and Japanese readings of *kanji* characters (Chinese ideograms) to represent Japanese phonetically.

The invention and spread of *kana* characters toward the end of the ninth century led to the emergence of many stories. (As kana are phonetic (each representing a single syllable), easy to write and of limited number, they greatly simplified the writing of Japanese.) The advent of kana, together with the shift of the center of political power to the nobility, laid the foundation for the productive Heian literary period, which peaked in the early eleventh century with the writing of *Genji Monogatari* (*The Tale of Genji*) by Murasaki Shikibu. In her story, she depicts the brilliant court life of the hero Hikaru Genji, who, although a prince by birth, fails to become emperor. *Genji Monogatari* is written in Japanese style, intermixed with *waka* poetry. Its portrayal of the thoughts and feelings of the characters is exquisite. Running to 54 books, this is the world's first full-length novel.

In the twelfth century, midst the incessant conflicts that accompanied the rise of the warrior class to power, people turned to religion. Buddhism spread among both the warriors and the common people. Reflecting this, the literature of the period is

17世紀初めに江戸幕府の創設とともに、動乱の世が終わりを告げた。平和な年月の間に商業の発展に伴い町人が経済力を身につけるようになり、町人中心の文化が誕生した。その代表的な存在が、井原西鶴と近松門左衛門であった。井原西鶴の代表作は『好色一代男』で、11世紀に書かれた『源氏物語』に倣って、世之介という好色の男の生涯が54章にわたって描かれている。近松門左衛門は浄瑠璃や歌舞伎の脚本をたくさん執筆し、当時の庶民の姿を巧みに描いた。義理と人情との葛藤に苦しんだ末に心中した、徳兵衛とお初という若い男女を描いた『曾根崎心中』は、特に有名である。また、俳句（別項258頁参照）を優れた芸術にまで高めた松尾芭蕉が活躍したのも、この時代である。芭蕉は、俳句以外にも作品を残しているが、なかでも奥羽・北陸の大旅行を題材とした『奥の細道』は、日本の紀行文学の代表作である。

　19世紀後半の明治維新以降、日本は西欧との交流を深め、その影響を受けてさまざまな文芸思潮や新しい作品が生み出された。近代文学の二大巨峰といわれるのが、森鷗外と夏目漱石である。ともに、西欧への留学を経験し、東西文化に精通して、鷗外と漱石は、どこの派にも属さず、独自の立場を守って多くの作品を生み出した。『舞姫』は、鷗外の処女作である。ドイツ留学中に真の自我に目覚めた官吏、太田豊太郎にかかわる小説である。ドイツ滞在中踊り子エリスとの恋愛におちいり、免官されてしまう。親友のはからいで帰国することになるが、そのため自由と発狂した恋人を棄てざるをえなくなる。こうした胸中の苦悩を描いた自伝的な色彩の強い作品である。また、『吾輩は猫である』は漱石の処女作である。中学校教師苦沙弥先生の飼い猫を主人公とした、擬人体で書かれている。飼い主の家族、周囲の人物とそこに起きるさまざまな事件が、飼い猫の目から、鋭い風刺とユ

dominated by works with an underlying tone that derives from the Buddhist concept of the impermanence of worldly things. The best work from the period is *Heike Monogatari* (*The Tale of the Heike*), whose author is unknown. The story appeared in the thirteenth century and was spread among the people of the time in the form of a narration accompanied by the music of the *biwa*, a stringed instrument. It tells the story of the rise to glory and eventual downfall of the Heike clan in the late twelfth century, a theme based on the Buddhist concept that the proud will surely be destroyed.

The period of civil wars came to a close with the establishment of the Edo Shogunate at the beginning of the seventeenth century. As commerce flourished and the merchant class gradually gained economic power during these peaceful years, a new urban culture developed. The leading writers to emerge were Saikaku Ihara and Monzaemon Chikamatsu. Ihara's best known work is *Koshoku Ichidaiotoko* (*Life of an Amorous Man*) which, in the style of the eleventh-century *Genji Monogatari*, devoted 54 chapters to the lifetime escapades of the lecherous Yonosuke. Monzaemon Chikamatsu wrote a large number of *joruri* and *kabuki* plays which are especially notable for their superb portrayal of the common people. Probably his most famous work is *Sonezaki Shinju* (*Love Suicides at Sonezaki*), the story of young lovers, Tokubei and Hatsu, who, torn between their love and their obligations, find suicide the only solution. Also of this period is Basho Matsuo, the poet who elevated *haiku* to a major poetic genre (see p. 259). While Basho is best known for his poems, he also produced a number of other works, most notably *Oku no Hosomichi* (*The Narrow Road to the Deep North*), a diary of his extensive travels through northern Honshu which is a classic among Japanese travelogues.

The deepening exchanges between Japan and the West following the Meiji Restoration in the late nineteenth century gave rise to various literary trends and new works. The two masters of this modern literature period were Ogai Mori and Soseki Natsume. Both studied abroad, were deeply versed in Western as well as Eastern culture, avoided involvement in any particular school, and produced many works that reflected their own independent views. Ogai's first work was *Maihime* (*The Dancing Girl*), a novel about Toyotaro Ota, a government worker who discovers his true self while studying in Germany. While there, he falls in

ーモアによって描かれている。

　そのほかに、翻訳版によって海外でよく知られている
作家・作品としては、次のようなものがある。大阪の豪
商一家の四人姉妹を題材に「源氏物語」的世界を描いた
『細雪』の谷崎潤一郎。近代叙情文学の古典といわれる
『雪国』を書いた川端康成（別項 368 頁参照）。金閣寺に
放火する青年の心理的過程を描いた『金閣寺』の三島由
紀夫。作者の内的な芸術的自叙伝とされる『人間失格』
の太宰治。砂の穴に落ち込んだ中学教師が、穴に住む女
と共同生活をする話を描いた『砂の女』の安部公房。障
害を持った子供の誕生に対する青年の葛藤を描いた『個
人的な体験』の大江健三郎（別項 368 頁参照）。

h) 短歌・俳句

　短歌は和歌の一形式で、5・7・5・7・7の5句
31 音の形式を持つ。この定型は、感情を表現する抒情
詩として、日本人の呼吸に極めて自然な長さであるとい
われている。最初の5・7・5を上の句、続く7・7を
下の句という。

　和歌の形式は、もとは長歌・短歌・旋頭歌など多様で
あったが、やがて短歌のみが優勢となり、平安時代以降
（8世紀末以降）は、和歌すなわち短歌と考えられるよ
うになった。
　短歌は短詩型抒情詩であるため、自然や人間生活の美
を尊重し、あこがれる心が重要な要素である。このあこ

love with a dancer, at the cost of losing his post. Although he manages to return to Japan with the help of a friend, he is forced to abandon both his freedom and his now crazed sweetheart. The story, which centers on Ota's anguish, has strong autobiographic overtones. Soseki's first work was *Wagahai wa Neko de Aru* (*I am a Cat*). It is written in the first person as if by a cat, the pet of a middle school teacher named Kushami. The story about this teacher, his family and the other characters and the incidents that occur, as seen through the eyes of the cat, is told with biting satire and considerable humor.

A short list of Japanese literary works that have become well known overseas in their translated versions would include the following. Junichiro Tanizaki's *Sasame Yuki* (*The Makioka Sisters*), which paints a *Genji Monogatari*-like world around four sisters belonging to a great Osaka merchant family. Yasunari Kawabata's *Yukiguni (Snow Country)*, often called a classic of modern lyric literature (see p.369). Yukio Mishima's *Kinkakuji (The Temple of the Golden Pavilion)*, which follows the mental processes of a young man who sets fire to a famous temple in Kyoto. Osamu Dazai's *Ningen Shikkaku (No Longer Human)*, considered a revealing of the writer's inner artistic sensibilities. Kobo Abe's *Suna no Onna (The Woman in the Dunes)*, the story of a middle school teacher who falls into a hole in the sand and takes up life with a woman who lives there. Kenzaburo Oe's *Kojinteki na Taiken (A Personal Matter)*, which describes a young father's preoccupation with the birth of his handicapped son (see p. 369).

h) Tanka and Haiku

Tanka is one form of *waka* (Japanese poetry), consisting of five lines of 5, 7, 5, 7 and 7 syllables. It is said that for a Japanese this is the most natural length for a lyric poem expressing emotion. The first three lines of 5, 7 and 5 syllables are termed the *kami no ku* ("upper poem") and the remaining two lines of 7 and 7 syllables the *shimo no ku* ("lower poem").

Waka originally encompassed a variety of forms, such as *choka*, *tanka* and *sedoka*, but tanka gradually became the predominant form until, from the Heian Era (late 8th century), the term waka came to be considered synonymous with tanka.

As a short form of lyric poetry, tanka stresses the beauty of life and nature, and a feeling of yearning is an important element.

がれの心の本質を、単純な形式のなかに、喜怒哀楽の諸感情が交錯した深みのあるものとして、表現することが求められるのである。こうして心に感ずることをいきいきとうたいあげたものは、豊かな連想を呼ぶ力を持つ。このように、31音の言外に感じられるものを余情といい、短歌一首の内容は、この余情をも含めたものというべきである。

俳句は5・7・5の17音による定型詩である。

江戸時代の中ごろ（17世紀末ごろ）、松尾芭蕉が俳諧連歌の発句を独立させて、「さび」（枯れた渋み）、「しおり」（おのずから句に表われた繊細な余情）、「軽み」（題材を日常的な事物のなかに求め、そこにあか抜けした面白みを見いだそうとするもの）を理念とする、人生詩・自然詩としての芸術性を確立した。

俳句という呼び名が一般に用いられるようになったのは、明治20年代（19世紀末）になって、正岡子規に始まる。

俳句の特色として、季節にあらわれる動物や植物、生活のなかの行事や風習などを用いた季語をよみこむ。たとえば、「すみれ草」という季語によって、春の暖かさや、すみれ草の咲く山道の自然の情景の連想を呼びおこし、それによって最短詩型でありながら、句に広がりと深さをかもし出す。俳句はその対象を客観的・即物的に描き出すのであるが、実景をそのまま細かく描写することは不可能で、対象のかなめをおさえながらの省略が不可欠であり、季語もその一つである。

短歌・俳句は、現在も国民の間に広く愛好されており、いわば国民的文芸となっている。

(2) 伝統演劇・芸能

a) 伝統的な演劇・芸能

日本の演劇には長い歴史があるが、過去のものが次第に発展変化して現在の演劇になったのではない。過去のものはそのままの形で伝わり、他方つぎつぎに新しいものが加わって、現在の多種多様な演劇が共存しているのである。

伝統的な演劇として、14世紀からの「能」、17世紀からの「文楽」・「歌舞伎」が知られている。これらには現

What is sought within this simple form is to express the essence of this yearning with a depth in which all the emotions are intermingled. The vivid expression of that which has touched the heart has the power to evoke a wealth of associations. This allusive feeling contained in these thirty-one syllables is referred to as *yojo*. In content, a tanka poem should include this yojo.

Haiku is a fixed verse form of seventeen syllables arranged in a five-seven-five pattern.

Basho Matsuo, in the middle of the Edo period (late 17th century), gave independent life to the *hokku* (opening verse) of the *haikairenga* (linked verse), and established it as an art form dealing with life and nature, using aesthetic values such as the austere elegance called *sabi*, *shiori*, in which there is a natural expression of delicate beauty, and *karumi*, which seeks a refined interest in plain everyday material.

General use of the name "haiku" for this form began with Shiki Masaoka, in the third decade of the Meiji Era (end of the 19th century).

A feature of haiku is inclusion of a "season word," referring to an animal, plant, event or custom of the season. For example, the season word *sumireso* (violets) will bring to mind the warmth of spring and violets in bloom along a mountain path. Thus, breadth and depth is given to haiku, the shortest of poems. Haiku gives an objective, fleeting picture of its subject. As it is impossible to depict an actual scene in detail, it is necessary to abbreviate to the essentials, and the season word is one such abbreviation.

Tanka and haiku are very popular nowadays too, and can be said to have become an art form of the people.

(2) Traditional Dramas and Entertainments

a) Traditional Theater and Entertainments

Theater in Japan has a long history. The theater forms of today, however, are not the results of gradual changes and developments over the ages. Instead, each has reached us in its original form, while at the same time new forms have been added so that many types of theater now coexist.

The well-known traditional forms of theater are *noh*, dating from the fourteenth century, and *bunraku* and *kabuki*, dating

在熱心な愛好者がいるが、日本人全体からするとごく一部の人である。

一方、伝統的な大衆芸能として「浪花節」・「落語」・「民謡」などがあり、むしろこれらの方がはるかに多くの日本人に愛好され、親しまれている。

伝統的な邦楽では、「箏曲」・「長唄」・「小唄」・「謡曲」などに、現在も比較的多くの愛好者がいる。

b）能

日本最古の演劇である「能」の起源は古いが、盛んになったのは 14 世紀以降である。「歌舞伎」や「文楽」が庶民の演劇であるのに対し、能は武士階級のものとされた。

能は独特な舞台の上で、曲につれて舞い踊る楽劇である。主役は面をかぶり、ゆっくりとした仕草で動き、劇的な要素は少ない。

能の曲は謡曲といわれ、これのみでも独立の芸術とされている。

能の題材は約 250 あるが、これらを分類すると神・男・女・狂・鬼の 5 種になり、思想的には仏教の影響を受けているものが多い。

主役のかぶる面の役は特定のものに決まっておらず、一つの面をいろいろのテーマのいろいろの役に使い分けている。能の面は個性的な表情に乏しいが、現実から昇華した形相（けいそう）のなかに表わされる奥深さが能面の真髄とされる。能面は、極度に抽象化された役者の動作と、単調な音楽とあいまって独自の芸術美を発揮する。能の衣装も面とともに、能の味わいの深さを構成する主要な要素となっている。

c）歌舞伎

歌舞伎は 17 世紀から盛んになった日本の代表的な庶民演劇である。現在、能や文楽よりも愛好者が多い。能や文楽の要素も取り入れているので、日本の伝統芸能の

from the seventeenth century. Although these have their ardent followers, such devotees make up only a very small fraction of the Japanese people.

Traditional forms of entertainment include *naniwabushi* (story-telling), *rakugo* (humorous story-telling) and *minyo* (folk songs), and a far greater number of Japanese enjoy and are familiar with these.

Many people also enjoy singing, playing or listening to traditional Japanese music such as *sokyoku*, *nagauta*, *kouta* and *yokyoku*.

b) Noh

The origins of *noh*, Japan's oldest theater form, go back to ancient times; but it was in the fourteenth century that it began to flourish. Whereas *kabuki* and *bunraku* were for the common people, noh was for members of the warrior or samurai class.

Noh is a lyric dance-drama, performed on a special stage to the accompaniment of music. Dramatic elements are few: the principal characters wear masks and the dance-movements are performed slowly.

The noh singing, called *yokyoku*, is also practiced as an independent art.

There exist about 250 noh plays, which are grouped roughly into five main classifications according to subject matter. These five classifications are *shin* (God), *nan* (man), *nyo* (woman), *kyo* (madness), and *ki* (demon). The concepts of most of the plays show Buddhist influences.

The masks worn by the actors are not limited to any one specific role, but are used for various roles in different plays. Noh masks are lacking in individuality of expression, and their essence lies in a profoundness in form that is a sublimation of reality. The noh mask combines with the extremely symbolic movements of the actor and the monotonic music to display a unique artistic beauty. The noh costumes, together with the masks, are the main elements which form the profoundness of the noh experience.

c) Kabuki

Kabuki is a popular dramatic art form that has been a favorite among the Japanese people since the seventeenth century. It is today more popular than either *noh* or *bunraku*, two classical

集大成的なものといえる。

　歌舞伎の舞台装置には、花道や回り舞台など独特のものがある。花道は、舞台に向かって観客席を貫いて設けられた通路である。これは俳優が登場・退場するためだけでなく、俳優と観客との交流をも、目的とするものである。

　演劇としての性格からいえば、歌舞伎は音楽劇であり、舞踊劇である。その多くの作品が三味線などによる日本固有の音曲を伴奏とし、台詞にも動作にも独特の音楽的リズム感が要求される。そして、省略・誇張・形式化された動きが一つの様式を生み出し、近代的リアリズムに立脚する演劇とは大きく異なっている。

　男優が女性の役に扮することや、瞬間的な衣装替えの技巧なども特色の一つである。

　歌舞伎の主題には、昔の貴族や武士の世界を描くものと、庶民の生活を描くものとの2種類がある。

　歌舞伎の俳優は、先祖の芸を受け継ぐよう幼少から育てられ、脚本にしたがって演ずるというよりは、俳優の芸を中心に脚本がつくられる。

d）文楽（人形浄瑠璃）

　「文楽」は一種の人形劇である。能・歌舞伎と並んで日本三大古典演劇の一つで、17世紀から盛んになった。

　文楽で使う人形は首・胴・手・足・衣装からなっていて、1mから1.5mの大きさである。

dramatic forms from which it borrows heavily. Because of its assimilation of various aspects of the other dramatic art forms, kabuki might well be called a summarization of traditional Japanese theatrical art.

Kabuki does, however, have a number of unique points. One of these is the *mawari butai* (revolving stage) which permits almost instantaneous changes of scene. Another is the *hanamichi*, a long, narrow, walk-like extension of the stage that runs through the audience to the back of the theater. Although the actors often enter and exit via the hanamichi, it is not primarily a passageway but a device for permitting the actors to come into closer contact with their audience.

Music and dancing are fundamental to the kabuki performance. Most kabuki plays are performed to the accompaniment of typically Japanese melodies played on several *shamisen* (a three-stringed instrument of the lute family) and other instruments peculiar to Japan. The actors are required to follow a specific "kabuki rhythm" pattern in both their speech and their movements. Differing greatly from modern drama, which lays primary emphasis on realism, kabuki is a formalized art in which the significance of omissions, exaggerations and many of the actors' movements are pre-defined.

Anyone watching kabuki for the first time will no doubt be surprised to learn that all roles, including those of female characters, are played by men. He will also be amazed by the rapidity with which the actors change costumes, often transforming themselves into totally different characters in a matter of seconds.

By subject matter, kabuki plays fall into two categories: those which deal with the fortunes of the noble and warrior classes and those which depict the lives of the common people.

The art of kabuki acting is passed on from father to son and training begins at a very early age. The actor is considered more important than the play; he does not change his acting style to fit the play but the play is changed to fit his particular skills.

d) Bunraku

Bunraku is one form of puppet theater. It has flourished since the seventeenth century and now stands with *noh* and *kabuki* as one of the three great classical forms of theater in Japan.

Bunraku puppets consist of a head, trunk, hands, feet, and costume, and range in size from about a meter to a meter and a

舞台の上で、人形を人形遣いが、1体につき3人で動かす。人形遣いは黒い衣で顔を隠しており、それぞれ首と右手・左手・足の動きを分担している。女の人形には足がなく、人形の衣装のすそさばきで巧みに表現する。人形は、三味線の伴奏と独特の節まわしで語る浄瑠璃にあわせて、さまざまな仕草をする。このため、文楽のことを人形浄瑠璃ともいう。

人形の首は約60種類あり、そのうち40種類は、一つの首をいろいろの役に使う。そのほかに一首一役の特殊な首がある。目や口が開閉するもの、眉が上下するもの、指の動くものもある。感情の動きなども、人形の微妙な動作で表現される。

e）邦　楽

日本古来の邦楽には、その発生時期にしたがって、古代の「雅楽」、中世の「能楽」、近世の「三味線」・「箏」の音楽があるが、各種の邦楽のうち、現在も比較的愛好者が多いのは「箏曲」・「長唄」・「小唄」・「謡曲」などである。

箏曲は、琴で演奏する音楽の総称で、16世紀後半に発展し、その後三味線・胡弓・尺八とも合奏されるようになった。現在は西洋音楽との交流も試みられている。

長唄は、三味線音楽による長編のうたいもので、17世紀後半に歌舞伎舞踊とともに発達し、その過程で謡曲・地歌・浄瑠璃・民謡などの歌詞や曲節が取り入れられたため、多様性があり、伴奏に笛・小鼓・大鼓・太鼓の囃子などを用いるので、曲詞が爽快で、はでなことが特徴である。

小唄は、15〜16世紀ごろ行われた庶民的な短い歌謡である小歌の流れをくみ、19世紀初めごろに生まれた小歌曲で、テンポが早く、声をおさえる発声法でうたわれ、伴奏の三味線は「ばち」を使わず「つまびき」をする。19世紀終わりごろに、個性的な作詩・作曲、独特な伴奏が行われるようになって様式が確立した。

half.

On the stage, each puppet is manipulated by three puppeteers. These puppeteers wear black robes with a flap that covers the face. One puppeteer manipulates the puppet's head and right hand, one the left hand, and one the feet. In the case of female dolls, which have no feet, the third man skillfully manipulates the skirts of the doll to give the impression of walking and other leg movements. The puppets perform the actions as the story is related in a special chant, called *joruri*, to the accompaniment of *shamisen* music. Because of this, bunraku is also called *ningyo-joruri* (puppet ballad-drama).

Altogether there are about 60 puppet heads. Around 40 of these are multi-role heads, while the others are limited to a single role each. There are puppets with eyes and mouth that can be opened and shut, with eyebrows that move up and down, and fingers that move. Emotions are expressed by subtle movements.

e) Japanese Music

Traditional Japanese music is classified by period of origin into *gagaku* (ancient), *nogaku* (medieval), and the music of the *shamisen* and *koto* (recent). Among the various subclasses of Japanese music, those having relatively large followings today are *sokyoku*, *nagauta*, *kouta* and *yokyoku*.

Sokyoku is the general name for music played on the koto (a kind of harp). This musical form which developed in the second half of the sixteenth century later came to be played in concert with the shamisen (three-stringed lute), the *kokyu* (Chinese fiddle) and the *shakuhachi* (five-holed bamboo clarinet). Present-day attempts have been made to blend sokyoku with Occidental music.

Nagauta is a kind of long epic song based on shamisen music which evolved together with *kabuki* dancing in the latter half of the seventeenth century. Having absorbed the lyrics and melodies of yokyoku, *jiuta* (regional music), *joruri* (puppet ballad-drama music) and *minyo* (folk music) in the course of its development, nagauta has become very diverse in form. It is performed in a lively, florid style to the accompaniment of flutes and full-sized drums.

Kouta is a form of short song or ditty which appeared in the early nineteenth century but which derives from popular short songs of the fifteenth and sixteenth centuries. The songs are sung

謡曲は、能の台本ともいえる性格を持つが、独立したかたちでもうたわれる。大部分15～16世紀ごろにつくられたもので、ことに観阿弥・世阿弥父子によるものが多い。

詞章は7・5調または5・7調の韻文が主体で、その多くは『古事記』や『日本書紀』、『源氏物語』や『平家物語』、鎌倉・室町時代の説話などに題材をもとめている。一般に能管・小鼓・大鼓・太鼓の伴奏で演奏され、シテ・ワキ・ツレなど登場人物のうたう部分と合唱する部分とからなっている。

f） 日本舞踊

日本舞踊は、「舞」と「踊」とに大別されるが、一般に「能」以前のものが「舞」、歌舞伎以後のものが「踊」と呼ばれてきた。

「歌舞伎踊」は今日も盛んに行われており、日本舞踊といえば、この歌舞伎踊を指すことも多い。

踊は15～16世紀ごろから、民俗舞踊として庶民の間で広く行われ、やがてそのなかから歌舞伎踊が生まれた。

その発展過程で舞の要素も取り入れられ、さらにたとえば、富士山の形を描いてみせるというような、演劇的表現の強い「振り」といわれる要素も加えられた。

女歌舞伎が禁止されて以後、専門の舞踊家は男子ばかりだったが、18世紀ごろから次第に芸者などの間に広まり、庶民の愛好者も増加した。

踊の流派も、「西川」・「花柳」・「若柳」・「藤間」など多くのものが生まれ、また20世紀初めごろからは西洋舞踊の影響を受けて、新舞踊運動が起こった。

at a quick tempo in a suppressed voice to the accompaniment of a shamisen plucked with the fingers instead of a plectrum, as is more common in other types of music. Kouta became established in its present form near the end of the nineteenth century as its devotees provided it with its own individual lyrics, melodies and style of shamisen accompaniment.

Yokyoku is the singing to which *noh* plays are performed and, for all intents and purposes, is itself the script of a noh play. It is also performed independently of noh. Most yokyoku date back to the fifteenth and sixteenth centuries and many were written by a composer named Kan'ami and his son, Zeami.

The verses generally follow a rhymed seven syllable-five syllable or five syllable-seven syllable pattern and the subject is usually a tale from the *Kojiki*, the *Nihonshoki*, *Genji Monogatari* or *Heike Monogatari*, or a story from the Kamakura or Muromachi era. Yokyoku is ordinarily sung to the accompaniment of flutes, hand drums and full-sized drums. The characters appearing in the story sing both individually and in chorus.

f) Japanese Dancing

There are two main types of Japanese dancing: *mai* and *odori*. Mai is a more static form associated with *noh* and odori a more dynamic form related to *kabuki*.

Odori (kabuki dancing) is by far the more popular at present, so much so that when people refer to Japanese dancing today, they almost always mean kabuki dancing.

Kabuki dancing grew out of various folk dances that became popular from around the fifteenth or sixteenth century.

As it developed, kabuki dancing borrowed certain aspects of mai (noh dancing). It also developed its own dramatic form of expression through gestures and postures. For example, if Mt. Fuji is mentioned in the accompanying song, the dancer may use the hands to suggest the shape of the mountain.

For many years following the prohibition of kabuki acting by women, all professional Japanese dancers were men. From around the middle of the eighteenth century, however, kabuki dancing became increasingly popular among *geisha* and was also taken up more by the general populace.

Today there are many different schools of Japanese dancing. A few of the better known are Nishikawa, Hanayagi, Wakayagi

現在では、主として女性が趣味として日本舞踊を習っている。

g）大衆芸能

　　現在多くの日本人に親しまれている、伝統的な大衆芸能をいくつかあげてみよう。

　　落語は、対話を主とした滑稽な話を独演し、聴衆を笑わせる大衆芸能の一つである。

　　落語の源流は16世紀にみられ、17世紀中ごろには、身ぶりもまじえて話すようになり、おかしさを効果的に盛り上げる方法として、話の終わりに「落ち」がつけられるようになった。

　　かけだしの落語家のことを「前座」というが、これは寄席で客が出揃うまでの時間を埋めるために、プログラムの初めの方に出演するということから出た呼び名である。芸の最も優れた落語家のことを「真（心）打ち」といい、寄席では最後に出演するが、これは客を呼ぶだけの値打ちのある、あるいは客の心を打つだけの優れた技量を持った落語家という意味である。

　　講談は、武勇伝・政談・人情話などを語り聞かせるもので、落語とともに日本特有の話術芸能の一種である。起源は17世紀で、はじめは棒読みだったが、その後調子をつけて独特なテンポで語るようになった。

　　浪花節は、三味線の伴奏に合わせて渋みのある独特の節まわしでうたう部分と、対話を主とした語りの部分からなり、これを独演する。

　　義理・人情や勧善・懲悪を内容とするものが多く、現在愛好者は年輩者に多い。「浪花節的」という言葉があるが、これは義理・人情に安易に傾きすぎていることをいう。

　　漫才は、2人のコンビで滑稽な軽口の掛け合いを行う演芸である。13～14世紀ごろから伝わる伝統的な万蔵（初春に悪魔をはらい、祝福をもたらすという習俗を演芸化したもので、2人で演ずる）を現代化したもので、19世紀末に関西に発生した。出し物は自作自演のものが多い。最近では、3人で演ずるものや楽器を持ち込むものもある。

and Fujima. There is also a neo-Japanese dancing movement which arose in the early 1900s under the influence of Western dance.

Today, far more women than men practice Japanese dancing as a pastime.

g) Popular Entertainment

Some traditional popular Japanese entertainments are:

Rakugo, the telling of long humorous stories, mainly in the form of dialogs.

Rakugo has its beginnings in the sixteenth century. By the middle of the seventeenth, the use of gestures and facial expression to accent the stories had become common and it had become the custom to include a "punch line," called the *ochi*, at the end of the story for added effect.

The storytellers are ranked according to their skill and experience. A beginner, for example, is referred to as a *zenza* (curtain raiser) from the fact that he is placed at the beginning of the program and performs while the audience is being seated. On the other hand, a rakugo master is called a *shin'uchi* (which can be interpreted either as "one of true value" or "one who strikes the heart") from his ability to draw large audiences because of his true worth as a story-teller or to move the hearts of his listeners. The shin'uchi is of course the last to perform.

Kodan, also a kind of storytelling but in this case the subject is a heroic tale, famous historical episode or human interest story. Kodan has its origins in the seventeenth century. Although in the early days the deliveries were flat and monotonous, the storytellers later began to chant their stories in a unique rhythm which remains a feature of the art right up to today. Rakugo and kodan stand together as two unique narrative forms.

Naniwabushi, a solo recitation partly sung in a special, sober intonation to the accompaniment of a *shamisen* and partly narrated in the form of a dialog.

The theme is usually one of love versus duty or good versus evil. Today, naniwabushi is popular mostly among older people. Naniwabushi has also given the Japanese language the word "naniwabushiteki" (naniwabushi-like) which means to be overly susceptible to the feelings of love and duty.

Manzai, slapstick and wisecracks by a comedy duo. Today's manzai developed in Western Japan toward the end of the

日本民謡には、仕事歌・神祭歌・遊び歌・酒宴の歌・子守歌などさまざまの種類がある。民謡の歴史は古いが、現在も聞かれるような曲節のものは、16〜17世紀ごろは仕事歌が中心であったが、次第に信仰や娯楽と結びついていった。

　　産業の機械化が進むにつれ、民謡は仕事を離れて宴席用の娯楽歌となったり、盆踊り歌などに変質しながら曲節のおもしろいものだけが残り、第二次大戦後は流行歌と同じような歌われ方がされるようになった。

(3)　伝統芸術・工芸

a)　いけばな

　　日本のいけばなは、切花を使った伝統的生活芸術で、16世紀ごろから盛んになった。

　　初期のいけばなは自然のままの素材と姿を重んじていたが、次第に素材は自然のものを用いながら、構成について理念的な意味づけが行われるようになった。

　　すなわち、いけばなの基本となる枝を天（宇宙）・地（地球）・人の3本とし、これらが調和のとれた大自然を表現する。

　　しかし伝統的ないけばなに対し、第二次大戦後、生命のない鉄片・石膏・ガラスなども素材にしてそれに生命感を与え、生きた形として表現しようとする前衛的ないけばなが生まれた。現在、いけばなの流派は3,000ほどあるといわれる。

　　いけばなの基礎技術としては、一つには素材を花器に定着させる方法、余分な枝葉の切り落とし方、素材の曲げ方、ゆがみの直し方など、造形上の技法がある。現在

nineteenth century as a modernized version of a dramatic form going back to the thirteenth or fourteenth century. (This traditional manzai, also performed by two persons, was based on a ritual for driving away demons and ushering in good fortune at the beginning of the new year.) Most manzai teams write their own material. In recent years there have been a number of innovations such as three-member teams and the use of musical instruments as a part of the act.

Japanese folk music covers a large number of types: work songs, sacred songs, play songs, drinking songs, lullabies. Although the history of folk music goes back to ancient times, most of the melodies popular today are based on work songs from the sixteenth and seventeenth centuries. What was originally a work song often came to be associated with religion or entertainment.

With increasing industrial mechanization, the melodies of work songs were readapted as party songs or for community dancing and, as a result of this process, only the more interesting tunes were preserved. In the postwar years, folk songs have come to be sung in the same way as popular songs.

(3) Traditional Arts and Crafts

a) Ikebana

Ikebana, the Japanese traditional art of arranging cut flowers, started to flourish in the sixteenth century.

At first, the emphasis in ikebana was on the materials and forms as they existed in their natural state; gradually, though, while continuing to employ natural materials, ideological significance became attached to the compositions.

That is, three basic sprays were used to signify, respectively, sky, earth and mankind, and their arrangement was to express the harmonic balance of Nature.

Since the Second World War, however, an avant-garde school of ikebana has appeared, the exponents of which, unlike those of the traditional schools, use lifeless materials such as iron, plaster, glass and the like arranged so as to give an impression of life through the vitality of form. There are estimated to be around 3,000 ikebana schools.

Many of the fundamental ikebana techniques are concerned

では室内装飾の一つとして、また生活を楽しむ趣味として、気軽に生活のなかに浸透している。

　なお、日本では以上のほかに、欧米流のフラワーデザインも趣味として行われている。

b）茶　道
　「茶道」は一定の作法にしたがって、主人と客が心の共感をもってお茶を飲む日本伝統のもので、安土桃山時代（16世紀後半）に千利休によって大成された。
　茶道では、抹茶という粉末状の精製された茶の葉を茶碗に入れて湯を注ぎ、茶筅（ちゃせん―竹の攪拌具）でかきまわして泡立てて飲む。
　茶道の礼法は、そのためにつくられた観賞価値のある独特の茶碗に、香り高い茶をたてて客にすすめる方法や、客がこれをいただく心得からなる。
　茶道の礼法には、武士の礼法や能の影響がみられ、これは日本の伝統的な礼儀作法に強い影響を与えた。形よりも心を重んじ、おのれをむなしうして客をもてなすのが茶道の心といわれている。
　茶室（茶をたてるためにつくられた専門の部屋）・露地（茶室の庭）・懐石料理（茶席で出す簡単な料理）・茶道具の取り合わせなど、すべてに客を迎える主人の細心の注意が払われる。茶会の客に初めて招かれた場合、茶道の礼法を知っているのにこしたことはないが、客として最も大切なのは、主人の心づかいに対する感謝の気持ちである。
　単にお茶を飲むという日常行為を、形式美をともなった一種の芸術に仕上げたところに茶道の特色がある。岡倉天心が英語で書いた『茶の本』は、日本の茶道を世界に紹介した本として有名である。

with structure, such as fixing the materials in the vase, cutting off unwanted leaves and twigs, curving the materials, correcting kinks, and so forth. Nowadays, ikebana is practiced as a form of interior decoration, or just as an enjoyable pastime.

Flower design is also practiced in Japan.

b) Tea Cult

Called *cha-no-yu* or *sado*, the tea cult is the traditional Japanese way of drinking tea in accordance with set rules of etiquette. Both the host and guests share a sense of togetherness during the ceremony. The cult was perfected by Rikyu Sen in the Azuchi-Momoyama period in the latter half of the sixteenth century.

In the tea ceremony, tea is made by putting powdered tea leaves into a cup and then adding hot water. It is then stirred till foamy with a tea whisk and drunk.

The "etiquette" of the tea ceremony concerns the manner in which the host serves the guests fine aromatic tea in a traditional tea cup of exquisite beauty and the manner in which guests show their appreciation to the host in the way they accept the tea.

The tea ceremony etiquette has been influenced by the etiquette observed by the *samurai* classes as well as by the form of *noh* dances. In turn, the tea cult has greatly influenced traditional Japanese customs and manners. Inner spirit is considered more important than the ritual form in the tea cult, and the heart of the ceremony lies in the "selfless manner" in which the host serves tea to the guests.

In inviting the guests to a ceremony, the host always takes utmost care in the preparation of his tea room, the adjacent garden, tea utensils and the provision of simple dishes for the guests in the tea room. Although a person invited to a tea ceremony for the first time is well advised to acquire some knowledge about the cult beforehand, still he should remember that the most important thing is the way guests express their sense of gratitude for the hospitality shown them by the host.

The tea ceremony is distinguished from other art forms in that it has taken a simple, everyday activity (tea drinking) and elevated it to the level of an art embodying the beauty of form. *The Book of Tea*, written in English by Tenshin Okakura, is well known as the book that introduced the Japanese tea cere-

c）書　道

　　書道は、漢字や仮名文字を毛筆と墨で書くことによっ
て、精神的な深さ、美しさを表わそうとする造形芸術で
ある。

　　西洋でも文字を美しく書くことは行われているが、中
国・朝鮮・日本では漢字が複雑で一字一字に意味がある
こと、軟らかくも硬くも、太くも細くも書ける毛筆があ
ったことにより、芸術として発達した。

　　作品の鑑賞は表現美（運筆・構成・墨色・配置など）
と内容美（風格・意味）によるが、書道は書家の人格の
表現であるから、鑑賞者の心を打つものがよいとされる。

　　正月2日に、めでたい言葉や縁起のよい詩歌などを毛
筆で書く「書きぞめ」は、現在も趣味家や小・中学生の
間で広く行われている。

d）日本画

　　日本画は、日本家屋に飾る絵としてふさわしく、その
愛好者も多い。日本画は絹地または和紙の上に毛筆で、
墨や岩絵具（群青・緑青・黄土などの鉱物を砕いたも
の）を用いて描く。

　　日本の絵画は、当初仏画として中国から伝わったが、
10世紀ごろになると日本の風景や風俗も描かれるよう
になり、大和絵が発生して日本画の基礎が築かれた。

　　水墨画は、禅宗とともに中国からもたらされ、15世
紀ごろには、日本画としても独自の発達をとげた。墨の
濃淡を用い、簡素・素朴で暗示的な表現を、特徴として
いる。

　　その後水墨画に大和絵の手法を取り入れるなど、いろ
いろな変遷をたどり、さらに近代以降は油絵の影響も受
けて、現代の日本画に至っている。

mony to the world.

c) Calligraphy

Calligraphy is a creative art form which attempts to express spiritual depth and beauty by means of *kanji* and *kana* characters written with a brush and *sumi* (ink).

The art of beautiful handwriting is practiced in the West, too; but because of the complexity of the kanji character, each of which has a meaning, and the use of a brush which allows the strokes to be made softly or firmly, thick or fine, calligraphy as an art is more highly developed in China, Korea and Japan.

Although appreciation of a work of calligraphy depends on the beauty of expression (brush strokes, structure, color of sumi, arrangement etc.) and content (style, meaning), as the writing expresses the personality of the writer, a good work is considered to be one that moves the observer.

On January 2 of each year, calligraphy devotees as well as many elementary and junior high school students take out their brushes to write auspicious words and poems in what is called the "First Writing of the New Year."

d) Japanese Painting

Japanese-style paintings are more appropriate for the traditional Japanese house, and thus have many devotees. Japanese paintings are done on silk or Japanese paper with a brush, using *sumi* and mineral colors (pulverized lapis lasuli, malchite, ocher, etc).

The Japanese style of painting has its origin in Buddhist painting introduced from China. From this beginning, there had, by around the tenth century, evolved the *Yamato-e* painting style which dealt with Japanese scenes and themes. It was this style that served as the foundation for what has come to be known as "Japanese painting."

The *suiboku-ga* style came into Japan from China together with Zen Buddhism and became established as an independent art form in about the fifteenth century. The suiboku-ga of that time were characterized by an allusive mode of expression that, based on lines and shades of sumi, was simple and unsophisticated.

Before reaching its present form, this style of painting underwent considerable change and development through the adop-

江戸時代の絵画で、現在でも広く鑑賞されているものに浮世絵がある。民衆的風俗画の一様式で、肉筆画も行われたが、とくに版画として普及した。その画題は、芝居の情操・美女・役者・力士の似顔絵を主とし、歴史画や風景・花鳥におよぶ。

　18世紀中ごろに、多色刷版画が鈴木春信により創始され黄金期を迎えた。浮世絵の代表的なものとして春画が外国に流布したことがあるが、これは浮世絵のほんの一部でしかない。

　浮世絵の画法が後期印象派の画家たち（ゴッホ、ゴーガンなど）に大きな影響を与え、新しい写実技法が展開したといわれている。

　　［補］国語辞典で浮世絵の項を見ると、第2番目の意
　　　　味として春画のこととなっている。外国では浮世絵
　　　　即春画と考えられることがあるので、表現には注意
　　　　を要する。

e）陶磁器

　日本の先史時代の呼称を、縄文時代・弥生時代などその当時の土器の名称で表わしているように、日本の陶磁器の伝統は長い。芸術品としての陶磁器は、5〜6世紀ごろ朝鮮・中国から技術の導入や技術者の渡来によって大きな影響を受けたのち、独特の発展を遂げた。

　英語で陶器のことを「チャイナ」というが、日本では、陶磁器のことを瀬戸物という。これは中部地方の瀬戸市付近が有名な産地であったからである。この地域では、13世紀から優れた陶磁器がつくられた。九州の唐津も陶磁器の産地として有名である。16世紀に朝鮮から来た陶工によって、優れた陶磁器がつくられたという。

　このほか、現在芸術的な意味での日本の陶器の代表的なものに、京焼・楽焼・志野焼・薩摩焼・織部焼などがある。

　磁器の代表的なものとしては、有田焼・清水焼・九谷焼などがある。

　原料の土に恵まれているため、各地にある伝統的な窯場で、優れた陶芸家が立派な陶芸品を数多く生み出している。

tion of Yamato-e techniques and under various other influences such as modern oil painting.

The *ukiyoe* paintings of the Edo period are very popular even today. A form of genre picture, some were painted by hand, but it is as prints that they became widely known. The most common subjects were scenes from the theater, and portraits of famous beauties, actors and *sumo* wrestlers, but historical themes, landscapes, birds and flowers were also depicted.

The development by Harunobu Suzuki of multi-color printing in the mid-eighteenth century gave rise to the golden age of color prints. One type of picture of beautiful women that had a circulation abroad was pornographic *shunga*, but this style accounts for only a small fraction of the ukiyoe genre.

It is said that the ukiyoe art of drawing had a strong influence on such postimpressionists as van Gogh and Gauguin, and resulted in the development of the new techniques of realism.

e) Ceramic Ware

From the fact that Japan's prehistoric periods are referred to by the name of the earthenware of the time, such as the Jomon or Yayoi period, it can be seen that Japan has a long tradition of ceramics. In the fifth and sixth centuries, Japanese artistic ceramic ware was greatly influenced by the introduction of techniques from Korea and China and by visits of skilled craftsmen from these countries. After this period of foreign influence had ended, the art began to follow its own unique path of development.

While ceramic ware is referred to as "china" in English, in Japan it is referred to as *seto-mono*, because the area around Seto City in the Chubu region is famous for this ware. This area has been producing fine ceramic ware since the thirteenth century. Karatsu in Kyushu is also famous for its ceramics. It is said that the very fine ceramic ware produced was introduced by potters who came from Korea in the sixteenth century.

Other representative artistic pottery of the present day include *kyoyaki, rakuyaki, shinoyaki, satsumayaki* and *oribeyaki*.

Typical chinawares (porcelain) include *aritayaki, kiyomizuya-ki* and *kutaniyaki*.

There is a plentiful supply of the right materials, and highly skilled ceramic artists at the traditional kilns in each district

f) 漆 器

　　漆器とは漆を塗った器などの美術工芸品である。漆が東洋特産のため、漆器は日本・中国・朝鮮・ベトナム・タイ・ミャンマー（ビルマ）などで発達した。とりわけ日本のものは世界的に名高い。

　　漆とは、ウルシの木の樹皮の下から浸み出てくる粘液である。これを精製して顔料を加えたものを塗って、ほどよい湿度で乾燥させると、接着性や防蝕・防湿性の強い被膜が得られる。通常、薄く塗っては乾かすことを何回も繰り返す。

　　漆の利用は古くから行われ、原始時代のものも発見されているが、芸術品としては法隆寺に残されている玉虫厨子（桧造りの上に黒漆が塗ってある。玉虫の羽根は漆塗りの上に張ってある）が最も古い。

　　7世紀以後、中国の技術も導入されて、箱・食器そのほかの家具・仏像・建築などの、美術工芸品に用いられている。

　　漆器に文様を画く方法にはいろいろある。漆で文様を描き、金属粉や色粉をまきつける「蒔絵（まきえ）」、色漆で文様を描く「漆絵」、漆を塗り重ねた面に文様を彫る「堆朱（ついしゅ）」や「堆黒（ついこく）」、漆面に文様を線刻して金をすりこむ「沈金」、木彫りの上に朱漆や緑漆を塗った「鎌倉彫」、貝殻や金属板を漆面にはめこんだり、張りつけたりする「螺鈿（らでん）」や「平文（ひょうもん）」などである。現在は輪島塗が最も有名である。

　　漆器は英語で「ジャパン」とも呼ばれている。

g) 七宝焼

　　七宝焼は、銀や銅などの金属または陶器やガラスを素

create countless beautiful pieces.

f) Lacquer Ware

The term "lacquer ware" means any artistically-crafted article which has a lacquer finish. Because lacquer is a product of the Orient, the best lacquer ware has developed in Asian countries such as Japan, China, Korea, Vietnam, Thailand and Myanmar (Burma). The lacquer ware of Japan, in particular, is renowned the world over.

Lacquer is a viscous liquid that exudes from under the bark of the lacquer tree. This liquid is refined and mixed with pigment. By applying a layer of the mixture to the surface of an object and then drying it in air of an appropriate humidity, a coating is obtained that is highly adhesive and resistant to damp and corrosion. Usually, a number of thin layers are applied, each layer being dried before the next application.

Lacquer has been utilized since early times, and some examples of its use in primitive times have been discovered. The oldest object that displays an artistic use of lacquer, however, is the Tamamushinozushi (a black lacquered miniature shrine made of Japanese cypress, the lacquer being overlaid with the wings of the *tamamushi* beetle) preserved in Horyu Temple.

Starting with the introduction of Chinese techniques from the seventh century, lacquer was used on artistically crafted items such as furniture, Buddhist images, buildings etc. as well as on boxes and eating utensils.

There are various ways of producing designs on lacquer ware, such as *makie*, where a pattern drawn in lacquer is sprinkled with metal or colored powder; *urushie*, where the pattern is done in colored lacquer; *tsuishu* and *tsuikoku*, where a number of coats of lacquer are applied and the pattern is carved into the finished surface; *chinkin*, where the lacquer is scored with pattern lines and gold-powder is then rubbed into the lines; *kamakurabori*, where a carved surface is coated with vermilion or green lacquer; and *raden* or *hyomon*, where shell or pieces of precious metals are set into or on the lacquer. At present, Wajima lacquer ware (from the district of the same name) is the most famous.

Another name for lacquer in English is "japan."

g) Cloisonné

Cloisonné is a form of decoration in which beautiful designs

地として、ガラス質のうわぐすりを焼きつけて、種々の色の花鳥人物などの美しい模様を現わし出したものである。模様の輪郭に針金を用いたものと、用いないものがある。

七宝焼はペルシアやヨーロッパから中国を経て日本に伝来したもので、わが国でも8世紀ごろつくられたがすたれてしまい、のち17世紀に改めて朝鮮から製法が伝えられ、19世紀以後とくに盛んになり技術も進んだ。

現在でも日本の特産品として、装身具・工芸品などがつくられている。

七宝焼という言葉は、7種の珍宝をちりばめたように美しい焼物という意味である。

h） 日本刀

日本刀は片刃で反りがあり、加熱した鋼を槌で打ってよく鍛練し、焼き入れを行うなど独特の製法によってつくられるので、折れたり曲がったりせず、切味の鋭いのが特徴である。

日本には中国・朝鮮などから刀剣の製法が伝えられたが、9世紀ごろになって反りのある日本刀がつくられるまでは、ほとんど直刀（両刃のものもある）で、これは古代刀と呼ばれている。

9世紀から12世紀にかけてつくられたものは、刀身の元幅と先幅の差が大きく、腰もとでの反りが強く、またこの時代から刀に作者の銘がきざまれるようになった。無銘のものも少なくないが、刀の特徴によって、現在では作者が確かめられているものが多い。

13世紀初めごろから、日本刀は武家の需要により、刀身の身幅が広くなるとともに、元幅と先幅の差が縮まり、切先が短かくなって豪壮さを加え、その黄金時代を迎えた。

14世紀末ごろからは、脇差し（守り刀として腰に差す小さな刀）が現れた。

of flowers, birds, people etc. are produced by baking vitreous enamels of various colors on a ground of metal, such as silver or copper, or of ceramic or glass. Some methods use wire to outline the designs, some do not.

The art of making cloisonné was introduced into Japan from Persia and Europe through China in the eighth century. However, it was practiced for a short period only and then died out. It was not until the seventeenth century that cloisonné production methods were reintroduced from Korea. The art has flourished particularly since the nineteenth century, and this same period has seen numerous improvements in technique.

Today Japan is known for its fine personal ornaments and craftwork articles of cloisonné.

The Japanese word for cloisonné is *shippoyaki*, the literal meaning of which is "a ceramic work that is as beautiful as if encrusted with seven types of precious stones."

h) Japanese Swords

The Japanese sword has a curved blade with a single cutting edge. Made by a special process that includes heating, hammer-forging and hardening, the sword is characterized by its great spring-like toughness and its extremely sharp cutting edge.

The art of swordmaking came to Japan from China and Korea. The early swords, what are today called ancient swords, were straight (and sometimes double edged), the curved blade not appearing until the ninth century.

Swords made between the ninth and twelfth centuries were much wider across the base than the tip and were curved sharply near the base. It was also during this period that swordmakers began stamping their names onto the swords they made. Today, while there are many unmarked swords from this period, in many cases they are accredited to specific swordmakers on the basis of distinguishing features in the craftsmanship.

Early in the thirteenth century swords began to undergo modifications to meet the needs of the *samurai*. The blade was made broader and the difference in breadth between the base and the tip was reduced. The tip was given a sharper angle and made shorter. These changes enhanced the splendor of the weapon and marked the beginning of the golden age of the Japanese sword.

The *wakizashi* (a short sword worn at the side mainly for protection) appeared around the end of the fourteenth century.

一般に、16世紀末ごろまでにつくられたものは古刀、それより新しいものは新刀と呼ばれている。新刀は身幅が広く、反りが少なく、先幅が細く、切先が長いのが特徴である。

　刀は武士の魂とみなされ、武家社会の象徴だったので、工芸品としても優れた名刀も多い。

　第二次世界大戦後は、日本刀はもっぱら美術品として鑑賞の対象となり、清く澄み切った冷たい美しさから、心の落ち着きを得るために、一部の人によって珍重されている。

　日本では日本刀を所持するには、許可証をとる必要がある。

i ）人　　形

　日本の原始時代の遺跡から土の人形（土偶）が発見され、古代の古墳から埴輪人形が出土するなど、大昔から日本人と人形の関係は切り離せない。

　日本の伝統芸術の一つである文楽は、大きな人形をあやつりながら演ずる大規模な人形劇である。（伝統演劇の項264頁参照）

　男の子の節句には武者人形を飾り、女の子の節句には華美な雛人形を飾る。

　日本で現在つくられている人形の種類は、ヨーロッパ式も含め非常に多い。最もポピュラーなものは「博多人形」と「こけし」であろう。

　「博多人形」は、土で形をつくり、素焼にしてから彩色するもので、九州福岡県の特産である。写実的で繊細な姿態と彩色を特徴とし、模写に優れ、世界各国の風俗、古今の美人画、歌舞伎俳優などの題材をこなしている。

　「こけし」は、東北地方伝統の木製人形である。ろくろでひいた円筒形の胴体に、丸い頭をつけて女の子の顔を描き、胴体に赤・青・黄など2〜3色で線や菊の花の模様を描く。素朴なものであるが、面相や彩色にひなびた味があって捨てがたい。

Swords made up to about the end of the sixteenth century are classified as "old swords" and those made after this time, as "new swords." New swords have a broader blade that is only slightly curved, and a long, narrow tip.

As the sword was considered to be the very soul of the samurai and became the symbol of the warrior class, many specimens show superb craftsmanship.

Since the end of World War II, the Japanese sword has come to be regarded solely as an object of art, often to be treasured for a sense of tranquility found in its cold, serene beauty.

One has to obtain a permit to own a sword in Japan.

i) Dolls

Dolls have played a part in the life of the Japanese people since time immemorial. Clay figurines have been discovered among protohistoric relics, and *haniwa* clay images have been unearthed from ancient burial mounds.

Bunraku, one of the traditional theater arts of Japan, is a large-scale puppet drama in which big dolls are manipulated to show the action of the play (see p.265).

Warrior-dolls are displayed during the Boy's Festival, and colorful *hina* dolls during the Girl's Festival.

A tremendous variety of dolls, of both Japanese and European style, are manufactured in Japan nowadays. The most popular are the *hakata* and *kokeshi* dolls.

Hakata dolls, which are molded from clay, fired, then painted, are the specialty of Fukuoka Prefecture in Kyushu, the southern island. Hakata dolls, which are characterized by a finely detailed realism and by the colors used, depict subjects old and new and from every land, such as beautiful women from all periods of history, and *kabuki* actors.

Kokeshi are the traditional wooden dolls made in the northeastern region of Japan. The dolls consist of a cylindrical torso, turned out on a lathe. A round head is fitted on the torso and a girl's face drawn in. Two or three colors, such as red, blue or yellow, are used to paint lines or a chrysanthemum design on the body. While unsophisticated, the face and colors give kokeshi dolls a certain rustic charm that is hard to deny.

j) 扇子（せんす）

扇子は日本で発明されたもので、もともと涼をとるためのものであったが、その後儀礼用や舞踊の用具として用いられるようになった。

はじめに桧の薄片を綴り合わせた桧扇がつくられ、その後紙扇がつくられた。

桧扇は7世紀ごろから宮廷で使われ、8世紀には、宮廷内での装束になくてはならないものとなった。

やがて紙扇もつくられるようになり、能や歌舞伎の用具としても取り入れられ、また宗教行事や庶民の日常生活のなかにも、盛んに用いられるようになった。

能や歌舞伎に用いられる扇子にはそれぞれきまりの文様があるが、庶民が日常使用する扇子には自由に歌や書や絵が描かれた。

桧扇や紙扇は中国や朝鮮にわたり、朝鮮扇は扇骨の数が増加し、中国では扇骨に彫刻をほどこすようになった。

西欧の扇が日本の方式にならって折りたたみ式になったのは、17世紀中ごろからである。

現在では扇子は、ほとんど舞踊の用具や装飾品として用いられている。

k) 羽子板

羽子板は新年の初めに遊ぶゲームで使う板で、長方形の柄がついている。遊び方はバドミントンに似ており、ふつうは着物をきた若い女性2人が「羽根」（黒くて固い種子に鳥の羽毛を植えつけたもの）を高く打ちあげて遊ぶ。「羽根」を地上に落とした方が負けになる。この遊びが最初に出てくるのは、室町時代（14〜15世紀）の文献である。

羽根は、蚊（か）を食うトンボに似せたもので、この遊びは子供の蚊よけ、厄病よけのまじないから生まれたともいわれる。室町時代には宮中の公家（くげ）や女官の遊びであったが、江戸時代に一般庶民の遊びとなった。

j) Folding Fans

The folding fan is a Japanese invention. Originally it was purely functional but it later became important in Japanese etiquette and dancing.

The first folding fans consisted just of thin sticks of Japanese cypress held together by ribbons. It was only later the sticks were covered with paper.

The cypress stick fans first appeared at the Imperial Court in the seventh century and by the eighth century they had become an indispensable part of Court attire.

Later, the paper fans came to be used extensively — in *noh* and *kabuki*, in religious ceremonies and in everyday life.

Although noh and kabuki fans are decorated with certain fixed painted or printed patterns, those for daily use come in all manner of designs, the most popular types being handwritten poems, artistically executed *kanji* characters and various painted patterns, landscapes and portraits.

The Japanese folding fan served as a model for similar fans in China, where the embellishment of elaborately carved ribs was added, and Korea, where the number of ribs was greatly increased.

The folding fans that first appeared in Europe around the middle of the seventeenth century were also derived from the Japanese fan.

Today the Japanese folding fan is used mainly in dancing and as an ornament.

k) Hagoita

The *hagoita* is a paddle used in a game played at the beginning of the new year. It consists of a board with a rectangular handle. The game is played somewhat in the manner of badminton, typically by two kimono-clad girls, with the players taking turns at hitting a shuttlecock (a hard black seed to which feathers have been attached) high into the air. The player who allows the shuttlecock to fall to the ground is the loser. The first references to the game are found in literary works of the Muromachi period (fourteenth and fifteenth centuries).

The shuttlecock is modeled after a mosquito-eating dragonfly and the game is thought to have grown out of a magical rite for protecting children from mosquitoes and sickness. In the Muromachi period, the game was played only by nobles and ladies

羽子板は、江戸時代には飾りものとしても使われるようになった。大形の羽子板には、船・美人・初日の出・花・鳥など豪華な絵柄を飾りたてたものもある。現在でも正月には、東京（昔の江戸）はじめ各地で羽子板市が開かれている。

l) 凧（たこ）

　　凧は遊び道具としては諸外国でも知られている。

　　日本では、平安朝時代（9〜12世紀）に中国凧から学んだ後、独自のタイプの凧が発達した。日本の凧には字凧と絵凧があり、形も多種多様になった。たとえば、角形・菱形（ひしがた）・六角形・人の形（やっこだこ）など多種のものがある。

　　凧あげは、今も正月のポピュラーな子供の遊びとして残っており、また地方では成人の競技になっているところもある。一辺が5m（16フィート）もある大凧あげや、凧どうしを戦わせる凧あげ合戦が行われている地方もある。

　　凧を表わす言葉は、国によってさまざまな起源がある。日本語では「風をはらむ帆布」、中国語では「風の琴（箏）」、英語では鳥の名前（トビ）、フランス語では「クワガタムシ」、スペイン語では「彗星」から出ている。

m) 庭　園

　　日本・中国・朝鮮の庭園は、自然の景観美を主とするものであって、幾何学的な美しさを重視する西洋の庭園とは対照的である。自然の景観美といっても、自然そのままの姿ではない。樹木・石など自然の材料を用いて自然の山水のたたずまいを象徴化し、あるいは強調して、一つのまとまりのある調和した人工的空間美を形成する。

　　1000年にわたる庭園の歴史のなかで、時代の推移とともにその様式も変化する。大別して、中心の池で大海を表わし、土を盛り岩を配して山を表わす形式（築山式）と、水を使用せず白砂を敷いて大海を、砂紋によって流れを表現し、青石を立てて滝を象徴させる方式（枯山水式）がある。

of the Imperial Court, but by the Edo Period it had become an amusement of the common people.

The Edo period also saw the hagoita become a decorative object. Huge specimens embellished with fancy pictures of ships, beautiful women, New Year's Day sunrises, flowers, birds and the like came into fashion. In early January even nowadays, stalls selling decorative hagoitas can be found around Tokyo (previously called Edo) and other parts of the country.

l) Kites

The kite is a universally known plaything.

Japan developed its own distinctive types of kites after learning about Chinese kites in the Heian period (ninth-twelfth centuries). Japanese kites are patterned with written characters (words) or pictures and come in various shapes: square, diamond, hexagonal, man-shaped (the *yakko* kite) and so forth.

Kite flying continues to be a popular pastime of children at the beginning of the year and in some areas has been elevated to a competitive sport among adults. The competition may be to see which individual or group can fly the largest kite (kites measuring 5 meters or 16 feet per side are not uncommon), or it may take the form of aerial kite fights.

In many languages, the word for "kite" has an interesting origin. The Japanese word comes from "sail swollen with the wind," the Chinese from "wind harp," the English from the name of a bird, the French from "stag beetle," and the Spanish from "comet."

m) Gardens

The main consideration in the gardens of Japan, China and Korea is on natural scenic beauty, which is in contrast to the gardens of the West in which the emphasis is on beauty of geometrical form. However, by "natural scenic beauty" is not meant nature in its original, unchanged forms. Rather, natural materials such as trees, shrubs and rocks are used to symbolize or emphasize the forms and features of the natural landscape, thereby creating an artificial spatial beauty that has a harmonic unity.

The history of landscape gardening spans a thousand years, during which styles have changed as one age gave way to the next. Broadly speaking, there are the miniature artificial hill style (*tsukiyama*), where a central pond symbolizes the sea, and

京都の天竜寺や西芳寺の庭園が前者の、竜安寺や大徳寺大仙院の庭園が後者の例である。

こうした日本庭園のそれぞれの特徴をすべて取り入れたうえ、庭園外の山や樹木をも遠景として活用した（借景）庭園としては、京都の円通寺が有名である。

n）盆　栽

盆栽は陶磁器の鉢に樹木を植え、その生育する力を利用して適切な培養を行い、自然の雅趣をかもし出すように姿を整えて観賞するものである。中国に生まれ、隋・唐の時代（日本の奈良・平安時代）に日本に伝えられ、日本で独自の発展を見た。

短期間観賞する鉢植えとは異なり、盆栽は数十年から数百年もの長期にわたって育成し、次第に古木の風格をつくり出していくものであり、そのために特殊な培養を行う。

盆栽の素材の代表格は松であるが、常緑樹、落葉樹、花や実のなる樹など多くのものを盆栽に仕上げることができ、それぞれに捨てがたい味わいがある。

盆栽は、自然の美を愛し、それを身近な生活に取り入れようとした日本人の生活の知恵の所産といえよう。

(4)　建築・住居

a）家　屋

日本の個人住宅は木造が多く、2階または平屋である。木造は火災や地震に弱いが、通風採光がよく、高温多湿な日本の風土に適している。また、材料である木の落ち

mountains are represented by banks of earth and arrangements of rocks; and the dry garden style (*karesansui*), in which the sea is symbolized not by water but by a layer of white sand, which is given a pattern of furrows to represent the rippling movement of the water, and waterfalls are symbolized by an arrangement of blue rocks.

The gardens of Tenryu Temple and Saiho Temple in Kyoto are examples of the former style, and those of Ryoan Temple and Daitoku Temple's Daisen-in, also in Kyoto, are examples of the latter style.

Famous examples of gardens which, in addition to incorporating the above features, utilize the views of surrounding mountains and woods (*shakkei*) include Entsu Temple in Kyoto.

n) Bonsai

Bonsai (dwarf trees) is an art form that consists of planting a tree in a ceramic pot and then, through a process of cultivation that draws on and accents the plant's vital powers, producing a natural elegance of form pleasing to the eye. It originated in China and was introduced to Japan during the Sui and Tang Dynasties (the Nara and Heian Periods of Japan), whereafter it developed independently in Japan.

Ordinary potted plants can only be appreciated for a short time, but bonsai last for periods ranging from decades to centuries, gradually gaining in character as they age. Special cultivation methods are used for this.

Pine trees are typical bonsai subjects; but many other types of trees can be used, such as various evergreens and deciduous trees, and trees that blossom and bear fruit, and each has its own unique attractiveness.

The ability to produce bonsai can be said to spring from the resourcefulness of the Japanese people who, in their love of natural beauty, have tried to bring it closer to their lives.

(4) Buildings

a) Houses

Most houses in Japan are made of wood and are of one or two stories. While wooden houses are easily damaged by fires and earthquakes, they are airy and light and, therefore, suited to the

着いた感触が日本人の好みに適合している。

　現在は、コンクリート造りあるいは鉄骨造りの住宅も増えている。また、家屋の形にヨーロッパ風も取り入れられている。

　都市およびその周辺には、三階建から 20 階建以上のアパートがある。

　和室の内装は、大体一定の型がある。一般に天井は木の板であり、壁は塗り壁、床は板を張った上に畳を敷いてある。畳の本体は米作の副産物であるワラでつくったマットであり、表に藺草（いぐさ）で織ったシートが張ってある。和室の境界には木の枠に紙を張りつけた襖や障子がある。これは敷居という横木に刻まれた溝の上を、左右に滑らせることにより開閉する建具である。

　障子は採光を考慮したものであり、襖は遮蔽を主目的とし、採光は考慮されていない。これらの素材は日本の多湿の風土によく適合しており（湿気を吸うので湿気を調整する機能がある）、長い間の生活の知恵から生まれたものである。

　洋間のつくりは、おおむね欧米の部屋と変わりはない。

　家に入る時は、玄関で靴を脱ぐ。ここで、スリッパにはきかえることもあるが、これも和室に入る前には必ず脱ぐ。

b）住宅の広さ

　第二次大戦によって都市の住宅が焼失したうえ、経済成長にともなって大都市への人口集中が激しくなった。このため都市部の家屋は集合住宅方式が多く、また、一戸あたりの面積は小さくならざるを得なかった。

　日本全国では世帯数を上まわる住宅があるが、一戸あたりの平均部屋数は 4.8 室、平均面積は 92.43 m²（110 平方ヤード）にすぎない（1998 年現在）。一戸建ては 57.5 ％、構造的には 64.4 ％が木造で、持ち家比率は 60.3 ％となっている。1998 年に新築された持ち家の平均部屋数は 6.0 室、平均面積は 120 m²（143 平方ヤー

hot, humid climate of Japan. Moreover, Japanese people feel more settled and relaxed in a house made of wood.

Recent years have seen an increase in the use of other materials, such as concrete, and, for the framework, steel; there has also been greater incorporation of Western styles.

Apartment houses, ranging in height from three to twenty or more stories, can be seen in urban centers and their environs.

The interiors of Japanese-style rooms follow fairly fixed patterns: the ceiling will be of wooden boards, the walls of plaster, and the floor of *tatami* laid on wooden floorboards. Tatami are thick mats made of rice straw and are thus a by-product of the cultivation of rice. They are finished with a cover of woven rushes (*igusa*). In a Japanese-style house, the rooms are partitioned by *fusuma* and *shoji*, sliding doors and screens made of a wooden frame with paper stretched over it. They are set in grooved beams (called *shikii*) so they can be slid to one side or the other.

Shoji permit the passage of light, whereas the purpose of fusuma is to act as a partition. Shoji and fusuma are eminently suited to the highly humid Japanese climate (they absorb and release moisture and thus even out humidity fluctuations), and were developed over a long period from the experience of the people in their everyday life.

Western-style rooms are built substantially the same as their counterparts in Europe and America.

When entering a Japanese house, whether of Japanese or Western style, one removes one's shoes at the entrance and, generally, puts on slippers. The slippers are removed on entering a Japanese-style (tatami-matted) room.

b) The Size of Houses

Many of Japan's houses were destroyed by the fires of World War II. Then, in the postwar years, since the growth in the economy was accompanied by very rapid concentration of people in the major cities, urban housing was built in blocks, and the area of each dwelling unit was unavoidably small.

The Japan of today has more housing units than households, but each has an average of only 4.8 rooms and an area of 92.43 square meters or about 110 square yards (1998). Stand-alone houses account for 57.5% of all units. Most (64.4%) are made of wood and 60.3% are owned by the occupant. The average owner

ド）で、5年前とほぼ同一水準である。

　日本では、住宅建設費や用地費は非常に高く、また世界一高い。
　日本の大都市およびその周辺では、庭つきの一戸建ての家をを持つことはなかなか難しい。

c) 建築物

　日本では 19 世紀以前の建築物は、すべて木造であった。それは良質な木材が豊富に採取できたこと、高温多湿の気候に適していること、地震や風に対しても構造を工夫すれば、かなり強い建物が造れることなどの事情による。
　7 世紀後半の建物といわれる法隆寺は、現存する世界最古の木造建築であり、また奈良の大仏のある東大寺は、世界最大（東西 57.3 m［188 フィート］、南北 50.4 m［165.35 フィート］、高さ 48.6 m［159.45 フィート］）の木造建築である。
　19 世紀にヨーロッパの建築技術が導入されて以来、レンガ造りや鉄筋コンクリート造りで大学・官庁・事務所などが建てられた。とくに鉄骨については、使用鋼材の改良と従来の剛構造から柔構造への設計思想の進歩もあり、1960 年以降は都市部には 40 階以上の高層建築物がたくさん建てられるようになった。現在では、70 階以上の建物もある。
　こうして、昔から日本の建築界を悩ましてきた地震に対する問題も一応克服できた。しかし、新技法による高層建築は、現実の試練に直面した経験が少ないので、倒壊・火災以外のトラブルに対する配慮が要望されている。

-occupied house built in 1998 had 6.0 rooms and a total floor space of 120 square meters (143 square yards), figures that have not changed substantially over the past five years.

The cost of house plots and construction is very high; such costs are, in fact, among the highest in the world.

Few people can afford to own an independent house with garden in or near a major metropolis.

c) Large Buildings

All buildings in Japan up to the nineteenth century were of wood. This was because, among other reasons, a plentiful supply of good wood could be obtained, and wood was suitable for the hot and humid climate; also, with skillful use, structures could be built that would stand up fairly well to earthquakes and strong winds.

The world's oldest wooden structure still standing is Horyu Temple, said to date from the latter half of the seventh century; and the world's largest wooden structure is Todai Temple, which houses a large statue of Buddha, and is situated in Nara. Todai Temple measures 57.3 meters (188 feet) from east to west, 50.4 meters (165.35 feet) from north to south, and is 48.6 meters (159. 45 feet) high.

After European building techniques began to be introduced in the nineteenth century, universities, government buildings, business offices and the like started to be constructed of brick or ferro-concrete. The use of steel frames, in particular, has shown a considerable increase, and with the improvements in the steel used together with the advance in design concept from rigid structures to flexible structures, many high-rise buildings of more than 40 stories have been constructed in cities since 1960. At present there are a few buildings of more than 70 stories.

It would therefore seem that the Japanese construction industry has managed to overcome the problem that has always existed in Japan—that of earthquakes. However, such high buildings constructed with these new methods have been little tested in actual circumstances, and though probably quite safe from collapse and fire, they may be susceptible to other troubles which must now be taken into account.

(5) スポーツ

a) スポーツ

スポーツで人気があるのは、野球・サッカー・ラグビー・バレーボール・バスケットボール・テニス・水泳・柔道・剣道・弓道（アーチェリーを含む）・空手道・登山・釣などである。

また、ウインタースポーツとしてスキー・スケート・アイスホッケーが盛んである。

ビジネスマンの間でもっとも普及しているのはゴルフである。

野球やサッカーなどにはプロのチームがあり、相撲・ゴルフ・ボクシング・レスリング・テニスなどには、プロの選手がいる。試合は、テレビで放映されてファンが多い。

b) ゴルフ

1960 年代にビジネスマンの間で始まったゴルフブームは、現在は自由業者・学生層などのグループにも普及している。日本のゴルフ人口は 1,000 万人といわれている。そしてビジネスその他の社交上、ゴルフが行われることも非常に多い。

ゴルフ場は全国で約 2,400 カ所もある。日本は土地の価格が高いので、ゴルフ場会員権も高く、賃金水準の上昇とともにグリーンフィー・キャディーフィーも高くなってきた。また、自然環境保護の観点から、ゴルフ場の新設もかつてのように自由にはできなくなってきた。

国際舞台で話題になる日本人プロゴルファーも何人かいる。

c) 相　撲

日本の相撲の歴史は、古代にまでさかのぼることができる。神話時代に神様同士が闘ったという伝説がある。相撲は単にスポーツとしてだけではなく、農業生活の吉凶を占い、神の心を伺う行事として行われてきた。16 世紀ごろからは見るスポーツとしても発展してきた。

現在の相撲は、直径 4.55 m（日本の古い尺という単位で 15 尺、14.9 フィート）の円形の土俵の中で力士 2 人が技を競う。力士は、素手で腰に「まわし」を締めただけの裸体で登場する。

(5) Sports

a) Sports

Popular sports include baseball, soccer, rugby, volleyball, basketball, tennis, swimming, *judo*, *kendo*, archery (both Japanese- and Western-style), *karatedo*, mountain-climbing and fishing.

The most popular winter sports are skiing, skating and ice hockey.

Golf is the most widespread sport among businessmen.

Professional team sports include baseball and soccer. S*umo*, golf, boxing, wrestling and tennis are also practiced by professionals, with competitions being televised and followed by numerous fans.

b) Golf

A golf boom that started among business people in the 1960s has in the meantime spread to writers, doctors, lawyers, students and other groups. There are estimated to be about 10 million golfers in Japan. Also, golf is used on a wide scale for business, socializing and the like.

There are about 2,400 golf courses in Japan. Land is very expensive, so the cost of golf club memberships is also high, and as the level of wages has risen, green fees and caddie fees have gone up. Moreover, the building of new courses has become increasingly difficult owing to environmental protection considerations.

Several Japanese professional golfers have won recognition on the international scene.

c) Sumo

The history of *sumo* goes back to ancient times in Japan. There is a legend that in mythical times the gods wrestled with each other. Sumo was not just a sport, but was an event used to tell whether crops would be good or not by seeking the divine intention of the gods. From about the sixteenth century it developed into a spectator sport.

In modern sumo, the wrestlers, two at a time, pit their skills against each other in the round sumo ring which is 4.55 meters in diameter (or 15 *shaku*—14.9 feet—using the old Japanese unit

2人は古式にのっとり、競技に入る前に左右の足を交互に上げ下げして準備運動をし（四股をふむ）、水で口をそそぎ（力水）、紙で体をぬぐい、清めの塩を土俵上にまく。2人は行司という審判の指図にしたがって、向かい合って相手の動作に合わせながら体を前かがみに低くし、両手をついて立ち上がる身構えをし、呼吸を整える。2人は呼吸の合ったところで同時に立ち合い、押し合い、突き合い、組み合って闘う。土俵の中で足の裏以外の部分が土につくか、体の一部が土俵の外に出た方が負けになる。

　プロの相撲団体が一つあり、年に6回、1回15日間の興業（「大相撲」と呼ばれる）を東京で3回、大阪・名古屋・福岡で各1回行っている。各回ごとに、勝率によって各力士の地位の入れ替えが行われる。

　力士の最高位は横綱で、過去300年間に67人（2002年）しかこの地位に上っていない。1993年に初めて外国人（アメリカ・ハワイ州出身）の横綱が誕生した。優勝すると天皇杯を賜るほか、外国大使館やいろいろの団体から賞をもらう。

　相撲は国技として人気があり、テレビ中継やラジオ放送によって全国民が楽しんでいる。

　プロの相撲のほか学生相撲もあり、また少年達は相撲で遊ぶことも多い。

d）柔　道

　嘉納治五郎という教育者（東京高等師範学校長になった人）が、私費を投じて講道館を1882年に開き、柔道の研究と指導を行った。ここで古来の武術である柔術から、近代柔道としての発展の基礎をつくったのである。

　柔道は単に勝負を競うのみでなく、これにより心身を錬磨するものである。20世紀になってから男子の中等学校以上の教育にも取り入れられ、大いに普及した。

of measurement). The wrestlers are bare-handed in their bouts and wear only a loincloth, called a *mawashi*.

Before the bout commences, the wrestlers perform a series of ceremonial warm-up exercises and rituals. They stamp their feet, wash their mouths out with water and dry themselves with paper, and toss salt onto the ring, a ritual purification symbol. The referee (*gyoji*) indicates when the wrestlers should get ready, whereupon they position themselves opposite each other, then bend forward and touch their fists on the ground to ready themselves for their charge. When both are ready they charge and start pushing, thrusting and grappling. The first one who touches the ground with any part of his body except the soles of his feet, or who is pushed out of the ring, is the loser.

There is just one professional sumo organization, which holds six tournaments (called *ozumo*) a year, three in Tokyo, and one each in Osaka, Nagoya and Fukuoka. Each tournament lasts fifteen days. The individual sumo wrestlers are moved up or down in rank according to how many victories they obtain in each of these tourneys.

Top of the ranks are the *yokozuna*, or grand champions: in the past three hundred years only 67 have reached this grade (as of 2002). In 1993, the first foreigner, a Hawaiian, was promoted to the rank of yokozuna. The winner of a tournament receives the Emperor's Cup, the top award, plus a number of prizes from foreign embassies and various organizations.

Sumo, as the national sport, is highly popular, and is enjoyed by people all over the country through television and radio broadcasts.

In addition to the professional sumo, the sport is also practiced in universities, and many children, too, play at sumo.

d) Judo

In 1882, the educator Jigoro Kano (who later became head of the Tokyo Higher Normal School) personally financed and opened the Kodokan for the study and instruction of *judo*. This formed the starting point of the development of modern judo from *jujutsu*, one of the traditional martial arts.

The aim in judo is not just to win contests; rather it is to train the mind and body. At the beginning of the twentieth century judo became part of the educational curriculum of boys from middle school onwards, and since then it has become very

柔道の競技方法は、上衣・下袴・帯から成る柔道着を着けた 2 人が、 5 間(9 m)四方 (50 枚の畳を敷いてある) の中で、互いに組み合い、投げ技と固め技によって勝負を競う。

　柔道の柔とは「やわらかい」という意味であり、「柔よく剛を制す」という原理により名付けられた。

　各人の力量を段と級で表わし、段のなかでは 10 段が最高、初段が最低、級は段に至らないもので、 1 級が最高、 5 級が最低である。そして段と級の区分により帯の色をかえる。10〜 9 段は紅、 8 〜 6 段は紅白のだんだら、 5 〜初段は黒、 1 〜 3 級は茶、 4 〜 5 級は白、初心者は水色になっている。

　1964 年以来男子柔道が、1992 年以来女子柔道が、国際スポーツとしてオリンピック正式種目になっている。

e) 剣道・弓道・空手道

　剣道・弓道・空手道は日本の伝統的な武道であるが、現在はスポーツとして親しまれている。最近では外国人の愛好者も非常に増加している。

　剣道は、剣で身を守り、敵をたおす道である。 7 〜 8 世紀ごろから行われ、16 世紀ごろに急速に発展して、いろいろな流派が生まれた。

　17 世紀以降、剣道は技術とともに精神を練ることに重きがおかれ、仏教や儒教、とくに禅宗の影響によって、道徳的に修練されるようになった。

　昔は木刀を多く用いたが、18 世紀に竹刀と面・胴・小手・たれなどの防具が考案され、今日に至っている。

　面打ち・小手打ち・胴打ち・突き (喉頭部) を技の基本とし、いろいろな連続わざ、応用わざや構え方がある。競技は通常 3 本勝負で行われ、 3 人の審判員のうち 2 人以上が有効な打ち・突きを認めれば 1 本となる。

widespread.

In a judo match two participants, each wearing jacket, trousers and belt, contest in an area 9 meters square (on 50 *tatami* mats), and each tries to win by using throwing techniques or grappling techniques.

The *ju* of judo means "soft" or "gentle," and the sport was named after the principle shown in the saying *ju yoku go o seisu* —"softness overcomes hardness."

The ability of judo practitioners is indicated by *dan* and *kyu* grades. Tenth dan is the highest of the dan grades, and *shodan* (first dan) the lowest. Kyu grades rank below dan, and first kyu is the highest and fifth kyu the lowest of the kyu grades. These various grades are indicated by the color of the belts worn; red for ninth and tenth dan, red and white for sixth to eighth dan, and black for first to fifth dan. First to third kyu wear brown belts, fourth and fifth kyu white belts, and beginners blue belts.

Judo has been recognized as an international sport and designated as an official Olympic event since 1964 for men and 1992 for women.

e) Kendo, Kyudo, Karatedo

Kendo, *kyudo* and *karatedo* are traditional Japanese martial arts which today are practiced as sports. In recent years all three have become extremely popular internationally as well.

Kendo is a kind of fencing in which the fencer uses a "sword" for protection and to attack his opponent. While kendo's origins go back to the seventh or eighth century, it was around the sixteenth century that it developed rapidly and various styles, or schools, appeared.

From the seventeenth century, it has been stressed that kendo involves spiritual as well as technical refinement, and under the influence of Buddhism and Confucian teachings and, especially, Zen Buddhism, kendo became associated with moral training.

Previously various woods were used for the swords, but in the eighteenth century the use of bamboo became established. It was also at this time that the protective gear—face-mask, body-protector, gauntlets, and tuille—that are still used today, were devised.

The fundamental fencing touches are cuts to the face, hands and body and stabs to the throat. In a bout, the fencers use various movement sequences, practical techniques and positions. A match is usually decided on the best of three bouts. A score is

弓道の伝来は中国説や南方説があり、必ずしも明らかではないが、8世紀には弓術が奨励された記録がある。

　弓は狩猟や武器に使われ発達したが、鉄砲の伝来（1543年）以来、次第に武器としての効用を失った。その後禅や儒教の思想を取り入れて、心身鍛練のための武道の一つとして発展した。

　射法の基本は、足踏み・胴造り・弓構え・打起し・引分け・会・離れ・残身（心）の8節からなっている。

　日本の弓は、木と竹を接合したもので、長さ約2m余りのものが用いられ、矢は身長の半分よりもやや長めのものを使用する。

　射距離は近距離（28m）と遠距離（60m以上）に分かれ、それぞれ的の大きさが異なる。

　空手道は、手の突きや足のけりを主体に、体の各部位を有効に使って身を防ぎ、相手を制する技（わざ）をきわめるものである。7世紀ごろ中国に発生し、14世紀に沖縄に伝えられた。

　試合には、組手と型の2種類がある。型の試合は、基本動作と移動転身による正しい姿勢、正確な突き・けり、気合の充実、動作の緩急などにより勝負を決する。組手試合は、気合の充実した正確な突き・けり・間合い・残心（身）などを重要な要素として、相手を倒しえたと判定される技をもって優劣を決める。

f) 野　球

　日本はアメリカに次いで野球が普及している。アマチ

awarded when at least two of three judges recognize a touch.

It is not certain where kyudo, or Japanese archery, originated. Most commonly mentioned are China and Southeast Asia. As for the date, it is only known that there are written records of archery being encouraged in the eighth century.

The bow had become widespread for hunting and fighting, but the introduction of firearms into Japan in 1543 led to the gradual demise of the bow as a weapon. Subsequent kyudo development was as a discipline of mind and body based on Zen and Confucian tenets.

The fundamentals of shooting are planting of the feet, stance (including mental attitude), nocking of the arrow, anchoring, drawing, concentration at full draw, release and follow-through.

The Japanese bow is a combination of bamboo and other woods and is over two meters long. The arrows are made of bamboo and should be slightly longer than half the height of the archer.

The shooting range is either 28 meters or over 60 meters, with a different size target for each range.

Karatedo is a system of self-defense in which the main emphasis is using the body to the greatest effect to defeat an adversary, by precise kicking and striking techniques. It is considered to have developed in China around the seventh century. In the fourteenth century it was introduced into Okinawa.

Karate *shiai*, or contests, are of two types, *kumite* and *kata*. Kata consists of a series of formalized movements and the points judges look for are correctness of posture in the basic techniques and the change from one technique to the next, the accuracy of the kicking and striking, the quality of the *kiai*, which is a vocal expression (usually a shout) of a contestant's mental concentration, and the overall pacing of the person's movement. In *kumite* ("sparring") contests the emphasis in judging the winner is on the accuracy of the striking and kicking accompanied by the kiai, *ma'ai* (timing and keeping of proper distance) and *zanshin* (posture following attack, deemed to show both physical and mental preparedness). A match is decided when the judges acknowledge that one of the contestants could have knocked down the other.

f) Baseball

Only in America is baseball more widespread than it is in

ュア野球は、むしろ本家のアメリカをしのぐ隆盛を示している。

日本に野球が伝えられたのは 1873 年である。1934 年にプロ野球ができるまでは、学生野球を中心として発展普及した。現在も、東京 6 大学（早稲田・慶応・明治・法政・立教・東大）のリーグ戦や、春夏の全国高等学校野球大会が多くのファンを湧かせている。2002 年夏の高等学校野球大会には、4,219 校が参加した。

プロ野球は第二次大戦後非常に人気を高め、今日に至っている。現在のプロ野球は、セントラルリーグとパシフィックリーグの 2 リーグ制で、各 6 球団計 12 球団がある。シーズン末には、両リーグの優勝チーム同士で日本シリーズが行われる。2001 年、セ・パ両リーグは年間 2,300 万人の観客を動員した。

日本の代表的プロ野球選手であった王貞治は、1977年に、ホームラン 756 本の世界記録を達成し、1980 年に引退するまで、通算 868 本のホームラン記録を樹立した。最近では、大リーグでも活躍する選手が出るようになった。

日本は、オリンピック正式種目となって以来、ずっと参加している。

g) サッカー

サッカーは野球・相撲・ゴルフなどと並んで人気のあるスポーツであり、子供から成人まで多くの人々に親しまれている。小学生・中学生・高校生・大学生・社会人など各層レベルの全国大会がある。

1993 年、プロの競技団体としての「日本サッカーリーグ」（J リーグ）が設立された。一部リーグの J 1 は16 チーム、二部リーグの J 2 は 12 チーム（2002 年）あり、世界のトップレベルへの仲間入りを目指している。98 年には、長年の夢であったワールドカップ（W 杯）への初出場を果たした。また、2002 年には韓国とワールドカップを共催し、韓国はベスト 4 、日本はベスト16 入りを果たした。

h) オリンピック

日本は 1912 年のストックホルム大会に初参加して以来、ほとんど毎回参加している。

Japan. Amateur baseball may be even more popular here than in the United States, the home of baseball.

Baseball was introduced into Japan in 1873. Its development centered mainly on student baseball until the advent in 1934 of the professional game. Even now the league competition of Tokyo's "Big Six" universities (Waseda, Keio, Meiji, Hosei, Rikkyo and Tokyo) and the spring and summer all-Japan high school baseball meets have a big following; in 2002, 4,219 schools participated in the high school baseball meets.

Professional baseball became extremely popular just after World War II, and this popularity has continued up to the present day. There are two leagues, the Central League and the Pacific League, each league consisting of six teams, giving a total for the two leagues of twelve teams. At the end of the season the two league winners compete in the Japan Series. In 2001 the two leagues drew a grand total of 23 million spectators.

In 1977 Sadaharu Oh, then the most famous professional in Japanese baseball, hit the 756th home-run of his career, for a new world record. At the time of his retirement in 1980, he had improved his home-run record to 868. Recent years have seen some Japanese players playing for U.S. major league teams.

Japan has sent a baseball team to each Olympiad since the game became an official Olympic sport.

g) Soccer

Soccer ranks in popularity with baseball, *sumo* and golf, and is enjoyed by large numbers of children and adults. National soccer tournaments are held at the elementary school, junior high school, high school, university and company levels.

The Japan Soccer League (the J League) was established as a professional sports association in 1993. The League has 16 teams in Division 1 (J1) and 12 teams in Division 2 (J2), and hopes to place them among the world's best. In 1998, Japan fulfilled its long-held dream of playing in the FIFA World Cup tournament. Japan and the Republic of Korea jointly hosted the World Cup in 2002. In the playoffs, Korea was among the top four teams and Japan among the top sixteen.

h) The Olympics

Japan first participated in the 1912 Stockholm Olympic Games, and has been represented in almost all Olympics since.

20年のアントワープ大会で、初めてテニスで銀メダ
ルを取った（熊谷一弥・柏尾誠一郎）。日本で最初の開
催は、64年の東京大会で、この第18回夏期大会では、
金メダル獲得数は16個に達し、世界第3位となった。

　72年札幌で開かれた第11回冬期大会で、70m級ジ
ャンプで一挙に3本の日章旗を揚げた。
　1998年、長野で冬季大会が開催され、日本選手は大
活躍をした。

(6)　宗教

a)　日本の宗教

　日本でのおもな宗教には、神道・仏教・キリスト教が
ある。
　統計によると、特定の宗教を熱心に信仰しているとす
る日本人は少なく、宗教には無関心とみずからいう者が
多い。
　この理由はいくつか考えられる。まず、日本人の現世
的・楽天的性格があげられよう。美しい自然と恵まれた
四季のなかで、日本人は、外敵の侵入も極端な天災もな
く、何世代にもわたって過ごしてきた。そのため、宗教
を熱心に求める気風ができなかったのかもしれない。
　また、元来多神教的であった日本古来の神道の影響か
ら、どの宗教に対しても伝統的に寛容であった。
　多くの日本人は誕生や結婚の儀式は神道により、葬式
は仏教による。同じ人間が神社に初詣（はつもうで）も
するし、お盆の寺参りもし、クリスマスも祝う。
　各宗教が自宗の信徒数として発表している数は、神道
1億800万人・仏教9,500万人・キリスト教180万人
（2000年、文化庁）である。宗教人口を合計すると、日
本の人口の約2倍に達するという事実は、外国には例が
ない。

The first medal won by Japan was a silver in the tennis doubles (Kazuya Kumagaya and Seiichiro Kashio) in the 1920 Antwerp Games. Japan first hosted the Olympiad in 1964, when the 18th Summer Olympic games were held in Tokyo. At this meet, Japan won a total of 16 gold medals to place third in the overall medal standings.

In the 11th Winter Olympics held at Sapporo in 1972, Japan swept the first three places in the seventy-meter jump.

Japanese athletes made a very strong showing at the 1998 Winter Olympics held in Nagano.

(6) Religion

a) Japanese Religions

The principal religions in Japan are Shinto, Buddhism and Christianity.

Statistics show that few Japanese are deeply devoted to a specific religion and that, in fact, many profess to have no interest in religion at all.

A number of reasons can be given for this lack of religious feeling. For one thing, the Japanese people are by nature optimistic and concerned mainly about worldly affairs. Inhabitants of a country blessed with the beauty of nature and a moderate four-season climate, the Japanese have for many generations led an easygoing existence free from the threat of extreme natural disasters and the invasion of enemies. Perhaps because of this, they have not developed any deep religious yearning.

Further, Shintoism, the religion of Japan from time untold, is polytheistic, and because of this the Japanese people have traditionally been tolerant of all religious sects.

The birth and marriage ceremonies of most Japanese are Shinto, while funerals are Buddhist. The same person will pay his respects to a Shinto shrine at the beginning of the year, visit a Buddhist temple during the Festival of the Souls in summer, and celebrate Christmas at the end of year.

The number of followers claimed by different religions are: Shinto, 108 million; Buddhism, 95 million; and Christianity, 1.8 million (2000, Agency for Cultural Affairs). The sum of these figures is nearly twice Japan's population, a situation without parallel in other countries.

日本では憲法で宗教の自由が保障され、厳格に実行されている。したがって国教というものはなく、国の行事も宗教とは一切無関係である。国公立の学校では、宗教教育が禁じられている。

b) 神　道

神道は日本固有の自然宗教であり、神道の神を祭るところが神社である。神道でいう神は無数にあり、初めは自然物や自然現象をも神としていた。そして次第に先祖を祭るようになった。したがって神道には特定の教祖はなく、教典もない。

日本神話では「八百万（やおよろず）の神」という言葉があるように、神々の数は極めて多かった。のち神道は仏教・儒教の影響を受け理論化もされてきた。19世紀以後は国教のような扱いを受け、天皇が神格化された。しかし、第二次世界大戦後は国家との関係を断ち切り、各地の神社ごとの信仰となっている。

日本人は誕生のときお宮詣りをし、結婚式を神前で行う。さらに神社に入学合格を願ったり、自動車を運転する人が交通安全のお札を受けたりする。家の中に神棚を祭ることが多い。正月には有名な神社に一家そろってお詣りし、また神社ごとに定めている年1度のお祭りには、その地域の住民が多く集まり、出店なども繁盛する。

このように神社との縁は深いが、大部分の国民は神道の教義には無関心であり、現代日本人に対する思想的影響は少ない。

c) 仏　教

仏教は6世紀に中国・朝鮮を経て日本に伝えられた。7世紀の初頭、当時の皇太子であり実際に政治を行っていた聖徳太子が、仏教を深く学んでこれを広める役割を果たした。12世紀ごろまでは、仏教は貴族のための宗

The Japanese constitution guarantees religious freedom, and this guarantee is strictly maintained. Therefore, there is no state religion, and no connection between national and religious functions. Religious instruction is forbidden at public schools.

b) Shinto

Shinto is the natural indigenous religion of Japan. Shinto gods, or *kami*, are worshipped at shrines (*jinja*). All natural objects and phenomena used to be considered as having kami, so the gods of Shinto were uncountably numerous. Gradually Shinto practice extended to the worship of ancestors. Accordingly, then, there were no specific leaders in Shinto religion, nor any books of scripture.

That the number of Shinto gods was extremely great can be seen from the existence in Japanese mythology of the phrase *yaoyorozu no kami*, meaning "eight million kami." Later, influenced by Buddhism and Confucianism, Shinto became ideologized. From the nineteenth century it came to be regarded as the national religion of Japan, and the Emperor became deified. However, after World War II the practice of religion was separated from the functions of state, and worship became limited to the shrines in each locality.

People go to shrines when a child is born, and marriage ceremonies are also conducted according to Shinto rites. Further, people offer prayers at shrines for success in passing university entrance examinations, and motorists visit shrines to receive charms designed to keep them from harm. Small Shinto altars are found in many homes. Families go to famous shrines at the beginning of the new year. Each shrine has its own festival once a year, attended by the people in the area and served by numerous stalls selling a variety of things.

Thus, the people have a deep relationship with shrines, but the majority of Japanese have no interest in the tenets of Shinto, and the influence of the religion on the thought of the Japanese of today is small.

c) Buddhism

Buddhism reached Japan in the sixth century via China and Korea. At the beginning of the seventh century the then-crown prince Shotoku, who was in charge of affairs of state, made a deep study of Buddhism, and this served to spread the belief. Up

教であった。しかし、13世紀から庶民の間でも非常に盛んになり、同時に武士には「禅」が普及した。これらは現在まで引き続いて日本人の宗教の中心になっている。

仏教は「みずから真理に目覚めることによってえられる悟り」を究極の境地とする。また「あらゆるものが無常であるにもかかわらず恒常のものと考え、すべてのものは実体を持たないにもかかわらず実体あるものと考える執着を絶つこと」を眼目とする。

仏教では神がなく、無限の愛をもって憎しみや怨みを捨てることを強調する。一般に狂信を排して寛容であり、同時に平等を貫ぬこうとする。

日本人の生活では仏教とのつながりが非常に強く、信徒でなくともお寺に参詣し、葬式を仏教式で行い、死後は仏教上の名前（戒名）をつけ、ほとんどの家庭が、自分の家に仏壇を設け、供物を置き、線香をたき、先祖の冥福を祈っている。日本の美術・文学・建築あるいは日本人の思想・道徳など、文化全般にわたって仏教が非常に強く影響を与えている。

d）禅

禅宗は仏教の一つである。禅とは、心を静めることによって得られる高次の宗教的・内面的体験である。

このように、心を静めるために座って静かに思いをこらすことが坐禅である。

禅宗は12〜13世紀に、中国から帰国した日本人僧侶（栄西・道元）によって伝えられた。

禅宗では、真理は我々の言語・文字による表現を超えているとされ、坐禅修道によって直接に自証体得することによってのみ把握されるものだとする。

禅宗は武士道や茶道・いけばななどのバックボーンになり、日本の思想や文化・生活全般に影響を与えた。

until the twelfth century Buddhism was the religion of the aristocracy only, but from about the thirteenth century it became very popular among the common people. At about this time *Zen* became widespread among the *samurai* class. Since those times and up to the present day, Buddhism has been the principal religion of the Japanese people.

Buddhism holds that the ultimate state is one of self-enlightenment attained by awakening to the truth. It is an objective, too, to rid oneself of the tenacious idea that everything is everlasting, although all is transitory, that everything has substance, although all is insubstantial.

There is no God in Buddhism; the emphasis is on ridding oneself of hate and jealousy through infinite love. Fanaticism is rejected; one should try to attain tolerance and equality.

Buddhism is a major presence in the life of the Japanese people. Even if they are non-believers they go to temples, are buried according to Buddhist rites and, after death, are given posthumous Buddhist names. Most families have a Buddhist altar in their homes, where they place offerings, burn incense and pray for the repose of their ancestors. Buddhism has exerted a tremendous influence on every aspect of Japanese culture, including art, literature and architecture, and on the morals and way of thought of the people.

d) Zen Buddhism

The *Zen* sect is one of the denominations of Buddhism. "*Zen*" is defined as an enlightened religious and mental state attained by achieving serenity of mind.

One of the practices used to obtain this serenity of mind is called *zazen* or "sitting in silent meditation."

Eisai, Dogen and other Japanese priests introduced the Zen sect to Japan in the twelfth and thirteenth centuries after studying in China.

According to the Zen sect, truth is something which transcends the expressions of language and letters. It can only be grasped through the direct proof of experience obtained in the practice of zazen.

The Zen sect has become the backbone of the *samurai* spirit, tea cult and *ikebana* or Japanese flower arrangement. It has exerted great influence on Japanese thought, culture and literally all aspects of Japanese life.

現在の日本では、禅宗の僧侶以外にみずから坐禅をして真理を追求している人は少ないが、精神修養の方法として、短期間禅寺に坐禅をしにいくことは一部に行われている。

e) キリスト教

日本に最初にキリスト教が伝えられたのは、1549年にカトリック教会のイエズス会士フランシスコ・ザビエルが鹿児島に渡来したときである。

はじめ支配層のなかには西洋の文物に対する関心もあって、イエズス会のカトリック布教に好意的な者もあった。17世紀初めの最盛期には、信徒が約75万人いたとされる。のち、封建秩序に有害であると考え、次第に抑圧禁止するようになった。信者は迫害を受け、1613年には外国人宣教師は国外に追放された。カトリック禁止後も、秘密に信仰を持ち続ける者も少なくなかった。

19世紀後半、欧米と国交を開いてから、再び日本におけるキリスト教布教が盛んになった。

1859年以降、プロテスタント宣教師がアメリカから派遣され、またカトリック・ロシア正教も布教活動を行った。これらの外国人宣教師は、日本で社会事業や教育事業にも従事し、日本におけるヨーロッパ・アメリカの文化導入に貢献した。

日本における近代文化とは、ほとんど欧米文化を意味したが、欧米文化の中心をなすキリスト教的思考・生活方式の一部、道徳なども日本に取り入れられた。現在の一夫一婦制などもその一例とされている。

現在日本のキリスト教信者は、プロテスタント41万人、カトリック46万人，その他93万人といわれている（2000年文化庁）。各派がつくった大学がある。また、宗派を超越した国際基督教大学も設立されている。カトリックの司教土井辰雄が、1960年日本人初の枢機卿に任命された。

In Japan today there are a good many people, besides the Zen priests, who pursue truth by practicing zazen. As a method of spiritual training, some people pay periodical visits to Zen temples for short sessions of zazen.

e) Christianity in Japan

Christianity first reached Japan in 1549 with the arrival at Kagoshima of Francis Xavier, a Catholic missionary belonging to the Society of Jesus.

At first, there were some members of the ruling class in Japan who were interested in Western culture and institutions and therefore friendly toward the propagation of the Catholic religion by the Jesuits. At its peak, in the early seventeenth century, it is estimated that there were about 750 thousand Christians in Japan. Later, though, it came to be considered a danger to the feudal order and was eventually repressed and banned. Christians were persecuted, and in 1613 foreign missionaries were banished from the country. Even after Christianity was prohibited, quite a few believers carried on practicing their faith in secret.

After Japan established diplomatic relations with Europe and America in the latter half of the nineteenth century, propagation of Christian faith again began to flourish.

From 1859, Protestant missionaries from America started to arrive, and the Catholic and Russian Orthodox churches also became actively involved in missionary work. These foreign missionaries also engaged in social and educational activities, contributing to the introduction of American and European culture into Japan.

By "modern culture" in Japan is meant almost entirely the culture of the West. So also introduced into Japan, then, were some of those Christian morals and modes of life and thought that are central to the culture of the West. The present monogamous system of marriage is considered an example of such influences.

At present there are in Japan about 410 thousand Protestants, 460 thousand Catholics and 930 thousand of other denominations (2000, Agency for Cultural Affairs). There are universities that have been established by these sects. There is also a university, the International Christian University, that is non-denominational. In 1960 Tatsuo Doi, then a bishop, became the first Japanese to be made a cardinal.

(7) 風俗・習慣・娯楽

a) 着物（和服）

　　　現在の着物は、江戸時代に正装になったもので、これは平安時代の貴族の正装の下着が次第に変化して、今日の形に発展してきたものだといわれている。

　　　現在日本人は、日常ほとんど洋服を着て生活しているが、和服は正装として、あるいは室内着として現在でも愛好されている。

　　　女性の着る和服は、キモノとして外国でもよく知られた美しい衣装である。このうち一番豪華なものは、花嫁が着る打掛けである。これは絹の布地に金銀の箔を織り込んだ金糸・銀糸で刺繍を施し、多くは花鳥の図案模様を描いたものが用いられる。

　　　このほか、未婚の女性と既婚の女性ではキモノの模様・色合いや袖の長さなどが異なり、正式の訪問か遊楽のためかなど外出の目的によっても、布地・模様・色合い・仕立方などが異なる。一般の女性がキモノを着るのは、正月・成人式・大学卒業パーティー・結婚式・同披露宴・葬儀などである。

　　　洋服が体形に合わせてつくられているのに対し、キモノは体形との相関関係がルーズであって、着付けによって体に合わせるため着方が難しい。日常洋服で生活している最近の若い女性の大部分は、自分ひとりでキモノを着ることができない。

　　　キモノの持つ奥床しさ、落ち着きの美しさは、染織の美しさによるということ以上に、キモノを着ることによってかもし出される雰囲気によるといわれる。

　　　男性がキモノを着るのは、現代では主としてくつろぎのための室内用に限られるが、正月などに自宅において客をもてなすときなどには、和服を着ることは珍しくない。和服の正装では羽織・袴をつける。

　　　最も軽便な室内着として、木綿地のゆかたがある。これはとくに夏期には、入浴後に着て室内の風通しのよいところで涼をとりくつろぐのには、最適の着物である。

(7) Customs, Manners and Pastimes

a) Kimono (Japanese Dress)

The *kimono* as known today first appeared as a formal outer garment in the Edo era, having evolved through gradual changes in the shape and color of the formal undergarments worn by the nobility in the Heian period.

For the most part, Japanese people today wear Western clothing in their everyday life, but the traditional kimono is still popular both as formal attire and as clothing for the home.

The kimono worn by Japanese women are well known abroad for their beauty. By far the most gorgeous is the *uchikake*, a long overgarment worn by the bride in a wedding ceremony. The silk fabric is embroidered with gold and silver threads, most commonly in patterns of flowers or birds.

There are various types of kimonos. Those of married and unmarried women differ in design, color, sleeve length and other aspects. Women also wear kimonos of different fabrics, designs, patterns and cuts in accordance with the occasion —formal or informal. Japanese women ordinarily wear kimonos during the New Year holidays, or on such occasions as the coming-of-age ceremony, college graduation parties, wedding ceremonies and receptions as well as funeral services.

Whereas Western dresses are tailored in specific sizes to fit the wearer, Japanese kimonos are made only in approximate sizes and the fit is adjusted by the manner in which it is worn. This is an operation requiring special technique. Most young Japanese women of today are accustomed only to Western dresses and cannot put on a kimono by themselves.

The elegance and refined beauty of the kimono derives more from the atmosphere created by the manner in which the kimono is worn than from the beauty of the cloth.

Men wear kimonos mostly at home when they wish to enjoy a relaxed, easy atmosphere. However, it is not uncommon for men to wear kimonos during the New Year holidays to receive guests at home. On formal occasions, they wear *haori* (a half-coat) and *hakama* (a divided skirt).

The cotton *yukata* is an informal kimono and is popular as a home garment especially for summer wear. It is an ideal kimono to wear while cooling off in a breezy part of the house after a bath in the summer.

b）主な年中行事

○元日（1月1日）：新年の門出を祝う日である。元日から1月3日までの3日間を、「お正月」または「三が日」といって完全に仕事を休む。「正月」とは本来「1月」のことであるが、慣習的にこの3日間を指すようになっている。神社に参詣したり、知人宅を訪問して新年のあいさつを交わし、酒を飲み、正月独特の料理（おせち料理）を食べたりして楽しむ。正月には、門には注連縄を張り、松飾りをつけ、または門松をたてる。門松は、神の降臨するための樹木をたてるという意味がある。松飾りのある期間は元日から7日まで（昔は15日まで）で、この期間を「松の内」ともいう。

○節分（2月3日または4日）：太陰太陽暦の立春の前日をいい、節分の夜に各家庭では「鬼は外、福は内」ととなえながら家の内外に大豆をまき、鬼（災い）を追い払って戸口を閉ざす行事が行われる。

○ひなまつり（3月3日）：女の子の将来の幸福を願うお祭りである。昔の宮廷の風俗を模したきれいなひな人形を桃の花と一緒に飾る。もち米の粥に麹をまぜて醸造した酒（しろざけ）を飲んで楽しむ。

○端午の節句（5月5日）：男の子が健やかに育つことを願うお祭りである。武士の人形を飾り、邪気を払うための菖蒲を軒に差し、鯉のぼりをたて、柏餅を食べて楽しむ。

○七夕（7月7日）：中国伝来の風習と、わが国固有の信仰とが結合したものといわれている。天の川（銀河）の両岸にある牽牛星と織女星とが、年に1度あうことを祝うお祭りである。庭前に供物（とうもろこし、なすなど）をし、歌や字を書いた5色の短冊を笹竹につけて飾り、織女星にあやかって女児の手芸の上達を祈る。

b) Main Annual Festivals

○ Ganjitsu (January 1): the day on which the birth of the new year is celebrated. Nobody works on the first three days of the new year, the period called *sanga nichi*, or *shogatsu*. Shogatsu originally referred to the whole of January, but now is used just to refer to these three days. On these days, the people go to shrines, visit friends and relatives, drink *sake* and eat special new-year dishes, called *osechi*. *Shimenawa*, sacred rice-straw ropes, are hung across the top of the gateway, which is also decorated with pine boughs or *kadomatsu* (gate pines). The kadomatsu symbolizes a tree provided for the descent of the gods. This pine decoration is left in place from January the first to the seventh (until the fifteenth in olden times), the period referred to as *matsu no uchi*.

○ Setsubun (February 3 or 4): the day before the beginning of spring according to the lunisolar calendar. On the evening of this day, people open the doors of their houses and drive the demons (i.e. bad luck) out of their homes and gardens by throwing handfuls of beans and shouting "Demons out! Good luck in!"

○ Hina matsuri (March 3): the Festival of Dolls. Also called Girls' Day Festival, this is the day on which wishes are expressed for the future happiness of girls. A set of dolls dressed in costumes which were worn in the royal court in ancient times are displayed together with peach blossoms as decoration. A sweet drink called *shirozake*, brewed from rice gruel mixed with fermented rice, is partaken of on this day.

○ Tango no sekku (May 5): the Boys' Festival for expressing the hope that each boy in the family will grow up healthy and strong. Warrior figures are set up in the house during this festival, iris leaves are placed under the eaves to fend off evil, and huge fish-like streamers are fastened to poles. Special rice cakes wrapped in oak leaves are eaten on this day.

○ Tanabata (July 7): the Star Festival, which is said to be a combination of Chinese tradition with beliefs peculiar to Japan. This festival celebrates the meeting, just once a year, of two lovers, Kengyu (the star Altair, personified as a cowherd) and Shokujo (Vega, as a weaving girl), who are separated by the Milky Way on the other days of the year. Pieces of bamboo are set up in the garden and adorned with strips of paper of five different colors on which are written poems associated with the legend, and offerings of food, such as corn and eggplant, are

○お盆（8月15日の前後数日）：種々の食物を祖先の霊に供えてその冥福を祈る。都会に働きに行っている者は郷里に帰る。なお、東京などの大都市では7月に行うところもある。各地の町や村で盆踊りが行われ、ゆかた姿で多くの人が参加するが、これは日本の夏の風物詩の一つである。

○月見（陰暦8月15日夜および9月13日夜〔満月の夜〕）：すすきを飾り、お酒とだんごを月に供え、月を見ながら秋の夜を楽しむ。

○お彼岸（春分の日と秋分の日を中心とした前後7日間）：彼岸とは向こう岸の意味で、仏教ではさとりの世界のことである。先祖の霊を呼び、仏事を行い、墓にお詣りする。

○七五三：男の子は3歳と5歳、女の子は3歳と7歳にあたる年の11月15日に、子供の成長を祝い、晴着を着せて神社に詣る。奇数をめでたい数とし、そのうちから三つを取ったものである。

○クリスマス：日本には洗礼をうけたクリスチャンの数は多くないが、かなりの人が一種のお祭り的なものとして、クリスマスイブを楽しむ。子供にとってはサンタクロースのプレゼントが楽しみである。

c）国民の祝日

　　法律で14の国民の祝日が定まっており、学校・官庁・会社が休日になる。
○元日（1月1日）：年の始めを祝う。

○成人の日（1月の第2月曜日）：大人になったことを自覚し、自ら生き抜こうとする青年を祝い励ます。各市町村は、その年成人になる人を集めて祝いの式を行う。

made. Also, young girls pray that their handicraft will become as proficient as Vega's was supposed to be.

○ Obon (around mid-August): the Festival of Souls. In this festival a variety of foods are offered to the spirits of ancestors, and their repose prayed for. People who have moved to the cities to work return to their home towns during this period. In Tokyo and other major cities this festival is celebrated in July. In towns and villages across the country people in *yukata* (light cotton *kimono*) gather for outdoor dances known as *bon-odori*. For many Japanese, summer wouldn't be summer without a bon-odori.

○ Tsukimi (night of the full moon on August 15 and September 13 of the lunar calendar): the days for "moon-gazing." Decorations of Japanese pampas grass are used, and moon-offerings of *sake* and *dango* (a kind of dumpling) are made as the people gaze at the moon, enjoying the autumn evening.

○ Higan (two periods of seven days with the middle day falling on the spring or autumn equinox): the word *higan* meaning "the other shore," or, in Buddhism, nirvana. During higan the spirits of ancestors are recalled, Buddhist rites carried out and family graves visited.

○ Shichi-go-san (November 15): the seven-five-three festival when parents with boys of five, girls of seven and either boys or girls of three dress their children in gay clothes and take them to shrines where they pray for their children's future. These three numbers were chosen since odd numbers are considered lucky.

○ Christmas: There are not many baptized Christians in Japan, but many people engage in festive activities on Christmas Eve. Children, especially, enjoy receiving presents from "Santa Claus."

c) National Holidays

Schools, companies and government offices close on these fourteen legally-established national holidays:

○ New Year's Day (January 1): day on which the start of the new year is celebrated.

○ Coming-of-Age Day (second Monday of January): day for congratulating those who have reached their majority and are now ready to make their own way in the world. Each city, town and village holds a congratulatory ceremony for those who come of age in that particular year.

○建国記念の日（2月11日）：建国をしのび、国を愛する心を養う（紀元前660年に第1代の天皇が即位したと伝えられる日を記念する）。

○春分の日（暦の上での春分日）：自然をたたえ、生物をいつくしむ（古来から仏教上のお祭りの日であった）。

○緑の日（4月29日）：昭和天皇が自然と親しまれ、ご在位中に全国を巡幸された際、各地で植樹されたことを記念する日（1988年までは、昭和天皇の誕生日として祝っていた）。

○憲法記念日（5月3日）：日本国憲法の施行を記念し、国の成長を期する（1947年5月3日施行）。

○子供の日（5月5日）：子供の人格を重んじ、子供の幸福をはかるとともに、母に感謝する（古来から5月5日が男の子のお祝いの日であった）。

○海の日（7月20日）：海に囲まれた国として、日本が海から受けているさまざまの恩恵に感謝するとともに、海洋国としての繁栄を願う（1941年に定められ、96年から国民の祝日になった）。

○敬老の日（9月15日）：多年にわたり社会に尽くしてきた老人を敬愛し、長寿を祝う。各市町村で高齢者を招いて演芸会などを開いたり、記念品を贈呈したりする。

○秋分の日（暦の上での秋分日）：祖先を敬い、亡くなった人々をしのぶ（古来から仏教上のお祭りの日であった）。

○体育の日（10月の第2月曜日）：スポーツに親しみ、健康な心身を培かう（1964年10月10日の東京オリンピック開会を記念する）。体育振興の行事が開かれることが多い。

○文化の日（11月3日）：自由と平等を愛し、文化を進める（1946年11月3日、日本国憲法公布の日を記念す

○ National Foundation Day (February 11): day for commemorating the founding of the nation and for fostering patriotic feelings. (Marks the anniversary of the accession to the throne of the first emperor, in the year 660 B.C.)

○ Vernal Equinox Day (on the day of the spring equinox according to the calendar): day for praising nature and showing love of all living things. (This has been a Buddhist festival day from ancient times.)

○ Greenery Day (April 29): day for commemorating the Emperor Showa's love for nature and the many trees he planted on tours throughout the country. (Up to 1988, this day was celebrated as the birthday of the Emperor Showa.)

○ Constitution Memorial Day (May 3): day for commemorating the enforcement of the Constitution and reaffirming hope in the growth of the nation. (The Constitution was enforced on May 3, 1947.)

○ Children's Day (May 5): day on which wishes are expressed that the children will grow up good and find happiness; it is also for expressing thanks to mothers. (May 5 has long been the celebratory day for boys.)

○ Marine Day (July 20): day for giving thanks for the many blessings Japan receives from the ocean as a country completely surrounded by water and also for reaffirming the people's desire to prosper as a maritime country. July 20 was designated as a day to remember the ocean in 1941 and became a national holiday in 1996.

○ Respect-for-the-Aged Day (September 15): day for showing respect and affection for the elderly who have devoted themselves to the society for so many years, and for celebrating their long life. In cities, towns and villages, the elderly are invited to entertainments and given gifts to mark the occasion.

○ Autumnal Equinox Day (on the day of the autumnal equinox according to the calendar): day on which ancestors are honored, and the deceased remembered. (This has been a Buddhist festival day from ancient times.)

○ Health-Sports Day (second Monday of October): day for sports and to foster a sound mind and body. (Commemorates the 1964 Tokyo Olympiad, the opening ceremony of which took place on October 10.) Many sporting events are held on this day.

○ Culture Day (November 3): day for celebrating love of freedom and equality, and promoting culture. (Commemorates the

る。ちなみに 1945 年以前には、明治天皇誕生の日として祝っていた）。

○勤労感謝の日（11 月 23 日）：勤労を尊び、生産を祝い国民互いに感謝しあう（天皇が新しく収穫した米を神に捧げる日を記念する）。

○天皇誕生日（12 月 23 日）：今上天皇の誕生日（1933年 12 月 23 日）を祝う。皇居で天皇・皇后両陛下が国民の参賀を受ける。

　〔注〕この他に、5 月 4 日は「国民の休日」である。

d) 郷土色豊かな祭りや伝統的行事

○秋田県横手地方の「かまくら」（正月行事の一つ）：縦横 2 m 位の雪室をつくり、中に祭壇を設け水神を祭る。夜、数人の子供達が雪室の中に集まり、甘酒や餅などを食べる。

　昔は小屋（正月小屋）にこもって飲食を慎しみ、不浄を避けた生活を送る風習が、日本の中部以東でかなり広く行われていた。その変形として、今は子供の楽しい行事となっている。

○札幌の雪祭（2 月第 1 金曜日〜日曜日）：動物・神話・伝説・人気マンガのキャラクター・有名な建物などを題材にした、大小さまざまの雪像が立ち並ぶ雪の祭典である。札幌の大通り公園で行われる。

○博多の「どんたく」（5 月 3 日〜4 日）：「どんたく」とは、オランダ語の Zondag のなまりで、休日の意である。馬に乗った神話の神様の仮装行列や、屋台に乗った着飾った子供の行列が、にぎやかに市内をねり歩くほか、種々の芸能大会が催される。

○東京の山王祭（6 月 15 日）：日枝神社の祭礼で、神田祭とともに江戸（現在の東京）の二大祭とされた。しかし、次第に豪華になり、氏子の負担がますます大きくなった。このため氏子の負担を軽減するために、1615 年以来、双方が隔年に行われるようになった。これらは天下祭または御用祭とも呼ばれ、山車（だし）行列は一般

promulgation, on November 3, 1946, of the Japanese Constitution. Prior to 1945, this day was celebrated as the birthday of the Emperor Meiji.)

○ Labor Thanksgiving Day (November 23): day for praise and celebration of labor and production. The people give thanks for the benefits of labor. (It is on this day that the Emperor makes an offering of newly harvested rice to God.)

○ Emperor's Birthday (December 23): On this day the Emperor, with the Empress, receives the congratulations of the people at the Imperial Palace. (The Emperor was born on December 23, 1933.)

May 4 is also national holiday—simply a day of rest.

d) Local Festivals and Traditional Events

○ Kamakura Festival at Yokote in Akita Prefecture (one of the New Year holiday events): A *kamakura* is an igloo-like snow house, about 2 meters square, which shelters an altar dedicated to the God of Water. At night, children gather in the kamakura to enjoy rice cakes and a sweet mild *sake* called *amazake*.

In olden times, it was a widespread custom among people in central and eastern Japan to build a small New Year's hut in which to spend a few days refraining from the pleasures of eating and drinking in order to purify themselves. This has now turned into a happy event for children.

○ Snow Festival in Sapporo (From the first Friday in February through the following Sunday): winter carnival at which an array of huge snow sculptures of animals, figures from legends and mythology, popular cartoon characters and famous buildings is exhibited in Sapporo's Odori Park.

○ Dontaku Festival in Hakata, Fukuoka Prefecture (May 3 to 4): the word *dontaku* deriving from the Dutch *zondag* meaning "holiday." The Dontaku Festival is marked by a gala procession of figures on horseback masquerading as deities from Japanese mythology and of floats with *kimono*-clad children aboard. Many and various shows are also held during the festival period.

○ Sanno Festival in Tokyo (June 15): this Hie Shrine Festival and the Kanda Festival were formerly considered to be the two major festivals of Edo (present-day Tokyo). Year by year, however, these festivals became more and more extravagant, and more burdensome for the shrine parishioners, until it was decided in 1615 to hold them in alternate years. The two festivals were

市民の入ることのできなかった江戸城内まで入ることができた。現在もこの伝統によって隔年に行われる。

○京都の祇園祭（7月1日〜29日）：八坂神社の祭礼で、9世紀末に疫病退散を願ったのが起源とされる。16日の夜には、町の旧家は軒に神灯や青簾をかけ、敷物をのべて花を飾り、屏風を立てて祭りに色彩をそえる。また、鉾山車（ほこだし）には、灯が明々とともり、祇園囃子が奏でられる。17日の豪華壮麗な鉾山車の巡行で、祭りの雰囲気は最高潮に達する。

○大阪の天神祭（7月25日）：天満宮の祭礼。神輿が堂島川を下る神幸式が中心である。お迎え人形船・ドンドコ船・かがり船・はやし船などが川いっぱいに豪華な船祭りをくりひろげる。

○青森の「ねぶた」祭（8月3日〜7日）：大きなはりこの人形・魚・鳥獣などをかついだり、車に乗せて、笛や太鼓の囃子にあわせて「らっせ・らっせ」の掛声にぎやかに市中をひきまわす。夜は内部から照明を照らし、幻想的な雰囲気につつみ込む。

6日夜から7日にかけて、これらを船に乗せて海上をねるのが見ものである。青森地方の夏を色どる風物詩である。

ねむいことを「ねぶたい」ともいうが、この語幹の「ねぶた」をとって、睡魔のことをいうらしい。この睡魔を払う行事が発端である。

○仙台の七夕祭（8日6日〜8日）：七夕の伝説（別項「七夕」参照）にちなんでの祭りで、全国で行われるが、とくに仙台のものが有名である。各戸に種々意匠をこら

designated "official" or "national" events and the parade of festival floats was allowed into the Edo Castle grounds, a place that commoners were ordinarily prohibited from entering. The practice of holding the festivals alternately continues to this day.

○ Gion Festival in Kyoto (July 1 to 29): festival of Yasaka Shrine said to have originated in an attempt to secure protection from a plague toward the end of the ninth century. On the evening of July 16, lanterns are hung from the eaves of the houses in the old sections of the city, special blue curtains are hung in the doorways, flowers are set out on cloth spreads and decorative screens are displayed, thus adding color to the festival. It is also on this evening that the float lanterns are lighted to the accompaniment of festive music. The climax comes on July 17, when a fleet of gorgeously decorated floats parade through the boulevards.

○ Tenjin Festival in Osaka (July 25): festival of the Tenman Shrine, the main event of which is the Shinkoshiki or the descent of Dojimagawa River by a *mikoshi* (portable shrine). Numerous boats, some decked out with life-size dolls, others with blazing torches suspended over the sides and still others carrying drummers and other musicians who provide lively music for the occasion, create a gorgeous scene as they spread across the river to greet the mikoshi.

○ Nebuta Festival in Aomori (August 3 to 7): a festival featuring as its main attraction a parade of huge papier-mâché dolls, fish, birds and animals which are carried through the city on shoulder or aboard wagons to the accompaniment of flute and drum music and the chants of the participants shouting "*Rasse! Rasse!*" At night the papier-mâché figures are lighted from the inside, creating a fantastic atmosphere.

From the night of August 6 into the morning of August 7, the figures are loaded on boats for a spectacular sea parade. This summer festival is the biggest annual event in the Aomori district.

The word "*nebuta*" is derived from "*nebutai*" which in the local dialect means "sleepy." It apparently refers to the demon of sleep and the festival originated from a local ritual aimed at chasing off this demon.

○ Tanabata Festival in Sendai (August 6 to 8): one of numerous Tanabata festivals held throughout the country (see section on Tanabata). The one held in Sendai is, however, especially

した短冊や吹流しを飾りつけた竹を立てて優美を競うが、ことに商店街では、軒並みに趣向をこらした豪華な飾りつけをして、雰囲気を盛り上げる。

○秋田の竿灯（かんとう）祭（８月５日〜７日）：秋田市で行われる七夕祭りの行事である。仕事の妨げとなる一年中の睡魔をはらうことを願うものである。

　１本の長い親竹に横竹を結びつけ、それに46個または48個の提灯をぶらさげたものを、バランスをとって頭上・肩先・掌上などに立てる。若者が太鼓の囃子につれて、倒さないように扱う技を競う。

○徳島の阿波踊り（８月12日〜15日）：16世紀末に、時の大名がこの地方に入城したのを祝って、住民が踊ったのがはじまりといわれる。

　三味線・太鼓・笛などの伴奏につれて、老若男女を問わず、ゆかたがけで踊る。踊りは単純活発で、手びょうし・足どりも面白く、全市をあげて夜を明かして踊り抜く。

○長崎の「おくんち」（10月７日〜９日）：諏訪神社の祭礼である。「おくんち」とは、太陰暦９月９日のことで、中国の重陽の節句（中国では、９は陽の数とされ、これを二つ重ねた月日にあたる）にちなんでいる。

　中国風の蛇踊りなどがあり、鎖国時代も唯一の開港地だった土地柄をしのばせる。

○京都の時代祭（10月22日）：平安神宮の祭礼である。京都に都がおかれていた、1000余年にわたる風俗・習慣などを、時代別にかたどった行列がくりひろげられ、日本歴史の絵巻物を、目のあたりに見るような美しさである。

○秩父の夜祭り（12月３日）：秩父神社の祭礼で、夜祭りとして有名である。神輿に続いて、ぼんぼりを無数にともした屋台と山車が行進する。はげしいリズムをもつ

famous. Each family in the city tries to outdo its neighbors in putting up bamboo poles colorfully decorated with streamers and strips of fancy paper with Japanese *haiku* or *tanka* poems written on them. The decorations are by far the most gorgeous and colorful in the shopping centers where elaborate adornments continue block after block and help to raise the festive mood to a high pitch.

○ Kanto Festival in Akita (August 5 to 7): Akita City's version of the Tanabata festival. It is held to drive off the demon of drowsiness that hampers the people's work throughout the year.

A *kanto* is a long bamboo pole with numerous cross bars on which forty-six or forty-eight lanterns are hung. The highlight of the festival is a competition among local youths who vie with each other in balancing the kantos on their heads, shoulders, and hands as they dance to the accompaniment of drums.

○ Awa Odori Dancing Festival in Tokushima (August 12 to 15): a festival dating back to the end of the sixteenth century when residents danced in the streets in celebration of their new warlord's move into the city's castle.

Men and women, young and old, don their *yukatas* (a traditional Japanese summer garment) and dance through the night to the music of *shamisen* (a three-stringed musical instrument), drums and flutes. The dance itself is simple, but very lively, and involves interesting hand and foot movements.

○ Okunchi Festival in Nagasaki (October 7 to 9): the festival of the Suwa Shrine in Nagasaki. "*Okunchi*" means ninth day of the ninth month according to the lunar calendar and the festival originated from one in China falling on the same day. (Nine is considered a lucky number in China and the double nine especially so.)

The festival features dragon dances in the traditional Chinese fashion and is reminiscent of the days of isolation when Nagasaki was the only port open to foreign countries.

○ Jidai Festival in Kyoto (October 22): the festival of the Heian Shrine highlighted by a unique procession of historical figures clad in costumes representing each of the historical periods of the ten centuries during which Kyoto was the capital. The parade is a beautiful reproduction of the history of Japan.

○ Chichibu Night Festival (December 3): the festival of the Chichibu Shrine and one of the most famous to be held at night. The *mikoshi* (portable shrine) at the head of the parade is

祭囃子は、秩父屋台囃子として知られている。

○男鹿半島の「なまはげ」（12 月 31 日）：古くから男鹿半島に伝わる変わった行事である。面をかぶり、わらや海草でつくった腰みのをつけて、鬼に仮装した青年達が、張子の出刃包丁・棒・かますなどを持って各家を訪れ、怠け者をいましめて歩く。

「なまはげ」は「なまみはぎ」（生身剝ぎ）の転訛であるが、なまみとは炉端で火にあたってばかりいるときにできる皮膚の火だこのことで、これができるような怠け者を指す。

e）外国と異なる日本の習慣

○入浴：日本人は入浴により体を洗うだけでなく、湯槽につかってゆっくり温まる習慣がある。体を洗い、汚れを流すのは湯槽の外で行う。湯槽の中の湯は加熱できるようになっており、湯の減った分は水を追加して温める。数人が順次同じ湯槽に入る。各家庭だけでなく、代金を支払って入る共同風呂の銭湯も同様である。

○不吉な数字：4 と 9 を嫌う。4 はシと読み、シは死を意味する。9 はクと読み、苦を意味する。ホテルの部屋番号でも、13 とともに 4 と 9 を除いているところがある。

○ノーチップ制：戦前は、旅館や交通機関の一部でチップを与える習慣があったが、最近はほとんどなくなった。
〔注〕日本と逆な西欧の習慣
　　　◇手招きのしかた…掌を上に向けて、指を曲げる。
　　　◇鋸（のこぎり）・鉋（かんな）の使い方…先方に押すときに力を入れて、切ったり、削る。
　　　◇マッチのすり方…手前に向けてする。

followed by floats lit up with countless paper lanterns. The parade progresses to the strong beat of the festival song, the well known Chichibu Yataibayashi.

○ Namahage Festival of the Oga Peninsula in Akita Prefecture (December 31): a unique event observed from ancient times in the Oga Peninsula. Young men dressed as dreadful demons and bearing big papier-mâché knives, clubs and straw bags go from house to house admonishing sluggards to mend their ways. The costume includes a demon's mask and a skirt of straw or seaweed.

"Namahage" is a corruption of *"namami-hagi"* which literally means "getting rid of calluses formed by excessive exposure of the skin to heat." The term is used to indicate the treatment required by a person so lazy as to sit warming himself at the fire long enough for such a callus to form.

e) Differences in Custom and Belief

○ Baths: Japanese people do not use baths just to wash themselves; they also like to warm themselves by soaking slowly in a deep tub full of hot water. The actual washing and rinsing is done outside the tub. Baths are constructed to allow the water in the tub to be heated directly, so when the level of hot water drops, it is topped up with cold water and reheated. A number of people use the same bath in turn. This is true not only of home baths but also of public, communal baths (meaning baths open to anyone for a fee).

○ Unlucky numbers: Four and nine are considered unlucky. Four in Japanese is *shi*, which has the same sound as the word meaning "death." The number nine is read *ku* in Japanese, which is associated with another word meaning "suffering." There are some hotels which do not have any rooms numbered four, nine or thirteen.

○ Tipping: Before the war, there was some tipping in inns and transport facilities, but this has almost disappeared in recent times.

◇鉛筆の削り方…鉛筆の先を、内側に向けて
削る。
◇釣銭のかぞえ方…足し算でかぞえる。

f) 名　刺

　日本では名刺が広く使われており、とくにビジネスマンが初対面のときに、姓名のほかに、勤務先企業・団体名・所属名・役職名・住所・電話番号が印刷されている名刺を、相互に交換する習慣がある。

　名刺の交換は、地位の低い人や若い人の方から先に相手に渡すのがエチケットとされている。名刺を渡すときは、相手の方に向けて差し出す。名刺を折ったり、不必要なメモをすることは、相手に対して失礼とされる。

g) 判　子

　日本では、西欧式のサインと同じような意味で、自分の姓や名を彫った判子による押印が用いられる。

　市町村の役所に登録してある印を「実印」と呼び、それ以外の「認め印」と区別する。この実印の印鑑証明によって、本人に相違ないことを確認することが法律上定められている。したがって、主要な取引や契約書作成には、印鑑証明が必要になる。

　このように判子は、ビジネス社会に限らず一般市民生活にも、極めて重要である。たとえば、日本では近年、銀行預金の出し入れのさい自動引出し用の「キャッシュ・カード」の利用が盛んになっている。しかし、この「カード」によらない銀行・郵便貯金通帳からの預金払い戻しや、郵便の書留の受取証・領収書発行などにも判子が必要である。

h) 風呂敷

　風呂敷は、日本で古くから物品の持ち運びや保存などに使用されている四角形の布である。風呂敷の名称が一般に用いられるようになったのは、江戸時代前期（17世紀ごろ）である。銭湯（別項 328 頁参照）の発達にともない、衣料をこの布に包んで運び、更衣をこの布の上で行ったため、風呂敷と呼ばれるようになった。

f) Name Cards

Name cards (calling and business cards) are used extensively in Japan. When business people meet for the first time, each invariably gives the other a card printed with his name as well as the name, address and telephone number of his company, the department he works in, and his position.

Etiquette calls for the lower ranking or younger person to offer his card first. When the card is extended, it should be turned so the other person can read it as he accepts it. It is considered impolite to use a damaged card or one that bears a memo not intended for the receiver.

g) Seals

Where a Westerner would put his signature on something, a Japanese will stamp it with a seal engraved with his name.

A Japanese may have more than one seal; the one he has registered at the local government office is called his *jitsuin* and the others *mitomein*. Under Japanese law, a person who has registered his seal can obtain a certificate of seal impression which he can use to prove his identity. Such a certificate is necessary whenever one makes a major transaction or concludes a contract.

Seals are very important not only in the business world but also in everyday life. For example, although the use of cash cards for making deposits and withdrawals at money vending machines is now widespread in Japan, a person who wants to withdraw money from a bank or postal savings account over the counter without his card will have to use his seal. He will also need it for receiving registered letters and making out receipts.

h) Furoshiki

A *furoshiki* (literally a "bath spread") is a square piece of cloth for bundling up various articles that one wishes to carry or store away. Furoshiki have long been used in Japan; the word itself dates back to the early part of the Edo Era (around the 17th century) when public, communal bath houses became popular (see p. 329). The name comes from one of the first uses for this

風呂敷は、物品の形・大きさなどにあまり関係なく自由に包装できる。また何も包まないときは、小さく折りたたんで持ち歩ける。物品を包装するさい、四角の布の対角線上の端を相互に結ぶ必要があるが、日本人の手先の器用さがその発達をうながしたといえよう。

風呂敷の大きさや材質は、用途に応じていろいろなものがある。ふとんを包むための木綿で唐草模様の実用一点張りのものや、絹織物に紋様や花鳥の模様をあしらった美しいものまである。

i) そろばん

日本古来からの計算器で、電卓が普及した現在でも用法が簡単で便利なために、広く使われている。横長浅底の木わくの内側に、上方に横に梁を設け、これを貫いて縦に木わくの上辺と下辺に竹串を等間隔に渡し、梁を隔てて各串の上部に珠を1箇おいて数字の5を、下部に珠を4箇（以前は5箇）おいて、1箇で1を表わす。この珠を上下して加減乗除を行う。

そろばんは16世紀ごろ中国から日本に伝わったといわれている。その後現在の形に改良が加えられた。

そろばんの技術を示す段や級が設けられており、その認定を受けたい者は検定試験を受ける。

j) じゃんけん

互いに片手の掌で石・紙・はさみの形を出し合って勝負を争う遊びで、掌を握ったものを石、掌を開いたものを紙、人差指と中指との二本を出したものをはさみとみなし、はさみは紙に、紙は石に、石ははさみに勝つ。

cloth—to carry a change of clothes in it to a public bath house and to change clothes on it.

The furoshiki is very handy since it is so freely adaptable to the size and shape of the article being wrapped, and when not in use it can be folded up and easily carried in the hand or pocket. The usual way of wrapping an article is to place it in the center of the furoshiki, and tie first one pair of diagonally opposite corners together over the article, followed by the other pair. As this is more easily done by nimble fingers, the dexterity of Japanese may well have had something to do with the popularity of the furoshiki in Japan.

Furoshiki come in various sizes and materials. There are large cotton ones with arabesque patterns for binding up quilts and dainty silk ones patterned with decorative designs, flowers and birds.

i) Abacus

The Japanese have been using the abacus for hundreds of years. Even today, in this age of the ubiquitous electronic calculator, this traditional calculating device remains highly popular for the ease with which it can be operated. The Japanese abacus consists of a rectangular wooden frame having a crosspiece running lengthwise slightly below the upper edge of the frame. Evenly spaced thin bamboo rods run vertically from the upper edge of the frame to the lower, passing through small holes in the crosspiece. Each of the rods carries beads, a single bead above the crosspiece which counts as five, and four (formerly five) beads below the crosspiece, each counting as one. These beads are moved up and down on the rods to carry out addition, subtraction, multiplication and division.

The Japanese abacus is believed to have been developed from one brought in from China in the 16th century.

Tests are held periodically to rank abacus operators by skill and speed. Anyone interested can take one of these tests.

j) Janken

Janken is a game in which each of two or more players thrusts out one hand while making it into the shape of a stone, a piece of paper or scissors, the winner being decided by the rule that stone is stronger than scissors, scissors stronger than paper and paper stronger than stone. Stone is made by clenching the fist,

17世紀に中国から伝わった「両挙」（りゃんけん）が変化したもので、最初は酒席のなぐさみに、その後子供の遊びとして広まった。

現在では、西欧でコインを投げてその表裏で事を決めるのと同様に、大人の間でもじゃんけんで順番を決めることが広く行われている。

k）賭け事

日本人には、賭け事や勝負事が好きな人が比較的多い。しかし、賭博は禁止されており、カジノはない。競馬・競輪・競艇・宝くじは公営で行われている。

競馬は、全国規模の27の重賞レースがある（2001年）。競馬の年間の売上げは3兆5,000億円（2000年）である。

宝くじは、地方自治体の財政資金を調達するために1946年以来発売されており、夢を買うということで、国民の間に根強い人気がある。現在の最高賞金は前後賞を含め3億円（2001年）である。

2001年3月には、サッカーくじ（愛称トト）の販売も開始された。

l）パチンコ

庶民のささやかな遊びとしてパチンコがある。

これは、ピンボールゲームに似た日本独得の遊びである。パチンコ台は、まっすぐに立ち、前面がガラス張りになっている。中の板面には標的の穴がいくつかあいていて、その周囲を多くのくぎがガードしている。プレーヤーは電動式ハンドルを操作して、大きな豆粒ほどの鋼鉄の玉を板面の上部をめがけて打ち出す。すると玉は上部からくぎの間をすり抜けて落ちてくる。玉が標的の穴に入れば、器械から5〜15個の玉が出てくる。プレーヤーは、出た玉を使ってゲームを続けることもできるし、十分溜まったらタバコ・食品などの賞品と交換することもできる。

パチンコは、日本で最も普及した大衆娯楽のひとつで

paper by opening the hand and scissors by extending the index and middle fingers.

Janken is a variation on *ryanken* introduced from China in the 17th century and was originally played mostly at drinking parties. Today it is a children's game played throughout the country.

Grown-ups also frequently use janken to decide turns, much in the way that people in Western countries toss a coin for this purpose.

k) Betting

Quite a lot of Japanese like betting and games of chance. However, serious gambling is forbidden, so there are no casinos. There are, however, publicly operated horse, bicycle and boat races as well as lotteries.

There are twenty seven "big-prize" horse races which attract the interest of fans throughout the country(2001). Annual takings from horse races amount to some ¥3,500 billion (2000).

Publicly operated lotteries were begun in 1946 as a way of raising funds for local governments. As they offer a chance to strike it rich on a very modest investment, these lotteries have remained popular. At present (2001), a lucky ticket holder can win up to ¥300 million if he holds the winning number and the ones before and after.

Soccer pari-mutuel tickets (popularly called "Toto" tickets) went on sale from March 2001.

l) Pachinko

A form of pinball game called *pachinko* is enjoyed as a pastime by many people.

Pachinko is played on a machine that has a vertical, glass-covered panel with target holes guarded by many protruding pins. The player operates an electric plunger to shoot steel balls the size of large beans to the top of the panel, from where they filter down through the pins. If a ball enters a target hole, the machine dispenses five to fifteen balls. The player can use the balls he wins in this way to continue the game or, if he accumulates enough of them, can exchange them for cigarettes, food items, or some other such prize.

Pachinko is one of the most common pastimes in Japan. Every town, no matter how remote, has at least one pachinko parlor.

ある。どんな地方の町にもパチンコ店がある。全国にパチンコ店は約17,200軒、パチンコ台は約480万台あり、総売上額は約21兆円もあった（1999年）。しかし、96年頃から若者層、高齢者層を中心とした客離れで、パチンコ業界もやや下火になっている。

パチンコは、1920年ごろアメリカから伝えられたコリントゲームから変化してきたといわれている。はじめは子供を対象とする遊びであったが、次第に大人向けのゲームとなり、専門の店ができるようになった。とくに第二次世界大戦後まもなく、名古屋でのパチンコブームが引き金になって、全国に急速に普及した。

日本でパチンコがこのように普及したのは、短時間に手軽に楽しめ、これが日本人の好みに合っていたからだろう。パチンコの人気がいつまでも衰えないのは、機械のメーカーがつぎつぎと新しい機種を開発して、大衆の関心をとらえて放さなかったためといわれている（終戦後から現在までに、考案された新機種は30種類以上ある）。

m) カルタ

日本の家庭で親しまれているカード遊びとして、カルタ取りがある。

カルタ取りのうち、古くから行われているものに小倉百人一首がある。これは、13世紀に7世紀以来の代表的な和歌百首を集めたものである。

和歌は、5音7音5音の上の句と、7音7音の下の句から成っている。遊び方としては、まず下の句のみ書いたカードを広げておく。何人かでこれを囲み、一人の人が和歌を読み上げるのを聞いて、対応するカードを拾う。たくさん拾った人が勝ちである。

上手な人は上の句を読み始めるとすぐカードを拾ってしまう。したがって、100の和歌を全部記憶しておかなければ勝負に勝てない。和歌の記憶を通じて、文化の伝承を行った古人の知恵といえよう。この遊びは家庭のみでなく、地域や職場などでの競技大会まであり、大人も子供も参加している。おもに正月に行われる。

The approximately 17,200 parlors located throughout the country have a total of about 4.8 million machines and take in around ¥21 trillion per year (1999). The pachinko business has seen a moderate decline since around 1996, owing to a decreasing number of young and elderly customers.

Pachinko is believed to derive from the Corinthian game imported from the U. S. around 1920. It started as a game for children but was gradually modified into one for adults and then turned into a business. It spread particularly rapidly in the early postwar years when a pachinko boom in Nagoya triggered a proliferation of pachinko parlors throughout the country.

Pachinko probably took hold in Japan because it is the type of amusement Japanese tend to prefer: something casual and not taking much time. Another reason for its continuing popularity may be that the pachinko machine manufacturers regularly come out with new machines sporting new features designed to hold the public's interest. (Pachinko machines have gone through more than 30 generations since the end of the war.)

m) Japanese Card Games

Some of the card games played in the Japanese home use cards peculiar to Japan.

One of the oldest such games is that of "one hundred *waka* poems." These waka, which are representative of this form of poetry, date back as early as the seventh century and were assembled together in the thirteenth century to form this game.

Each of these waka consists of 31 syllables arranged in 3 lines of 5, 7 and 5 syllables respectively in the first part and 2 lines of 7 syllables each in the second part. To play the game, first the cards that have only the second part of the waka printed on them are laid face up. A number of people sit around these cards, listen to one person read out the waka and try to pick up the matching card. The winner is the one who picks up the most.

An expert is able to pick up the correct card as soon as he hears the beginning of the first part. So it means that if you want to win you have to memorize the whole of the one hundred waka. Devising this method of transmitting the culture of Japan in this way, through the memorization of waka, shows the wisdom of our ancestors. This game is played not only in the home but also in regional and factory tournaments, with both adults and children taking part. It is mostly played around New

このほか、子供用にことわざなどを読み上げ、そのことわざの最初の文字および関係ある絵を書いたカードを拾うイロハカルタもある。そのほかさまざまなカルタが考案されている。

n) 碁・将棋・麻雀

日本で最も普及している室内の娯楽には、碁・将棋・麻雀などがある。

碁は361箇の目のある正方形の碁盤の上で、2人の対局者が白と黒の碁石を交互に並べて、囲み取った目の数で勝負を決めるゲームである。

上手の者が白石を持ち、黒石を持った者が先手となる。対局者の実力の差に応じて、いくつかの黒石を碁盤の目の一定の場所にあらかじめ並べておくというルールがあり、こうしてハンディキャップをつけることにより、実力に差のある者同士でも互角に戦うことができる。

碁は8世紀に中国から伝わり、初めは当時の貴族の遊びであった。13世紀ごろから次第に広まり今日におよんでいる。

将棋は2名の対局者が、81箇の区画が描かれた将棋盤の上で、交互に駒を動かして、相手の王将を早く追い詰めた方が勝ちとなるゲームである。

駒は8種類あり、それぞれが合計20枚を持ち、最初に将棋盤の所定の位置に並べる。

将棋は8世紀に中国から渡来し、次第に改良が加えられて日本将棋として発展し、相手からとった駒を自分の持ち駒として再び使用できる独特のルールが生まれ、ゲームが変化に富んだものとなった。

段位の差のある者同士の対戦では、上位者が自陣の駒の一部を落として、戦力のバランスをとることになっている。

Year.

For children there are also similar games with cards that have proverbs and sayings on them, the cards to be picked up sometimes having the first parts of the proverbs and matching pictures on them instead of words. There are also various other Japanese card games based on this same idea.

n) Go, Shogi, Mah-jong

Go, *shogi* and mah-jong are the three most popular indoor games in Japan.

Go is played by two players on a square board marked with a grid having 361 intersections. The players take turns placing stones (black for one, white for the other) on the intersections in such a way as to surround as much territory as possible. The player who encloses the greater area is the winner.

The more skillful player has the white stones, and black moves first. Rules allow for the use of handicaps to even out the effect of differences in skill, thereby allowing a more evenly matched game even when the levels of two players are considerably different. The handicap consists in black being able to put stones at specified locations on the board prior to the start of the game. How many stones he is allowed to place naturally depends on how much better the other player is.

Go was introduced to Japan from China in the eighth century. At first it was played only by the aristocracy, but from the thirteenth century its popularity gradually spread, and has continued to do so up to modern times.

Shogi is played by two players, moving in turn, on a board of 81 squares. As with chess the object of the game is to immobilize the opposing King so that he cannot evade capture.

Each player has twenty pieces, of eight different ranks, set up in accordance with the rules.

The shogi now played in Japan has developed from the game originally brought from China in the eighth century. One of the many changes is that captured pieces can be re-used.

A player who is considerably better than his opponent may remove one or more of his own pieces from the board before starting play, in order to ensure a more balanced contest.

Go and shogi players are ranked according to ability. For advanced players these rankings range from first *dan* (grade) up to ninth dan. In addition, tournament winners are awarded such

碁・将棋の段位は実力に応じて上位に向かって初段から九段までである。さらに名人・棋聖・十段位などのタイトルがある。初段の下は１級で、２級、３級となるほど下位になる。

　碁・将棋いずれの場合もプロにとっては厳しい勝負の世界であり、人間形成の場でもある。したがって昇段基準も厳しく、アマチュアとの対比では、同じ段位でも、実力の差はかなりあるようである。

　麻雀は136個の牌を用いて４人で得点を争うゲームである。４人がそれぞれ13個ずつの牌を持ってゲームを開始し、牌に刻まれた記号が解からないように裏返しに並べられた残りの牌を順番に１個ずつ引き、代わりに不要の牌を１個ずつ捨てながら、手持ちの牌の組み合わせを定められた形に整えていく。最も早くその形ができ上がった者を勝ちとし、でき上がった形の種類によって得点が計算される。

　日本には1920年代に、中国やアメリカからの帰国者によってつぎつぎに伝えられ、第二次世界大戦後は麻雀人口が急速に増加した。しかし、近年レクレーションの多様化にともない、麻雀人口は、ひところより減少している。

ｏ）歌謡曲

　西洋音楽の影響を受けて、日本の伝統的なうたである詩吟・音曲・民謡などとは異なる独特なふしまわしの歌謡曲が生まれ、国民大衆に愛好されるようになった。

　日本の歌謡曲の発生は、1914年にトルストイ原作の『復活』の劇中でうたわれた「カチューシャのうた」がはじまりといわれている。その後、毎年多くのヒット曲がつくられ、ひろくうたわれ、大衆の心のいこいとなってきた。

　テレビやラジオでの歌謡曲の放送は、根強い人気があるが、プロの歌手のみでなく、一般視聴者が出演する素人のど自慢の放送もたびたび行われている。

titles as *meijin*, *kisei*, tenth dan, etc. Below the dans are a number of grades for novices called *kyu*. The highest kyu is first kyu, so the higher the number of the kyu grade a person holds, the less skillful he is.

In both go and shogi the world of professional play is a grueling one and requires considerable dedication and ability. The standards on which promotion is based are correspondingly rigorous and because of this a professional player is usually considerably stronger than an amateur, even when they both possess the same dan ranking.

Mah-jong is usually played by four people with 136 pieces shaped like small tiles, each identified by a *kanji* character inscribed on the face. At the start of the game each player has a "hand" of thirteen pieces. The remaining pieces are placed in the middle of the table, face down. The players take turns at picking up a piece from the center pool and discarding an unwanted piece from their hand, as each tries to build up various combinations. The first player to meld wins the hand, and is credited with a certain number of points calculated on the basis of the particular combination of pieces making up the hand.

Mah-jong first started to be played in Japan in the 1920's, when it was introduced by Japanese returning from China and the U. S., but it was following the Second World War that the game attained its immense popularity as the numbers of players grew by leaps and bounds. The number of devotees has declined somewhat in recent years as recreational activities have grown more diverse.

o) Popular Songs

The *kayokyoku*, or Japanese popular song genre, displays in its melodic structure the considerable part Western music has had in creating and shaping it. This type of melody differs markedly from traditional Japanese forms such as *shigin* (the chanting of ancient Chinese poems) , *onkyoku* (in which singing is accompanied by the music of the *shamisen*) and folk songs.

Some trace the beginnings of kayokyoku to a 1914 song, "Kachusha Song," which was sung during a stage performance that year of Tolstoy's "Resurrection." Since that time such popular songs have appeared in great numbers every year and enjoyed widespread popularity among the people.

Kayokyoku programs broadcast on television and radio have

毎年末には、その年に最もヒットし評価の高かった歌謡曲の歌手や作詞・作曲者を選ぶレコード大賞や歌謡大賞の選定がある。

　選ばれたその年の人気歌手が、男性と女性のチームに分かれて各自のヒット曲をうたい、チームの総合評価を競い合う「紅白歌合戦」は、毎年12月31日放映される。年末をしめくくる恒例の番組として親しまれ、このテレビ放送を見て年を越す人も多い。

　最近は「カラオケ・ブーム」といわれる。メロディだけで歌詞が入っていないテープやディスクの伴奏に合わせて各人がうたい、歌手気分を味わって楽しむことが、気安い仲間同士の宴会や家庭で一般化している。「カラオケ」とは、歌の入っていないオーケストラ（空のオーケストラ）という意味の日本語の略称である。このシステムは、現在では東南アジアをはじめ諸外国にもかなり広がっている。

p) **日本映画とグランプリ**

　第二次世界大戦後、日本映画は、国際的に高い評価を受けるようになった。そのきっかけとなったのは、1951年に黒沢明の『羅生門』が、ベネチア国際映画祭でグランプリを獲得したことである。

　その後日本映画は、各地の国際映画祭で多くの賞を得ているが、そのいくつかを紹介すると、衣笠貞之助の『地獄門』が、54年のカンヌ映画祭でグランプリを受賞するとともに、ニューヨーク映画批評家賞で外国映画賞首位に輝いている。61年には新藤兼人の『裸の島』が、モスクワ国際映画祭のグランプリを獲得した。黒沢の『隠し砦の三悪人』は、59年にベルリン映画祭で銀熊賞を、『影武者』は、80年にカンヌ映画祭でグランプリを得ている。また1983年のカンヌ映画祭では、今村昌平の『楢山節考』がグランプリを得た。

　その後、ベルリン映画祭では、86年に熊井啓の『海と毒薬』が銀熊賞、87年に、原一男の『ゆきゆきて、

immense grass-roots popularity. On such programs may often be heard the vocal efforts of non-professional singers—ordinary listeners who are convinced that they are talented singers.

At the end of each year awards are presented to singers, lyricists and composers of songs which have enjoyed the greatest popular and critical success during the year.

On the last day of the year the singers who have been chosen as the year's most popular appear in the "Red and White Singing Contest," which is aired by NHK on the evening of the thirty-first of December. The singers are divided into two teams (the "Red" and the "White "), the women in one and the men in the other. For many Japanese the show is the traditional way of seeing out the old year and welcoming in the new.

In recent years there has been in boom in *karaoke*. These are tape or disk players with voice mixing facilities and are used to provide musical accompaniment for solos or singalongs whenever required, such as at parties, where they provide an atmosphere of cheerful comaraderie, or in the home. The "kara" of kara-oke means empty, while the "oke" is a Japanese abbreviation of the English word orchestra. The combination is intended to imply an orchestra without a vocalist. Karaoke systems have also come into fairly wide use in Southeast Asia and other parts of the world.

p) Award-Winning Japanese Films

The Japanese film first received international critical acclaim in 1951, when "Rashomon," directed by Akira Kurosawa, was awarded the Grand Prix at the Venice film festival. In the following years Japanese films received many awards at international film festivals around the world.

Some of the most famous of these films are Teinosuke Kinugasa's "Gates of Hell," which in 1954 received the Grand Prix at the Cannes film festival and also won the American Academy Award for best foreign film of the year; Kanehito Shindo's "Naked Island," the 1961 Grand Prix winner at the Moscow international film festival; Kurosawa's "Hidden Fortress," Silver Bear Prize winner at the Berlin film festival of 1959; Kurosawa's "Kagemusha," which received the Grand Prix at the 1980 Cannes festival; and Shohei Imamura's "Narayamabushi-ko," which received the Grand Prix at the 1983 Cannes festival.

In addition, Kei Kumai's "The Sea and Poison" won the

神軍』がカリガリ映画賞を得た。ベネチア国際映画祭では、89年に熊井の『千利休・本覚坊遺文』が銀獅子賞を、91年には竹中直人の『無能の人』が、国際映画批評家協会賞を得た。さらに、97年のカンヌ映画祭では、『うなぎ』で今村がパルムドールを受賞し、二度目のグランプリを獲得した。また、同年、ベネチア国際映画祭で、北野武の『HANA―BI』がグランプリにあたる金獅子賞を受賞した。

q）日本のマンガ

　　今日の日本で見られるマンガが生れたのは、明治時代（1800年代後半）で、新聞マンガが最初である。風刺絵に近いマンガから始まり、現在でもほとんどの日刊新聞に掲載されている4コママンガに発展した。

　　ストーリー性を重視したマンガも第二次世界大戦前に生まれ、主として少年向きの人気キャラクターが活躍するマンガが呼び物になった。この分野のマンガで、第二次世界大戦後もっとも広く国民に親しまれているのは、長谷川町子の『サザエさん』である。

　　戦後のマンガブームの先駆者は、手塚治虫である。彼は映画的手法を初めて日本のマンガに導入した。マンガの読み手は、はじめは主として子供であったが、1960年代になると「劇画」が生まれ、そのリアルな絵と社会的なテーマによって、大学生を中心に大人の読者を増やして行った。その後も多くのマンガ家が多彩な表現に挑戦し、娯楽性をもったものだけではなく、芸術的・文学的価値を持つ作品が生み出された。これらの中には翻訳され、海外で楽しまれているものもある。

　　1997年、日本における出版物の年間総発行部数約68億冊のうち数10％がマンガである。なかでも劇画スタイルが最も多く、週刊誌として刊行されているもののなかには数100万部も売れていたものもある。その後、人気はやや下降気味であるが、まだなお相当な人気を保っている。

　　87年には、情報マンガが市民権を得た。たとえば、87年大ベストセラーになった『日本経済入門』などのように、経済・法律・流通など経済の仕組を解説したものや、現代社会の動向を題材にしたものもある。95年にはマンガ文庫ブームも再来した。今日ではマンガは、

Silver Bear Prize at the 1986 Berlin film festival, Kazuo Hara's "The Emperor's Naked Army Marches On" won the Caligari Prize at the same festival in 1987, Kumai's "The Death of a Tea Master" took the "Silver Lion Award" at the Venice film festival in 1989 and Naoto Takenaka's "Nowhere Man" received the FIPRESCI Prize in 1991. At the 1997 Cannes film festival, Shohei Imamura won the Palme d'Or, the festival's highest award, for "Unagi." This was Imamura's second Grand Prix at Cannes. Also in 1997, Takeshi Kitano was awarded the Venice film festival's top award, the Golden Lion, for "Hana-bi".

q) Japanese Comics

Cartoons and comic strips of the kind seen in Japan today got their start in the newspapers of the Meiji Era (late 1800s). Beginning as caricature-like cartoons, they evolved into the four-frame comic strips that can be seen in almost every daily newspaper today. Comics with a story line appeared before the Second World War and in most cases featured the escapades of characters that appealed to boys. The most popular of the story comics in the postwar years was *Sazaesan*, created by Machiko Hasegawa and loved by readers of all ages.

The postwar comic book boom was pioneered by Osamu Tezuka, the first cartoonist to apply motion picture techniques to Japanese comics. With the advent in the 1960s of a style (the *gekiga* style) that used realistic pictures to tell stories dealing with topics of social import, comic book readership expanded beyond boys, the main readers up to then, to college students and other adults. Once adults had been brought into the fold of comic book aficionados, numerous other cartoonists began experimenting with a wide range of cartooning genres and techniques, creating not only comics that entertained but also works with artistic and literary merit. The translated versions of some of these have an overseas following.

Comic books accounted for 10% of the 6.8 billion books published in Japan in 1997. Most were in the story comic (gekiga) style and some of those published weekly had circulations of a few million. The popularity of comic books has since slipped slightly but still remains very high.

Information comics came into their own in 1987. These include business oriented specimens with titles like *Introduction to Japanese Economics*, one of the top best sellers of 1987, that

新聞や雑誌には必要欠くべからざるものであり、企業の会社案内パンフレットにさえ姿を現わす。こうしてマンガは、老若すべての日本人にとって不可欠の表現手段となっている。

r) 日本のアニメーション

　　日本のアニメーション映画は、戦前から存在したが、その多くは、教育・国策 PR 用に、制作されたものであった。

　　日本のアニメーションが本格的になったのは、戦後テレビに登場してからである。とくに、マンガ家・手塚治虫主宰の虫プロの制作した『鉄腕アトム』をはじめとする一連のテレビシリーズは、その後の日本アニメに大きな影響を与えた。

　　1974 年には、宇宙 SF『宇宙戦艦ヤマト』のテレビシリーズの劇場版が大ヒットし、それを契機に劇場用アニメーションが盛んにつくられるようになった。最近の作品では、「ポケモン（ポケットモンスター）」や、宮崎駿監督による「もののけ姫」「千と千尋の神隠し」など、高度な技術を駆使して、大人も満足させる内容の冒険アニメーションフィルムも生まれている。これらの多くは海外でも好評を博している。「千と千尋の神隠し」は、2002 年のベルリン国際映画祭で最高賞にあたる金熊賞をアニメ映画として初めて受賞した。

　　また、日本のテレビアニメーションは、東南アジアをはじめ、ヨーロッパ・アメリカなど全世界に輸出されている。海外のテレビ局はこれらをシリーズとして放映している。

(8)　食物・飲み物

a)　食生活

　　日本人の食生活には、伝統的に主食と副食という考えがあって、米を主食とし野菜や魚などを副食としてきた。肉食も相当古くから行われていたが、仏教の普及により

explain the workings of the economy, the legal system, the distribution system and the like, as well as comics that focus on current social trends. Sub-pocketbook-sized comic books made a comeback in 1995. Today the story comic has become an integral part of newspapers and magazines, and is even used in corporate brochures. Comics and cartoons in general have become essential reading for Japanese of all ages.

r) Japanese Animated Cartoons

Animated cartoon movies existed in Japan before the Second World War but most were produced for use in education and government PR.

It was not until the advent of television in the postwar years that animated cartoons came into full bloom. Probably the greatest influence on the course of Japanese animated movies came from *Tetsuwan Atomu* (Atom, the Boy with Arms of Steel) and a number of other TV cartoon series produced by Mushi Productions, a company founded by cartoonist Osamu Tezuka.

The unprecedented success of the movie version of the 1974 TV series *Uchusenkan Yamato* (Spaceship Yamato) set off a flood of other full-length cartoon cinemas. More recent offerings, such as Pokemon (Pocket Monster), and Mononoke Hime (Princess Mononoke) and Sen to Chihiro no Kamikakushi (Spirited Away), both directed by Hayao Miyazaki, employ highly sophisticated techniques to create animated action films that are fascinating even for adults. Many of these have also been well received overseas. Sen to Chihiro no Kamikakushi won top prize, the Golden Bear, at the 2002 Berlin film festival, a first for an animated film.

Japanese TV cartoons are exported throughout the world, mostly to Southeast Asia, but also to Europe, the United States and many other countries. Overseas TV stations generally broadcast them in serial form.

(8) Food and Drink

a) The Japanese Diet

The daily diet in Japan has traditionally been considered as consisting of a main, or staple, item of food supplemented by subsidiary items. Rice has long been the staple, and vegetables,

肉食を禁忌するようになり、中世以降すたれ、明治以後復活した。

　第二次世界大戦後、学校給食の影響でパン食が普及し、経済成長とともに肉類や乳製品などの摂取も大幅に増加した。さらにインスタント食品の普及もあり、食生活は多様化している。
　米食には、野菜や魚または肉などの煮物・揚げ物・焼き物などに、味噌汁・漬物をそえる。副食には、西洋風あるいは中華風の料理もたくさん取り入れられている。
　日本の食生活では、節約という観念が古くから定着している。たとえば、魚の利用にあたっては、「身は刺身（または焼物）に、アラは煮物に、骨は汁」というならわしがある。
　また、不作のときに備えるための保存食として漬物（野菜）、魚・肉の塩蔵物、乾物などが古くから定着している。
　食事をするには、一般に箸（多くの場合木製）を用いる。
　朝食は簡素で、昼食も比較的軽く、夕食に最も重点をおく。
　最近の傾向として、社会構造・生活様式の変化にともないグルメ指向、外食の利用と食生活は一層豊かにかつ多様化してきている。

b) **日本料理**
　日本料理は、日本列島で生まれ発達した日本独特の料理である。新鮮な魚介類の持味を生かした料理が多く、ほとんどが米食と日本酒に調和するようにつくられている。材料や調理法に季節感を重んじており、食器の色・形・材質がさまざまで、盛りつけにも繊細な配慮が加えられる。これは、日本料理が舌だけでなく目で楽しむことも大切にしているからである。

fish and so forth the subsidiaries. Meat has been eaten in Japan since fairly early times, but with the rise of Buddhism the eating of meat became tabooed, and consequently meat disappeared from the table from the middle ages and was only to reappear during the Meiji Era.

After the Second World War bread became part of the diet, an effect of its inclusion in school meals. With the growth of the economy there was also a great upsurge in the consumption of different kinds of meat and dairy products. Moreover, instant foods became widespread, and the items making up the daily meals became further diversified.

A Japanese meal with rice as the staple will include vegetables and boiled, fried or roasted fish or meat as well as *miso* (mixture of fermented beans, barley and rice) soup and pickled vegetables. Many supplementary dishes cooked in Western or Chinese styles have now also become part of the meal in Japan.

In the preparation of food in Japan the idea from ancient times has been to avoid waste. For instance there is an expression concerning the utilization of fish that says, to use the meat for *sashimi* (sliced raw) or to grill it, to boil the lean parts of the meat, and to use the other parts (except the innards) for soup.

Also, preserved foods have been used since long ago to make up for shortages in lean years; preservation methods include pickling for vegetables, and salting or drying for fish and meat.

The food is generally eaten using chopsticks, which are nearly always made of wood.

Breakfast is rather plain and simple, and lunch fairly light, the main emphasis being on the evening meal.

In recent years, changes in the social structure and lifestyles have led to more luxurious and varied eating habits, with many people now seeking out gourmet foods and frequenting restaurants.

b) Japanese Cuisine

Japanese cuisine is unique to the Japanese archipelago where it originated and developed over the centuries. The majority of Japanese dishes are contrived to accent the natural flavors of fresh fish and shellfish and almost all are prepared so as to go well with rice and *sake*. The season of the year is the prime factor in the selection of materials and the choice of the manner in which to prepare them. As Japanese cuisine is supposed to

飯・汁・香の物のほか、前菜・刺身・焼き物・揚げ物・煮物・あえ物・酢の物などが加えられる。

　味は醤油・酒・酢・砂糖などで調味するが、材料そのものの持味を生かすようにし、あまりゴテゴテした濃厚な味つけをしない。汁・煮物・揚げ物のつけ汁などには、旨味を出すため鰹節・椎茸・昆布その他を用いる。また、「隠し味」と称してある種の調味料（たとえば塩）を少量加えることにより、材料の持味のある要素（たとえば甘味）を引き立たせる用法もある。砂糖を用いるようになったのは近代以後であり、現代においても高級な日本料理では砂糖を多く使用しない。

　外国人に好まれる日本料理として、鮨・天ぷら・すき焼などがある。鮨は酢で味をつけた飯に魚介類・のり・野菜をあわせた料理で、日本全国各地にそれぞれ異なった製法・形・味のものがある。東京のにぎり鮨というのは、一握りの飯の塊の上に、鮮度のよい生の魚介類の切身をのせただけの簡単なものである。職人の腕を客の前で見せる「粋」な感覚が特徴で、全国に普及している。生の魚介類すなわち刺身を食べる日本の習慣は、広く外国にも知られるようになり、多くの国々で「刺身愛好者」も増えている。

　天ぷらは魚介類・野菜類に水でといた小麦粉の衣をつけて油で揚げた料理である。

　すき焼は日本の伝統的な料理ではないが、19世紀後半以後普及したもので、牛肉を薄く切ったものを野菜などと一緒に煮て、主として醤油と砂糖で味をつける。

delight the eye as much as the palate, utmost care is used in arranging the foods on dishes of various colors, shapes and materials.

In addition to rice, soup and pickles, there are hors d'œuvres, *sashimi* (slices of raw fish), grilled fish, deep fried and boiled foods, vegetables and fish in various dressings, and vinegared dishes.

In seasoning, special efforts are made to enhance the natural flavor of the materials. Typical seasonings are soy sauce, sake, vinegar and sugar, but in no case is the seasoning so heavy as to make the dish strong or cloying. In making broths for soups and boiled foods and sauces for fried foods, stocks prepared from such materials as dried bonito, *shiitake* mushrooms, and tangle (an edible seaweed) are used to bring out added flavor. One common technique in Japanese cooking is the use of a "hidden seasoning" which is not itself perceptible to the people enjoying the dish but which accents some natural flavor of the materials. For instance, a small amount of salt is added as a "hidden seasoning" to bring out the natural sweetness of a dish. Use of refined sugar goes back only about one hundred years, and even today, sugar is used but sparingly in the best Japanese cooking.

Among the Japanese foods liked best by foreign visitors are *sushi, tempura* and *sukiyaki*. Sushi is slightly vinegared rice overlaid or mixed with raw fish, shellfish, laver or vegetables. The method of preparation, shape and taste differ somewhat depending on the locality. *Nigirizushi*, which originated in Tokyo, is a simple variety of sushi consisting of small oblong balls of vinegared rice topped with a thin slice of raw fish or shellfish. It is usually eaten in *sushi* shops where it is prepared before the customer's eyes by cooks who go about their work in a smart and lively manner that gives these establishments a special atmosphere. Nigirizushi is popular throughout the country. The Japanese custom of eating raw fish and shellfish (*sashimi*) has become widely known throughout the world and the number of "sashimi epicures" is on the rise in many countries.

Tempura is a fritter-like dish of fish, shellfish and vegetables dipped in a flour-and-water batter and deep-fried in vegetable oil.

Although not a traditional Japanese dish, sukiyaki has been quite popular from about the late nineteenth century. Slices of beef are braised together with vegetables in a small amount of

日本人が祝い事のとき食べる料理に、赤飯と鯛の尾頭付がある。赤飯はもち米に小豆を入れて蒸したもので、小豆の色が米について赤くなる。赤は火の色、太陽の色を表し、昔から縁起の良い色とされている。

　　鯛は日本語でめでたいという言葉と語呂があい、色も赤く縁起の良い魚とされている。祝の席には、頭から尻尾まで完全な形のまま焼かれた鯛が出される。これには、形の完全さによって人を祝福するという意味がある。

c）日本における外国料理

　　日本では、世界の主な料理が食べられる。東京や大阪などの大都会では、それぞれの国の料理を食べさせる専門店がある。しかし、日本人の平均的好みに合わせて日本化されている場合が多い。

　　家庭でも、世界各国の料理が日常の食生活のなかに取り入れられている。家庭で最も普及している外国料理は、目玉焼き・ハンバーグステーキ・カレーライス・スパゲッティ・サラダなどである。

○中国（中華）料理：日本で最も普及している外国料理で、中国人が経営している店も多い。横浜・神戸・長崎には中国料理店のたくさん並んだ街がある。とくに一般の日本人には、めん類・ギョーザ・まんじゅうなどが好まれる。

○韓国料理：日本中どこにもあり、多くのファンがいる。焼き肉・ナムル・キムチに人気がある。

○フランス料理：日本では、西洋料理の正統的なものは、フランス料理とされている。各種の前菜・グラタン・ソテーなどは家庭料理にも取り入れられている。このほかフランス製のぶどう酒と、皮の堅いフランスパンが好まれている。

○イタリア料理：気候、魚介類の豊富なこと、米料理・めん料理を好んで食べることなど、イタリアと日本はよく似ている。日本人の好きなイタリア料理は、魚介類の

liquid seasoned mainly with soy sauce and sugar.

The Japanese celebrate particularly happy occasions with red rice (*sekihan*) and sea bream (*tai*) prepared with head and tail intact. Sekihan is made by steaming glutinous rice (an especially sticky variety) together with red beans which turn the rice red. The Japanese have long considered red to be a lucky color because of its association with the color of fire and the sun.

The Japanese word for sea bream, *tai*, sounds similar to the word "*mede-tai*" or "felicity" and, what is more, it is auspiciously red in color. On festive occasions the tai is served broiled completely whole from head to tail. The wish for good luck is thought to be better conveyed through the full and perfect shape.

c) Foreign Cuisine in Japan

In Japan you can find examples of the cuisine of almost every country of the world. In big cities, such as Tokyo and Osaka, there are restaurants which specialize in the food of various countries. Many of these, however, have adjusted their fare to suit Japanese tastes.

In the home, too, dishes from many countries are prepared as part of the day's meals. The most popular foreign dishes are fried eggs, hamburger, curry and rice, spaghetti, and salads.

○ Chinese: The most common foreign cuisine in Japan is Chinese, with many of the restaurants being run by Chinese. In Yokohama, Kobe and Nagasaki can be found streets with rows of Chinese restaurants. Most Japanese are especially fond of noodles, *gyoza* (a kind of dumpling stuffed with minced pork and vegetables), and *manju* (buns filled with minced pork and vegetables or bean-paste).

○ Korean: Korean restaurants can be found everywhere in Japan and they have a large number of regular patrons. Grilled meat dishes, *namuru* and *kimuchi* (hot pickled Chinese cabbage) are popular.

○ French: In Japan, French cuisine is considered the cuisine of the West. Various types of hors d'œuvres, *gratins* and *sautés* are used in meals prepared in the home. In addition, many people have taken a liking to French wines and crusty French bread.

○ Italian: There are many similarities between Japan and Italy, such as the climate, the abundance of sea foods and the liking for rice and noodles. Italian dishes that are particularly popular in Japan are the various seafood preparations, spaghetti and maca-

料理・スパゲッティ・マカロニである。
○インド料理：カレーライスは、日本人の好物の一つであり、とくに子供が好む。ただし、日本では子供用の場合あまり辛くしない。

d) 海外における日本料理

現在では、世界各地の都市で日本料理を食べることができる。主要国の大都市には、必ず何軒かの日本料理店がある。その中には、「すしバー」と呼ばれている店も多いが、大抵は鮨に限らず天ぷら・すき焼などの日本料理を食べさせてくれる。

海外で出される日本料理は、味つけ・材料などの点で、国内で食べられる食事と微妙に異なる場合が多い。たとえば、たねにアボカドを使った鮨などは、日本では考えられない独創的なメニューである。また料理の出し方にも違いがある。たとえば、アメリカの鉄板焼レストラン（醤油味の肉と野菜を客の目の前で料理して出す）では、料理人のナイフさばきをみせるショー的要素が取り入れられている。

海外の日本料理店の常連客は、日本料理について複雑な感情を持っているようである。一方では、生ものを食べるのでこわいと思いつつ、他方では、油をあまり使わず魚や野菜が中心となっているので、健康によいという評価もしている。

日本料理の素材のなかで、海外で最も普及しているのは醤油（ソイソース）であろう。肉・魚の料理に醤油を使う料理法は、近年世界各国の料理に見られるようになった。また醤油の海外生産も、アメリカをはじめいくつかの国で行われている。

日本の味噌や豆腐も、まだ一般的ではないが、醤油に続いて徐々に使用されていく傾向にある。

e) 酒

日本では、日本酒（アルコール含有量15～16％）をはじめ、世界中の酒が飲まれている。

日本酒は米からつくられる醸造酒である。全国各地でつくられるが、良い水のでるところ、あるいは良い米のできるところに、有名な酒の産地がある。なかでも兵庫県の灘、京都の伏見、広島の西条などが有名である。日本酒は、温めて飲むのが普通である。

roni.

○ Indian: Japanese, especially children, are very fond of curry and rice but curries prepared for children are not very hot.

d) Japanese Cuisine Outside Japan

Japanese food is eaten in cities around the globe. Every major city in the world has at least a few Japanese restaurants. Many are referred to as *sushi* bars, though in addition to sushi they often serve *tempura*, *sukiyaki* and other dishes considered typical of Japanese cuisine.

The Japanese food served overseas is often subtly different from that eaten in Japan as regards seasoning, materials and other points. Some dishes, such as sushi made with avocado, are ingenious innovations not available in Japan. Differences in the way food is served are also seen. For instance, in American *teppanyaki* restaurants (serving soy sauce-seasoned meat and vegetables prepared on a griddle before the customer's eyes) the cooks juggle their knives and otherwise make a show of the food preparation.

Frequenters of overseas Japanese restaurants express mixed feelings about the fare. They are anxious about getting sick from eating foods raw but recognize the health advantages of dishes that are low in fat and prepared mainly of fish and vegetables.

The ingredient of Japanese food most widely used overseas is probably *shoyu* (soy sauce). Meat and fish recipes that call for soy sauce have recently appeared in many countries and soy sauce is now being produced in the United States and several other countries.

Japanese *miso* (fermented bean paste) and *tofu* (bean curd) are following in the path of soy sauce. Although still not generally known, their use is increasing steadily.

e) Sake and Other Drinks

Not only *sake* (which has an alcoholic content of from 15 to 16%) but drinks from all over the world are popular in Japan.

Sake is a fermented beverage obtained from rice. Although it can be made anywhere in Japan, famous sakes are produced in regions that have a supply of good water, or good quality rice. Nada in Hyogo Prefecture, Fushimi in Kyoto and Saijo in Hiroshima are some famous sake-producing regions. Sake is

また、ビールもよく飲まれるが、ほとんど国産である。ウィスキーやぶどう酒もかなり飲まれており、これらは国産のほか輸入されるものも多い。ほかにブランディ・マオタイ・ウォッカなども輸入している。

　日本の酒類の消費量は、年間約1,000万キロリットルである。生産量は約940万キロリットルで、そのうちビール（発泡酒を含む）が76％、日本酒は8％、しょうちゅうは8％を占めている。（2000年）

　日本では、勤務時間後、上司や同僚あるいは仕事上の相手と酒をくみかわししながら、本音で話し合ったり、人間関係を深めたりすることが多い。

f）飲み物

　日本人の最もポピュラーな飲み物は緑茶である。使用する原料の葉の品質によって、大まかに玉露・煎茶・番茶に分けられる。

　玉露はあまり高温でない湯を用い、煎茶・番茶は高温の湯を用いる。このほかに、玉露級の良質の茶を粉状にして湯を注いで、そのままこさずに飲む抹茶がある。緑茶には砂糖やミルクを入れない。

　コーヒーも現代日本人に広く愛好されている。コーヒー好きの人は、好きな豆を買って自宅で調製して飲む。喫茶店でもコーヒーはよく飲まれる。一般の家庭でコーヒーを飲む習慣は、インスタントコーヒーが出現して以来、著しく普及した。

　紅茶も広く普及し、各種の銘柄が好まれている。

　その他の飲料としては、戦後80年代前半まではコーラの普及が著しかった。最近ではコーヒーが目立った伸びを示しているほか、各種のスポーツドリンク・ジュース・ウーロン茶、緑茶など、非常に多様な飲みものが飲まれている。

usually drunk warm.

Beer, most of which is domestically produced, is very popular. Whisky and wine, some of which is domestically produced and some of which is imported, are also quite popular in Japan. Other imported drinks include brandy, *mao tai* and vodka.

Japan consumed 10.00 million kiloliters (2.64 million U. S. gallons) and produces 9.40 million kiloliters (2.48 million U. S. gallons) of alcoholic beverages a year. Of the amount consumed, 76% is beer, 8% sake and 8% *shochu* (distilled spirits). (2000 figures)

Many Japanese workers enjoy going out after work for a few drinks with their colleagues, superiors or subordinates from the same company or with business associates from other companies. These occasions are used for frank exchanges of opinion and make for deeper personal relationships.

f) Beverages

The most popular beverage of the Japanese people is green tea. Green tea is graded into three categories depending on the quality of the leaf: refined, medium and coarse.

The water used to make refined green tea (*gyokuro*) is not so very hot, whereas the temperature of the water used to make medium-grade (*sencha*) and coarse-grade (*bancha*) tea should be quite high. In addition, there is a tea called *matcha* which is made by powdering quality gyokuro. Hot water is added to the tea powder and the tea is drunk without straining. No milk or sugar is used with green tea.

Coffee is also very popular nowadays. Those who are especially fond of coffee buy the particular kind of coffee beans they prefer and prepare their own coffee at home. Coffee is also widely drunk in coffee shops. Since the appearance of instant coffee there has been a great increase in the number of people who drink it at home.

Black tea is also quite popular, and there is a demand for all the famous types.

Among other beverages, cola drinks enjoyed rapidly increasing popularity from shortly after the Second World War up to the early 1980's. Recently, canned coffee drink sales have risen sharply, and a very wide variety of other canned beverages— isotonic drinks, pop, oolong tea etc.—are being drunk in large quantities. The Japanese purchased about 30 billion cans of

また、ミネラルウォーター・天然水の販売量も急増している。

g）タバコ

　　1986年、日本は成人一人あたりのタバコ消費量で、アメリカを抜いて世界第1位となった。成人男子の52％、女子の14.7％がタバコを吸っている（2001年）。しかし、喫煙者の地位は弱くなっている。非喫煙者の禁煙権の主張が強くなっているからである。多くの国々と同じように、職場、公共乗り物、レストランなどでは禁煙がますます広がっている。

　　外国産を含め20種以上のタバコがある。銘柄別ではマイルドセブンが、20年連続で販売本数首位であった。が、98年にはこれのタール分より低タールのマイルドセブン・スーパーライトがトップになった。喫煙者の健康志向の高まりで低タール、低ニコチン化志向が一段と進行している。

　　日本では、タバコは1985年に公社から民営化された日本たばこ産業株式会社によって販売されている。タバコの売値のおよそ50％前後が税金である。

⑼　日本人について

a）国民性

　　日本人の国民性の特徴として多くの人が指摘しているもののうち、共通性のあるものをいくつか取り上げてみよう。
1）日本人が何人か集まると、たとえば、年齢とか社会的地位など何らかの基準によりお互いの序列が意識され、それにより行動様式も影響を受ける。また日本語は敬語が非常に発達しているが、これらは日本人が上下関係を重視することによるものである。

2）欧米人は自分の意思や意見を直接相手にぶつけて強く自己主張するのに対し、日本人は相手の気持ちや立場を察して、それも考慮に入れて発言したり行動したりする傾向が強い。さらに、日本人にはイエ

beverages from vending machines in 1994.

Sales of mineral and spring water have also been increasing rapidly.

g) Tobacco

In 1986, Japan overtook America to become the country with the highest per capita consumption of tobacco in the world. Fifty -two percent of adult males and 14.7% of females smoke (2001 figures). The status of smokers is weakening, however, as nonsmokers become more assertive of their right to a smoke-free environment. As in many countries, smoking is being increasingly prohibited in workplaces, public conveyances, restaurants and the like.

More than 20 domestic and imported brands of cigarettes are available. In 1998, Mild Seven, the best-selling brand for 20 years, yielded top place to Mild Seven Super Lights, a cigarette with a lower tar content. Owing to rising concern about the effects of smoking on health, the trend in smoker preference toward low-tar, low-nicotine cigarettes is accelerating.

All tobacco products are sold through Japan Tobacco Inc., which was formed by the privatization of a public corporation in 1985. About 50% of the price of tobacco products is tax.

(9) About the Japanese

a) The Japanese Character

Below are some common features of the Japanese that have been pointed out by many people.

1) When Japanese people gather together in any numbers, their behavior is influenced by an awareness of the order and rank of each person within the group according to age, social status and other such considerations. Both this and the fact that the honorific forms of speech in the Japanese language have reached such an advanced level of sophistication are because of this emphasis the Japanese place on vertical relationships.

2) In contrast to Western people who are more likely to express their opinions openly in a self-asserting way, Japanese tend to speak and act only after due consideration has been given to the other person's feelings and point of view. Further-

　　　　ス・ノーをはっきり表明しない傾向がある。日本人
　　　　がこのような行動をとり、また相手にもそれを期待
　　　　するのは、日本人の同質性、無用の摩擦を避けよう
　　　　とする古くからの伝統などに基づくものであろう。

　　3）日本人は人間と自然との調和を尊重する。建築や庭
　　　　園の様式でも、日本では自然をそのまま生かして素
　　　　材としていこうと努める。

b) 日本人の集団帰属意識

　　　　日本人が個人より集団を重視する傾向が強いことは、
アメリカのE・O・ライシャワー教授はじめ多くの研究
者によって指摘されている。そして、日本人の集団帰属
意識が、稲作文化の歴史とかかわりがあるとする見方も
広く認められている。

　　　　日本の水田稲作農業では、集団作業と共同秩序が必要
とされた。一定時間に集中的に行われる田植や稲刈など
の作業には、近隣同士、力をあわせて共同作業をする必
要があったし、田にひく水の割当なども近隣同士の配分
の秩序が必要であった。このことから農民は、農村とい
う地域社会への帰属意識を持たざるを得なかった。

　　　　また、中国から伝わった儒教の道徳が広がるにつれ、
家に対する帰属意識が強まり、支配階級である武士は、
自分の属する藩に対する帰属意識も持つようになった。

　　　　サラリーマンの企業への帰属意識も、このような歴史
的基盤の上に、さらに日本の企業経営の特徴である終身
雇用制や年功序列あるいは企業内福祉により強められて
きた。

c) 武士道

　　　　武士道は、鎌倉時代から発達し、江戸時代（17世紀
から19世紀半ばまで）に儒教的思想に裏付けられて大
成した武士階層の道徳体系である。忠誠・犠牲・信義・
廉恥（れんち）・礼儀・潔白・質素・倹約・尚武・名
誉・情愛などを重んずる。

more, there is a habit of not giving a clear-cut yes or no answer. The fact that Japanese behave in this way and take these attitudes for granted in their dealings with each other can be partly explained by their homogeneity and a tradition of avoiding unnecessary friction.

3) The Japanese put much importance on harmony between man and nature. Even in the design of buildings and gardens, an effort is made in Japan toward preservation of the natural form.

b) Japanese Group Consciousness

Dr. Edwin O. Reischauer of the U.S. is one of many scholars who have pointed out that Japanese tend to put group interests before personal ones. It is also widely acknowledged that the Japanese group consciousness is related to Japan's longstanding culture of rice cultivation.

The wet-paddy rice cultivation method used in Japan made it necessary to work in groups and have a system of joint cooperation. The people in an area had to band together during the regular periods of intensive work involved in the planting and harvesting of the rice, and it was also necessary for these groups to institute some system among themselves for allocating the water for the paddies. All this instilled in the agricultural workers a consciousness of belonging to their localized farming communities.

Also, with the spread of the Confucian ethic from China there was a strengthening of the concept of belonging to a family group, and among the warrior class, of belonging to a clan.

Against this historical background, the modern employee's sense of belonging to his company is further strengthened by the system of lifetime employment, ranking according to the numbers of years of service and internal welfare schemes, which are features of company management in Japan.

c) Bushido

Bushido is the moral code of the *samurai* class. Based on Confucian ideas, it originated in the Kamakura period and reached perfection in the Edo period (1603–1867). It puts emphasis on loyalty, self-sacrifice, justice, sense of shame, refined manners, purity, modesty, frugality, martial spirit, honor, affection, etc.

武士が支配階級となる前、専ら戦うことを職業として
いた時代、死を讃える考え方が大きな比重を占めた。こ
れは平和な江戸時代にも残り、佐賀藩では「武士道とは
死ぬことである」という思想（葉隠精神）が強調された
が、これは日本の武士道の全体系の中の一部の考え方で
ある。

武士道の特徴の一つは尚武・名誉である。すなわち相
手に勝つことである。勝つということは、ただ単に力ず
くで他者を圧倒することではない。自分自身に勝つこと
によってのみ他者に勝ちうるという、精神的な構造の錬
磨をも含むのである。強さは自己に勝つとき形成される
ものであり、それは他者を精神的に圧倒し、他者から一
目おかれる精神的な高さの表現でもある。このような精
神的な強さを表現することの一部として、礼儀が重んぜ
られた。

ヨーロッパの騎士道はキリスト教の影響を受けて発達
し、勇気・敬神・礼節・廉恥・名誉・鷹揚（おうよう）
などの徳を理想としている。騎士道はこのように武士道
と多くの点で共通性を持つが、主従関係が契約的性質を
持っていたため、この点で武士道が絶対的忠誠を重視す
るのと異なる。

d）切　腹

切腹とは、武士が責任をとって自害する方式のことで、
平安時代以来始まったといわれている。もちろん、現代
日本では、切腹は自殺の手段としても刑罰としても行わ
れていない。1970年に著名な作家である三島由紀夫が
切腹した事件は、極めて例外的な事柄であり、日本人自
身も驚いている。

日本では、精神修養のできた立派な人を腹のできた人
といって尊敬する気風が強い。

封建時代の武士は、腹を精神のやどるところとして尊
重したので、武士として責任をとるために死ぬときに腹
を切ったのである。

The glorification of death which prevailed in samurai thinking goes back to the days when these warriors fought strictly as professionals, before they became the dominant class, but such thinking remained strong even into the Edo Period when peace prevailed. In the Saga clan, for example, strong emphasis was put on the concept that "Bushido is the way of death." However, this is only one aspect of the entire system of bushido.

Two other important aspects are martial spirit and honor. That is to say, emphasis is on prevailing over others. But this does not mean simply winning over others by physical force. Rather, in bushido one is encouraged to pursue spiritual training for the purpose of conquering oneself, for only through conquering oneself is it possible to conquer others. Strength is deemed to derive from victories in self-discipline and it is strength obtained in this manner which spiritually overpowers and commands the respect of others as a manifestation of spiritual stature. Refined manners were considered to be an important aspect in the expression of spiritual strength.

In Europe, chivalry developed under the influence of Christianity and gave much weight to such virtues as courage, reverence, a sense of shame, honor and generosity. Although chivalry had much in common with bushido, it was different from bushido in that the relation between a knight and his lords was contractual while bushido stressed absolute loyalty.

d) Seppuku

Seppuku means the ritual form of suicide that used to be practiced by members of the *samurai* class to show they accepted responsibility for their actions. It has its beginnings in the Heian Period, about one thousand years ago. In present-day Japan, of course, seppuku is not practiced either as a form of suicide or as a punishment. The suicide of Yukio Mishima, the famous novelist, by seppuku in 1970 was an extremely exceptional case, and astonished even the Japanese.

In Japan, a man who is respected as being a person of high moral character is said to "have stomach," meaning that he is a man of definite principles.

In feudal times warriors used to respect the abdomen because it was considered to be the receptacle of the spirit, so when they assumed responsibility as warriors for some action or course of conduct and had to die, they would cut open their abdomen.

江戸時代、切腹は武士に対する死刑の方法となった。これは、武士の人格・名誉を重んずる意味で、自ら死なせるという形をとったものである。切腹の失敗を防ぎ、無残な苦しみを早く断つために、自ら腹を切ったときにほかの人が首を切り落とした。

e) 日本人の微笑

　　長く日本に滞在して帰化したイギリス出身の文学者であるラフカディオ・ハーン（1850〜1904）は、『日本人の微笑』という随筆で次のようにのべている。

　　日本人の微笑から受ける第一印象は……まず、たいていの場合、すばらしく愉快なのが通例である。日本人の微笑は、最初はひどく魅力的なのだ。それが見る人に、へんだなと首をかしげるようになるのは、よほど後になってからのことで、同じ微笑を常とはちがう場合に――たとえば、苦しいときとか、恥かしいときとか、がっかりしたときとかに見せられると、はじめは何だか妙てけれんな心持になってくるのである。……笑顔は、目上にものを言うときでも、対等の相手と話をするときでも、愉快な場合はもちろんのこと、愉快でない場合にも用いられる。だれにとっても一番愛想のいい顔は笑顔なんだから、できるだけ愛想のいい笑顔を、両親・身うちのもの・先生・友達・そのほか好意を持ってくれている人にむかっていつも見せる。――これが生活の掟になっているのだ。……心は千々に乱れているようなときでも、顔には凜とした笑顔をたたえているというのが、社交上の義務なのである。」（小泉八雲全集『知られざる日本の面影』平井呈一訳）

　　このように、ラフカディオ・ハーンは、日本人の文化として定着している自制としての微笑に言及している。親愛・同調・共感などを示す微笑は、外国人にも共通であり理解されるが、この自制としての微笑は時に外国人をまどわせるようだ。

f) 日本人の自己紹介のしかた

　　日本では、特殊な職種を除いて大部分の従業員は、職種により採用されるのでなく、一般的潜在能力により採用されている。そして、会社が本人の希望や適性を加味

In the Edo Era seppuku became the mode of capital punishment for members of the samurai class. To allow the warrior to die by his own hand showed respect for his character and honor. To avoid mishaps occurring during the act of seppuku and to cut short needless suffering, another person would be standing by to cut off the head of the person as soon as he had cut open his abdomen.

e) The Japanese Smile

Lafcadio Hearn, an English man of letters who adopted Japanese citizenship and lived in Japan from 1890 until his death in 1904, wrote the following in his essay, *The Japanese Smile*.

"[The] first impression is, in most cases, wonderfully pleasant. The Japanese smile at first charms. It is only at a later day, when one has observed the same smile under extraordinary circumstances—in moments of pain, shame, disappointment—that one becomes suspicious of it. ... But the smile is to be used upon all pleasant occasions, when speaking to a superior or to an equal, and even upon occasions which are not pleasant; it is part of deportment. The most agreeable face is the smiling face; and to present always the most agreeable face possible to parents, relatives, teachers, friends, well-wishers, is a rule of life... Even though the heart is breaking, it is a social duty to smile bravely." (From The Writings of Lafcadio Hearn, *Glimpses of Unfamiliar Japan*, published by Houghton Mifflin Co.)

Here, then, Lafcadio Hearn refers to the Japanese smile as a form of the self-control rooted in the culture of the Japanese. Smiles to indicate affection, agreement, sympathy etc. are the same wherever one goes; but this smile of self-control is something that on occasion seems to puzzle people from other countries.

f) How Japanese Introduce Themselves in Business Situations

In Japan, the general rule is that people are employed according to their general abilities, rather than according to their occupational skills. And, while taking some account of a person's wishes and aptitude, the decision as to where he or she

しながら、各職場からの配属要求に基づいて、配属先を決定する。その後も地位の上昇あるいは事業の展開によって、経験のない職場にかわることはごく普通である。とくにホワイトカラーの場合、職種という観念が乏しい。

このようなことから、仕事の内容を表わすのには、会社名と現在の所属部門をいうのが、一番的確であるということになる。

g) 日本の企業内での呼びかた

日本では古来、実名敬避の習慣があり、自分より年齢の高い人、地位の高い人の名前を口にするのは失礼にあたると考えられている。これは、中国の影響ともいわれ、日本最古の小説である『源氏物語』でも、登場人物は固有名詞でなく役職名で表わされている。

こういう伝統が習慣化し、日本の企業では、相手が自分より地位の高い人であるときは、「社長」・「部長」など職階名で呼ぶ。相手が 2 人以上で識別が必要なときは、「経理課長」など役職名で呼ぶか、「山田課長」というように名前と職階名をいっしょに呼ぶのが一般的である。

家庭内でも、親や兄姉など目上の人に対しては名前を呼ぶことはせず、「お父さん」・「お兄さん」・「お姉さん」というような呼び方をする。

h) 日本人のノーベル賞受賞者

現在までにノーベル賞を受賞した日本人は、次の 10人である。

1) 湯川秀樹（1949 年、物理学賞）：陽子と中性子との間に作用する核力を媒介するものとして、中間子の存在を予言した。

2) 朝永振一郎（1965 年、物理学賞）：「超多時間理論」と「くりこみ理論」で有名で、量子電磁力学分野の基礎的研究につくした。

is to be assigned is based on the needs of the different sections which comprise the organization. Later, as well, it is quite usual for personnel to be moved, because of promotion or commencement of a project, to a post for which they have no experience. Particularly with white-collar workers, there is little concept of job classification by ability.

Because of this, the most precise way of indicating the nature of a person's work is for the person to mention the name of his or her company and the section to which he or she is assigned at the time.

g) How Japanese Address Each Other in the Workplace

In Japan, since ancient times, the custom has been to avoid the use of personal names out of politeness. That is, when addressing someone older or of higher rank, it is considered rude to utter his name. This can also be ascribed to Chinese influence. Even in Japan's oldest novel, *Tale of Genji,* the characters are indicated not by name but by their official titles.

This tradition gradually became the custom, and so in Japanese companies when speaking to a person who is higher in the hierarchy than yourself, you address him as *shacho* (president) or *bucho* (general manager) as the case might be; that is, by his official title. When there are two or more managers present, for example, they are usually distinguished by referring to one as say, "Accounts Manager" or by use of his name and position together, such as in "Manager Yamada."

Even in the home, one does not call one's parents or elder brothers and sisters by name; instead, they are addressed as "father," (elder) brother" or "(elder) sister."

h) Nobel Prize Winners

Listed below are the ten Japanese who have won a Nobel prize.

1) Hideki Yukawa (1949, Physics)

Yukawa won his prize for work predicting the existence of the meson as providing the nuclear force between the proton and the neutron.

2) Shinichiro Tomonaga (1965, Physics)

Tomonaga's famous super-many-time and renormalization theories have become fundamentals in the field of quantum electromagnetics.

3 ）川端康成（1968 年、文学賞）：人生の哀歓の幻想と
美をみごとに描いた『雪国』は、近代日本抒情文学
の古典といわれる。
　　『伊豆の踊子』・『古都』・『千羽鶴』・『山の音』な
ど多くの名作を残している。

4 ）江崎玲於奈（1973 年、物理学賞）：半導体・超電導
体トンネル効果について研究し、エサキダイオード
を開発した。

5 ）佐藤栄作（1974 年、平和賞）：日本の首相として国
を代表して核兵器保有に終始反対し、太平洋地域の
平和の安定に貢献した。

6 ）福井謙一（1981 年、化学賞）：「フロンティア電子
軌道理論」を開拓し、化学反応過程に関する理論の
発展に貢献した。

7 ）利根川進（1987 年、医学・生理学賞）：「多様な抗
体遺伝子が体内で再構成される理論」を実証し、遺
伝学・免疫学に貢献した。

8 ）大江健三郎（1994 年、文学賞）：核時代の人間の救
済、障害をもつ子との共生などを思想の背景に、
『個人的な体験』『万延元年のフットボール』などの
作品を発表した。

9 ）白川英樹（2000 年、化学賞）：絶縁体と考えられて
いたプラスチックに導電性を持たせることに成功し、
現代社会を支える電子機器の開発・普及に貢献した。

10）野依良治（2001 年、化学賞）：必要な型だけを合成
する「不斉合成」とよばれる手法を開発し、医薬・
食品を安全かつ大量に生産することに貢献した。

⑽　観光

　　日本では自然を中心と、それに歴史や文化を加えた観

3) Yasunari Kawabata (1968, Literature)

Kawabata's *Snow Country*, with its masterly depiction of the beauty and fleeting joys and sorrows of life, has become a modern Japanese classic. Other masterpieces by Kawabata include *Dancing Girl of Izu*, *The Old Capital*, *Thousand Cranes*, and *The Sound of the Mountain*.

4) Reona (Leo) Esaki (1973, Physics)

For research on the tunnel effect in semiconductors and superconductors, and development of the Esaki diode.

5) Eisaku Sato (1974, Peace)

Sato received the prize for his efforts as Prime Minister to keep Japan directed away from possession of nuclear weapons and his contributions to the stability of peace in the Pacific region.

6) Kenichi Fukui (1981, Chemistry)

Fukui pioneered the frontier orbital theory which contributed to advancing theories related to chemical reaction processes.

7) Susumu Tonegawa (1987, Physiology or Medicine)

Tonegawa contributed to genetics and immunology by showing how pieces of genes form millions of combinations which can produce a vast number of antibodies.

8) Kenzaburo Oe (1994, Literature)

Much of Oe's work derives from his ideas regarding the redemption of humans in the nuclear age and living together with physically and mentally impaired children. His works include *A Personal Matter* and *The Silent Cry*.

9) Hideki Shirakawa (2000, Chemistry)

Shirakawa succeeded in imparting electrical conductivity to a plastic that is ordinarily an insulator. His achievement contributed enormously to the development and utilization of electronic equipment that is now an essential part of the infrastructure of modern societies.

10) Ryoji Noyori (2001, Chemistry)

Noyori developed a method called asymmetric synthesis that can produce only the useful form of molecules that come in two forms. Thanks to Noyori's research, many medicines and foods can now be more safely produced in large volumes.

(10) Sightseeing

Many places in Japan offer the tourist an opportunity to

光ができる多くの拠点がある。来日外国人の数は、2000年には年間約527万人であり、そのうち269万人は観光客であった。

〔注〕国籍別入国者数は巻末〔統計資料〕欄(19)参照

a）日本の自然景観の楽しみかた

日本には山岳・渓谷・河川・湖沼などが多く、海岸線も複雑で地形が変化に富んでいること、四季の移り変わりがはっきりしていることなどから、美しい自然や景観を楽しめる観光地が多い。また、火山が多いので温泉地に恵まれており、それぞれ、よい保養地となっている。これらの代表的なものは、国立公園（28カ所）や国定公園（55カ所）に指定されている。また、松島（宮城県）、天の橋立（京都府）、宮島（広島県）は日本三景といわれ、水戸の偕楽園、金沢の兼六園、岡山の後楽園は日本三庭園として知られている。

b）日本の歴史や文化をたずねる観光地

一方、日本の長い歴史を背景にした古都や史跡をたずね、古い寺院・神社の建物や庭園などの見学、仏像や美術工芸品の鑑賞などを楽しみながら、日本文化の歩みを少しでも多く知ることができる。

さらに、各地の郷土の伝統や特色をいかした地方色豊かな祭りや行事も、日本をいろいろな面から理解するのに役立つ。

奈良は、8世紀に日本の首府として約70年間続いた古都である。神社・仏閣・仏像・彫刻・絵画など、国宝や重要文化財の宝庫である。

高さ16.21 m（53.18フィート）の大仏（752年開眼、その後度々修復）がある東大寺や、五重塔が猿沢池に美しい影をうつす興福寺、さらに放し飼いの鹿がたくさんいる春日大社などが、とくに有名である。また、東大寺には正倉院という特殊な防湿構造（校倉「あぜくら」造りという）の木造倉庫がある。ここには、当時の天皇の遺愛品、東大寺の寺宝・文書など奈良時代の美術品のほか、中国やペルシアなどからの伝来品9,000余点が収められている。

immerse in natural beauty while also pursuing historical and cultural interests. Japan had 5.27 million visitors from overseas in 2000. Of these, 2.69 million were tourists.

a) How to Enjoy Japan's Natural Scenery

The rich topographical variety produced by many mountains, gorges, rivers, lakes, marshes and a complex coastline, together with the clearly defined four seasons, provides Japan with many sightseeing spots where the beauties of nature can be enjoyed. Also, the presence of many volcanoes provides an abundance of hot spring areas, many of which have become health resorts. The most representative of these have been designated national parks (28 areas) or quasi-national parks (55 areas). Also, there are what are known as the three famous beauty spots of Japan: Matsushima (Miyagi Prefecture), Ama-no-Hashidate (Kyoto Prefecture) and Miyajima (Hiroshima Prefecture); and the three famous gardens of Japan: Kairakuen, in Mito; Kenrokuen, in Kanazawa; and Korakuen, in Okayama.

b) Historical and Cultural Places in Japan

Those who wish to learn something about the progress of Japanese culture may do so by visiting Japan's old cities and other spots which form a backdrop to Japan's long history, by looking at old temples, shrines and gardens and by admiring images of Buddha and objects of fine art.

Also, the many provincial festivals and events that show the traditions and characteristics of each particular area help one to understand many facets of Japan.

The ancient city of Nara was the capital of Japan for about seventy years, starting in the early eighth century. With its many shrines, Buddhist temples, statues of Buddha, carvings and paintings, it is rich in National Treasures and Important Cultural Assets.

Particularly famous are Nara's Todai Temple with its 16.21-meter-high (53.18 feet) statue of Buddha (dedicated in the year 752 and renovated several times since), Kofuku Temple with its five-storied pagoda facing the beautiful pond called Sarusawa-no-ike, and Kasuga Shrine with its many tame deer which are allowed to roam free. Todai Temple also has the Shoso-in, a wooden treasure-house with a special construction (called *aze-*

奈良国立博物館は、仏教美術の粋を集めている点で日本第一である。

　奈良近郊には、現存する世界最古の木造建築である法隆寺がある。また隣接する飛鳥地方は、6〜7世紀ごろ、日本文化の開花した地方で、日本仏教の発祥地でもあり、天皇の御陵や古墳・史跡などが点在している。1972年に、極彩色の壁画が発見されて有名になった高松塚古墳もこの一角にある。

　京都は、8世紀末から約1000年余り皇居のあった古都である。清水寺・三十三間堂・銀閣寺・金閣寺・平安神宮および東・西本願寺・大徳寺・西芳寺・竜安寺・京都御所・二条城・桂離宮など多くの寺社や史跡があり、その建築美や庭園美は訪れる人達を魅了する。

　また、東山・嵐山・嵯峨野・加茂川など景勝地も多く、西陣織・友禅染・京人形・清水焼・京扇子などの名産品もある。

　東京近郊の鎌倉は、12世紀末から約150年間、武家政権の所在地となったところである。鶴岡八幡宮・長谷の大仏・建長寺・円覚寺などの史跡が多い。

　日本の各地には、石垣・建物・配置などに日本独特の様式を持つ城が残されている。三名城といわれる姫路城・名古屋城（金の鯱鉾で名高かった。戦災で焼けたあと修復された）・熊本城のほか、大阪城・松本城・犬山城（その天守閣は、現存するもののうち最古）などが有

kura) which is resistant to moisture. Stored in this are more than nine thousand items, including fine art objects which belonged to the emperor of that time, Todai Temple treasures and manuscripts of the Nara period, plus items which came from countries such as China and Persia.

As far as assembling the cream of Buddhist art goes, Nara National Museum is without peer in Japan.

On the outskirts of Nara is Horyu Temple, the world's oldest wooden structure still in existence. Also, the nearby Asuka district was where the culture of Japan flowered around the sixth and seventh centuries, and as such was the cradle of Japanese Buddhism; in this area can be found Imperial mausolea, burial mounds and historical relics. One such place is Takamatsuzuka, which became famous when a tumulus with brilliantly colored wall paintings was discovered in 1972.

The ancient city of Kyoto was the Imperial seat for more than a thousand years, starting at the end of the eighth century. Among its many historical places of interest are such temples and shrines as Kiyomizu Temple, Sanjusangendo, Ginkaku Temple, Kinkaku Temple, Heian Shrine, the East and West Hongan Temples, Daitoku Temple, Saiho Temple and Ryoan Temple. Other important sights are Kyoto Gosho, Nijo Castle and Katsura Imperial Villa. Each of these places has architectural and landscape beauty that leaves the visitor entranced.

In addition, there are many places of scenic beauty, such as Higashiyama, Arashiyama, Sagano and the River Kamo, and many famous local products, such as *nishijin* brocade, *yuzen* dyed fabrics, *kyo* dolls, *kiyomizu* ware and *kyo* fans.

Kamakura, which is not far from Tokyo, became the seat of the military government for a period of one hundred and fifty years, starting from the end of the twelfth century. The many historical places that can be seen there include Tsurugaoka Hachiman Shrine, the Great Buddha of Hase, Kencho Temple and Engaku Temple.

In various regions of the country are found castles which are uniquely Japanese in their stone walls, architectural style and choice of location. The three most famous ones are Himeji Castle, Nagoya Castle (famous for its golden dolphin; destroyed by fire during the war, this castle was later rebuilt) and Kumamoto Castle, and other famous ones include Osaka Castle, Matsumoto Castle and Inuyama Castle (the tower of which is the

名である。

なかでも姫路城は、14世紀中ごろにつくられ、その後次第に拡張され、その規模の雄大さ、純白の天守閣の美しさなどで、一頭地を抜いている。別名、白鷺城とも呼ばれる。

城郭の石垣の積み石は、重さ1トン前後のものが多いが、大阪城にはとくに大きなものが使用されている。大阪城の石は、遠く110km（68マイル）もはなれた小豆島から運ばれたもので、とくに重い石の場合は、海中に石をつるし、浮力分だけ軽くして運ぶ石釣船が使われたという。

皇居は、徳川時代の将軍の居城であった江戸城の跡で、毎年1月2日と天皇誕生日には、国民参賀が行われるので、その一部が参観できる。

c) 日本にある世界遺産

世界の顕著な普遍的価値を有する文化遺産と自然遺産を認定、保護する条約が、1972年ユネスコ総会で採択された。2001年12月現在、722の遺産が、このリストに登録されている。このうち、日本の遺産は下記の11件である。

1) 法隆寺地域の仏教建造物（1993年12月登録）（別項372頁参照）
2) 姫路城（同上）
3) 屋久島（同上）

この島は、九州南方65kmに位置する。年間雨量が10,000mmに達し、植物の宝庫として世界に知られている。ここには、樹齢数千年（最高7,200年）の屋久杉もある。

4) 白神山地（同上）

青森・秋田の両県の日本海側に広がる世界最大級のブナ原生林で、稀少な動植物も多い。

5) 古都京都の文化財（京都市、宇治市、大津市）（1994年12月登録）（別項372頁参照）
6) 白川郷・五箇山の合掌造り集落（同上）

岐阜・富山県境の山岳地帯に発達した合掌造りの集落である。この地域の豪雪と自然環境にもマッチして、合

oldest in existence).

Himeji Castle was built in the middle of the fourteenth century and gradually enlarged until now it is unrivaled for its size as well as for the beauty of its pure white tower. Another name it is known by is Shirasagi Castle.

Most of the stones of the terraced walls of the castles weigh about 1 ton each, but the stones of Osaka Castle are particularly large. These stones had to be brought 110 kilometers (68 miles) from Shodo Island, and it is said that particularly large stones were suspended in the sea so that the buoyancy lightened them slightly, making it easier for the boats to transport them.

The present Imperial Palace was built on the site of Edo Castle, headquarters of the feudal government in the Tokugawa Era. A part of it can be visited on the second day of each year and on the Emperor's birthday, at which times the people are allowed to enter to offer their congratulations to the Emperor.

c) World Cultural and Natural Legacies in Japan

At its general meeting in 1972, UNESCO adopted a convention concerning the identification and protection of world cultural and natural heritage of outstanding and universal value. As of December 2001, the list of registered world legacies had reached 722, including eleven in Japan.

1) Buddhist monuments in the Horyu Temple Area (Registered December 1993) (see p. 373)

2) Himeji Castle (Registered December 1993)

3) Yakushima (Registered December 1993)

An island located 65 km south of Kyushu, Yakushima receives up to 10,000 mm of rain annually and is known internationally as a botanical treasure house. Some of the island's cedars, the *yakusugi*, are thousands of years old (the oldest, 7,200 years).

4) Shirakami Sanchi (Registered December 1993)

One of the world's largest virgin beech forests extending along the Japan Sea sides of Aomori and Akita prefectures. Home of many rare animals and plants.

5) Historic Monuments of Ancient Kyoto (Kyoto, Uji and Otsu Cities) (Registered December 1994) (see p. 373)

6) Historic villages of Shirakawa-go and Gokayama (Registered December 1994)

Nearly all of the houses in these villages are of the *gassh-*

掌造りの農家は三角形の結合をベースにした独特の構造で、巨大な茅葺き屋根からもすぐにわかる。建築学上も大きな関心がもたれている。

7)　厳島神社（1996 年 12 月登録）
　　17 棟他からなる厳島神社の鮮やかな朱塗りの建造物が、深々とした緑に覆われた山容を背景として、陸上から海上にまで展開している。日本 3 景の一つ「安芸の宮島」で知られる。

8)　原爆ドーム（1996 年 12 月登録）
　　このドームは、第 2 次世界大戦で、広島市に投下された原子爆弾によって破壊された広島県産業奨励館の残骸で、当時のまま保存されている。

9)　古都奈良の文化財（1998 年 12 月登録）
　　東大寺や興福寺など日本で独自の発展を遂げた仏教建築群、春日大社とその原始林、そして平城宮跡が指定範囲である（別項 370 頁参照）。

10)　日光の社寺（1999 年 12 月登録）
　　徳川将軍の霊廟として 1617 年に創建された日光東照宮を中心とした社寺の建造物群で、周辺の自然と一帯となって文化的景観を形成している。

11)　琉球王国の城・遺産群（2000 年 12 月登録）
　　現在の沖縄県、琉球王国は東南アジア、中国、朝鮮半島、そして日本の間にあり、それらの文化・経済の中継地としての地位を築いている地域である。

d）東京の見どころ

　　日本の政治・経済・文化の中心として、東京には各種

ozukuri style that developed in the mountainous region along the border between Gifu and Toyama prefectures. Well adapted to the extremely heavy snows and other natural features of this region, the gasshozukuri farm house has a unique structure based on interconnected triangles and is immediately recognizable from its enormous thatched roof. It has attracted considerable architectural interest.

7) Itsukushima Shinto Shrine (Registered December 1996)

Located on Itsukushima Island southwest of Hiroshima City, the shrine consists of seventeen bright vermillion buildings and other structures spreading down a deeply forested hillside to, and even onto, the sea. Itsukushima Shinto Shrine is the main attraction of Aki no Miyajima, long known as one of Japan's "three beauty spots."

8) Hiroshima Peace Memorial (Genbaku Dome) (Registered December 1996)

This dome is what remains of the Hiroshima Prefecture Industrial Promotion Hall destroyed by the atomic bomb dropped on Hiroshima City near the end of World War II. It has been preserved in its condition following the bombing.

9) Historic Monuments of Ancient Nara (Registered December 1998)

Included are a group of Buddhist buildings, most notably Todai Temple and Kofuku Temple, of a style that evolved independently in Japan, Kasuga Shrine and the surrounding virgin forest, and the Heijokyu ruins (see p. 371).

10) Shrines and Temples of Nikko (Registered December 1999)

These are a group of shrine and temple buildings including the centrally located Nikko Toshogu built in 1617 as the mausoleum of the shogun (feudal era general) Tokugawa Ieyasu. They blend with the surrounding natural environment to present a culturally intense panorama.

11) Remains of the Ryukyu Okoku castle (Registered December 2000)

Ryukyu Okoku was a kingdom that developed in the region of today's Okinawa Prefecture. Located midway among Southeast Asia, China and Japan, it established itself as a cultural and economic crossroads.

d) Around Tokyo

All types of institutions and facilities are concentrated in

の機関や施設が集中している。西部が台地になっていて山の手と呼ばれ、東部の低地部は下町と呼ばれている。

中心部に皇居があり、松の深い緑と大きな石垣を堀の水にうつしている。その近くに、東京駅がある。

霞ヶ関・永田町およびその近辺は官庁街で、その一角に国会議事堂・最高裁判所などもある。

丸の内・大手町一帯はビジネス街で、ここには日本の代表的企業の本社がある。

明治神宮は、明治天皇をまつるお宮で、大きな森に囲まれている。その外苑を「神宮外苑」といい、そこには東京オリンピックの主競技場となった国立競技場・体育館・屋内プール・野球場などがあって、一大スポーツセンターとなっている。

上野公園には、国立博物館・西洋美術館・動物園などがあり、桜の名所でもある。そのほか日比谷公園、芝公園などの公園や、後楽園・新宿御苑などの公開された庭園がある。芝公園の中には高さ 333 m（1,092.5 フィート）の東京タワーがそびえ、名所の一つとなっている。

NHK 放送センター・国立劇場・歌舞伎座・国会図書館など、文化的な施設も数多くある。

買物を楽しむには、銀座や新宿・渋谷などの繁華街がある。銀座は高級品を並べた老舗や有名店が多く、新宿は戦後の都市計画で、副都心として位置づけられ栄え、最高 243 m の高層ビルを有する都庁も 91 年ここへ移転した。また、外国人や若者がよく集まるしゃれた街として、六本木・青山・原宿などがある。

下町の浅草は、浅草寺を中心にたくさんの出店や興業街があり、庶民の町として独特な雰囲気を持っている。

東京の西部郊外には、神代植物公園や井の頭公園などがあり、数十年前まで雑木林におおわれていた武蔵野のおもかげを残している。

東京ディズニィーランド・ディズニィシーは、夢の世界を楽しむ人々で年間を通じてにぎわっている。

Tokyo, the political, economic and cultural center of Japan. The plateau on the west side is called the Yama-no-te district, and the lowland on the east is referred to as Shitamachi, or downtown.

In the center is the Imperial Palace, the deep green of the pines and the massive stone walls of which are reflected in the waters of the moat. Nearby is Tokyo Station.

Government offices are located in the Kasumigaseki and Nagatacho area, near which can also be seen the National Diet building and the Supreme Court.

Marunouchi and Otemachi form the business center. The head office of many of Japan's leading corporations are located here.

Meiji Jingu, a shrine dedicated to the Emperor Meiji, is ringed by a thick wood. In Jingugaien, the outer garden of the shrine, is located a large sports center made up of the National Stadium, one of the main sites of the events of the Tokyo Olympiad, a gymnasium, indoor swimming pools and baseball grounds.

In Ueno Park are the National Museum, Western Fine Arts Museum, and a zoo. This park is also famous for its cherry trees. In addition, there are Hibiya Park and Shiba Park, and gardens which have been opened to the public, such as Korakuen and Shinjuku-gyoen. One famous sight in Shiba Park is Tokyo Tower, which is 333 meters (1,092.5 feet) in height.

Tokyo also has numerous cultural facilities, such as the NHK Broadcasting Center, National Theater, Kabuki Theater and National Diet Library.

For shopping there are the bustling streets of Ginza, Shinjuku and Shibuya. In Ginza are many old-established and famous shops selling goods of the best quality. Shinjuku, a thriving satellite city center that resulted from post-war urban planning, has a skyline punctuated by numerous towering buildings, the tallest of which is the 243-meter high Tokyo Metropolitan Government Office built in 1991. The Roppongi, Aoyama and Harajuku districts are fashionable places which attract foreigners and young people.

Asakusa, in Shitamachi, with its many small shops and entertainment enterprises clustered around Senso Temple, has a special atmosphere as a town of the common people.

In Tokyo's western suburbs are Jindai Botanical Gardens and Inokashira Park, the last vestiges of the forests which covered the Musashino plain up until a few decades ago.

Tokyo Disneyland and Disney Sea bustle with fantasy seekers

幕張には、国際モーターショーなどが開かれる大規模な見本市会場（メッセ）がある。周辺一帯は新しいハイテク衛星都市となっている（ディズニィーランド・ディズニィシーと幕張は千葉県にある）。

e) 日本での宿泊

日本の宿には、日本式と西洋式がある。

西洋式のものは、設備・サービス・食事・会計など欧米の場合と大体同様である。

日本式の宿の各部屋は、日本家屋と同様に畳敷である。便所は部屋ごとについている場合もあるが、便所・浴室ともに共同の場所に設けられていることもある。とくに温泉地では、共同浴室が売物なので広く豪華である。

料金は通常、夕食・宿泊と翌日の朝食代が含まれている。食事は日本料理であるが、ふつうは客が選択するのではなく、宿側が用意したものが出される。また、食事は各部屋に運ばれてくるが、最近では人手不足と労務費の節約から、食堂式に簡略化されている場合もある。食事をとらないときは、もちろん料金を割り引いてもらうことは可能であるが、日本式の宿では食事の内容も含めて客をもてなすという考え方があるため、食事込みでない客はあまり歓迎されない。

西洋式・日本式を問わず、所定料金・税金のほかに、所定料金の 10〜15 ％位のサービス料を出発時の会計で一括請求される。したがって、特別に世話になったとき以外は、従業員に心付け（チップ）を渡す必要はない。

観光シーズンには、観光地の宿はたいへん混雑するので、早めに予約しておく必要がある。シーズン外でも予約しておいた方がよいが、もし予約なしで旅行するような場合は、下車駅や空港の交通公社や旅行案内所に、安心して泊まれる宿を斡旋してもらうとよい。

throughout the year.

Makuhari is home to a mammoth exhibition hall where international motor shows and other large events are held.The area surrounding the hall has become a new high-tech satellite city center. (Tokyo Disneyland, Disney Sea and Makuhari are in Chiba Prefecture.)

e) Lodgings in Japan

There are two types of (hotel) lodging in Japan, Japanese-style and Western-style.

In the Western-style establishments, facilities, service, meals and method of charges are roughly the same as in Europe and America.

In the Japanese-style places, the floor of each room is covered with *tatami* mats, as in Japanese homes. At some places each room has its own toilet while at others toilets and baths are provided for the common use of all the guests. Particularly in hot-spring resorts, where bathing is the attraction, the communal bathrooms are large and luxurious.

Charges usually include dinner, the night's stay and breakfast the following morning. The meals are Japanese style, and guests ordinarily do not choose the dishes, but are served whatever the management has prepared. By tradition, meals are served in the rooms of the guests. Recently, however, in order to combat staff shortages and rising labor costs, some places require guests to come to the dining room for meals. Naturally, the charge will be reduced if meals are not required, but the general thinking at such places is to include meals, and the hotels are not too keen on having guests who do not require meals.

When checking out of a Western-style or Japanese-style place, the guest is required to pay a service charge of 10 to 15%, as well as tax. This means that it is not necessary to tip any of the staff, unless you feel that someone particularly deserves it.

Lodgings at popular sightseeing spots become very crowded during the tourist season, so it is necessary to book well in advance. It is of course best to book even in the off-season; but if you do travel without booking, ask the Japan Travel Bureau or a travel guide office at the station or airport to find a suitable place for you to stay.

［付　録］

〔統 計 資 料〕

(1)　主要各国の面積
(Area of Selected Countries)

国　　　　名	面　　積	
	$(1,000 \text{ km}^2)$	$(1,000 \text{ sq.mile})$
アメリカ（U. S. A.）	9,364 千 km²	3,616 千平方マイル
カナダ（Canada）	9,971　〃	3,850　〃
ブラジル（Brazil）	8,547　〃	3,300　〃
イギリス（U. K.）	243　〃	94　〃
ドイツ（Germany）	357　〃	138　〃
フランス（France）	552　〃	213　〃
イタリア（Italy）	301　〃	116　〃
ロシア（Russia）	17,075　〃	6,593　〃
オーストラリア（Australia）	7,741　〃	2,989　〃
インドネシア（Indonesia）	1,905　〃	736　〃
マレーシア（Malaysia）	330　〃	127　〃
中華人民共和国（China）	9,597 [1]　〃	3,706　〃
（台湾）	36　〃	14　〃
（香港特別行政区）	1.1　〃	0.4　〃
（マカオ特別行政区）	0.018　〃	0.007　〃
サウジアラビア（Saudi Arabia）	2,150　〃	830　〃
アルジェリア（Algeria）	2,382　〃	920　〃
日本（Japan）	378　〃	146　〃

「日本国勢図会」（2002）

[1]台湾を含み，香港とマカオを含まない。

(2)　大陸別面積と人口

(Area and Population by Continent)

地　　域 (Region)	面　積 (Area)		人　口 (Population)		人口密度 (Population Density Persons/km²)
	百万 km² (In Miliones of km²)	%	百万人 (In Miliones)	%	1 km²につき 人
アジア (Asia)	31.8	23.5	3,672	60.6	115.6
アフリカ (Africa)	30.3	22.3	794	13.1	26.2
ヨーロッパ (Europe)	23.0	16.9	727	12.0	31.6
アメリカ (America)	42.1	31.0	833	13.8	19.8
北中アメリカ	24.2	17.9	487	8.0	20.1
南アメリカ	17.8	13.1	346	5.7	19.4
オセアニア (Oceania)	8.5	6.3	31	0.5	3.6
世界計 (Total)	135.6	100.0	6,057	100.0	44.7

「日本国勢図会」(2002)

面積は国連 "Demographic Yearbook"（1999 年版）による 1999 年の数値。人口は国連 "Population and Vital Statistics Report"（シリーズ A, 第 50 巻, 第 4 号）による 2000 年 7 月 1 日現在の国連の推計値。面積・人口ともトルコはアジアにハワイは北中アメリカに含める。バルト 3 国を除く旧ソ連構成国は, ロシア, ウクライナ, ベラルーシ, モルドバがヨーロッパに, アゼルバイジャン, アルメニア, ウズベキスタン, カザフスタン, キルギス, グルジア, タジキスタン, トルクメニスタンがアジアに含まれる。100 ％になるように調整。

(3) 日本の年齢・男女別人口および割合（2000 年 10 月 1 日現在）
(Japanese Population by Age and Sex)

年　齢 (Age)	人　口(万人) (Population(10,000))			割　合(%) (% of total)		
	男 (Male)	女 (Female)	計 (Total)	男 (Male)	女 (Female)	計 (Total)
0〜4 歳	302	288	590	4.9	4.4	4.7
5〜9 〃	308	294	602	5.0	4.5	4.7
10〜14 〃	335	319	655	5.4	4.9	5.2
15〜19 〃	383	365	749	6.2	5.6	5.9
20〜24 〃	431	411	842	6.9	6.3	6.6
25〜29 〃	497	483	979	8.0	7.4	7.7
30〜34 〃	444	434	878	7.1	6.7	6.9
35〜39 〃	410	402	811	6.6	6.2	6.4
40〜44 〃	392	388	780	6.3	6.0	6.1
45〜49 〃	447	445	892	7.2	6.9	7.0
50〜54 〃	521	523	1,044	8.4	8.1	8.2
55〜59 〃	429	444	873	6.9	6.9	6.9
60〜64 〃	375	399	774	6.0	6.2	6.1
65〜69 〃	336	375	711	5.4	5.8	5.6
70〜74 〃	267	323	590	4.3	5.0	4.6
75 歳以上	319	580	900	5.1	9.0	7.1
年令不詳	15	8	23	0.2	0.1	0.2
0〜14 歳	946	901	1,847	15.2	13.9	14.6
15〜64 〃	4,328	4,294	8,622	69.7	66.2	67.9
65 歳以上	922	1,278	2,201	14.8	19.7	17.3
総数[1]	6,211	6,482	12,693	100.0	100.0	100.0

「日本国勢図会」(2002)

総務庁統計局「2000 年国勢調査報告」による。

(4) 日本の主要都市人口 （2000年10月1日現在）
(Population of Selected Cities in Japan)

都　市　名	人口 (In thousands)
東京23区　（Tokyo）	8,135 千人
横　　浜　（Yokohama）	3,427 〃
大　　阪　（Osaka）	2,599 〃
名 古 屋　（Nagoya）	2,172 〃
札　　幌　（Sapporo）	1,822 〃
神　　戸　（Kobe）	1,493 〃
京　　都　（Kyoto）	1,468 〃
福　　岡　（Fukuoka）	1,341 〃
川　　崎　（Kawasaki）	1,250 〃
広　　島　（Hiroshima）	1,126 〃
さいたま*　（Saitama）	1,024 〃
北 九 州　（Kitakyushu）	1,011 〃
仙　　台　（Sendai）	1,008 〃
千　　葉　（Chiba）	887 〃
堺　　　　（Sakai）	792 〃
熊　　本　（Kumamoto）	662 〃
岡　　山　（Okayama）	627 〃
相 模 原　（Sagamihara）	606 〃
浜　　松　（Hamamastu）	582 〃
鹿 児 島　（Kagoshima）	552 〃
船　　橋　（Funabashi）	550 〃
八 王 子　（Hachioji）	536 〃
東 大 阪　（Higashiosaka）	515 〃
新　　潟　（Niigata）	501 〃

「日本国勢図会」（2002）

総務省統計局「2000年国勢調査報告」による。

＊さいたま市は、2001年5月1日に埼玉県の浦和、大宮、与野の3市が
合併して誕生した。

(5) 日本の統治機構 (2002年)
(Government of Japan)

(行政)
Executive Branch

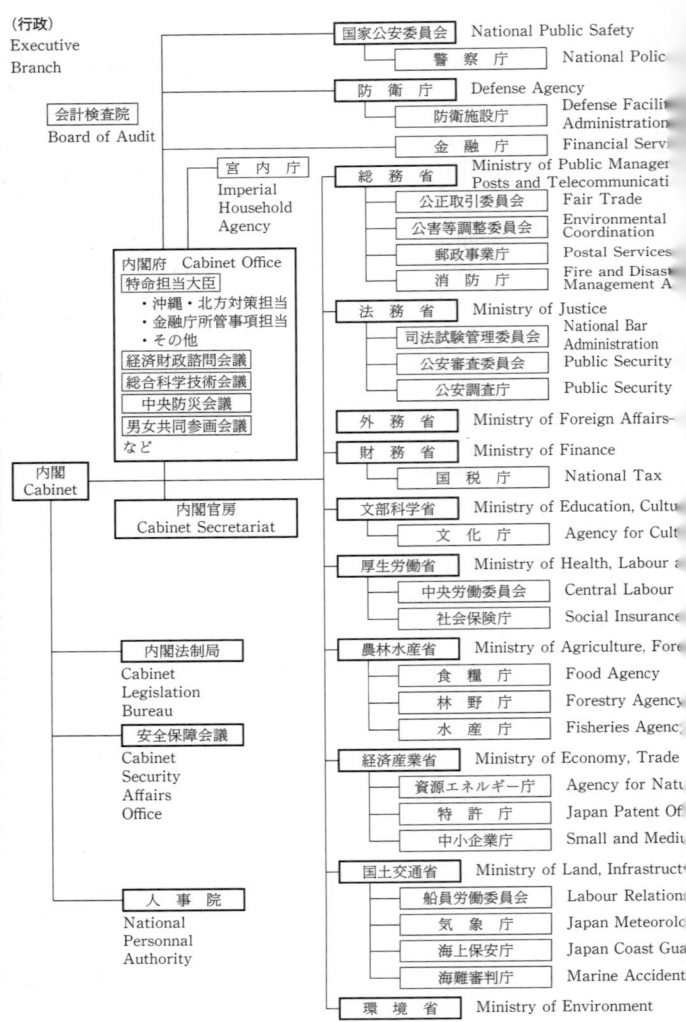

国家公安委員会	National Public Safety
警察庁	National Polic
防衛庁	Defense Agency
防衛施設庁	Defense Facili Administration
金融庁	Financial Servi
総務省	Ministry of Public Manager Posts and Telecommunicati
公正取引委員会	Fair Trade
公害等調整委員会	Environmental Coordination
郵政事業庁	Postal Services
消防庁	Fire and Disas Management A
法務省	Ministry of Justice
司法試験管理委員会	National Bar Administration
公安審査委員会	Public Security
公安調査庁	Public Security
外務省	Ministry of Foreign Affairs
財務省	Ministry of Finance
国税庁	National Tax
文部科学省	Ministry of Education, Cultu
文化庁	Agency for Cult
厚生労働省	Ministry of Health, Labour a
中央労働委員会	Central Labour
社会保険庁	Social Insurance
農林水産省	Ministry of Agriculture, Fore
食糧庁	Food Agency
林野庁	Forestry Agency
水産庁	Fisheries Agenc
経済産業省	Ministry of Economy, Trade
資源エネルギー庁	Agency for Natu
特許庁	Japan Patent Of
中小企業庁	Small and Mediu
国土交通省	Ministry of Land, Infrastruct
船員労働委員会	Labour Relations
気象庁	Japan Meteorolo
海上保安庁	Japan Coast Gua
海難審判庁	Marine Accident
環境省	Ministry of Environment

会計検査院
Board of Audit

宮内庁
Imperial Household Agency

内閣府　Cabinet Office
特命担当大臣
・沖縄・北方対策担当
・金融庁所管事項担当
・その他
経済財政諮問会議
総合科学技術会議
中央防災会議
男女共同参画会議
など

内閣
Cabinet

内閣官房
Cabinet Secretariat

内閣法制局
Cabinet Legislation Bureau

安全保障会議
Cabinet Security Affairs Office

人事院
National Personnal Authority

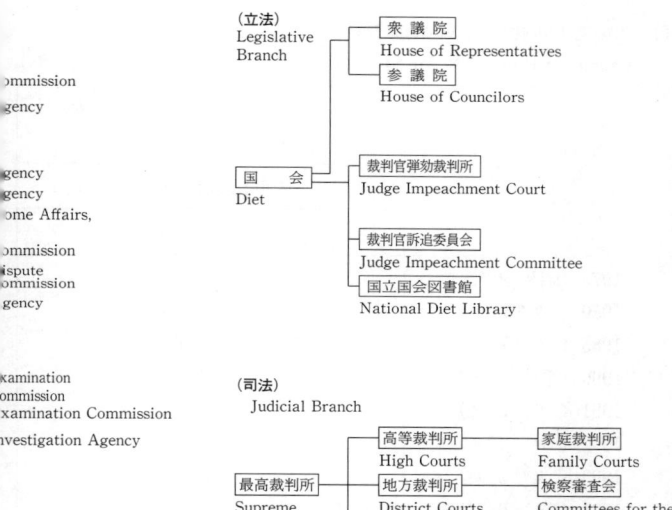

ommission
gency

gency
gency
ome Affairs,

ommission
ispute
ommission
gency

国　会 Diet	衆　議　院 House of Representatives
	参　議　院 House of Councilors
	裁判官弾劾裁判所 Judge Impeachment Court
	裁判官訴追委員会 Judge Impeachment Committee
	国立国会図書館 National Diet Library

xamination
ommission
xamination Commission

nvestigation Agency

dministration

ports, Science and Technology

ffairs

Velfare

Relations Comission

gency

nd Fisheries

ndustry

Resources and Energy

Enterprise Agency

and Transport

Commission for Seafarers

Agency

Inquiry Agency

（司法）
Judicial Branch

最高裁判所 Supreme Court	高等裁判所 High Courts	家庭裁判所 Family Courts
	地方裁判所 District Courts	検察審査会 Committees for the Inquest of Prosecution
	簡易裁判所 Summary Courts	

*

| 在外公館
Overseas Establishments |
| 大　使　館
Embassies |
| 総 領 事 館
Consulates-General |
| 領　事　館
Consulates |
| 政府代表部
Permanent Missions and Delegations |

(6) 円の対ドル相場（銀行間直物）

    (Exchange Rate of ¥ for $)   （単位：円，%）

年　　　末	インターバンク相場（東京市場） （1米ドルにつき円）
	スポット・レート
	終　　　値
1975（昭和 50 年）	305.15
1980（ 〃 55 〃 ）	203.60
1985（ 〃 60 〃 ）	200.60
1990（平成 2 年）	135.40
1991（ 〃 3 〃 ）	125.25
1992（ 〃 4 〃 ）	124.65
1993（ 〃 5 〃 ）	111.89
1994（ 〃 6 〃 ）	99.83
1995（ 〃 7 〃 ）	102.91
1996（ 〃 8 〃 ）	115.98
1997（ 〃 9 〃 ）	129.92
1998（ 〃 10 〃 ）	115.20
1999（ 〃 11 〃 ）	102.08
2000（ 〃 12 〃 ）	114.90
2001（ 〃 13 〃 ）	131.47

「日本の統計」（2002）

(7) 各国の国民総生産と1人あたり GNP

(GNP and Per Capita Income)

	国民総生産 (億ドル)				1人あたり (ドル)	
	1997	1998	1999	2000	1999	2000
アメリカ合衆国	83,184	87,815	92,686	98,729	33,990	35,082
日本	43,128	39.407	44,935	47,652	35,479	37,560
ドイツ	21,111	21,453	21,042	18,669	25,633	22,762
イギリス	13,274	14,235	14,584	14,272	24,510	23,987
フランス	14,060	14,521	14,387	12,951	24,343	21,991
イタリア	11,669	11,967	11,805	10,743	20,520	18,674
中国	9,035	9,645	9,912	10,800	782	…
ブラジル	8,077	7,870	5,294	5,955	3,201	3,550
カナダ	6,339	6,081	6,446	6,995	21,142	22,749
メキシコ	4,012	4,204	4,803	5,747	4,895	5,903
スペイン	5,616	5,880	6,027	5,612	15,290	14,218
韓国	4,766	3,174	4,067	4,572	8,679	9,672
ロシア	4,285	2,778	1,846	2,511	1,268	1,726
インド	4,174	4,262	4,545	…	461	…
オーストラリア	4,047	3,617	3,916	3,778	20,645	19,718
オランダ	3,769	3,934	3,985	3,692	25,203	23,277
スイス	2,561	2,621	2,585	2,396	36,259	33,412
スウェーデン	2,389	2,398	2,415	2,276	27,252	25,664
ベルギー	2,440	2,502	2,489	2,267	24,329	22,120
トルコ	1,902	2,005	1,848	2,002	2,872	2,971
オーストリア	2,060	2,112	2,101	1,899	25,967	23,444
デンマーク	1,690	1,746	1,762	1,626	33,050	30,452
ノルウェー	1,550	1,478	1,536	1,619	34,435	36,048
フィンランド	1,225	1,290	1,284	1,213	24,833	23,425
ポルトガル	1,065	1,116	1,140	1,051	11,530	10,500
チェコ	530	569	546	507	5,308	4,938
ニュージーランド	657	535	546	495	14,329	12,919
ルクセンブルク	175	183	193	189	44,949	42,936
アイスランド	74	81	86	85	30,788	30,410

「日本国勢図会」(2002)

内閣府「2000年度国民経済計算参考図表」および同「月刊海外経済データ」(2002
年2月号）による（原資料は OECD, IMF 等資料による）。中国には台湾，香
港，マカオを含まず。名目値。米ドル。暦年。

(8) 日本の経済活動別国内総生産（暦年）（単位　十億円）

(GDP by Industry in Japan)

	1997	1998	1999	2000	〃 (%)
農林水産業	8,363	8,251	7,583	6,996	1.4
農業	6,294	6,438	5,963	5,474	1.1
林業	554	573	355	347	0.1
水産業	1,515	1,240	1,265	1,174	0.2
鉱業	810	743	655	636	0.1
製造業	119,417	113,472	110,989	110,927	21.6
うち食料品	12,716	12,708	12,951	13,685	2.7
繊維	1,458	1,296	1,169	1,103	0.2
パルプ・紙	3,359	3,244	3,081	3,199	0.6
化学	9,865	9,245	9,647	8,938	1.7
石油・石炭製品	6,378	6,155	6,070	6,024	1.2
鉄鋼	6,117	4,916	4,718	5,265	1.0
金属製品	6,985	6,304	5,829	5,679	1.1
一般機械	12,295	11,349	10,227	10,365	2.0
電気機械	21,253	19,724	20,000	20,772	4.0
輸送用機械	11,387	12,055	12,027	11,253	2.2
印刷・出版	6,334	5,866	6,031	6,131	1.2
建設業	41,301	39,740	38,496	37,636	7.3
電気・ガス・水道業	14,185	14,543	14,424	14,312	2.8
電気	9,669	9,870	9,748	9,559	1.9
ガス・水道・熱供給	4,516	4,674	4,676	4,753	0.9
卸売・小売業	80,630	77,382	73,099	71,451	13.9
卸売	51,173	49,496	45,555	43,697	8.5
小売	29,457	27,886	27,544	27,754	5.4
金融・保険業	30,244	29,316	33,045	32,644	6.4
不動産業	63,196	64,099	65,130	66,490	12.9
うち住宅賃貸業	53,609	54,512	55,527	56,843	11.1
運輸・通信業	35,464	34,652	32,936	32,909	6.4
運輸	25,209	24,394	23,901	23,936	4.7
通信	10,255	10,258	9,035	8,974	1.7
サービス業	96,165	100,008	100,726	104,182	20.3
産業計	489,774	482,204	477,081	478,182	93.1
政府サービス生産者	44,084	45,177	45,875	46,430	9.0
対家計民間非営利 サービス生産者	9,331	10,095	10,001	9,341	1.8
小計	543,188	537,476	532,958	533,953	104.0
輸入税	3,165	2,929	2,941	3,165	0.6
（控除）総資本形成 に関わる消費税	3,462	3,611	3,329	3,512	0.7
（控除）帰属利子	25,028	24,855	24,807	23,738	4.6
統計上の不突合	3,998	3,897	4,074	3,666	0.7
国内総生産	521,862	515,835	511,837	513,534	100.0

「日本国勢図会」（2002）

内閣府「2000 年度国民経済計算」による。構成比（%）は原資料掲載のものを
そのまま引用し，各項目の内訳の調整を行っていない。

(9) 主要国のエネルギー自給率 (1998年) (%)

(Self-sufficiency in Energy)

	日本	アメリカ合衆国	ドイツ	イギリス	フランス
一次エネルギー[1]	22.4	79.6	39.6	120.5	49.1
石炭[2]	2.8	110.4	63.5	68.5	22.5
原油	0.2	40.3	2.7	149.0	1.9
天然ガス	3.4	88.7	21.0	102.2	5.1
	カナダ	ロシア	中国	オーストラリア	サウジアラビア
一次エネルギー[1]	151.8	166.0	104.2	203.1	507.6
石炭[2]	191.3	99.8	101.8	360.6	—
原油	125.7	177.8	93.0	75.4	467.6
天然ガス	205.3	154.2	114.9	149.9	100.0

「日本国勢図会」(2002)

国連"1998 Energy Statistics Yearbook"による。自給率は，生産量÷消費量(供給)×100で算出。 1) 石油換算　2) 無煙炭と瀝青炭のみ。

(10) 日本の原油輸入先 (2000年)

(Source of Petroleum Imports)

	千kl	%		千kl	%
アラブ首長国連邦	62,876	25.2	オーストラリア	3.797	1.5
サウジアラビア	62,863	25.2	イラク	3,642	1.5
イラン	29,556	11.8	ベトナム	2,872	1.1
カタール	22,928	9.2	メキシコ	2,392	1.0
クウェート	21,036	8.4	計×	249,814	100.0
インドネシア	12,365	4.9			
オマーン	11,403	4.6	OPEC計	216,079	86.5
中国	5,927	2.4	中東計	214,540	85.9

「日本国勢図会」(2002)

日本関税協会『日本貿易月表』による。×その他とも。

(11) 日本の主要耐久消費財の普及率（全世帯）　　　　（単位%）

(Ownership of Consumer Durables by Japanese Households)

品　　目	全　世　帯		
	平成 7 年 (1995)	平成 12 年 (2000)	平成 13 年 (2001)
じ　ゅ　う　た　ん	59.0	64.6	63.4
応　接　セ　ッ　ト	38.3	38.1	37.8
ユ　ニ　ッ　ト　家　具	19.3	21.6	22.3
ベ　　ッ　　　　ド	53.1	56.7	59.6
温　水　洗　浄　便　座	23.6	41.0	43.2
洗　髪　洗　面　化　粧　台	30.8	43.9	46.7
システムキッチン	28.2	39.9	40.8
温　　水　　器	30.4	33.4	33.0
ガ　ス　瞬　間　湯　沸　器	58.3	51.2	49.1
電　気　冷　蔵　庫	97.8	98.1	98.4
電　子　レ　ン　ジ	87.2	94.0	95.4
電　気　洗　た　く　機	99.0	99.3	99.4
衣　類　乾　燥　機	19.4	21.7	21.7
ふ　と　ん　乾　燥　機	38.1	36.5	37.0
電　気　掃　除　機	98.3	98.2	98.3
ミ　　シ　　ン	79.1	72.0	72.5
石　油　ス　ト　ー　ブ	67.7	60.4	58.9
温　風　ヒ　ー　タ　ー	66.3	69.4	69.5
ルームエアコン	77.2	86.2	86.3
電　気　カ　ー　ペ　ッ　ト	63.1	68.0	68.3
カ　ラ　ー　テ　レ　ビ	98.9	99.1	99.2
衛　星　放　送　受　信　装　置	27.6	38.9	39.2
Ｖ　　Ｔ　　　　Ｒ	73.7	78.5	79.3
ビ　デ　オ　カ　メ　ラ	31.3	37.9	36.8
ビデオディスプレーヤー	15.3	14.3	15.7
カ　ラ　オ　ケ　装　置	15.2	11.5	9.9
ス　テ　レ　オ	57.7	55.5	52.9
CD　プ　レ　ー　ヤ　ー	55.9	61.8	62.1
ワ　ー　プ　ロ	39.4	39.1	37.7
パ　ソ　コ　ン	15.6	38.6	50.2
ファクシミリ	10.0	32.9	35.5
プッシュホン	58.3	75.5	77.2
乗　用　車	80.0	83.6	85.4
オートバイ・スクーター	24.5	21.7	21.4
自　転　車（大　人　用）	79.4	81.3	81.2
カ　　メ　　ラ	85.7	83.9	83.2
ピ　　ア　　ノ	22.2	21.4	22.8
電　子　鍵　盤　楽　器	16.8	17.5	17.6
ゴ　ル　フ　セ　ッ　ト	38.3	39.1	40.0
ゴ　ル　フ　会　員　権	7.4	7.3	6.8

「日本の統計」(2002)

『消費動向調査』（3 月末現在）による。調査対象：一般世帯のうち単身者世帯および外国人世帯を除く約 5,040 万世帯。

　　資料　内閣府経済社会総合研究所景気統計部消費班『消費動向調査年報』
　　　　　『消費動向調査四半期報』

(12) 東京の主要食料品の小売物価 (2000年)
(Retail Food Prices in Tokyo)

品　目 (Items)	単位(Unit)	価格(Price)
米　　　　(Rice)	10kg	￥4,934
食パン　　(Bread)	1kg	422
牛　肉　　(Beef)	100 g	393
豚　肉　　(Pork)	100 g	157
牛　乳　　(Milk)	200mℓ	93
チーズ　　(Cheese)	150 g	282
鶏　卵　　(Eggs)	1kg	309
しょう油　(Soy Sauce)	1 ℓ	307
み　そ　　(Miso)	1kg	333
砂　糖　　(Suger)	1kg	211

「日本の統計」(2002)

(13) 各国の食用農産物自給率 (1999) (%)
(Self-sufficiency in Food Crops)

品目 (Items)	日本 (Japan)	アメリカ (U.S.A.)	イギリス (U. K.)	ドイツ (Germany)	フランス (France)	イタリア (Italy)
穀物(Grains)全体	24	134	100	123	195	86
米(Rice)	92	169	0	0	19	226
小麦(Wheat)	9	182	102	128	187	73
いも類(Potatoes)	78	101	87	114	109	72
豆類(Legumes)	37	150	108	84	171	25
野菜類(Vegetables)	82	97	51	37	89	125
肉類(Meat)	56	108	80	93	109	80
卵類(Eggs)	99	102	97	82	102	97
魚介類(Fishes and Shells)	58	80	39	24	38	32

「世界の統計」(2002)

⒁　粗鋼生産量・粗鋼1人あたり消費量

(Production and Per Capita Consumption of Crude Steel)

国　　　名	粗鋼生産量 (Crude Steel Production)		粗鋼1人あたり消費量 (Per Capita Consumption)	
	1997	2000	1996	1999
	（千トン）	（千トン）	(kg)	(kg)
中　　国　(China)	108,911	127,236	90	108
日　　本　(Japan)	104,545	106,444	665	557
アメリカ　(U. S. A.)	98,485	101,517	445	458
ロシア　(Russia)	48,502	59,098	135	133
ドイツ　(Germany)	45,009	46,376	417	469
韓　　国　(South Korea)	42,554	43,107	865	757
ブラジル　(Brazil)	26,153	27,865	88	99
イタリア　(Italy)	25,800	26,420	427	552
ウクライナ　(Ukraine)	25,627	31,373	150	61
インド　(India)	24,415	26,924	29	30
フランス　(France)	19,773	21,002	264	326
イギリス　(U. K.)	18,530	15,306	256	266
台　　湾　(Taiwan)	15,598	16,840	1,006	1,109
カナダ　(Canada)	15,459	16,496	486	604
トルコ　(Turkey)	14,475	14,325	170	189
メキシコ　(Mexico)	14,218	15,659	114	123
スペイン　(Spain)	13,670	15,841	313	469
ポーランド　(Poland)	11,585	10,504	106	205
ベルギー　(Belgium)	10,738	11,637	—	—
オーストラリア　(Australia)	8,831	8,511	333	341
世　界　計　(Total)	798,000	848,000	134	138

「鉄鋼統計要覧」(2001)

粗鋼の消費量は（粗鋼生産＋輸入－輸出）÷総人口

(15) 産業別就業人口割合（15 歳以上　％）（2000 年）

(Breakdown of Industrial Sector of Employed Persons 15 Years Old and Over)

	日本	アメリカ合衆国 [5) 6)]	イギリス [6)] (1999)	ドイツ	ロシア (1999)
農林水産業	5.1	2.6	1.5	2.7	11.8
鉱業	0.1	0.4	0.4	0.4	2.0
製造業	20.5	14.7	17.8	23.3	19.1
電気・ガス・水道業	0.5	[7)] 1.1	0.7	0.8	2.6
建設業	10.1	7.0	7.0	8.5	5.7
商業[1)]	[3)] 22.9	[3)] 20.6	19.8	17.5	13.3
運輸・通信業	6.4	6.1	6.6	5.5	9.1
公務・サービス業[2)]	[4)] 33.8	[8)] 47.5	45.9	41.2	36.4
分類不能	0.6		0.3	—	—
計	100.0	100.0	100.0	100.0	100.0
実数（千人）	64.460	135,208	27,442	36,604	60,408

	イタリア [9) 10)]	中国 [5)]	韓国 [5)]	ブラジル [12)] (1999)	オーストラリア [5)]
農林水産業	5.3	46.9	10.9	24.2	4.9
鉱業	0.3	0.8	0.1	1.1	0.8
製造業	23.2	11.3	20.1	11.6	12.7
電気・ガス・水道業	0.8	0.4	0.3	[13)] —	0.7
建設業	7.6	5.0	7.5	6.6	7.8
商業[1)]	19.7	6.6	27.2	[14)] 13.4	24.8
運輸・通信業	5.6	2.9	6.0	[15)] 3.9	6.6
公務・サービス業[2)]	37.5	[11)] 3.4	27.9	[16)] 39.2	41.8
分類不能	—	22.7	—	—	—
計	100.0	100.0	100.0	100.0	100.0
実数（千人）	21,225	711,500	21,061	71,676	9,010

「日本国勢図会」（2002）

ILO（国際労働機関）『労働統計年鑑』（2001 年）による。1) 飲食業・ホテル業を含む。2) 金融・保険・不動産業などを含む。3) ホテル業を除く。4) ホテル業を含む。5) 軍隊を除く。6) 16 歳以上。7) 衛生業を含む。8) ホテル業を含み，衛生業を除く。9) 徴兵を含む。10) 14 歳以上。11) 対事業所サービスを除く。12) 10 歳以上。一部地域の農村地域の人口を除く。13) 鉱業に含まれる。14) 飲食業・ホテル業を除く。15) 倉庫業を除く。16) 飲食業・ホテル業，倉庫業を含む。

(16) 主な国の失業率の推移 (各年平均)
(Unemployment)

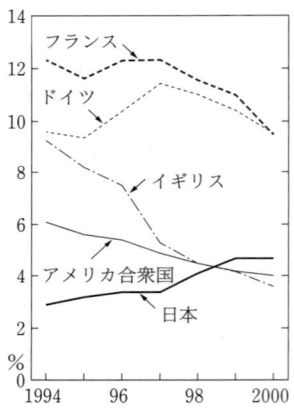

「日本国勢図会」(2002)
総務省統計局「労働力調査」による。原資料は各国資料。

(17) 人口自然増加率
(Rate of Natural Population Increase) (人口千人につき　人)

	調査年	出生率	死亡率	自然増加率
日本	2000	9.5	7.7	1.8
アメリカ合衆国	2000	14.0	8.5	5.5
イギリス	2000	11.4	10.3	1.1
ドイツ	1999	9.4	10.4	-1.0
フランス	2000	13.2	9.1	4.1
中国*	1995〜2000	16.2	7.0	9.2
インド*	〃	26.4	9.0	17.4

「日本国勢図会」(2002)

国連 "Population and Vital Statistics Report" (2001年10月) による。*国連推計。中国には台湾，香港，マカオを含まず。自然増加率は出世率から死亡率を減じたもの。

(18) 日本の学校体系図

(Japanese School System)

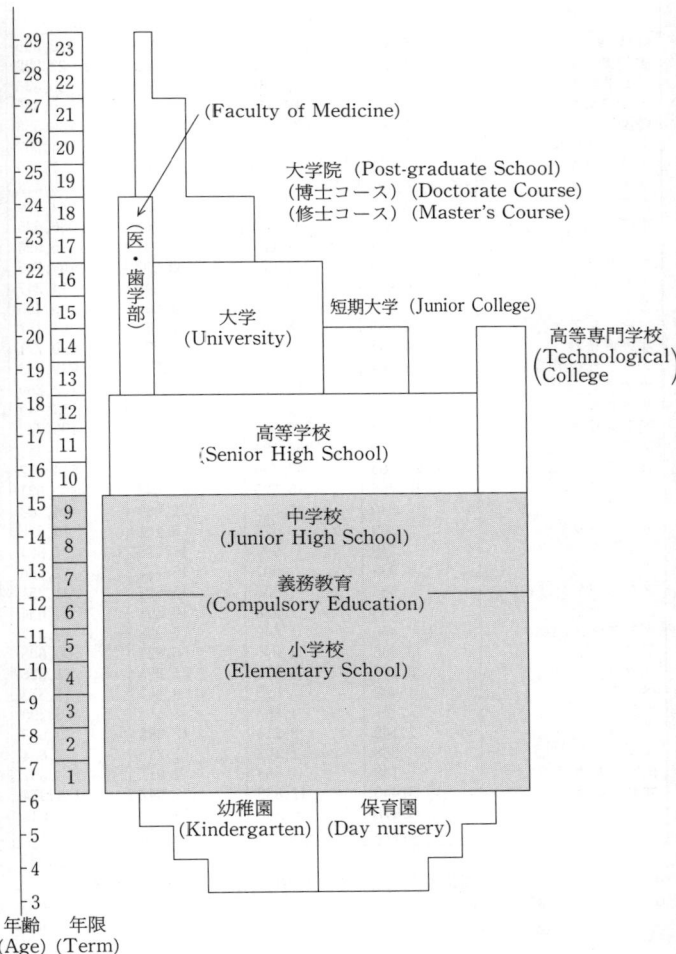

⑲　登録外国人数および正規入国者数

(Foreigners Living in Japan and Coming into Japan)　　　　　　(人)

国 (地域)	在日発録外国人数(12月末日現在)		正規入国外国人数	
	1990	2000	1990	2000
総数 a	1,075,317	1,686,444	3,504,470	5,272,095
アジア	924,560	1,244,629	2,164,373	3,222,982
インド	3,107	10,064	20,623	39,845
インドネシア	3,623	19,346	32,605	39,389
韓国	b 687,940	b 635,269	978,984	1,286,583
シンガポール	1,194	1,940	43,512	74,967
スリランカ	1,206	5,655	5,005	7,350
タイ	6,724	29,289	69,477	73,472
台湾	c …	c …	610,652	944,019
中国	c 150,339	c 335,575	118,065	386,635
トルコ	251	1,424	4,141	5,690
フィリピン	49,092	144,871	108,292	169,755
ベトナム	6,233	16,908	2,149	14,247
香港	c …	c …	38,622	49,423
マレーシア	4,683	8,386	58,112	64,157
北アメリカ	44,643	58,100	644,525	890,771
アメリカ合衆国	38,364	44,856	564,958	749,343
カナダ	4,909	10,088	64,791	122,260
メキシコ	786	1,740	9,950	13,049
南アメリカ	71,495	312,921	92,863	135,770
ブラジル	56,429	254,394	67,303	101,513
ヨーロッパ d	25,563	47,730	516,450	814,912
イギリス	10,226	16,525	212,043	391,621
イタリア	940	1,579	29,969	34,262
オーストリア	309	476	8,261	10,322
オランダ	749	904	17,715	27,864
スイス	980	907	16,784	17,896
スウェーデン	586	1,158	15,827	21,251
スペイン	856	1,338	16,391	14,654
デンマーク	450	542	7,928	10,347
ドイツ	3,606	4,295	66,827	90,605
フランス	3,166	5,371	51,995	81,528
ベルギー	402	525	8,901	11,373
ロシア	…	4,893	…	30,290
アフリカ	2,140	8,214	12,095	20,643
エジプト	368	1,103	1,827	2,854
南アフリカ	108	353	2,011	4,357
オセアニア	5,440	12,839	71,547	184,974
オーストラリア	3,975	9,188	53,252	150,046
ニュージーランド	1,275	3,264	16,396	32,142

「世界の統計」(2002)

a　無国籍を含む。b　北朝鮮を含む。c　中国は台湾および香港を含む。
d　旧ソビエト諸国を含む。

⑳　渡航先別出国日本人数

（Japanese Leaving Japan）　　　　　　　（単位　人）

渡　航　先	1990	2000	観光等	短期商用・業務
総数 a	10,997,431	17,818,590	14,582,476	2,599,173
アジア	5,245,528	8,481,472	6,661,687	1,648,217
インド	34,569	70,578	49,874	18,459
インドネシア	199,091	444,113	386,599	49,334
韓国	1,369,189	2,386,544	2,117,958	247,967
シンガポール	606,230	585,159	461,250	104,252
スリランカ	10,980	10,154	7,191	2,497
タイ	420,975	885,938	734,546	132,389
台湾	878,658	844,977	554,901	278,034
中国	366,550	1,468,492	1,012,524	413,312
トルコ	15,384	50,384	44,668	4,761
フィリピン	187,171	352,640	282,794	62,502
ベトナム	2,810	115,857	88,112	25,435
香港	999,662	810,526	580,249	208,874
マレーシア	102,937	268,322	191,292	67,990
北アメリカ	3,901,968	5,519,652	4,720,592	528,257
アメリカ合衆国	3,679,738	5,073,673	4,336,954	495,568
カナダ	201,794	373,693	325,110	22,564
メキシコ	15,333	52,826	42,557	7,578
南アメリカ	47,473	68,420	44,493	15,847
ブラジル	30,348	35,337	21,064	8,681
ヨーロッパ b	1,219,449	2,374,845	1,884,983	343,378
イギリス	281,873	401,844	282,524	64,397
イタリア	111,389	451,844	402,630	39,198
オーストリア	34,104	72,694	63,412	6,081
オランダ	31,111	78,560	54,900	18,037
スイス	54,696	147,735	129,203	13,384
スウェーデン	12,196	22,673	14,522	5,935
スペイン	79,067	162,316	144,741	13,033
デンマーク	13,540	21,783	15,733	4,525
ドイツ	179,096	335,625	235,512	77,962
ノルウェー	7,467	19,618	16,798	2,274
フィンランド	8,077	27,577	22,101	4,546
フランス	306,433	389,206	310,506	56,325
ベルギー	13,661	42,258	30,331	8,987
ロシア	…	45,370	31,467	10,138
アフリカ	43,122	106,470	89,274	14,331
エジプト	21,808	55,275	51,367	3,330
南アフリカ	3,119	9,804	5,588	3,630
オセアニア	535,054	1,267,492	1,181,271	49,143
オーストラリア	423,414	699,867	636,819	36,097
ニュージーランド	72,762	143,270	128,593	6,070

「日本の統計」（2002）

a　南極大陸および不詳を含む。　b　旧ソビエト諸国を含む。

(21) 海外在留邦人数
(Japanese Living Abroad by Country)　　　　　　　　　　　　　　(人)

国（地域）	1990			2000		
	総　数	長　期 滞在者	永住者	総　数	長　期 滞在者	永住者
総数	620,174	374,044	246,130	811,712	526,685	285,027
アジア	86,886	79,195	7,691	168,434	160,979	7,455
インド	1,190	1,153	37	2,035	1,937	98
インドネシア	7,031	6,931	100	12,254	11,586	668
韓国	5,826	5,312	514	16,446	15,751	695
シンガポール	12,701	12,454	247	23,063	22,074	989
スリランカ	625	596	29	868	836	32
タイ	14,289	11,755	2,534	21,154	20,405	749
台湾	7,729	7,364	365	14,041	13,613	428
中国 a	8,269	6,205	2,064	46,090	45,424	666
トルコ	645	557	88	1,030	788	242
フィリピン	4,025	3,337	688	9,227	7,980	1,247
ベトナム	99	99	0	2,682	2,604	78
香港	13,980	13,540	440	22,924	22,399	525
マレーシア	6,116	5,815	301	11,625	11,024	601
北アメリカ	263,863	170,803	93,060	339,067	206,623	132,444
アメリカ合衆国	236,401	158,918	77,483	297,968	188,360	109,608
カナダ	21,846	8,515	13,331	34,066	13,580	20,486
メキシコ	3,286	1,842	1,444	4,158	2,588	1,570
南アメリカ	130,565	7,283	123,282	99,496	6,432	93,064
ブラジル	105,060	3,980	101,080	75,318	2,674	72,644
ヨーロッパ b	111,933	97,720	14,213	146,774	117,958	28,816
イギリス	44,351	40,953	3,398	53,114	43,646	9,468
イタリア	4,849	4,147	702	7,997	6,549	1,448
オーストリア	1,568	1,403	165	1,826	1,247	579
オランダ	4,334	3,691	643	6,481	5,722	759
スイス	4,456	2,566	1,890	5,694	2,632	3,062
スウェーデン	1,510	472	1,038	2,142	728	1,414
スペイン	4,195	3,740	455	4,683	3,717	966
デンマーク	870	577	293	960	339	621
ドイツ c	20,913	18,479	2,434	25,021	21,237	3,784
フランス	15,026	12,750	2,276	25,574	20,632	4,942
ベルギー	4,551	4,551	0	4,936	4,936	0
ロシア	…	…	…	1,484	1,446	38
アフリカ	5,491	5,320	171	5,992	5,546	446
エジプト	925	848	77	912	735	177
南アフリカ	530	500	30	1,210	1,085	125
オセアニア	21,398	13,685	7,713	51,909	29,107	22,802
オーストラリア	15,154	9,786	5,368	38,427	21,614	16,813
ニュージーランド	2,006	1,065	941	7,780	4,077	3,703

「世界の統計」(2002)

a　1999年以降は香港を含む。　b　旧ソビエト諸国を含む。
c　1990年は旧西独地域。

(22) 犯罪件数および検挙率

(Number of Crimes and Arrest Rate)

	アメリカ合衆国	イギリス	ドイツ	フランス	日本
1997					
認知件数(千件) ………	13,175	4,461	6,586	3,493	1,900
発生率 ……………………	4,923	8,543	8,031	5,972	1,506
検挙率(%) ……………	*21.6*	*28.2*	*50.6*	*29.5*	*40.0*
1998					
認知件数(千件) ………	12,476	5,109	6,457	3,566	2,034
発生率 ……………………	4,616	9,745	7,869	6,072	1,608
検挙率(%) ……………	*21.3*	*29.3*	*52.3*	*28.7*	*38.0*
1999					
認知件数(千件) ………	11,635	5,301	6,303	3,568	2,166
発生率 ……………………	4,267	10,061	7,682	6,097	1,709
検挙率(%) ……………	*21.4*	*25.2*	*52.8*	*27.6*	*33.8*

「日本国勢図会」(2002)

法務省法務総合研究所「犯罪白書」による。原資料は各国統計書。主な犯罪の比較。主な犯罪の定義は各国でそれぞれ違うが, アメリカは放火を含まず, ドイツ, フランス, 日本は交通犯罪を含まない。発生率は, 人口10万人あたりの認知件数の比率。

〔参考文献一覧〕

〈全般〉

日 本 国 勢 図 会			矢野恒太記念会
世 界 国 勢 図 会			矢野恒太記念会
日 本 の 統 計	総務省統計局編		財務省印刷局
世 界 の 統 計	総務省統計局編		財務省印刷局
日 本 の 100 年			矢野恒太記念会
経 済 要 覧	内閣編		大蔵省印刷局
鉄 鋼 統 計 要 覧	鉄鋼統計委員会編		日本鉄鋼連盟
世 界 史 年 表	亀井高孝・三上次男 林健太郎・堀米康三 編		吉川弘文館
標 準 日 本 史 年 表	児玉幸多編		吉川弘文館
情 報 ・ 知 識 imidas			集英社
知 恵 蔵			朝日新聞社
現 代 用 語 の 基 礎 知 識			自由国民社
新 府 省 庁 ガ イ ド ブ ッ ク			財務省印刷局
日 本 大 百 科 全 書 (1987)			小学館
世 界 大 百 科 事 典			平凡社
日 本 国 語 大 辞 典			小学館
広 辞 苑	新村出編		岩波書店
朝 日 年 鑑			朝日新聞社
毎 日 年 鑑			毎日新聞社
読 売 年 鑑			読売新聞社
時 事 年 鑑			時事通信社
世 界 大 百 科 年 鑑			平凡社

〈地理・歴史〉

理 科 年 表	国立天文台編		丸善
防 衛 白 書	防衛庁編		大蔵省印刷局
日 本 列 島 の 誕 生	平 朝彦		岩波書店
新 詳 説 日 本 史	石井 進・笠原一男 児玉幸多・笹山晴生		山川出版社
日 本 を 決 定 し た 百 年	吉田 茂		日本経済新聞社

〈政治〉

外 交 青 書	外務省編		財務省印刷局
わ が 外 交 の 近 況	外務省		大蔵省印刷局
世 界 の 憲 法 集	阿部 照哉 畑 博行編		有信堂

〈経済〉

経 済 白 書	経済企画庁編		大蔵省印刷局

日 本 経 済 の 現 況	経済企画庁 調査局編	大蔵省印刷局
通 商 白 書	通産省編	大蔵省印刷局
戦後日本経済躍進の根本要因	高橋 亀吉	日本経済新聞社
ライシャワーの見た日本	エドウィン・O・ライシャ ワー 林 伸郎訳	徳間書店
日本経済・世界経済の 新たな危機と日本	吉冨 勝	東洋経済新報社
日 本 型 成 熟 社 会		野村総合研究所
鉄 鋼 業 の 基 礎 知 識		新日鐵調査部
日 本 経 済 の 真 実	吉冨 勝	東洋経済新報社
労 働 力 調 査 年 報	総務省	日本統計協会

〈企業経営〉

労 働 経 済 白 書	厚生労働省編	日本労働研究機構
労働白書のあらまし	労働省編	大蔵省印刷局
労 働 時 間 白 書	労働省労働基準局 賃金時間部 労働時間課	日本労働研究機構
日本的経営を 説明するための辞書	引野 剛司 長野 晃	ダイヤモンド社
日本的経営と異文化の労働者	駒井 洋	有斐閣
日 本 の 企 業 行 動 比 較	通産省編	大蔵省印刷局
日 本 的 経 営 の 特 質	高田 馨他	ダイヤモンド社
日本の経営から何を学ぶか	アベグレン 占部 都美監訳	ダイヤモンド社
日 本 の 経 営 システム	吉野 洋太郎	ダイヤモンド社
日 本 の 経 営	野田一夫、現代経 営学全集第 16 巻	ダイヤモンド社
日 本 的 経 営 の 論 理	津田 眞澂	中央経済社
日 本 の 熟 練	小沢 和男	有斐閣
日 本 的 経 営 を 考 え る	占部 都美	中央経済社
グローバル経済と日本の進路		通産省通商調査室
セ オ リ ー Z	ウィリアム・O・オーウチ 徳山二郎訳	CBS ソニー出版
労 働 統 計 要 覧	厚生労働大臣官房 統計情報部	財務省印刷局
日・米経営のコンセプト	松阪 麻樹生	にっかん書房
図 説 日 本 産 業	武藤博道/日本経 済研究センター	日本経済新聞社
ザ・ジャパニーズ・カンパニー	ロドニー・クラーク 端 信行訳	ダイヤモンド社

〈社会〉

環 境 白 書	環境省	(株)ぎょうせい
循 環 型 社 会 白 書	環境省	(株)ぎょうせい
日本の人口・日本の家族	厚生省人口問題研	東洋経済新報社
国 民 生 活 白 書	経済企画庁編	大蔵省印刷局
世界の中の日本の暮らし(図説)	総務庁統計局編	大蔵省印刷局
地球環境と資源問題	森 俊介	岩波書店
我 が 国 の 教 育 水 準	文部省	大蔵省印刷局
文 部 統 計 要 覧	文部省編	大蔵省印刷局
厚 生 労 働 白 書	厚生労働省編	厚生問題研究会
OECDレポート、日本の経験・ 環境政策は成功したか?	環境庁国際課監修 国際環境問題 研究会訳	日本環境協会
熱 帯 林 っ て な ん だ	馬橋 憲男	築地書館

〈科学技術〉

科 学 技 術 白 書	文部科学省	財務省印刷局
学 術 白 書	文部省編	大蔵省印刷局
国際比較 日本の技術力	森谷 正規	祥文社
日 本 人 の 創 造 性	飯沼 和正	講談社
技 術 と は 何 か	村上 陽一郎	日本放送出版協会
日本型技術が世界を変える	石井 威望	PHP研究所
「技術大国日本」の未来を読む	西澤 潤一	PHP研究所
電 子 工 業 年 鑑		電波新聞社
未 来 の た ね	アイリック・ニュート	NHK出版

〈文化〉

日 本 美 の 探 究	吉田 光邦	日本放送出版協会
日 本 人 の 探 究	会田 雄次編	日本能率協会
日 本 人 と は 何 か	宮城 音弥	朝日新聞社
日 本 論 の 視 座	網野 善彦	小学館
「日 本 文 化 論」の 変 容	青木 保	中央公論社
日 本 と は 何 な の か	梅原 猛	日本放送出版協会
日本の繁栄は、揺がない	渡部 昇一	PHP研究所
二 周 目 の 人 生 設 計	石井 威望	講談社
閉ざされた言語 日本語の世界	鈴木 孝夫	新潮社
日本人と日本の文化	日鐵商事編	日鐵商事
外国人労働者と経済社会の進路	内閣編	大蔵省印刷局
日 本 文 化 史	家永 三郎	岩波書店
キャッチフレーズの戦後史	深川 英雄	岩波書店
アメリカは何を考えているのか	ジョージ・R・ パッカード	講談社
現 代 日 本 (そ の 自 画 像)	新日本製鐵 秘書部広報室	学生社
日 本 人 の 国 際 性	祖父江 孝男	くもん出版

海外からみたニッポン	今田一夫、丸山晃、富永恭四郎、他33名	学生社
異国ニッポン・グラフィティ	国際教育情報センター	JATEC出版
日本 VS アメリカ	日米比較研究会	PHP研究所
アメリカ人の思考法	E・スチュワート	創元社
アメリカ人の日本人観	宮本 美智子他	草思社
日の丸の履歴書	吹浦 忠正	ネスコ
現代日本人の意識構造	NHK世論調査	日本放送出版協会
日本人まるわかり事典	PHP研究所編	PHP研究所
日本タテヨコ	学習研究社編	学習研究社
世界の中の日本の暮らし	坂東 真理子編著	大蔵省印刷局
日本人ことはじめ物語	米山 俊直	PHP研究所
日本人の考え方を英語で説明する辞典	本名 信行	有斐閣
日米「逆」の発想	ベイツ・ホッファ脇阪 昭	学生社
不思議の国の特派員	デビット・パワーズ	日本放送出版協会
日本の心・世界の心	田宮模型編集	学生社
ヒト不足社会	NHK世論調査部	
ほんとうの豊かさとは	岩波書店編	岩波書店
日本人の意識	日本放送協会放送世論調査所	至誠堂
日本人の人間観	千石 保	日本経済新聞社
日本人の信仰心	磯部 忠正	講談社
宗教年鑑	文化庁編	(株)ぎょうせい
世界の宗教	村上 重良	岩波ジュニア新書
日本人の微笑	ラフカディオ・ハーン下田 衛註解	学生社
あなたはどれだけ日本を説明できるか	藤田 幸正	潮文社
英語になった日本語	エバンス・M・年恵	ジャパンタイムズ
「異質の国」ニッポンを斬る	浜野 崇好	日本放送出版協会
勝者・日本の不思議な笑い	ギュンター・エーデラー	ダイヤモンド社
日本人にとって和とは何か	高際 広夫	商学研究社
日本という存在	ジョン・ネスビッツ木村 尚三郎訳	日本経済新聞社
「縮み」志向の日本人	イー・オリョン	学生社
日本とは何か	堺屋 太一	講談社

漢　字 〜生い立ちとその背景〜	白川　静	岩波書店
日本その日その日1．2．3	Ｅ・Ｓ・モース	平凡社
しぐさの日本文化	多田　道太郎	筑摩書房
日　本　人 ーそのユニークさの源泉ー	グレゴリー・クラ ーク、村松増美訳	サイマル出版会
日　本　入　門（全　3　巻）	早稲田大学編	早稲田大学出版部
日　　本　　の　　心 文化・伝統と現代	新日本製鐵 秘書部広報企画室	丸善
外国からきた新語辞典	齋藤　栄三郎	集英社
二　つ　の　顔　の　日　本　人	鳥羽　欽一郎	中央公論社
国際摩擦はなぜ起るか	鳥羽　欽一郎	PHP 研究所
甘　　え　　の　　構　　造	土居　健郎	弘文堂
誤解ーヨーロッパVS日本ー	エンディミョン・ ウィルキンソン 徳岡　孝夫訳	中央公論社
日　本　人　と　英　米　人	ジェイムズ・カー カップ 中野　道雄訳	大修館書店
民族と風土の経済学	竹内　宏	東洋経済新報社
風　土・人　間　的　考　察	和辻　哲郎	岩波書店
知られざる日本の面影	ラフカディオ・ハ ーン 平井　呈一訳	恒文社
タテ社会の人間関係	中根　千枝	講談社
コンサイス外来語辞典	三省堂編修所	三省堂
外国社会とつきあう法	三井物産協力	日本工業新聞社
日　米　も　の　の　み　か　た	ジャック・スワー ド	匠出版
日　本　人　と　ア　メ　リ　カ　人 こ　こ　が　大　違　い	我妻　洋	ネスコ
日本人の知らないアメリカ人	加藤　恭子	TBS ブリタニカ
アメリカ人の知らない日本人	マイケル・バーガ ー	TBS ブリタニカ
しぐさの比較文化 ージェスチャーの日英比較ー	リーシャー・ブロ ズナハン	大修館書店
日　本　文　明　77　の　鍵	梅棹　忠夫編	創元社
日　本　人　の　国　民　性	文部省統計研究所	至誠堂
日本人ーその構造分析ー	祖父江　孝男	至誠堂
出　　版　　年　　鑑		出版ニュース社
国　土　交　通　白　書	国土交通省編	大蔵省印刷局
建　築　統　計　年　報		建築物価調査会
国　民　生　活　時　間　調　査	NHK 放送文化研 究所	大空社

〔年 表〕

世紀	時代	史 実		
		日 本	東 洋	世 界
紀元前	縄文・	8000ごろ 縄文文化期に入る 300ごろ 弥生文化期に入る	2500ごろ インダス文明・仰韶文化 1400ごろ 殷王朝繁栄 771 春秋時代に入る 486ごろ シャカの死、仏教おこる 3世紀ごろ 箕子朝鮮王国おこる 221 秦の始皇帝中国統一、万里の長城を築く 202 漢建国 190ごろ 衛氏朝鮮王国おこる 37 高句麗おこる	3500ごろ メソポタミア文明おこる 3000ごろ エジプトの統一 1100ごろ ギリシア人、ペロポネソス半島に定住 753 ローマ建国と伝えられる 508 ローマ共和政の成立 334 アレクサンダーの東征
一世紀	弥	57 九州地方の王、後漢に使者を送る	25 後漢建国 67 仏教中国に伝わる	4ごろ イエス誕生（〜30） 79 ポンペイ市の埋没
二世紀		180ごろ 邪馬台国、女王卑弥呼が立つ	184 黄巾の乱おこる 196 朝鮮に帯方郡できる	新約聖書成る 117 ローマ帝国領土最大期
三世紀	生	239 卑弥呼、魏に朝貢	220 後漢滅亡、三国時代となる（魏・呉・蜀）	226 ササン朝ペルシアおこる
四世紀	大	350 このころ大和国家成立	346 百済建国 356 新羅建国	375 ゲルマン民族大移動はじまる 395 ローマ帝国東西に分裂
五世紀	和	このころ仁徳天皇陵築造、大陸文化（漢字・儒教・暦・技術等）伝来 478 倭王武が中国に使を送る	439 南北朝時代はじまる	449 アングロサクソンがブリタニアに移住 476 西ローマ帝国滅亡 486 フランク王国建国

世紀	時代	史 実		
		日 本	東 洋	世 界
六世紀	大	538 仏教伝来 593 聖徳太子摂政となる	589 隋，中国を統一	571 マホメット誕生。このころササン朝ペルシア隆盛
七世紀	和	604 十七条憲法制定 607 遣隋使（小野妹子）派遣 　　法隆寺建立 645 大化改新	608 隋の煬帝大運河を開く 618 唐建国 676 新羅朝鮮半島を統一	610 イスラム教おこる 622 イスラム暦元年 642 サラセン帝国できる
八世紀	奈良	701 大宝律令制定 710 奈良（平安京）遷都 712 「古事記」撰上 720 「日本書紀」撰上 752 東大寺大仏開眼 759 「万葉集」編纂 794 京都（平安京）遷都	712 玄宗皇帝即位，唐文化全盛期 755 安禄山の乱おこる 780 唐，両税法を施行	732 カール・マルテル，サラセン軍を敗る 768 チャールズ大帝即位
九世紀	平	858 藤原良房摂政となる 887 藤原基経関白となる 894 遣唐使の停止 　　かな文字の発生	禅宗の隆盛 875 黄巣の乱おこる	829 イングランド王国成立 870 フランク王国フランス，ドイツ，イタリアに分裂
十世紀	安	905 「古今和歌集」撰進 927 延喜式なる 935 将門の乱 1000 清少納言「枕草子」なる	907 唐滅亡 936 高麗が朝鮮半島を統一	962 神聖ローマ帝国成立
十一世紀		1007 紫式部「源氏物語」なる 1016 藤原道長摂政となる 1086 白河上皇の院政はじまる	1069 王安石の改革	1037 セルジューク・トルコおこる 1066 ノルマンのイングランド征服 1096 十字軍遠征はじまる

世		史			実	
紀	時代	日　　　本		東　　洋		世　　界
十二世紀	平安	1167　平清盛太政大臣となる 1185　平家滅亡 1192　源頼朝鎌倉幕府を開く		1127　南宋の創建		1143　ポルトガル王国できる
十三世紀	鎌倉	1221　承久の変，北条政権成立 1274　文永の役 1281　弘安の役 1297　徳政令出る		1209　チンギス・ハン，モンゴル統一 1271　元建国（〜1367） 1294　ジャワにマジャパヒト王国建国		1215　イギリス，マグナカルタ（大憲章）制定 1265　イギリス議会はじまる 1299　マルコ・ポーロ「東方見聞録」出る
十四世紀	室町	1334　建武の新政 1336　南北朝の対立 1338　足利尊氏将軍となる 1392　北朝が南朝を吸収 1397　義満，金閣を造営		1368　明建国 1392　李氏朝鮮王国おこる		高炉法出現 1338　英仏百年戦争はじまる 1378　教会分裂
十五世紀		このころ能狂言大成 1467　応仁の乱 1483　義政，銀閣を造営 1490　このころ各地に土一揆おこる		1433　韓国ハングル文字成立		1414　コンスタンツ宗教会議開始 1442　アラゴン家が南イタリア，シチリアを統一 1492　コロンブスのアメリカ発見 1498　バスコ・ダ・ガマ，インド航路発見 1500　ポルトガル人カブラル，ブラジル発見

世紀	史実			
	時代	日　　本	東　　洋	世　　界
十六世紀	室町		1506　このころ，西遊記，金瓶梅などできる	1503～6　このころレオナルド・ダ・ビンチ，モナリザを描く 1504　ミケランジェロ，ダビデを彫刻 1517　ルター宗教改革をとなえる 1519　マゼラン世界周航に出発 1526　ムガール帝国おこる 1531　ポルトガル人ブラジルに植民開始
十六世紀	室町	1543　ポルトガル人，鉄砲を伝える 1549　キリスト教伝来		1503～6　このころレオナルド・ダ・ビンチ，モナリザを描く 1504　ミケランジェロ，ダビデを彫刻 1517　ルター宗教改革をとなえる 1519　マゼラン世界周航に出発 1526　ムガール帝国おこる 1531　ポルトガル人ブラジルに植民開始
十六世紀	安土・桃山	1573　足利幕府滅亡 1592　文禄の役。朱印船就航 1600　関ケ原の戦い	1592　韓国，壬辰の乱(文禄の役) 1596韓国，丁酉の乱(慶長の役)	1543　コペルニクス地動説をとなえる 1595　オランダ，インドネシアへ進出
十七世紀	江戸	1603　江戸幕府開幕 1609　平戸オランダ商館設置 1612　キリスト教禁止令 1639　鎖国 歌舞伎おこる 1694　「奥の細道」完成	1636　清おこる	1602　オランダ東インド会社がインドネシア統治 1603　オランダ船オーストラリア発見 1607　アメリカ，ジェームズタウンの建設 1609　ガリレー望遠鏡を発明 1613　ロシアロマノフ王朝はじまる 1620　メイフラワー号によるピューリタンの植民 1642　イギリスの清教徒革命 1687　ニュートン万有引力の法則発見 1688　名誉革命おこる

世		史		実	
紀	時代	日　本	東　洋	世　界	
十八世紀	江 戸	1702　赤穂浪士事件 1716　徳川吉宗将軍 　　　となる 蘭学おこる 1796　エトロフ島日 　　　本領とす 浮世絵全盛期	1716　中国，康熙字 　　　典完成 1717　中国，チベッ 　　　ト領有。キリスト 　　　教禁止 1786　韓国，キリス 　　　ト教禁止	1701　プロシア王国 　　　成立 1717　オーストリア 　　　のイタリア支配 1720　イタリア，サ 　　　ルディニア王国成 　　　立 1742　フランクリン 　　　電気発見 1722　イギリスに産 　　　業革命おこる 1789　フランス革命 　　　おこる 1795　ナポレオンが 　　　イタリア征服	
十九世紀	 明 治	1853　ペリー来日 1854　開国 1857　大島高任洋式 　　　高炉に火入れ 1867　大政奉還 1868　明治元年 1889　明治憲法公布 1893　君が代を学校 　　　儀式用唱歌曲とし 　　　て制定 1894　日清戦争はじ 　　　まる	1840　中国，アヘン 　　　戦争おこる 1842　南京条約 1876　韓国，江華島 　　　条約（日鮮修好条 　　　約） 1890　ジャワ原人発 　　　掘 1894　韓国，東学党 　　　の乱おこる 1897　韓国，大韓帝 　　　国と改称 1899　中国，義和団 　　　事件おこる	1804　ナポレオン皇 　　　帝となる 1818　スチーブンソ 　　　ン蒸気機関発明 1823　アメリカ，モ 　　　ンロー主義宣言 1859　ダーウィン種 　　　の起源を発表 1861　イタリア王国 　　　成立。アメリカ南 　　　北戦争はじまる 1863　アメリカ，奴 　　　隷解放 1871　ドイツ帝国成 　　　立 1893　エジソン活動 　　　写真発明 1895　マルコーニ無 　　　線電信発明 1896　アテネで第1 　　　回国際オリンピッ 　　　ク大会開催	

世紀	時代	史　　　　実		
		日　本	東　洋	世　界
二　十　世　紀	明治	1904　日露戦争はじまる	1906　韓国，日本の保護国となる 1910　韓国，日本に併合	1903　ライト兄弟初飛行に成功 1914　第一次世界大戦はじまる
	大正	1923　関東大震災 1937　日華事変はじまる 1941　太平洋戦争はじまる 1945　ポツダム宣言受諾 1946　新憲法公布 1947　労働基準法・独占禁止法・教育基本法公布 1951　平和条約，日米安保条約調印 1954　自衛隊発足 1956　国連加盟 1964　IMF8条に移行。OECD加盟。オリンピック東京大会。新幹線開通 1965　日韓基本条約締結 1968　小笠原諸島復帰 1970　日本万博開かる。国産人工衛星打上げ 1972　沖縄復帰。冬期オリンピック札幌大会。日中国交正常化 1973　第一次石油危機 1976　ロッキード事件発覚 1977　王選手ホームラン756本世界記録達成 1978　日中平和友好条約調印	1912　中華民国成立 1927　南京国民政府成立 1946　フィリピン独立 1947　インド・パキスタン独立 1948　大韓民国，朝鮮民主主義人民共和国成立。ビルマ独立 1949　中華人民共和国成立 1950　朝鮮動乱おこる 1953　朝鮮動乱終結 1961　ヴェトナム戦争はじまる 1963　韓国，朴正煕大統領就任 1965　韓国，日本と基本条約を結ぶ。アメリカ，ヴェトナム北爆開始 1966　中国，文化大革命はじまる 1970　インドネシア，スカルノ大統領死去 1972　ニクソン米大統領訪中。中国，日本との国交正常化 1976　中国，周恩来首相死去。華国鋒首相就任。毛沢東主席死去。江青ら四人組逮捕。統一ヴェトナム社会主義共和国成立	1917　ロシア革命おこる 1919　アメリカ，禁酒法成立 1922　ソビエト連邦成立 1929　世界大恐慌はじまる。バチカン帝国成立 1932　オリンピックロスアンジェルス大会 1933　アメリカ，ニューディール政策開始 1939　第二次世界大戦はじまる 1945　第二次世界大戦終結。国際連合，ユネスコ成立 1948　OEEC発足 1949　NATO発足 1957　ソ連スプートニク1号打上げ 1960　オリンピックローマ大会 1963　アメリカ，ケネディ大統領暗殺 1969　アポロ11号月面着陸に成功 1973　拡大EC発足。第四次中東戦争おこりアラブ諸国石油戦略をすすめる 1974　アメリカ，ウォーターゲート事件でニクソン大統領辞任（フォード大統領就任） 1977　アメリカ，カーター大統領就任
	昭和			

世	史			実
紀	時代	日　本	東　洋	世　界
二 十 世 紀	昭 和	1979　第二次石油危機。東京サミット開催 1982　東北新幹線開業 1983　ロッキード事件で田中元首相に有罪判決 1985　電電公社民営化されNTTとなる。日本たばこ産業会社発足。男女雇用機会均等法成立 1986　東京の三原山大噴火 1987　国鉄分割民営化。次年度予算案の防衛費対GNP比1％枠を超える	1979　ソ連軍アフガニスタンに介入 1980　韓国，全斗煥体制発足 1981　中国，胡燿邦国家主席就任 1984　インドのガンジー首相，シーク教徒に暗殺される。英国と中国，'97年香港返還に正式調印 1986　フィリピンのマルコス政権崩壊し，アキノ夫人大統領に就任 1987　中ソ境交渉9年ぶりに再開。韓国大統領直接選挙，盧泰愚就任	1979　イラン革命，ホメイニ派制圧。エジプト・イスラエル和平条約成立 1980　エジプト・イスラエル国交樹立 1981　アメリカ，レーガン大統領就任。アメリカ，有人宇宙船スペース・シャトル初飛行成功。サダト・エジプト大統領死去 1982　フォークランド紛争 1983　フランスのモンタニエ，エイズウイルス発見 1985　アメリカ，レーガン大統領再任。ソ連ゴルバチョフ書記長就任。 1986　スペースシャトル・チャレンジャー号爆発。ソ連チェルノブイリ原発事故 1987　米ソINF（中距離核戦力）全廃条約調印
世 紀	平 成	1988　農産物が日米貿易摩擦の焦点となる。青函トンネル鉄道開業。瀬戸大橋開通 1989　昭和天皇崩御。皇太子明仁親王即位，年号「平成」と改まる。消費税スタート（3％） 1991　海上自衛隊掃海部隊のペルシャ湾派遣。雲仙・普賢岳で大規模火砕流	1988　ソウル・オリンピック開催 1989　北京天安門事件。ソ連軍のアフガニスタン撤退完了	1988　イラン・イラク戦争終結。 1989　アメリカのブッシュ，大統領に就任。マルタで米ソ首脳会議，（冷戦終結宣言）。「ベルリンの壁」撤去 1990　東西統一ドイツ誕生 1991　多国籍軍によるイラク攻撃（湾

世紀	時代	史 実 日　本	東　洋	世　界
二十世紀	平成	1992　国連平和維持活動法（PKO法）制定，活動部隊カンボジアへ派遣 1993　自民党分裂。日本初プロサッカー（Jリーグ）発足 1994　関西国際空港開港 1995　阪神淡路大震災。地下鉄サリン事件 1996　O-157食中毒 1997　消費税，5％へ。大手金融機関の破綻 1998　冬季オリンピック長野大会。サッカーのW杯日本初出場。戦後最悪の不況，各種経済対策 1999　臓器移植法に基づく日本初の脳死者からの臓器移植 2000　介護保険制度スタート	1992　モンゴル共和国社会主義を放棄 1993　カンボジア統一選挙実施，連立政府成立 1997　香港返還 1998　インド，パキスタン核実験 2000　南北朝鮮首脳会議	岸戦争）。ソ連邦のロシア共和国でエリツィンが大統領就任。ワルシャワ条約機構（WTO）完全解体。旧ソ連邦および東欧諸国における共産党の一党独裁制瓦解。旧ソ連邦解体，代わりに独立国家共同体（CIS）創設。南アフリカ共和国，アパルトヘイト（人種隔離政策）撤廃 1992　EC，マーストリヒト条約（欧州同盟新憲法）調印。ブラジルで環境と開発に関する国連会議（地球サミット）開催 1993　アメリカ，クリントン大統領就任。イスラエルとパレスチナ解放機構（PLO）がパレスチナ暫定自治協定に調印 1995　中仏両国地下核実験（〜96） 1997　アメリカ，クリントン大統領再任 1999　EU統合通貨「ユーロ」の使用開始
二十一世紀		2001　中央省庁再編，BSE（狂牛病） 2002　サッカーW杯日韓共催	2001　アフガニスタン，バーミヤンの大仏破壊	2001　アメリカ，ブッシュ大統領就任。9月アメリカで同時多発テロ。多国籍軍によるアフガン攻撃 2002　イスラエルとパレスチナの対立激化

〔索　引〕

太字はくわしい説明のある頁です。

Printed in Japan

日 本 ―その姿と心―

NIPPON
THE LAND AND ITS PEOPLE

1982年 7 月20日	第 1 版初刷発行
1984年 5 月 1 日	第 2 版初刷発行
1988年 5 月25日	第 3 版初刷発行
1993年11月25日	第 4 版初刷発行
1997年 4 月 1 日	第 5 版初刷発行
1999年 9 月30日	第 6 版初刷発行
2002年 9 月30日	第 7 版初刷発行
2002年10月30日	第 7 版 2 刷発行

監　修	新日本製鐵株式会社	東京都千代田区大手町 2-6-3
©著者	㈱日鉄ヒューマン	千葉県千葉市美浜区中瀬1-3-A
	デベロプメント	新日鐵幕張研修センター内
発行者	鶴　岡　一　郎	

	本　　社	（〒102-0074）東京都千代田区九段南2-2-4
	編集・販売	（〒123-0864）東京都足立区鹿浜3-27-14
		電　話　東京　03（3857）3031
		Ｆ Ａ Ｘ　東京　03（3857）3037
		http://www.gakusei.co.jp
発行所	株式会社 学 生 社	info@gakusei.co.jp
		振　替　00110-9-18870番
		壮光舎印刷／田中製本印刷

ISBN4-311-70037-7

編集担当　児玉有平　⑱0210